How To Preach

This remarkable book by Sam Wells is a three-fold gift: collected sermons by one of our finest preachers, honest reflections and best wisdom about his process of preparing them, and an invitation to us to examine our own sermons more deeply than we often dare to do. Don't be surprised if How to Preach leads you to a startling and unexpected reckoning about yourself as a preacher and human being—and when it does, don't turn away. Wells is the preacher's vicar. Everything he offers here is from the heart, as encouraging as it is empowering. This book will change your preaching life.

Anna Carter Florence, Peter Marshall Professor of Preaching,
Columbia Theological Seminary

How to Preach

Times, Seasons, Texts, Contexts

Samuel Wells

© Sam Wells 2023

Published in 2023 by Canterbury Press
Editorial office
3rd Floor, Invicta House,
108–114 Golden Lane,
London EC1Y 0TG, UK

www.canterburypress.co.uk

Canterbury Press is an imprint of Hymns Ancient & Modern Ltd
(a registered charity)

Hymns Ancient & Modern® is a registered trademark of
Hymns Ancient & Modern Ltd
13A Hellesdon Park Road, Norwich,
Norfolk NR6 5DR, UK

All rights reserved. No part of this publication may be reproduced,
stored in a retrieval system, or transmitted,
in any form or by any means, electronic, mechanical,
photocopying or otherwise, without the prior permission of
the publisher, Canterbury Press.

The Author has asserted his right under the Copyright, Designs and Patents Act
1988 to be identified as the Author of this Work

British Library Cataloguing in Publication data

A catalogue record for this book is available
from the British Library

Scripture quotations are from New Revised Standard Version Bible: Anglicized
Edition, copyright © 1989, 1995 National Council of the Churches of Christ in
the United States of America. Used by permission. All rights reserved worldwide.

978-1-78622-521-4

Typeset by Regent Typesetting
Indexes created by Meg Davies

For Maureen

Contents

Preface ix

Introduction xi

Part 1: Times

1. Preaching about Politics 3
2. Preaching about Society 18
3. Preaching about Freedom 30
4. Preaching on War 42
5. Preaching about Disability 57

Part 2: Seasons

1. Preaching on Advent Sunday 71
2. Preaching in Advent Season 82
3. Preaching before Christmas 95
4. Preaching at Christmas 109
5. Preaching in Epiphany 116
6. Preaching in Lent 130
7. Preaching at Easter 144
8. Preaching in Easter Season 152
9. Preaching at Ascension and Pentecost 167

Part 3: Texts

1. Preaching on Old Testament Narratives — 181
2. Preaching on Old Testament Poetry — 197
3. Preaching on Miracles — 207
4. Preaching on Parables — 218
5. Preaching on Paul — 233
6. Preaching on the Epistle — 248

Part 4: Contexts

1. Preaching at a Funeral — 261
2. Preaching at a Wedding — 275
3. Preaching at a Baptism — 288

Index of Biblical References — 303
Index of Names and Subjects — 305

Preface

Preaching may look like a lone art, but it isn't: behind it sits a host of companions, teachers, scholars, critics, family members and sources of inspiration; alongside it sits a chorus of colleagues, musicians, fellow leaders of liturgy and inspirational congregation members. So my first thanks go to those with whom the majority of these sermons have taken shape: among clergy, Sally Hitchiner, Richard Carter, Jonathan Evens, Cath Duce, Angela Sheard, Harry Ching; among choir leaders, Andrew Earis, Jennifer Sterling, Tom Williams; among administrators, Sian Conway, Harriet Merz, Jasmine Oakes; together with countless others who have contributed to worship and congregational life at St Martin-in-the-Fields during my time, particularly during the last five years when most of these sermons were preached.

Among those who have read sermons and given helpful comments, I'm especially grateful to companions who have told me the truth when I've sought guidance concerning their experience of sensitive issues. I'm also indebted to those who have told me about, or given me, books to read, suggested a film or play, or opened my eyes to new ways of seeing things. Most of my 'original insights' are, in fact, forgetting where I read or heard or saw something.

One remarkable experience that has contributed in indefinable ways to this book has been offering the weekly Sermon Preparation Workshop on the HeartEdge web page with Sally Hitchiner. Sally is a lively and thoughtful dialogue partner and it's been her imagination and energy, together with HeartEdge colleagues, that have gathered several thousand followers of the hour-long event that began on the stroke of the first 2020 lockdown and has continued since. Sally's questions and provocations have elicited a good number of the guidelines included in this book and I'm grateful for her part in helping me articulate my reasoned reflections and personal prejudices about preaching.

Christine Smith has been a faithful follower of the livestream and publisher of many of my books. I'm grateful to her for her confidence in me and for the conversations that led to the idea for this book. I'm thankful for Anne Gidion and her invitation to speak on these subjects in Budapest and Berlin, also fostering the idea of the book, and for Ian Markham, for the invitation to publish (and permission to adapt for the first chapter of this book), 'Getting the Basics Right' in Ian S. Markham and Crystal J. Hardin, eds, *Prophetic Preaching: The Hope or the Curse of the Church?* (New York: Church Publishing, 2020), pp. 109–21.

As always, I've been blessed by the company of family and friends who have enveloped me as I put this book together, making it an adventure and a joy.

The book is dedicated to Maureen Knudsen Langdoc who, in a way rather idealized by teachers but that nonetheless occasionally comes true, was first a student in class, then a distant contact, then an occasional correspondent, then a supervised doctoral student, then a more informed correspondent and adviser on fine details about Augustine and John Wesley, and finally conversation partner, source of wisdom and friend. It is in such diverse forms of companionship that the fruits of the Spirit are most evidently found.

Introduction

What this book is not

This is not a comprehensive handbook to enable a beginner, regardless of social location, to preach in any context with minimum preparation. Let me break down the components of that disclaimer.

It is not comprehensive. Most obviously, it only includes sermons from one preacher. I have a friend who likes to say to students, 'I don't want to teach you to think for yourselves: I want to teach you to think like me.' It's not a statement of arrogance, still less narcissism. When he explains, he refers to the 'boring old answers' students tend to come up with when invited to think for themselves. He's saying, 'Once you've undergone the discipline and humility of training, of developing inherent talents, honing learned skills and developing healthy habits, then you can think for yourself and come up with something worth saying. But for the time being, consent to letting me show you some good ways to go about things, and some places where treasure is to be found.' So this isn't a compendium of my favourite sermons from preachers around the world: it's an ordered assemblage of my best efforts to address the tasks that many preachers face. Of course, it's only one way of doing things. But it's a way honed in a variety of contexts – post-industrial town, suburbia, outer-urban deprived estate, chic urban village, elite American research university and central London gathered minster congregation – over 30 years, matched with pastoral ministry and academic study, and rooted on the border between church and world. It's the best I can do.

It's not a handbook. It doesn't train the reader in how to read a commentary (or what commentaries to read), in how to plan or write, on the merits of extempore versus scripted sermons, on which novels to read, which films to watch, how to make notes to keep your memory of long-past experiences sharp, how to deliver, how to stand, what to do with your hands, how long to speak for, what rhetorical techniques to cultivate. I do have views about some things: for example, I believe in planning and writing a sermon nine days before I preach it, for that way the liturgy can be shaped around it, the music and intercessions informed by it, and it can be shared with colleagues or those whose lives touch on the issues raised, and thus improved by comments or corrections. The number of times subsequent news or community events require substantial or entire rewriting I estimate as about one in 40; hardly a percentage to worry about. But I'm not setting out to be a coach. To be a coach requires a genuine relationship. This is a book of teaching by example.

This isn't for beginners. I hope beginners might gain from it: I learned a great deal from preachers like Harry Williams, William J. Bausch, Will Willimon, Richard Holloway, Peter Nott, John Inge and Ian Paton when I was starting out, from sitting-at-the-feet and from reading books of sermons. I wish there were several women on that list, and a greater ethnic and racial diversity; this was another era. But mostly I learned from trial and error, and from observing others and concluding what not to do as much as resolving what to imitate. I also owe much to inspired commentators like Ched Myers, F. D. Bruner, Walter Brueggemann, Warren Carter and Wes Howard-Brook, who instigated the ways I started to read the Bible for myself. If I could be on a list such as those for others, I'd be glad. But this isn't a beginners' manual. It's a guide for those who, like me, have learned by having a go, and who no doubt have their own dos and don'ts, and might find some benefit in comparing them with mine, or when stuck might derive some inspiration from one or more of the sermon examples offered here.

This book comes from a particular social location. When I started preaching in the late 80s, the talk was all about poverty and climate. (Yes, really – at the end of my first year studying theology, one student thanked the principal for his sermon about the environment – 'It gets better every time I hear it.') It became all about gender and sexuality; and now it's all about race and poverty and ... climate again. Such contributions as I've made about race, climate, sexuality and justice in general are published elsewhere, so if it feels like there are some significant things missing here, that's why. I'm blessed to have spent ten years of ministry in deprived urban neighbourhoods, seven years in the US and eleven years in central London in the most diverse (class, race, sexuality, disability, age) church I've ever encountered, so my congregations have taught me a great deal. I have Jewish, German and Ukrainian heritage and was born in Canada, so I'm a little more complex than appearances might suggest. But I've also had the advantage of an education and a support structure many don't get to enjoy. So there are bound to be people who hear or read my sermons and pick up shortcomings attributable not just to the weaknesses of my character but to the flaws in my social commitments.

This isn't a book that would fit neatly into any context. Most of the sermons included here, and most of the guidelines offered here, assume a congregation that's ready and willing, if not eager, to hear a 12–15-minute sermon engaging seriously with the Bible and drawing on a wide range of literature, experience, emotion and reflection, facing theological and existential questions with a minimum of jargon but a maximum of expectation. That wasn't my context in one church I served, where people weren't used to listening to one person talk for so long, and where instead I would offer interactive presentations in which congregation members would speak and spontaneously respond. A preacher and a congregation have to get used to one another and overcome irritations in both directions via accommodation and adaptation. But even after such mutual hospitality emerges, this style of preaching doesn't work in every context. I understand that. But there are plenty of contexts where it does, and could work better with greater reflection, example and experimentation, which is why I've written this book.

Likewise, this book might not be a good fit in some conservative Christian circles. I like to think I read Scripture closely and listen to its voice faithfully. But these sermons differ in form and content from most sermons preached in such a context. They're not line-by-line chase-the-reference Bible studies; and they assume an ethic with which preachers in such a culture might be at odds. Nonetheless, I've no desire to antagonize or exaggerate differences and I hope those from such contexts may find here food for their souls, too.

Perhaps most obviously, this isn't a pick-up-and-go instruction manual. It arises from 30 years of taking preaching seriously, seeking to enrich it from intentional study and eclectic observation, consulting with colleagues and companions about how to make improvements and broaden approaches and techniques, and choosing for this volume only those examples that seemed best fitted to the headings identified. What I'm talking about is a vocation. This is a book for those who want to enhance their existing vocation; for those who want to explore such a vocation; and for any who want to digest the fruits of such a vocation in written form. I hope it's a blessing to those who read it.

What this book is

You can read this book in at least three ways. You could forget the sermons and just consider the guidelines and how they apply to your experience and your context. You could forget the guidelines and just read the sermons, treating them as works of prose or rhetoric, regarding them as aids to devotion, perhaps reading one a day in Lent (there are around 50 in all), or as an introduction to theology. Or you could read sermons and guidelines together and reflect on the methods and considerations of each sermon and to what extent the sermons outmeasure the guidelines or the guidelines fail to be met in the sermons.

Some people like to go to a football match, enjoy the action, come away and talk about the game, or maybe discuss something else, and generally they've had a rewarding afternoon. Others are drawn into wanting to understand tactics, why a team changes its shape depending on who it's playing, how it alters its approach when it goes a goal behind – and look forward to the interview with the manager afterwards to explain the early substitution and the unusual formation. This is a book for those who enjoy the game, but also want to know why a team played the way it did, how much was intent and how much spontaneous, what in general makes a football team good and how it feels to play in such a team.

There's a paradox that if a composer publishes a collection of anthems, people will welcome it, peruse it for ones they can enjoy and sing frequently, and set aside the ones that are too difficult or don't match their tastes. Yet if a preacher publishes a book of sermons, there's a different reaction: 'Who does he think he is?'; 'Sermons are for the spoken moment, not for the written volume'; 'Everyone has their own style, what have I got to learn from this?'; 'This is just boasting – he's just trying to make me feel small.' These are among the inhibitions I've had to overcome in compiling this book. I've actually previously published six books of sermons, so I've travelled this road before; but this is the first time I've actually called them sermons, rather than pretending they were something else; this is the first time I've suggested they might be examples for others to follow and had the temerity to offer guidelines that they might find helpful in doing so.

There's a difference between a composer and a preacher, of course: a composition is made for performance by others, not the composer alone; it's made to be performed frequently, not just once; and composers earn a living by composing, whereas preachers – at least in the UK – are supposed to be nonchalant about preaching, regarding it as a long way behind pastoral care and increasing the number of young people among priorities of ministry.

So it may seem especially presumptuous to present these sermons, not just in a workbook, manual or guide, but as works of theology in their own right, the way a theologian might offer a book of essays, or a choir a CD of anthems. But that's what this book is. The sermons, rather than the guidelines, are the principal teacher; the guidelines are there if you want direction in how to preach, or at least produce, sermons like this – like this theologically, like this rhetorically, like this exegetically, like this pastorally, like this oratorically, like this as works of prose.

INTRODUCTION

For me, preparing a sermon, even more than delivering one, is an act of worship – of prayer. As I prepare a sermon, I'm reflecting on the Scripture and its origin in revelation to God's people centuries ago. I'm standing in a tradition of those who have proclaimed this message and sought to live it throughout the history of Israel and the church. I'm full of gratitude for those who have enriched me with teaching, example, scholarship, correction, patience and wisdom. I'm moved with compassion for those whose plight in today's world makes them closest to God's heart. I'm mindful of those across the globe who by the Holy Spirit live the implications of this text and my reading of it far better than I ever will. And I'm preoccupied with those who will hear – and those who perhaps will later read – this sermon, and how its words and arguments will land in their hearts, stir them to action or reflection and draw them close to God. Compiling this book has been the same.

PART I

Times

I

Preaching about Politics

I have two kinds of sermons. The first I call exegetical and the second I call pastoral.

When I prepare the first, I am captivated by a passage of Scripture, which is almost always one of the set readings for the day or given to me by the occasion or the person inviting me – it's almost never of my own choosing. I'm not always struck straightaway, but as I ponder, examine and read about that passage, either the structure, the terminology or the argument strikes me. Sometimes just one phrase or sentence jumps out. Thereafter, I seek to identify what is so special about that passage, sentence or phrase, and I prepare a sermon crafted to arouse in the congregation a thirst to wrestle with a conundrum or resolve a quandary to which that passage, sentence or phrase is an answer or a resolution. I almost never start with the passage, sentence or phrase itself; that would be like blurting out the punch line before you tell the joke. I don't usually introduce the passage in question until the congregation is already eager to resolve a tension that my opening remarks have identified. It may not be a tension the listener was aware of before, but in a few sentences, I seek to make the listeners aware of it so acutely that they are on tenterhooks to know what the resolution will be. The sermon is satisfying to the extent that the attention and expectation aroused is in keeping with, and on a theme identical with, the resolution that the exposition of the passage, sentence or phrase provides. Most satisfying of all is being able to return to an insignificant element of the material with which I began and show, at the end, that it has an even greater significance than was previously disclosed. Ideally that will be a Christological dimension that was abiding in the passage but had not been apparent until that point.

The second kind of sermon doesn't begin with a scriptural passage. It begins with a question in the hearts and minds of the congregation. It may be that something significant has come to pass in the congregation's life, planned or accidental: perhaps Giving Sunday, in the former case; a family tragedy in the latter. It may be that a major event has taken place in the national or global domain, anticipated or sudden: the hosting of the Olympic Games, perhaps, or the death of a monarch or noted politician.

It may be that the church, locally or denominationally, is consumed with a pressing theological or ethical question. It may be that the wider culture is wrestling with a question that is so timely it simply demands homiletical engagement. Or it may be that there is a question the wider church and culture are not actively discussing that I sincerely believe they should be, and I wish to put forward some framework for the conversation. The way I do this is rather different from the first approach. I usually start with a theological insight. It may be from church history or from a classic theological controversy. Sometimes it will be a careful procedural move, like the methods of overaccepting and reincorporation I discuss at some length in my own writing.[1] I then ponder where in the Scriptures that insight is most aptly expressed. In almost every case the passage I arrive at has more interesting things to say than just the part I was thinking of, and so I pause to explore how there is more to say from this part of Scripture than I originally imagined. Then I construct an argument based in most cases on an attempt at an even-handed overview of the issue, a move that draws in the existential and emotional depth and range of the question, and a recognition of where the pressure points lie.

From this point on, the two kinds of sermons are broadly similar, even though they have emerged from different thought-processes and serve different purposes. If I am seeking to address a pastoral issue on a Sunday morning, I almost always seek to do so from one of the texts set for the day. The only exception might be in the event of a major unexpected congregational or global crisis such as 9/11 or the sudden death of a very visible member of the community.

So-called prophetic sermons fall almost entirely into the second kind – occasions when a pastoral need makes it necessary or unavoidable to tread on contested ground, within church or world or both. If people like what I'm saying they may call it prophetic; if not, they call it misguided, unwise, inappropriate, taking advantage, imposing your convictions or venting. I want now to offer an example of this more edgy kind of pastoral sermon and to provide a commentary on it, before summarizing my suggestions. My hope is that the reader, if the reader is also a preacher, may find that if they preach an edgy pastoral sermon and face criticism, they may then, if they follow the guidelines I offer, recognize the costs of ministry. If they don't follow the guidelines, they may acknowledge that they might have got it wrong this time.

The following sermon I preached twice on the same day. In the evening, I was explicitly asked to speak on the subject of Brexit for a service at

---

1 Samuel Wells, *Improvisation: The Drama of Christian Ethics*, 2nd edn (Grand Rapids, MI: Baker Academic, 2018).

a Cambridge college, as part of an eight-part series entitled 'Christian Engagement with Public Debates'. Somewhat lazily, I noticed that Revelation 21 was among the assigned readings for the morning service at my own church and I decided to preach a longer version of the same sermon that morning. What follows is the longer version.

Discovering who we are
Revelation 21.1–4
4 November 2018

Two years ago, in the Brexit referendum, this country was divided between leavers and remainers. In truth, few remainers believed the European Union was the fount of every blessing, while few leavers really thought Britain would finally realize its eternal destiny the moment it left the EU. Instead, for both sides, the issue of whether or not to remain in the EU became a touchstone about other issues closer to people's hearts, about multiculturalism, democracy, belonging and rapid social change. I want today to take a step back from the intensity of chaos and controversy and explore what this is really all about.

Let's start with a story that I hope is relatively uncontroversial. After the hangover of VE Day and VJ Day, Britain woke up in 1945 to find itself in a different world. The United States now sat at the head of the table, Russia glowered at it from the far end, the empire was disintegrating, Europe was half destroyed, and a way had to be found to restore Germany without it yet again finding itself at war with France and Russia. For a long period, it looked like the answer to almost all these questions was the European Union. Yet underlying the European Union was a vision to which Britain never adhered, a vision of full economic and eventual political union. After nearly 20 years of trying, Britain joined the EEC in 1973, but, crucially, Edward Heath made the case on economic grounds rather than on questions of identity.

Britain continued to see its identity largely elsewhere – as a Security Council member, in the so-called 'special relationship' with the United States, at the head of the Commonwealth. Whenever critical questions of economic and political union surfaced, Britain always dragged its feet. The habit of assuming that we could have the parts of Europe we wanted and discard those we didn't was most evident in the refusal to join the single currency. You may know the story of the silent monastery. After ten years a monk was invited to his first audience with the abbot and was granted two words. He said: 'Food cold.' Ten years later he was granted his second audience and was allowed two more words:

'Room cold.' After 30 years the monk was granted his third audience and announced, 'I'm leaving.'

'Good riddance,' the abbot replied, 'you've done nothing but complain ever since you've been here.' That's been the story of Britain in Europe these last 45 years.

There's always been a simmering discontent within Britain about membership of the European Union. Some of that has been political: many have expressed disquiet about ceding sovereignty to Brussels. There's some irony underlying this: concern about sovereignty is greatest in England, but England, unlike Scotland, Wales and Northern Ireland, with no political institutions of its own, is notoriously a nation without a state; a democratic deficit that seems to trouble almost no one. Some discontent has been economic: the free movement of goods, services, capital and persons was all very well so long as the EU was made up of countries of broadly similar levels of prosperity, but the entry of several former Eastern Bloc countries has upset the equilibrium and made migration a significant part of many lives, some of whom perceive it not as a gift but as a threat.

Which brings us to the third element of discontent: identity. Identity invariably rests on narrative. Britain has its own narrative, somewhat different from the mainstream European Union narrative. The European narrative is that the tension between France and Germany had caused a half-century of devastating war, and that the whole of Europe needed to gather round the two giants to forge a better future together, a future of economic prosperity based on free trade and on the emergence of a European entity to rival the United States, Russia, Japan and, in due course, India and China. Britain's narrative is different. It's based on a memory of being in the vanguard of the Industrial Revolution and at the head of a global empire, with a corresponding mixture of duty, superiority and entitlement. Consider the song 'Football's Coming Home'. It keys into the sense that Britain (or England) invented all the games anyway, and has patiently let the upstarts win for much too long. But in the 20 years after the Second World War, Britain became obsessed by the narrative of economic, political and social decline. The question for Britain became whether membership of the EU reversed that decline, by charting a new, collaborative, confident identity – or epitomized that decline by allowing the grand old country to be swallowed up by a European leviathan.

One morning about a year ago, I was sitting in the green room at Broadcasting House, listening to the *Today* programme, and waiting to offer my Thought for the Day, when I was overwhelmed by the desire to walk into the studio, set aside my carefully constructed and minutely edited script, and simply say, 'Let's face it, everyone, Brexit may be a train crash but at least it's done what it was originally designed to do – unite the Tory party.' There's no doubt that the Conservatives have been plagued by contrasting feelings on Europe for a generation, and the somewhat unexpected return of a Tory majority at the 2015 election meant that their quandary immediately became the nation's quandary. But the civil war in the party that's characterized the period since the triggering of Article 50 is an indication of the fact that the 52 percent leave vote in June 2016 was a temporary coalition of those whose opposition to EU membership was based on economic, political and identity grounds. And as soon as Article 50 was triggered and the actual future relationship had to be defined, that coalition broke up into smithereens.

Christians have all kinds of political, social and economic views, but for me the central question of our time is one of identity. Britain was taken into the EEC by Edward Heath with economic arguments that hid political commitments. David Cameron chose to fight the 2016 Brexit campaign on economic arguments, just as he had the Scottish independence vote two years previously. In both cases, I believe he fought the battle on the wrong territory. The real issue in both was identity. In my view, Remain deserved to lose the Brexit vote because it failed to describe a multicultural European vision that Britain would be in every way impoverished to leave. The trouble is, the Brexiteers have had two years to identify a restored British identity that was worth all this trouble to re-establish, and towards doing so they have made no progress whatsoever.

Not long ago I walked up to the Penshaw Monument near Houghton-le-Spring and my companion pointed out the Nissan car factory whose workers overwhelmingly voted Leave, even though they knew it would likely mean the eventual closure of the factory and the loss of thousands of jobs in County Durham. They weren't thinking about economics: they were thinking about identity. Those who were happiest the next day were glad because they had recaptured a glimpse of an identity they had feared was lost. Those who were saddest, and I include myself, were horrified because they didn't recognize themselves in that identity.

Christians may have a range of views about economics and politics, but faith is fundamentally about identity. Who are we? What are our lives for? What is Britain's future role in the world as a small nation with a long history of punching way above its weight?

We live in a culture where such questions of ultimate purpose are seriously out of fashion. They are the territory on which the church should be very much at home, because the church has a very clear message of identity. That message is that our dignity derives from God's longing to be in relationship with us. Our freedom derives from Christ's cross, in which he frees us from the curse of our past, the damage we've inflicted and the hurt done to us. Our hope derives from Christ's resurrection, in which he opens to us the promise and prospect of eternal life, releasing us from the prison of death. The purpose of life is therefore to exercise that freedom and build on that hope, creating communities that demonstrate the reconciliation they together make possible.

The Feast of All Saints is a moment we focus on those in the history of the church whose lives have shown us the character of the holy city that we've just heard about in Revelation 21. By describing our eternal home as a city, Revelation is telling us there will always be politics in our lives. We will always be in the business of making alliances with those to whom we feel connected and trying to persuade those whose differences from us lead to tension. There is no disembodied peace in which problems go away and honest dialogue is no longer required. That's not heaven – that's laziness. The saints show us the politics of heaven, which in this world continues to require sacrifice, courage, witness and patience. Britain never completely got Europe right, and now it's about to embark on another chapter of how it relates to its international neighbours, near and far. Challenges and trials are sent to us to disclose who we really are and to reveal where our commitments truly lie. Only in the face of challenge do we discover gifts we never realized the Spirit was giving us. Right now, the gift we as Church and nation need is the grace to live with those who see the world very differently from the way we do. That grace is a fruit of the Spirit too, along with the love, joy and peace we'd rather be given.

This is the territory on which we need to be having the conversation, regardless of which negotiating position the government finally settles upon. What we're talking about is a diversity of visions of what it means to be human, what it means to join together with people who are different from ourselves, and how we can make a future together. 23 June 2016 exposed the fact that people have a variety of views on these things, far too wide in fact to be captured helpfully by a yes/no vote. But politics is about encompassing such diversity and making it fruitful, and it always has been. And so is church. We should always have known that.

The Brexit debate, both before the 2016 vote and even more afterwards, ignited gut-level feelings and soured otherwise amicable relationships like no other political issue in Britain in my lifetime. The outcome of the referendum took almost everyone by surprise, winners and losers. What had not been anticipated was that a vote to leave the EU left a host of choices and unanswered questions, with no obvious procedure available to resolve them – particularly after the 2017 general election left the Conservative Party no majority in the House of Commons. Everyone was cross, almost no one has changed their mind about anything, and there was no easy way out of the impasse.

At St Martin-in-the-Fields, the mood in June 2016 was almost universally one of shock, sorrow and bewilderment, and my clergy colleagues and I sought to reflect that mood in the days that followed the vote, particularly in light of our staff and congregation hailing from more than 25 different countries. But it quickly became clear that, while in the tiny minority, the Leavers were unapologetic, vocal and assertive in the rightness of their cause, and that while almost overwhelming, the Remainers in the community could not take the universality of their convictions for granted, even in such a diverse and famously progressive environment. So for two years the subject went almost entirely unmentioned in sermons, and intercessions contained mysterious pleas that the Holy Spirit would 'give wisdom to all exploring the future role of this country in relation to Europe and the rest of the world.' Much the same culture was true of the Cambridge college, which voted overwhelmingly to remain, but among whose faculty were conspicuous, ardent and articulate spokespeople and campaigners for the Leave cause. It was while reading a book written by one of these professors that I realized I was beginning to discover something that might need to be said that wasn't simply amplifying what everyone else was saying (and no one was listening to). I was also aware that, while its clergy had voted by a huge majority to remain, the laity of the Church of England had voted marginally to leave, and this was a reality with which the church as a whole was struggling to come to terms.

As I prepared the sermon, some things became clear. The first was that the theological point at stake was identity. In other words, this was, whether I made it explicit or not, fundamentally a sermon about baptism. The second was that in each setting the congregation would be apprehensive. There are so many ways to get things wrong when you are addressing a controversial subject, and few in either congregation seriously believed I would avoid all the pitfalls. The most obvious pitfalls were these: to give the impression I was using the privilege of everyone's attention to tee off on my own personal prejudices and inflict them on a captive congregation; to pretend I was neutral on a question on which I have yet to find a UK citizen who is neutral; to show no connection between my argument and the theological convictions and formation that had won me the honour of speaking from a pulpit; to suggest that those who disagreed with me were not only misguided but foolish and sinful;

and to lack the humility to recognize that I might be wrong. So I set about telling a story that would be genuinely interesting (and thus not incline the listener to feel I was merely repeating information endlessly discussed in the media), in which each person could locate themselves without too much difficulty and that steered clear of the name-calling and reductionism of most of the debate. I then included an element of humour, not just to lighten the mood, but to introduce a note of reality about what the last 40 years might have looked like from a non-UK perspective. Then, recognizing that the debate had been almost entirely on political and economic grounds, I made the single 'great leap' of the sermon – to say that I didn't believe this was really about politics or economics, but about identity. This leap had to be established and argued; but once made, created the space to make two crucial points, both intended in an ecumenical, reconciling spirit. The first was that Christianity was about an identity that went deeper than national or any other ancillary identity. (The Cambridge sermon, being shorter, left out the part about All Saints and this argument was weaker as a result.) The second was that politics is about navigating a host of different and sometimes conflicting identities, and church politics is not in most respects any different. If the first point was an invitation to all present to acknowledge a higher loyalty than their temporary divisions, the second point was designed to finish on a rather crestfallen note of humility that deep division shouldn't really be taking us by surprise. Success was going to be about persuasion, understanding and grace, and never about pummelling the opposition into submission or regarding them as mad, bad, ignorant or ridiculous.

It's always risky for the preacher to try to judge the reception of a sermon, so I relied on wise observers on each occasion to gauge the mood of the respective congregations. On both occasions there was such universal anxiety that I was going to fall into one or all of the five pitfalls noted earlier that the most tangible feeling afterwards was the relief and surprise that it seemed, to most, that I had not. I can't blame the Cambridge congregation for this, but I was still rather grieved that my regular congregation, whom I had, by that stage, served for six and a half years, were still anxious on this score. It simply shows how nervous a congregation is that a preacher will misuse the privilege of the pulpit – a nervousness only exacerbated when the subject matter is so notoriously divisive. The congregation can only have become so nervous from exposure to bad examples, in this setting or elsewhere. The second response in Cambridge was a more cheerful, 'Well, something for everybody' – which initially seemed lame, but on reflection I took as gratifying, since it was a jovial reaction to a subject that has brought untold grief. The second response in London was a sense of pride, that people felt we were in a community where we could talk about difficult things in the light of shared faith and reach new insight born of close attention and careful restraint. The third response in Cambridge was delight that the much-maligned 'Church' could enter a public debate and have something fresh and helpful to add. The third response in London was negative: from the voice of the Leave party who could only hear any reference to Brexit as a self-righteous preening of the righteousness of the remain position and couldn't seriously listen to the sermon for fear of receiving further wounding – wishing instead for further calls for reconciliation and unity.

I spent seven years preaching in the United States. I dislike the term prophetic preaching (almost never used in the UK and, in my experience, unique to the US context), because it too often takes the virtue-signalling path dismantled by Jesus in his words about the Pharisee who went up to the temple to pray, and because it too quickly leaves Scripture trailing behind in its specific policy proposals that are remarkably aligned with the platform of one particular political party. So many times I have heard the intercession, 'Lord, may those in positions of authority take the guns out of the hands of those bent on slaughter, and help us to speak up in places where discrimination and prejudice abide.' It's not that I have any admiration for US gun laws or any skin in the game of defending discrimination or prejudice, it's that such prayers could be translated (in *The Message* edition) as, 'Lord, you exist to make the world more like us: hasten in your purpose.'

In a quest to enrich pastoral preaching, therefore, I offer in humility the following guidelines about taking on controversial subjects.

1. Get a reputation for your understanding and insight in scriptural exegesis, theological nuance and pastoral depth before you take on edgy, divisive subjects outside the regular theological orbit. People really want to know about how to forgive and what to hope for when they die more than they want to know what the president should be doing about climate change. Remember, a sermon is almost always about God. Revelation is about the new thing that God is showing us. Sermons are about revelation. So a sermon is about the new thing God is showing us – who God is, who we are, how the two are inextricably linked and what to do about it.
2. Don't take on a big, weighty subject (like Brexit) more than one time in ten. And don't keep on and on about the same things. To make every sermon an attack on the president or prime minister isn't prophetic, it's boring and predictable. And it's the fact that it's boring and predictable that demonstrates that it's not the gospel, but rather it's politics. The gospel is never boring and predictable.

3. Don't be a 'Saturday night preacher' – show your edgy sermon to trusted critics who will be able to suggest ways to make your deepest points more clearly heard and enable you to jettison material where your heart has overruled your head. Show it to those preparing music and prayers so that a rounded perspective can be presented in the liturgy as a whole. Do your best to gauge the views of a dozen diverse congregation members in advance, to assess their fears and learn from their own investment in the issue, integrating their wisdom anonymously as appropriate.
4. Publicize your sermon theme in advance through website, email and social media so that those for whom the issue is sensitive (for example, on an issue such as abortion, should their life experience touch on it significantly) can keep their distance if they want or need to.
5. Avoid 'glancing blows' – in other words, don't make stray references to big subjects in sermons that distract from whatever else you're saying and can't possibly do justice to a complex issue.
6. Don't pretend to be neutral when you're not. Part of what you're modelling is how to be gracious and perceptive even if you feel very strongly and are convinced right is on your side. If people are critical, courteously follow up with them and so discover ways in which you might be better able to understand and speak with your people.
7. Remember 'the personal is the political' – in other words, it's more helpful to empower people to reflect on particular changes in their lives, which together make a big difference, than to call on faraway people who aren't listening to change the world all at one go.
8. If you are so passionate about an issue that you can't speak charitably about those who take a different view and can't in any significant way present another perspective than your own, it may be best to handle a difficult subject through a town-hall or open-microphone-style meeting than through a sermon.
9. Never underestimate the diversity of even the most apparently monochrome congregation. Even when you are sure you are speaking 'for us all' you almost certainly are not, and if you are indeed speaking for us all it may not be necessary to speak at all. You can't call it prophetic if no one's disagreeing with you. Be very careful about using the word 'we'.
10. It shows no insight and no humility to call on everyone to change but yourself. An argument carries a lot more weight if you say, '… and I recognize that to uphold this policy is going to require sacrifices from you and me.' Actions speak louder than words. Don't advocate for more liberal migration laws without at the same time cultivating a policy for welcoming, integrating or supporting migrants.

The problem with prophetic preaching is not that it's too often too prophetic, it's that it's too often terrible preaching – not about God, not new, not good news, not interesting, little or nothing to do with Scripture, not about our own transformation. If we get the preaching right, the prophecy will most likely look after itself.

The following sermon seeks to heed these ten guidelines. It doesn't address a specific political issue, although the Brexit context is almost unavoidable; instead, it affirms the politics of church – not so much the relations of Christians with each other, but the difference made in the world by there being a church.

Citizens of Heaven
Philippians 3.17—4.1
17 March 2019

'Are you a Londoner?' a journalist asked me last week. I found it a hard question to answer. I grew up in the West Country, although none of my family live there now. I was born in Canada, although my parents weren't there very long. My mother was a refugee from Berlin, although her parents weren't German. My father lived in London for several years, as did my sister, although they each moved away in their early thirties. I lived in America for many years, although never planned to settle there permanently. I've now lived in London longer than anywhere else in my adult life – but I somehow resist being pinned down to having to support Spurs or Arsenal or pining for the sound of Bow Bells.

So when Theresa May said at the Conservative Party conference in 2016, 'If you believe you are a citizen of the world, you are a citizen of nowhere,' I wondered if she was talking to me. Whatever you think about her accusation, she certainly put her finger on something important. A recent book claims the significant divide in British politics is not between capitalism and socialism, but 'between the people who see the world from Anywhere and the people who see it from Somewhere.'[2]

'Anywheres' dominate British culture and society. They thrive at school, go to prestigious universities, work in cities at some stage, marry late and populate the cultural elites. They are self-made. They are proud of being tolerant, meritocratic, egalitarian, autonomous, open to change, internationalist and individualist. They often live a long way

---

2 David Goodhart, *The Road to Somewhere: The New Tribes Shaping British Politics* (London: Penguin, 2017).

from their parents. They comprise about 25% of the population and almost all voted Remain.

'Somewheres' are about 50% of the population. Their identity is designated: they are a Scottish farmer, a working-class Geordie, a Cornish housewife. They mostly live within 20 miles of where they lived when they were 14. They are generally more local in outlook, communitarian, stable, patriotic, traditional, mindful of security and tied to specific places. They have larger families and give more to charity.

David Goodhart, the author of the book, contrasts what work means to the respective groups. (If you've got a tidy mind and are wondering about the other 25%, they're the In-Betweeners.) Anywheres work because they seek a good income and they wish to exercise their skills. Somewheres obviously need income, but are much more concerned to contribute to the lives of others, both family and the wider public. There's an irony that Anywheres proclaim the equality of diverse family structures, but themselves tend to live in stable nuclear families; whereas Somewheres tend to have a more conservative view of the home but their actual domestic lives tend to be less stable. The paradox of our society, in these terms, is that we're a population largely made up of Somewheres, whose cultural, educational, commercial and political leaders are mostly made up of Anywheres.

Rather than argue over the details of this analysis, I want today to identify the more general point that our lives are more centred on identity and belonging than on ideas or convictions. The experience of unemployment is of course about loss of income, but even more about not knowing who we are or where we belong. The great decisions of our lives are seldom prudent calculations of benefit and risk, and more often gut-level realizations of our true character and the people who we want and need around us. Our family and friends are those who most fully know who we are and see things about us that we hide from ourselves. The great political debates of our day aren't fundamentally about human rights or economic benefits or legitimate migration or coarsening public discourse: they're about profound identity, deep belonging, and about how we each can find a balance between securing our own sense of who we are while appreciating and encouraging the flourishing of those whose identity and belonging is different from our own.

It's into this context that Paul in his letter to the Philippians speaks some powerful words. In the midst of controversy over the person of Jesus Christ and over what kind of lifestyle was faithful to his legacy, Paul announces a revolution in our notions of identity and belonging. He says, 'Our citizenship is in heaven.' That might sound like familiar

Bible language – so I want to pause for a moment to recognize how transformational those words really are, for Anywheres and Somewheres alike. Paul literally shifts the centre of the universe, from this existence and our daily reality, to the realm of essence, the things that last forever, the habitation of God and of those whom God has called to share the life of eternity. Rather than earth being the source and testing ground of truth and coherence, heaven becomes the measure of all things. When we're assessing whether something is right or wrong, the question now is, does it stand the test of eternity? Will it abide with God forever? Or does it belong to the world that is passing away?

Consider the cliché of our time, 'I hear where you're coming from.' When we're confronted with a disputatious work colleague or an enervating in-law or a troublesome fellow passenger on a bus, and we have the will to come alongside them but still somehow win the argument, we say, with a hint of understanding perceptible within our weariness, 'Look, mate, I see where you're coming from…' and then we show that we really do appreciate what's making them act in this exasperating way. But there's always a 'but' and sure enough, after a short or long time, we eventually say, 'But see what it looks like for me,' and subtly suggest that our perspective is better, wiser, more comprehensive or more authoritative, and must prevail. You could say that's our cultural problem today: we're not really hearing where each other are coming from.

But Paul turns this kind of argument on its head. By saying we're citizens of heaven, he's saying, 'It's not finally about where you're coming from – it's about *where you're going*.' See what a colossal transformation this involves. If we try to reconcile where we're coming from, we'll never manage it – we'll be defeated by difference, deflated by diversity, discouraged by divergence. That all changes if we follow Paul and start to concentrate on where we're going. We're going to heaven – where there is more than enough love for all, more than enough joy, more than enough truth, more than enough space for everyone to flourish. So we arrive at a definition of the church: a bunch of people who all come from different places but are all going to the same place. Yes, it's interesting where we're coming from – but what's vital is where we're going.

So being a Christian transforms our identity. No longer are we trying to assert our assumptions as normal, demanding that everyone hear how much we've suffered to ensure they excuse our eccentricities, imposing our prejudices on others so we never have to be challenged or changed. Now we are a people pooling our resources for a journey we make together to a place none of us have ever been. There are no experts, because we're all citizens of a country we've never visited and longing for a home we've never known. How do we prepare for that journey?

Well, we start by consulting the guidebook. In the guidebook we start to learn a new language, begin to practise new habits, commence making new companions. For example, we stop saying 'life isn't a rehearsal' – because actually it is – or 'life's too short' – because the life that really matters goes on forever. We stop taking the largest piece of pie or the biggest slice of cake because we believe we're all one body and you eating is the same as me eating. We cease trying to make ourselves omnicompetent because we know that for a community to flourish, everyone has to have moments when they need to ask for help and moments when they're in a position to offer help. We cease seeing others as a threat and start to perceive the ways in which they are a gift.

Once we've got this new language, new habits and new companions, we can explore the next stage. And that's living as if we were already there. The experience of what it's like to feel like you're already in heaven is what we call the kingdom of God. Living as if we were already in heaven means being able to sit together in silence, because silence is no longer dead time but time in which we are most fully aware that God, rather than us, is the major actor in history, and we are blessed to be created by one in whose eyes we are precious, honoured and loved. It means keeping Sabbath, because Sabbath is a constant experience of not striving to secure our own salvation but resting in the grace that all the real work has already been done by God. It means sharing in worship in a way that recognizes that we all bring different things to the table but receive back the same. It means seeking to help others while being constantly aware of the ways in which they are helping you.

And when we've got used to living as if we were already in heaven, there's only one more step to take: and that's to let go of our own belonging, release our constant effort to establish and maintain our own identity and instead allow ourselves to be wholly owned by God. This is, of course, what baptism enacts. But it's no simple thing. You may know the story of the man who fell off the cliff. Somehow, as he fell, he clung on to a branch growing out of the rocky edge. Desperate, he shouted, 'Is anybody up there?' After a pause, a quiet voice said, 'My son, I am with you. Let go of the branch and I am here.' He thought for a moment and finally shouted, 'Is anybody else up there?' It's no simple thing to give up our own identity and allow our belonging to be refashioned. But it's the secret of eternal life.

The quest to discover where we're each coming from is a never-ending and finally fruitless one. The turn to realize where we're all going is a life-giving and joyful one. As Paul puts it, the Holy Spirit is turning the body of our humiliation so that it may be conformed to the body of Christ's glory. That's real transformation. That's what being a Christian is all about.

Once again, the tactic is to turn a question over identity into an opportunity to affirm the deeper identity bestowed through baptism. Through turning the question round from 'Where are you from?' to 'Where are you going?' the intractability of identity divides is overcome at a stroke; the issue shifts from created difference to eschatological convergence. The rest of the sermon is laying the ground for and underlining this point. If you've got a single important point to make, you construct the whole sermon around it.

2

Preaching about Society

Preaching about society is often more dangerous than preaching about politics. That's for two reasons. The first is that preachers, always liable to communicate rather more about their assumed social location than is wise or helpful, are especially so when speaking about society. The other is that the church, almost universally in the popular imagination and unfortunately often in reality, is immersed in nostalgia for a time when people were good, churchgoing was normal, the rate of change was digestible and all was well with the world. Recent critiques have exposed how racist, sexist and impervious to the climate emergency such assumptions invariably are; but they remain widely held and too many preachers are in thrall to a time when they suppose the church got it right. I once began a conversation with the leader of a prestigious church from a rather different tradition from mine by saying, 'I'm sure we disagree on a lot of things, but one thing I'm guessing we can agree on is that we can be confident that if our congregations were ever to stop believing in God, they would still believe in the 1950s.'

There's a quasi-holy approach in some styles of preaching that seems to believe that lament for the follies and complexities of our current age is a form of faithfulness to the gospel. Christian convictions give the preacher no especial insight into the malaises of this or any other era – and certainly no privileged knowledge that this is an especially benighted time. What those convictions do offer is good news about the inbreaking realm of God. It's quite in order to engage compassionately with those most disadvantaged in one's current time, and sometimes helpful to employ a dose of irony in highlighting how, despite the veneer of sophistication, our contemporary struggles make us no better or worse than those of other eras; but it's seldom appropriate to launch into a lament about ways in which things that could be taken for granted once upon a time cannot now, since this usually means the valorizing of one social context over another, unhelpfully privileging the speaker's own background. It can gain superficial consent from a congregation, but at the cost of substituting a particular context for a universal gospel.

In the following sermon, I seek both to empower and to challenge the congregation by suggesting that society isn't something a faceless *they* are depleting but something a very present *we* can be replenishing. The real issue in preaching on Revelation, in particular the final two chapters, is whether eschatology is something pie-in-the-sky and largely otherworldly or whether Christianity in fact works backwards by setting a vision for transformed existence and then imploring us to live that future now. The following sermon takes the latter view, considering a fascinating sociological study and deriving from it significant implications for church and God's realm.

The Holy City
Revelation 21.10, 22—22.5
26 May 2019

In 1995, an extraordinary heatwave afflicted the city of Chicago, killing around 750 people. Later, the sociologist Eric Klinenberg made a detailed examination of who died and who didn't. What he found was that the intense heat affected diverse neighbourhoods and social groups differently. Perhaps unsurprisingly, eight of the ten worst-hit neighbourhoods were African American. In such neighbourhoods, individuals, especially the elderly, would hunker down in the shadow of poverty and crime, keeping windows shut to curb burglaries. Such people would become isolated with the result that, come the heatwave, no one checked up to see if they were becoming dehydrated or experiencing heat exhaustion, and so many of them died. But Klinenberg also found some things he wasn't expecting to find. Three of the ten neighbourhoods with the *lowest* death rates were *also* poor and African American. Why? In the resilient neighbourhoods, diners, parks, minimarkets and barbershops were within easy walking distance: people came to know each other well enough to miss one another during the heatwave; it was easy to check on them, so lives were saved.

Klinenberg discovered that the biggest factor in determining people's well-being was not their level of income, but whether their neighbourhood had good social infrastructure. The difference of longevity between those in the good and those in the poor infrastructure neighbourhoods could average as much as ten years.[1]

---

1 Eric Klinenberg, *Palaces for the People: How to Build a More Equal and United Society* (London: Bodley Head, 2018).

Social infrastructure is a sophisticated name for the informal places where good things happen. Andrew Carnegie, dollar for dollar the greatest philanthropist in modern history, built 2,811 lending libraries and called them Palaces for the People. Libraries are the epitome of social infrastructure. They are places where people unrelated by family, tribe, race or class naturally meet, connect, have conversation and make relationships born of shared interests and passions. Other such places are the hairdresser, the gym, the cared-for park and playground, the outdoor swimming pool, the community garden, the market, the bookshop and the communal lounge with free Wi-Fi. These are spaces where people are welcome to congregate, linger and strike up conversation with strangers.

We all know the great threats to the developed world: climate change, profound inequality, serious poverty, an aging population and explosive racial and ethnic divisions. How can we address such challenges unless by developing stronger bonds and genuinely shared interests? It's common to lament chronic underinvestment in hard infrastructure – bridges, sewage works, railways, roads, communications and storm protection. But hard infrastructure only improves society when social infrastructure accompanies it – and when hard infrastructure fails, as in the Chicago heatwave, it's social infrastructure that determines our fate. Klinenberg concludes that 'social isolation and loneliness can be as dangerous as more publicised health hazards, including obesity and smoking.' The answer isn't technocratic or civic, but something in between – the hidden networks and taken-for-granted systems that underpin collective life.

We've just read together words from the last chapter of the Bible, Revelation 22. Here we discover that when all is literally said and done, what we're given is a new city. Notice it's not a cloud with an angel and a harp; it's not a garden with herbaceous borders; it's not a clearing in a primeval forest. It's a city. At first glance there's an awful lot of 'no'. There's no temple, because the whole city is holy, and God is there in person, so there's no need for a holy place. There's no sun or moon, because the city is bathed in the glory of God. There are no shut gates, because there are no enemies to keep at bay. There's no night, because on its spinning orbit the city will never turn away from the glory of God. There'll be no need of lamp or sun, because people will be so close to God they'll walk in the ways of justice and peace without any path to follow.

But see what there *is* in this holy city that comes from the heart of God. There's the utter presence of God. The people will see the face of God, something not possible since the creation of the world; they will bear God's name on their foreheads; and they will worship. There's the glory of God and all earthly glory. The river of the water of life flows through the holy city, just as the river ran through the Garden of Eden; and it flows from the throne of God, just as blood and water flowed out of the side of Christ when his body was pierced on the cross. And right there at the centre of the city is the tree of life, just as in Eden, but this time, instead of its fruit producing sin and death it has 12 kinds of fruit to encompass the 12 tribes of Israel and its leaves are for the healing of the nations.

We may think, 'Well that's all very lovely – and if eternity's like that then you can count me in.' But I want to point out the connection between what Eric Klinenberg discovered about cities and the holy city as described in the final book of the Bible. The holy city isn't a place that needs large infrastructure projects. It doesn't have the usual roster of social malaises. It isn't a deeply conflictual place where everyone is cautious about neighbours and mistrustful of strangers. But it does have one crucial thing in common with the Chicago of 1995. It needs people to make connections, form relationships and establish trust. What I want to point out is what a challenge this constitutes for what we usually think of as church.

Here's what we think of as church. We worship God, we seek to grow as disciples and we take the good news of the kingdom to the waiting world. Sometimes we take that news in verbal form and communicate the wonder of God in Christ through telling the story and challenging the listener and hoping for a response. Other times, we turn the good news into actions of goodness and mercy that seek to show what love can do and model what selfless kindness looks like. See what all of these forms of church have in common? They all assume that we know better, act better, understand better than the rest of the world and that mission is transferring wisdom, compassion or resources from us to them.

But what Klinenberg is describing isn't like that. He's not saying the best thing we can do is to find more and more ingenious and appropriate ways to demonstrate our beneficence and, out of our abundance, meet people in their scarcity. He's suggesting something much simpler and humbler. He's proposing we actively participate in the informal processes by which strangers come to establish communities of trust. Rather than approach every social situation thinking, 'How can I exercise my superiority by being generous or magnanimous?' this means looking for contexts where the Holy Spirit will make something good happen that isn't necessarily limited to our own vision or under our control.

In my all-time favourite TV advert, you hear a bell and then see a godly figure and a devilish figure meeting in a neutral space between hellfire and Elysian clouds. The godly figure breaks a Kit Kat in half and shares it. After a few munches, the devilish figure says, 'Oh well! No rest for the wicked,' and heads back to the flames. It's a playful scene that makes me wonder where and how I encounter and learn to coexist with those who are in every way different from me.

Let's imagine you're at the launderette. It's an interesting place, because once you've put your coins in, you're more or less stuck there for 40 minutes till the cycle's complete. Of course, you can get out your phone or read a book; but you can also ask the person using the next-door machine if they saw the game yesterday or whether they'd recommend what they're reading. Likewise on the train. Everyone knows you're not allowed to talk to strangers on a commuter train or the tube. But on a long-distance train it says on your seat where you're travelling to and a myriad of mysteries can begin with the words, 'Going to Peterborough?'

We've got it into our heads that you can tell we are Christians by our activity, our busy-ness, our constant advocacy for the poor or witness for the planet or justice for the migrant. But maybe mission is rather simpler and a lot more stationary. We're facing a period in history where our lives are more permeated by strangers, and a larger and larger number of people never have a real face-to-face conversation from one day to the next. They don't necessarily need rescuing from starvation or turning from their wicked ways; their need is for connection, humanity, common ground, a listening ear. In a lot of ways, we'd rather save them, because it spares us the relationship; but that way they're just saved for another stretch of loneliness and isolation.

Among the most important parts of St Martin's are our cafés. You'll notice few people go into the café alone. The cafés are places to talk, deepen relationship, find understanding, show concern. But just as important is the foyer at the base of the staircase. Without spending any money, people can linger, rest, strike up conversation, find common humanity. The significance of this is that this is how we'll all be spending eternity. We'll be in this holy city, with no lamp or sun, bathed in glory, with no social problems to fix – just opportunities to be with one another and God. So every time we strike up such a conversation we're rehearsing eternal life.

But we're also doing something even more significant. We admire, worship and adore Jesus. We believe he shows us the way God sets the world straight. But we also believe in the Holy Spirit. The Holy Spirit shows up when people meet, when relationships begin to form, when we discover the sheer goodness of the gift of one another. There's a temptation that many of us share, and that's to want to be Jesus so successfully that there's nothing left for the Holy Spirit to do. We want to save the world ourselves; and that's not a bad thing, unless it suggests that Jesus hasn't actually already done it. Maybe a more faithful and thoughtful approach is to create situations, cultivate circumstances and advance opportunities where the Holy Spirit will show up, with surprises, gifts, coincidences and miracles.

We can read the account of the holy city in Revelation as a faraway tale of utopian bliss. Or we can see it as a challenge to say, if we stopped thinking about what's missing from our lives, and how material change would make things better, how would we invest more imagination and energy in creating and sustaining real connection and relationship with people who we'd never meet through our work and home and regular life? And isn't such encounter where our real work as the church and our greatest contribution to our fractured society truly lies? Might we ask ourselves, 'This week, how may I cultivate connection with one person just for the sake of experiencing the abundance God has to give me through them?' Instead of waiting around for someone else to build social infrastructure, maybe, without realizing it, we could become that infrastructure ourselves.

This sermon employs insights not just from Eric Klinenberg's book but from John McKnight's ABCD (Asset-Based Community Development) movement, which shift the emphasis from what professionals aren't doing to what locals can do. It also challenges the assumption that mission is basically structured to make Christians the providers of expertise and models of benefaction, and asserts instead that mission is about discovering what the Holy Spirit is doing and joining in.

Here are some guidelines for preaching a sermon about society.

1. Ask yourself, 'Why do I have this impulse toward lament?' Are you colluding in an assumption that church or society once got all this right and (in a British context) uncomfortably close to a colonial assumption that a particular manifestation of church, with a sense of cultural superiority, is called to impose its character on others?
2. Look for the social implications of the narratives and injunctions the Bible offers. Don't just look for a personal takeaway of how an individual is going to live their life differently in the week to come.
3. Adopt an approach of appreciative enquiry toward another culture, thus ensuring you avoid conflating your own culture with the realm of God. If you can offer the directness of your own personal experience of that other culture, well and good; if instead you can present

succinct analysis provided by a third party in a book or article, just as good – provided you can focus on just a few salient points and avoid offering too much detail.
4. Find a way to show how Christianity affirms aspects of society while challenging others. A gospel that has no time for the abiding habits of growing healthy communities will in the end disrupt everything around it and have nothing with which to replace it.
5. Ensure you're communicating that you yourself are discovering and exploring, rather than speaking from a place of arrival waiting patiently or patronisingly for the congregation to catch up. This is a journey we're all already on, rather than one some of us have completed and are now communicating to others.
6. Try to offer illustrations of common practices from your own community that have wider significance, rather than communicate to your community that it has nothing to commend it and all the good examples come from elsewhere.

The following sermon differs from the previous one in that it's about a specific situation, indeed a specific three-word phrase that was ubiquitous at the time the sermon was preached – during the short premiership of Liz Truss. In some ways, it's more of a homily than a sermon, in that it turns round one phrase like a prism, before overturning it by placing it in a theological context. However, because the two modes of this sermon – exploring the context of this key phrase and then reframing it in narrative/theological terms – are so explicit, some subtle messages can be conveyed along the way, even while apparently relating things we all already know.

I never apologize for communicating the end of a novel or film, by saying 'Spoiler alert' or some such disclaimer. Whenever I preach about a story like this, a good number of people ask for details of publication or release, and I've never had anyone complain that I've given the game away or suggest they're less likely to engage with the account because I've revealed the climax. The point is to avoid getting so immersed in the story that you relate unnecessary detail: you only articulate such information as is crucial to the point of the sermon – in this case, to the reframing of the key term, 'cost of living'.

The cost of living
Harvest Festival
2 October 2022

How are you going to end the energy crisis, Prime Minister? How are you going to end the war in Ukraine, help people cope with the catastrophic rise in inflation, support the NHS, deal with the Northern Ireland protocol, address a small delicacy with the IMF, and a thousand other things? There's only one answer to all these questions – and it's a very short one: 'It depends.' The truth is all these things and most of the critical issues facing our country are to some degree related, and the way the new Prime Minister addresses one will affect the others. Meanwhile, many of the chief factors are way beyond the government's control. It's never an adequate answer, but it's almost always the most truthful answer: 'It depends.'

There's a set of jargon for this realization in management-speak. It's the notion of dependencies. A dependency describes the relationship among activities and specifies the particular order in which they need to be performed. Like a lot of management-speak, it's glorified common sense. If I can't start cooking dinner until you've brought the shopping home, then that's known as a finish-to-start dependency, because you can't cook without food. But if I've already got the mince, the chopped tomatoes, the herbs, onions and pasta, and all you're bringing home from the shops is the parmesan cheese, then that's a finish-to-finish dependency, because I can start before you've finished but I can't finish till you've finished. A key skill of management is to keep control of all your dependencies so you're not paying a workforce to sit idle in a factory waiting three weeks for the raw materials to arrive.

That's tough enough when managing a company. Imagine trying to manage all the dependencies when you're running a country. We find ourselves in a crisis right now because the dependencies have got way out of control. The pandemic led to supply-chain delays and a fall-off in demand for energy. The resumption in economic activity and the Ukraine war have hugely exacerbated both problems, and the rising cost of gas has increased the cost of fertilizers, thus inflating food prices. The labour shortage due to Brexit exacerbated the supply-chain delays, and it turns out the UK's gas reserves were much too low. It's a car crash of international and national dependencies – a textbook nightmare scenario, most affecting fuel, food and energy, three basic resources for every household.

What we're experiencing is what happens when our degree of dependency is exposed and our vulnerability is laid bare. It's a horrible feeling to discover how vulnerable you are and to feel so exposed. Not to be able to pay for fuel, not to afford food, not to imagine how you can cover a utility bill. But wait. Once we've got used to this alarming and, we trust, temporary reality, we perhaps need to attend to what this sense of vulnerability is telling us. It's revealing the host of dependencies that, when they go well, we take for granted.

We press a switch and a light goes on. We turn a knob and a gas flame catches fire on an oven top. We turn a key in the ignition and a car starts. We dial a number and a phone connects us to someone. And that's just the technology. We dial 999 and an ambulance comes. We wait by a sign and a bus comes. We give the checkout assistant some cash and we walk away with some groceries. On a larger scale, we go to bed in the dark and next morning the sun rises. We take in a breath and our lungs rise and fall. We see a leaf drop and a few months later a leaf grows from the same branch.

If any of these things don't happen as we expect, we become truly exasperated or deeply terrified. These are the foundations of our existence – as creatures in the world, as citizens of society, as members of a sophisticated communication network. But think what each of these things tells us about the myriad of interdependencies that underpin our lives. Most such things aren't goods or services we can pay money for; they're just things we believe we can take for granted – so much so we feel entitled to them.

I want to suggest to you a phrase that might describe those things we utterly depend on which someone else or something else is constantly sustaining, and without which we feel completely bereft. That phrase is the 'cost of living'. Now, you may have heard that phrase before. You may in fact have heard the phrase 'cost-of-living crisis' used almost constantly in the last few months to refer to the way the price of essential goods has been increasing far more rapidly than household incomes, resulting in people having to go without essential goods. But I want you to dwell more precisely on that phrase: cost of living. For our living – for my living, for everyone's living – there's a colossal, unimaginable, indescribable cost, which we seldom consider and almost never talk about.

I want you to think of this cost on three levels – three dimensions of dependency, if you like. The first level is everyday dependency. I use a laptop and a mobile phone a great deal. I have no idea how these things work, and yes, I pay some money for them, but I'm powerless without the people who make them and repair them and understand how their systems go. I go outside and there are buses and trains and shops and a whole social network of things that make my life possible. When things go wrong, there are doctors and opticians and dentists and police and lawyers and social security and insurance payments that exist to put them right. When we talk about things like postcolonial thinking, what we're identifying is the degree to which, in both explicit and hidden ways, the affluence of some societies depends on the exploitation of others; just because our country no longer has an empire, it doesn't mean our relative wealth doesn't rest on sweatshops and pitiful wages in client countries.

On the next level there's cosmic dependency. There's a planet, whose ecosystem we've woken up and realized is more fragile than we thought. There's my parents, without whose existence there would have been no me in the first place. There's weather and crops and livestock and transport and food processing, and on a grander scale, a bunch of meteors that haven't yet struck the earth but could blow us all apart one day.

But there's a third level we can call divine dependency. God made all things in order to be with us in Christ. We have no idea what it cost God to make all things. But we can see what it cost God to be with us in Christ, because we rejected Christ and crucified him. We have no idea how God raised Christ from the dead, but we can see the risen Christ in the work of the Spirit in great things and small. The cost of our living is a cost paid by God in Christ. The cost of our living with God forever is a cost we could never afford, astronomically beyond our capacity or ability to pay.

In Marius Gabriel's gripping novel *Goodnight Vienna*, published earlier this year, Gretchen is a 12-year-old neurodivergent Viennese girl who can neither read nor write, but has an incredible gift: she can listen once to a piece of music and then play it perfectly on the piano. Her caregiver is a frustrated trainee doctor, Katya, who's had to leave Glasgow in 1937 and move to Austria because her parents ran out of money. When the Nazis take over Austria, Gretchen is at risk of being sent to a medical research laboratory. Katya stops feeling sorry for herself and realizes she has to get young Gretchen out of the country. They have a series of near misses and dangerous adventures until they find themselves with forged passports on a train with a Jewish wheelchair-user, Shulamit.

When they reach the Hungarian border, the Gestapo guards scrutinize the passports closely. They're looking for a woman travelling with a 12-year-old child. It looks like the game's up. At the moment Katya and Gretchen's true identity is about to be revealed, Shulamit ridicules the guards for not realizing she's a Jew and claims she's plotting to kill the Führer. The guards march Shulamit off the train in her wheelchair and forget all about Katya and young Gretchen. Gretchen can't believe what's happened; but Katya says, 'I think she'd planned to do that all along, if she saw you were in danger.' Gretchen sobs, 'I can't even thank her.' Katya replies, 'I think she knows you will thank her with everything you do in your life.'

Goodnight Vienna is a novel about dependency. Katya rages at her dependency on her feckless parents. She initially sees neurodivergent Gretchen as pitifully dependent, before realizing the girl's true gifts and character. The two of them depend on the grace of several courageous people to escape Austria, and in the end Gretchen's life is saved when Jewish wheelchair-user Shulamit lays down her own life in Gretchen's place. Shulamit's death is the cost of Gretchen's living.

The cost-of-living crisis has exposed our dependencies; for some of us in humiliating and impoverishing ways. What I believe it's also showing us is the absurdity of our attempts to manage our dependencies as if the whole of existence could be charted on a project manager's spreadsheet or a finance director's PowerPoint presentation. Not only does this make us ignorant of how much our conventional living costs hidden people; even more it brackets out our maker, sustainer and companion, who bears the true cost of our living at all. Remember Gretchen, sobbing in grief and humility, and saying, when she realizes Shulamit's borne the cost of her living, 'Why did she do that? For me? She gave her life for us. I didn't even say thank you.' And remember Katya's reply: 'I think that was her plan all along.'

This sermon seeks to embody the six guidelines presented earlier. It doesn't take significant time listing the categories of people particularly suffering from the cost-of-living crisis: the congregation is familiar with that information. It doesn't infantilize the congregation by assuming a parental government should just sort everything out. Instead, it invites the congregation to enter into the complexity of the government's situation by engaging with a process some or all of which many members of the congregation will be familiar: assessing dependencies. The notion of a risk register has become widespread in recent years, and covers similar ground, but dependency is a much richer notion that invites humility rather than control, gratitude rather than anxiety.

The sermon could be criticized as abrupt in two ways. It's quite a sudden shift from outlining three notions of dependency to plunging into a novel about 1930s Austria. I'm assuming the listener will not have left off thinking about divine dependency, the third point among the list of dependencies. But the abruptness of the shift is deliberate, making the listener alert to how the notion of dependency and the emerging story are connected. Likewise, the ending of the sermon is sharp. This could lose some listeners; but the technique is to let the listener do the work of realizing real dependency is not just on God in general, but on Christ's utter grace in particular and thus for the listener to glean the satisfaction of putting the two halves of the sermon together, realizing the transformation in the whole notion of the cost of our living. The two moves are deliberate, but require close concentration on the part of the congregation, which can usually be ensured by providing a well-told story.

The common assumptions outlined at the beginning of the chapter mean that many congregations anticipate that every sermon will be a society sermon. This chapter has aimed to show what's profoundly flawed in those assumptions, yet how to ensure that, when you do preach a society sermon, you can actually preach the gospel, and that gospel may have both insight and novelty.

3

Preaching about Freedom

Christianity is about freedom: freedom from guilt and bitterness about the past, and freedom from anxiety and terror about the future. The caricature of preaching about freedom is that in the face of oppression externally it proclaims freedom internally, thus failing to confront injustice and subjugation and promising instead inner peace and eternal assurance. Thus, the task of the preacher is to steer a path that proclaims the joys and consequences of freedom while avoiding the inadequacies of a freedom that doesn't deserve the name.

Freedom is what almost every politician offers. This brings the twin dangers of cliché and empty rhetoric. But it offers the twin opportunities of asserting a truer notion of freedom and recognizing the cost of freedom. This opportunity constitutes the dwelling place of preaching about freedom. The most common approach is to demonstrate how freedom (for oneself) is one of those attainments that is not reached by seeking, but that you realize you have entered while seeking something beyond – something less self-centred, less commodified. The journey is from striving for freedom to accepting the freedom Christ brings.

Any preaching has to identify the power of the concept, and its hold on the contemporary imagination – a hold demonstrated on how many people long for it (note the exhilaration of the Arab Spring of 2011) and how many people are anxious about the ways they may be about to lose it (note the attention given to the appointment of justices to the US Supreme Court in, before and during Donald Trump's tenure as president). But every sermon, while acknowledging that power, has to redefine freedom away from the assumptions made by those who believe its definition belongs to them.

The heart of preaching about freedom is to demonstrate, with imagination and joy, the freedom the Bible proclaims and the ways that that freedom outnarrates the freedom the politicians (particularly the most manipulative ones) claim to offer. Perhaps the definitive account of freedom is given by Paul in Galatians; so I begin this chapter with a discussion and illustration of what Paul is telling us there.

A living parable
Galatians 5.1, 13–25
30 June 2019

The world is captivated by freedom; and never more so than when that freedom seems to be in jeopardy. Three years ago, Donald Trump claimed the American presidency by telling a story that American 'greatness' had been stolen by politically correct elites and racial, ethnic and religious others. The same year, the Brexit campaign won the day by lamenting that British sovereignty had been stolen by European bureaucrats and manipulated by profiteering citizens of nowhere. We were made for freedom, so the story goes, but are constantly in danger of being enslaved.

At Christmas 1989, as Eastern Europe began to unravel, and just after the death of President Ceauşescu, a BBC journalist toured Romania searching for someone who spoke English well enough to be interviewed. Finally, he found a woman who, in 12 words, expressed not just the mood of the time but the whole human condition: 'We have freedom, but we don't know what to do with it.'

When Paul is writing to the church in Galatia, in the centre of modern Turkey, 15 years after the death and resurrection of Jesus, he's dealing with the same question. How are we to keep our freedom and not simply lapse into another kind of slavery? He gives examples of the kinds of obsessions people commonly fall into: alcohol, sexual desire, envy, personal enmity, indulgent escapism, rivalry and ambition. What these all have in common is that they begin as, seem and even feel like good and free things but end up consuming us. Paul wants us to be truly free.

The 2009 film *My Sister's Keeper*, originally a 2004 book by Jodi Picoult, is a modern parable about how the pursuit of freedom can consume us. It tells how easy it is to fall into slavery and where freedom can be found. Sara and Brian have two children, Kate and Jesse. Their daughter Kate develops leukaemia aged 4. Her parents are told the only hope is for them to conceive by in vitro fertilization a sister for Kate who can donate organs, blood and tissue to keep her alive. And so a third child, baby Anna, is born. When Kate is 15, her kidneys fail, and the time has come for 11-year-old Anna to donate one of her vital organs. But to her parents' horror, Anna refuses. When her parents express dismay, and she realizes her mother will go ahead and force her to have her kidney removed against her will, Anna hires a lawyer and asserts her rights to her own body on the grounds of 'medical emancipation'. Her mother Sara, who is herself a lawyer, is dismayed by Anna's selfishness and bewildered that her fanatical efforts over the previous eleven years to keep Kate alive are set to be thwarted. But her husband Brian perceives that they've spent the last eleven years using Anna like a mechanic uses an old car, for body parts and fuel to help her sister, to the point that Anna's future life will be curtailed. Sooner or later there has to be a limit. Anna is not just a means toward her sister's survival. She has to be allowed to live her own life.

As the story reaches an impasse, one wonders how a family where mother and daughter are taking each other to court can possibly function in a caring way, and how young Anna can maintain a loving relationship with her dying sister when she's made it clear she's not prepared to do the one thing that can keep her sister alive. All the tensions in the family boil over when the dying Kate asks to clear out of the hospital and go to the beach one last time. It's a statement that she knows her life is over and she wants to be with her family to create one last memory. But her mother Sara is having none of it. Still determined to work for recovery, Sara loses all control and rails against the idea, to the point where Brian threatens her with divorce if she won't be part of this last family outing. Later that day, Sara sees sense and comes to join in the expedition. The family have the kind of slow-motion perfect day at the beach that only Californian nuclear families have in the movies.

But the momentous day in court nonetheless comes, and Sara gets to cross-examine her own daughter at the witness stand about why Anna won't give up a kidney to save her sister's life. Anna's answers ring increasingly hollow; there's no question her mother is turning into a harridan, but she has a point – why wouldn't you constrict your own life to save your beloved sister? Anna's refusal does seem to be uncharacteristically and inexplicably selfish. Finally, Jesse, the silent, suffering presence in the story, stands up in the courtroom and demands that his younger sister finally tell the truth. And the transformative truth that no one, not campaigning mother or sympathetic father or gripped audience is ready to hear, but that all three children already know, is this: refusing the operation was not Anna's wish; it was Kate's. Kate has been trying to tell her mother that she'd realized it was time to die, but her mother couldn't hear it. So the only way was to persuade Anna to refuse to give up her kidney on contrived grounds and so bring about a crisis in which her mother would finally get the message. At last seeing reason, Sara, finally at peace with both her daughters, leaves the courtroom and lies down in the hospital bed beside Kate, who dies later the same day.

The story is a study in the contrast between being with and working for. Sara's passionate commitment to the necessity of working for Kate obliterates any understanding of her dying child's best interests. Sara is unable to be with Kate except at the beach, when she's been threatened with losing her whole family, and in Kate's dying moments, when Sara has finally realized she doesn't even have Kate's support in her passionate campaign. Sara loses all ability to be with her family, as she becomes enslaved to the cause of saving Kate. Eleven-year-old Anna does work for her sister, by lying and saying she has no desire to donate her kidney and even suing her parents. But Anna's working for is fundamentally grounded in her deep and lifelong being with Kate, and is only entered into reluctantly and as a last resort. You can even see Anna's working for Kate as a drastic way of enabling the whole family to be with each other, because the only way for the family to be with one another is for Sara to cease her obsessive pursuit of Kate's recovery and simply enjoy the time they have left together. Brian spends the whole story trying to be with both his wife Sara and with his daughter Anna. The attempt tears him apart. Jesse feels powerless to work for either of them and ends up being able to be with no one, until finally in desperation he makes the crucial intervention that tells the truth about Anna and forces Sara to face the truth about Kate and so enables the family to be with one another for just those last few hours – but crucially, enables the surviving members of the family to be with one another into the future without bitterness or resentment.

The paradox at the heart of the story is that the lawyer's passionate pursuit of freedom ironically imprisons herself and her family, instrumentalizes and thus enslaves her younger daughter, and deprives her elder daughter of the one thing that by the end of the story she really wants, making her instead a slave to now-pointless medical treatment. The story works as a parable by showing how easy it is to subject relationships in particular to the tyranny of causes, and more generally to make the passionate pursuit of freedom itself a form of slavery. What makes the story particularly satisfying is that a daughter suing her mother seems like the most ghastly abandonment of family relationships and surrendering of love to law, but it is only in the law court that the loving truth emerges: it's not that selfish Anna is making Kate suffer and die out of a narcissistic desire to live a materially free and acquisitive life of her own; it's that loving Anna is laying down her life and jeopardizing all her most precious relationships so that Kate can exercise her choice to end pointless treatment. The story begins with Sara and Brian instrumentalizing Anna to seek body parts for Kate; but the story ends with Kate instrumentalizing Anna to make Sara see sense. Everyone uses Anna.

And that brings us back to Galatians. Sara is the embodiment of what Paul is warning the Galatians about. She becomes consumed by envy, rivalry, competitiveness, anger, strife, jealousy, quarrels, dissensions, factions. What she's doing, she's doing for apparently the noblest of reasons – she's giving up her job, imperilling her relationships and devoting her whole life to the cause of saving her daughter. But it imprisons her, enslaves her elder daughter, instrumentalizes her younger daughter and alienates her whole family.

Meanwhile, Anna is the embodiment of everything Paul is commending. Love, joy, peace, patience, kindness, generosity, faithfulness, gentleness and self-control. And she's only 11 years old. The point Paul is making is this. Forget for a moment the analysis of the complexity of *My Sister's Keeper*, and the way it's a parable for our times: just ask yourself, which character in the story represents anger, strife, quarrels, factions, and which represents patience, kindness, generosity, faithfulness, gentleness. To use a term not found in the original Greek, Paul says, 'It's a no-brainer.'

And now take that contrast and apply it to tensions and confrontations in your own close relationships, in politics today, in the Church of England right now, in social activism, in public debate, in all the issues that matter in our lives. Who's being Sara, totally sure they're right, and in the end fostering division and strife and factions that quickly imprison others and enslave themselves? And who's being Anna, embodying peace, patience, faithfulness and gentleness, and taking the consequences of others' petulance with generosity, kindness and self-control? And which one are you?

And this is where we realize that Galatians isn't about a tiny church in the middle of Asia Minor 2,000 years ago. And *My Sister's Keeper* isn't simply about the pathologies of middle-class America. They're both about Jesus. The forces that put Jesus to death were envy, strife, faction, anger; the perpetrators were not bad people, they were like Sara – consumed by passions and convictions that enslaved them and those around them. In the face of those enslaving forces, Jesus responded, like Anna, with love, joy, peace, kindness. And like Anna, he paid the price of the one who showed and lived the truth.

Freedom isn't a perfect, unassailable state we attain after passionate campaigning and wilful struggle. It's an experience we can attain right now by living, like Jesus, in the face of enslaving temptations, with patience, gentleness and generosity. Then we may call our lives, and the life of this church, a parable for our times.

The most obvious thing about this sermon is that two-thirds of it is spent exegeting a secular novel and finding in it an interpretative key to explaining a familiar yet still complex passage in Galatians. The exegesis hinges on my own work delineating the categories of working for, working with, being with and being for, and the way being with not only best characterizes the shape of Jesus' life, but best anticipates the life of heaven. It was undoubtedly an easier sermon to preach given a good half of the congregation were familiar with those four categories, at least in broad outline.

It offers an opportunity to reflect on how to preach when making the whole story of a novel or film the majority of a sermon. I'm not a fan of the phrase 'sermon illustration' because it suggests a didactic approach where the preacher almost formulaically makes a series of points, each illustrated briefly and succinctly. This may be easy on the ear, but it rules out the potential for one of those 'illustrations' to be more than a simple amplification, but instead something with enough depth and texture to be a whole sermon in itself. Beginners at preaching often succumb to the anxiety to pummel the congregation with ideas and visual images, lacking the confidence to discern if just one of those ideas or images could be more salient than the rest put together.

It takes a lot of practice to convey the nuances of a story, including five characters and plot twists that are received differently by different characters, in a succinct yet successful way. By 'successful' I mean that the congregation can follow the story, and its layers, without getting tangled up in the names of the characters or confused by the pace of the plot such that it wants to shout, 'Slow down!' The preacher has to be content to leave out significant parts of the story; sometimes it's not necessary to relate the beginning or the end. In this case, however, the dénouement reveals which of Sara and Anna will be vindicated and you can't understand the dénouement without the preceding details. There's no substitute for simply reading your account to a third party and asking the simple question, 'Did you get lost?'

Part of the satisfaction of the sermon is that the story itself is deeply satisfying, and, like a parable, speaks for itself without needing interpretation; yet at the same time, once set side by side with Paul's famous words in Galatians about the fruits of the Spirit, the comparison is undeniable; and then when interpreted through the categories of being with, a third dimension of significance becomes apparent. There's then very little work left to do to challenge the listener to draw conclusions for life and relationships. The story has done most of the work and commentary on the story has done the rest. An experienced preacher begins reading every novel or watching any film aware that the story may offer fruitful analogies for, or parables of (but seldom illustrations of), the gospel. But it's a very small number that merit their plot relating in full.

Returning to freedom, the preacher needs to be mindful of the way freedom has become a secularized (or to use a theological term, realized) notion of heaven, and thus how anyone who positions themselves as a struggler for liberation is automatically assuming a status no right-minded person could oppose. The skill is to harness that enthusiasm and passion, but not uncritically to assume it's the same thing Paul was talking about. The secret is to see, as Paul explains but many sermons miss, how many things that look and feel like freedom end up becoming prisons – and that not all those things are obviously bad things; who, after all, could possibly think a mother seeking her daughter's survival could be a bad thing? I tried in this sermon to find a place to reflect on Paul's 'negative' list, conscious of how many sermons read the passage as if it only contained the nine fruits.

Here are some guidelines for preaching about freedom.

1. Avoid uncritical adoption of the latest liberation movement as an automatic extension of Christian freedom, or an affirmation that Christianity and liberation are synonyms. Preaching and cheerleading are not the same thing.
2. Recognize your own social location in relation to freedom – the ways in which you get to take some things for granted that others long for, but also that your experience of oppression is not necessarily normative for, or on a par with, all experiences of oppression.
3. Appreciate that, while a movement's goal may be admirable, its method of achieving that goal may impose oppression either on others or on members of the movement itself. Don't tie the scriptural notion of freedom to one particular contemporary manifestation.
4. Ensure you are talking about a holistic notion of freedom – freedom to, not just freedom from; freedom in body, mind and spirit, not just inner peace.
5. Demonstrate humility that others' commitment to and insight into freedom may be a better embodiment of your argument than taking the opportunity to highlight your own causes.
6. Avoid becoming boring – a sermon should have a moment of the unpredictable, a flash of disclosure or surprise, that prevents it becoming simply a reiteration of everything everyone in the congregation already thinks.
7. Work hard to ensure that what you're describing is a Christocentric vision, not a world that would work perfectly well without Jesus.

The following sermon perhaps skirts dangerously close to 'inner peace in the face of external chaos' territory. As I acknowledge early on in the sermon, it was chiefly intended to inspire those who flee or fear conservative

Christianity to believe that Paul wrote Romans for them and that it is a letter with priceless treasure for them to unearth. I couldn't find a way to do this without appearing to criticize other Christians, something I generally believe is off-limits for the preacher. I only do it here because it's the elephant in the room, and naming it is unavoidable if I want the congregation to hear what I go on to say. By rooting the sermon in the personal narrative of a woman who spent eleven fruitless years looking for peace, I seek to encourage the listeners to realize that, just because their search may be long, it doesn't mean it's without wisdom or possibility.

The employment of faith, hope and love is hardly original, but its purpose is to demonstrate how the grammar of Christian language works in ways that are designed to empower the congregation. The same effect is created by the last line of the sermon, which connects the message of the sermon with the familiar practice of sharing 'the peace' before a eucharistic congregation comes to the table. Few things are more effective than reintroducing a familiar notion in a new context, thus enriching both by association with the other. I'm attempting to stay close to Paul's text while exploring what freedom actually feels like; the implied contrast is that some movements for freedom don't feel very much like freedom at all, but rather rapid judgement with no mercy.

The joy of peace
Romans 5.1–8
18 June 2017

After leaving school at 16, Ffyona Campbell set off walking around the world. She crossed the United States, strode up from Cape Town through Africa and continued north through Europe. When she described her motivation to the psychiatrist Anthony Clare, she talked of asking a group of French children, 'Have you ever taken the long route home from school one day because you were cross? Well,' she said, 'I was very, very cross.'

It transpired that her military father had moved house 24 times during her childhood, meaning she attended 15 schools. Mobility was in her DNA – but so, also, it emerged, was resentment. In the climax of her BBC interview, she described how, at the end of her epic walk, she marched up from Land's End to a hill near Bodmin and, in a scene that for me had all the echoes of Dr Frankenstein finally coming face to face with the monster, sat down with her Royal Marine father. After a silence that stretched the limits of what radio can convey, she said, tearfully, 'He gave me his green beret.' Dr Clare gently yet respectfully pointed out that this didn't seem to have given her closure. 'But you see,' she said, 'I didn't deserve it.'

I wonder whether you know what it feels like to find peace so elusive. To hear Ffyona Campbell's story is like watching a decade-long civil war unfold in someone's soul and family. Can you imagine walking 20,000 miles in eleven years and, at the end, being as unreconciled with yourself and your father as when you started? Maybe you can. It's sometimes been said that peace and joy are the same thing in different modes: peace is joy taken over a long, sober, gentle stretch; joy is peace in an effervescent, galvanizing moment – dancing, laughing, exalting. Where are that peace and joy to be found?

That's the question that Paul is addressing in the fifth chapter of his letter to the Romans. There's a tendency for some parts of the church to neglect Romans. It's taken to be full of complicated explanations of how Christ's death was necessary and how the Jews still fit in God's purposes, and it starts by seeming to make a critical remark about gay sex, so in general most of the church tends to set it aside and leave it to the evangelicals. But that's to miss out on a precious gift God is giving the church in this and every age, a gift that points the way to peace. I want to look with you at the first eight verses of Romans 5 to discover the peace and joy for which we all long.

Ffyona Campbell's story shows us the three things peace is not. Peace is not an achievement. Walking 20,000 miles is an amazing feat but peace does not simply follow from it, like a row of potatoes after an afternoon of digging and months of watering. Likewise, again, peace is not a reward. The way the story ends, you expect Ffyona and her father somehow to be reconciled and all to be happy, like a prodigal son and his father or perhaps brother, all reunited at the banquet. But it doesn't work out like that. You can't snatch peace against the odds like a wily and nimble child in a game of Capture the Flag, nor can you be handed peace like a medal after finally crossing the marathon finish line. Nor, again, is peace an entitlement. Ffyona's family clearly had class, money, status and talent, but those things didn't entitle her to peace – quite the contrary, as it turned out; they just exacerbated the turmoil.

Paul is clear that peace only comes through the knowledge that our desire for achievement, reward or entitlement can't get us what we crave. Peace is none of these things. Instead, peace is a gift. It is pure gift. There's nothing we can do to deserve or earn or claim or qualify for it. Peace comes in the form of our crucified saviour. That is to say, peace is about our reconciliation with God. It is something that comes about because God takes the initiative and makes it possible. And it comes at great cost. In other words, the achievement, reward and entitlement is all God's and not in the slightest ours.

But you get the impression that Paul's heard that talk at the youth group about how Jesus changes everything and he has the same tendency a lot of Christians have, which is to glaze over when either Christ in general or the cross in particular are offered rather casually as the answer to every one of life's questions. So he breaks things down a little more helpfully and explains what that means in three very familiar words.

The first word is faith – there it is in verse one: 'justified by faith'. Faith means accepting that God in Christ has done the work of reconciliation and there's nothing we can do to deserve, earn, claim or qualify for it, nor even thwart it. Just as we did nothing to bring ourselves into the world, there's nothing we can do to bring ourselves into the new world, God's kingdom. That may make us feel powerless but powerlessness in the face of grace translates as gratitude. Faith is a mixture of trust and gratitude.

The second word is hope – there it is in verse 2: 'our hope of sharing the glory of God.' Hope means two things. It means that death is not the end, sin does not ruin us or God's purpose, failure is not the last word. But it also means that eternal life is about sharing – participating with God and one another and the restored creation in an experience Paul calls glory. Being with God won't be about fear or shame or loss or humiliation but about glory, and life eternal won't be about isolation or survival but about sharing and enjoying ultimate wonder together.

The third word is love – there it is in verse 5, 'God's love has been poured into our hearts through the Holy Spirit that has been given to us.' Now, Paul's notion of love is rather different from ours. We have an ideal of love as kindness, generosity, compassion and trust, and maybe also electric attraction and passionate desire. But the love Paul is talking about isn't our love; it's God's love. And the point about God's love is that it's about grace – in other words, it's a love that keeps on pumping out whether we appreciate, honour and reciprocate it or not.

So these are the characteristics of God's peace. It's a soul full of trust and gratitude, a spirit inspired by the anticipation of shared glory, and a heart overflowing with a love that goes beyond what we can express. But Paul doesn't just describe what peace feels like. He goes on to suggest what difference that peace makes to our actions and demeanour.

People of peace stand. Paul refers in verse 2 to 'this grace in which we stand.' I once worked in an institution where the cleaner was the best-known and most authoritative person in the building. He did his job to perfection, had it almost finished by the time the first employee arrived in the morning and welcomed dignitaries at the door as if he were the boss. He never stooped, avoided eye contact, mumbled or shuffled. He stood tall, chest out, full of dignity. And everyone respected him. When Paul says peace makes us able to stand, I think of that cleaner. Even after 20,000 miles, Ffyona Campbell couldn't do that. That cleaner knew peace.

People of peace endure. Paul is so confident about the quality of what God gives us that he says even suffering can be withstood and made part of the experience of peace. I remember a woman of advanced years I used to visit in my first parish. She would always say, 'How've you been? All of a busy?' That phrase 'all of a busy' always made me feel shame – that here was she, in pain, with no prospect of recovery, facing an inevitable decline into discomfort and death; and suddenly all my running around and feeling important was exposed as an avoidance strategy from what she was looking at all the time. Yet she had a peace, a peace I hadn't found, a peace the world cannot give. In her, suffering produced endurance, endurance produced character and character produced hope. For her, and in Paul's mind for all of us, suffering doesn't contradict God's peace, but instead provides a context for us to experience it. She knew peace.

And people of peace surge with joy. Twice Paul uses the word 'boast': we boast in our hope and we boast in our sufferings. I recall 15 years ago I was at the lake, my daily walking spot. I was head down, listening to a friend who needed to talk. Suddenly, I missed a pitter-patter, a wag, a breathy, furry companion. My dog. No sign of her – and for how long? Then I looked out into the lake and saw a bobbing golden head, pursuing a nonchalant but quickening duck. She was far away. She had never swum this far. How far could she go? Was she the best judge? My concentration wavered; my conversation partner noticed. Her tragedy seemed a little less significant than perhaps it should have. Unfolding at the limits of my sight was something truly remarkable. My dog had emerged from the water and was shaking herself down over a patient fisherman. My dog had swum across the whole lake. Hear this, unwary world: this dog is an astonishing dog. My heart burst with pride. This was truly sensational.

I boasted. It felt like the most unambiguous boast of my life. I had done nothing to train, encourage or enhance such talent. It was just gift. However miserable my friend was, I couldn't not share that glorious surge of joy. That's what happens with the gift of peace. It issues in joy and you can't not share it. That afternoon I knew joy and peace.

Sometimes people sit alone in this church, and when you ask them if they're OK, they say, 'I just want a bit of peace.' Paul tells us how to find a lot of peace. Have faith in the reconciliation only Christ can give. Cherish hope in the glory you will one day share with God. Receive love that only the Spirit can infuse. And then you can stand and not be ashamed, you can endure and find joy in even the worst suffering, you can be so filled with wonder at what God has done that you surge with an irresistible impulse to express it.

Why do we come to church? To find that peace. Why do we read Romans? To find that peace. Why do we worship God in Christ? Because there, only there, do we find a peace that passes understanding, a peace people can walk 20,000 miles looking for; a peace the world cannot give.

The peace of the Lord be always with you.

While listeners can sometimes remember what a preacher says, what they never forget is how they felt when the preacher said it. A sermon like this works by contrasting the desolation of Ffyona Campbell with my own exaltation at my dog's swimming exploits. The former is somewhat exotic but desperately sad; the latter unsophisticated but hard not to share. The simple question is, 'Which of the two is your life oriented towards?' The answer lies not in the head but in the heart.

4

Preaching on War

War exposes the fragility of preaching. It's the ultimate manifestation of the fact that things haven't got any better since Christ ascended into heaven. It's impossible to reduce to personal ethics of how individuals should believe and act. It's a blatant contradiction of the claim that Christ's sacrifice is the end of sacrifice. It's terrifying, scarring, damaging and depressing.

It's useless to say war is wrong. It's not just useless, it's often thoughtless and insensitive too, because soldiers mimic Christ in laying down their lives for those they love, including those they've never met, and few have chosen to fight this particular war with all its flaws – and in many cases, certainly in the case of world wars, few have chosen to fight any war at all. Everyone knows war is wrong. But employing such convictions to criticize those whose lives have been ineradicably damaged by war is another matter.

The sermon below takes a different approach. It considers those left behind.

Testament of lament
Centenary of the outbreak of War
3 August 2014

We don't know how to talk about the First World War. If we speak of mindless slaughter, we risk naïveté in the face of the global politics of the early twentieth century. If we speak of courage and sacrifice, we risk glorifying the ugliness of carnage and the crimes of bungled generalship. If we look at Flanders fields of white crosses or litter our memories with red poppies, we risk making abstract what was a personal scar on almost every household in the country. If we condemn and moralize, we risk implying that somehow today we know better, and we fear dishonouring those who had to do and die and didn't get any say in the reasoning why. So our carefully-crafted minutes of silence mask our dumbfoundedness about how to express horror, how to honour bravery, how to recognize grief, how to acknowledge folly and how to confess the little we have learned.

In 1933, Vera Brittain, whose commemorative plaque stands in our Dick Sheppard Chapel in the crypt downstairs, published her memoir, *Testament of Youth*. It covers the years 1900–25 in the life of a young middle-class woman and thus gives us a glimpse of her story before, during and after World War One. The early chapters give us a picture of a life that we could look back on as calm and flourishing – but the tremors beneath the surface are clear. Vera's father is a paper manufacturer. Straightaway, we have two key dimensions of Britain's pre-war character: a nation dominated by the empire that drove the nation's economic ambitions and cultural identity, and by the razor-sharp class struggles that were rearing up at the time war broke out. Meanwhile, Vera's longing to go to Oxford embodies the suppression of women's gifts and flourishing in a stifling era of social conformity and control. Let's not forget that a lot of people saw the outbreak of war as a moment of opportunity to transform a lot of things in this country that we might now recognize as ripe for change.

Vera adores her brother Edward, and takes to her heart his three closest friends, Roland, Geoffrey and Victor. Indeed, she falls in love with Roland and he becomes her fiancé. It's because of her devotion to these four men that she finds herself drawn into the innocent idealism of those who enter the war with spirit and relish. She's caught up in the language of glory and later reflects, 'The War made masochists of us all.' But the heart of Vera's testimony lies in the harrowing account she gives of the way first one, then another, then finally all four of these young men she loves meet their end in the conflict. Most painfully, she eagerly picks up the phone one night before Christmas, expecting to hear of her beloved Roland's anticipated return home for the holiday season – only to be told that he is dead. He was 20 years old.

The loss is overwhelming. She says, 'There seemed to be nothing left in the world, for I felt that Roland had taken with him all my future and Edward all my past.' One night, she says, 'Too miserable to light a fire or even to get into bed, I lay on the cold floor and wept with childish abandon. "Why couldn't I have died in the War with the others?" I lamented … "Why couldn't a torpedo have finished me off … I'm nothing but a piece of wartime wreckage, living on ingloriously in a world that doesn't want me!"'

We see Vera's efforts to play her part in the war effort – to live a life worthy of the men who are sacrificing so much at the front. She worked in London, France and Malta, making no pretence that it was her natural calling, and wearing herself out in offering care and compassion. But we also see another side of what it was like not to be among the soldiers who were and are at the centre of the world's attention about the war. It was impossible to voice dissent about the struggle without seeming disloyal to swathes of sacrifice and appearing to dishonour the dignity of the dead. Thus the madness of slaughter multiplied in the face of the powerlessness of the onlookers.

Testament of Youth, and its sequel *Testament of Experience*, also show us what life was like after the war. Vera's fury and energy are unabated: she becomes a passionate pacifist and turns her stricken grief into desire for no repetition of the ghastly curse that stole her most precious relationships from her. She feels deeply the outrage that so many households passively let their sons be taken away to die, like sheep going to market. She lost her heart and soul in the war – but we become aware that many others remember differently, or desire to forget more assiduously. Despite her voracious and undying longing for Roland, Vera eventually settles to marry another man, Gerald, and, in that marriage, we see both realism and a different kind of love. And yet Gerald has to live with the reality that Vera's heart will always be shaped by her love for Roland and Edward, and she will never outgrow the circumstances of their loss. The war, for Vera, will never end. Likewise, Vera's father can never come to terms with his son Edward's death and commits suicide in 1935. He too feels like a piece of wartime wreckage, living on ingloriously in a world that doesn't want him. The shards of war stretch deep and woundingly into an indefinite future.

We also, in following Vera's life, come to dwell on what one does with such a profound experience as the decades pass. Vera takes up other causes that, to her, share a trajectory with her pacifism – she protests for peace and nuclear disarmament and against colonialism and apartheid. Here lies a challenge to quantify how much the experience of the First World War was unique, and how much it was part of a larger struggle and what that struggle might mean today.

Vera Brittain. Think about that name. Vera. It means true. Brittain. It means the country we're sitting in right now. It's a name that pushes us to see this testimony as the story of what the First World War truly meant to the people of this country. It's not primarily about an archduke shot in Sarajevo, or alliances made by colonial-dominated empires, or the logistics of trench warfare, or the Russian Revolution, or most of the things that history records. It's about a broken heart, a sense of being stricken beyond recovery, a life dominated by might-have-beens, an open wound that could never truly heal, a decimation of a generation of young men who could have been the light and life of the world, an immeasurable weight of grief among those who missed them and whose lives were dislocated beyond measure by war. Vera Brittain. Britain's true story.

But think also about the name Vera Brittain chose for her account: Testament. It's the name we give to each of the two parts of the Bible. It's a challenge to the reader to set Vera's account alongside what we call Scripture, and see what the one says to the other. The nineteenth century was a time of great confidence in human capability. The philosophy of the Enlightenment and the growth of science and the range of technological invention had turned attention from God as the creator and redeemer to humankind as the measure of all things. One German theologian epitomized the positive spirit of the day by speaking of the kingdom as the brotherhood of man under the fatherhood of God. People really started to believe we could all get this human flourishing thing right. The First World War was one huge smack in the face to any such grandiose ideas about human potential. If we had become more sophisticated, it was only in finding more complex ways to kill one another in larger numbers.

As we look back on the Testament of this terrible war, perhaps this is the simplest lesson to learn: that we should be very cautious in talking about human progress and potential. Whenever we say, 'in this day and age,' or start arguments with the words, 'Here we are in the twenty-first century, and I can't believe that we're still...', we're presupposing a narrative that assumes humanity gets better. When we call someone a dinosaur or say, 'Sorry, Grandad' to a person with youth still on their side, we're suggesting that the categories of bad and good map neatly onto the eras of past and future. But World War One should teach us differently. And what happened to Germany in the lead-up to World War Two should settle the debate beyond dispute. Vera Brittain's testimony starts as an account of progress – the emerging voice and power of women whose role had been suppressed for too long. But her life became one of loss and grief and horror and tragedy as a much less upbeat narrative devoured everything before it. And we don't want to remember the World War One because its Testament tells us a whole bunch of things we don't want to face up to about humankind.

The war should also have killed off a bunch of things we shouldn't ever have believed about God. That God is our talisman who ensures we win all the battles we fight. That there's something particularly godly about our nation that makes us on the right side of every battle we enter. That God is leading us gradually from benighted ignorance to glorious enlightenment. That such convictions exacerbated the slaughter of the World War One is cause for lament. That such convictions are still with us is cause for repentance. After seeing the horror of carnage that began 100 years ago, the astonishing thing is not that we still believe in God. It is that God still believes in us. That's the most amazing testament of all.

When preachers get in a tangle about how to speak on Remembrance Sunday, it reveals a lack of imagination about the number of angles from which war can be surveyed. There's certainly a strong case for a profound theological account of pacifism – but Remembrance Sunday is not the day for it.

Here are some guidelines for preaching on war.

1. Don't preach your anti-war sermon on Remembrance Sunday. It will persuade no one and antagonize many. Save it for another day and consider it as part of a discussion alongside just war and crusade.
2. Consider all the people involved in war – the left behind, the injured, the too old or too infirm to fight, the parents of combatants, their children, the people who ended up becoming friends, those caught in the crossfire, the nurses and doctors and auxiliaries. There's a limitless range of angles to pursue.
3. Make the most of the enormous literature of war, from the *Iliad* to *Birdsong*. Few of the questions we're asking are new, and most are beautifully and brilliantly portrayed in fiction and biography.
4. Keep it personal. Personal stories are vivid and moving, and provided they're balanced and unsentimental, are the simplest way to cut through the complexity of geopolitics.
5. The key points of theology – sin, incarnation, resurrection, church, eschatology – are likely to be more help than conventional exegesis.
6. Don't be too proud to type into Google the key words or emotions you want to evoke and see where it takes you. Narrative is invariably the most appropriate model for a sermon on war.

In the following sermon, I sought to follow these guidelines and blend narrative with personal encounter, embracing all within a theological shape.

Somebody else's fight
Remembrance Sunday
8 November 2020

I want you to imagine what it was like to be in a tank in World War Two. You haven't showered in three weeks. You're squeezed with others into a small metal capsule. If a shell gets through the inadequate cladding, it'll ricochet like a murderous pinball. Concussion would be a comparatively good outcome; more often your bones are shattered and your body becomes a blancmange. Soldiers called tanks a crematorium on wheels. Mechanics and maintenance men would cry when they came out from cleaning a tank.

Clarence Smoyer was 19.[1] It was 6 March 1945. Blond, curly-haired Clarence from Armstrong County, Pennsylvania, was in a Pershing tank, rumbling towards a crossroads through the desolate bombed-out cityscape of Cologne. 'Gentlemen, I give you Cologne,' his commander shouted down the radio. 'Let's knock the hell out of it!' Clarence had already lost a cousin and a brother-in-law in battle. He said, 'Amen to that.' He exchanged fire with a German tank, which quickly slipped behind a row of houses. Then suddenly a colleague in his tank shouted, 'Staff car', and Clarence saw a vehicle crossing the debris-strewn terrain of the crossroads. Immediately he unleashed a string of bullets. The car hit the pavement, and out flung the body of a young, unarmed, civilian, wavy-brown-haired woman.

Clarence's guts emptied and he tried to look away. But war doesn't stop for tragedy. His tank was facing a German Panther, whose gun was so powerful that its shells could splice one American tank and plunge through into the next. Clarence destroyed that fearsome tank and became a hero for doing so. But he never celebrated. The face of the woman in that car haunted his dreams for decades after the war. Finally, 50 years later, he was sent a videotape of the battle. It showed everything – his tank, the German adversary, the car and the wavy hair of the dead woman.

Now in his seventies, Clarence started having nightmares. He'd wake up fighting, punching the bedclothes, afraid he'd hit his wife. Medication couldn't calm him down. He couldn't function. He saw the woman before him, day and night. He had one desperate thought.

---

[1] The whole story can be found here: John Blake, 'A World War II hero returns to Germany to solve a mystery – and meet an enemy', *CNN*, 10 November 2018, www.edition.cnn.com/2018/11/10/us/ww2-reunion-us-german-veterans/index.html (accessed 2.05.2023).

Maybe he wasn't the only one who shot that woman. Could gunfire have come from the German tank too? And then he did a remarkable thing. He thought, 'I wonder if the German tank gunner is still alive. Maybe I could meet him, and ask him.'

In March 2013, 68 years after their tank guns had been poised to destroy each other, in the very same city of Cologne, Clarence Smoyer met Gustav Schaefer, all five feet of him – the gunner in the tank Clarence had destroyed that afternoon. Clarence was terrified at what Gustav would say – but Gustav extended a hand and, in a gentle voice, said, 'The war is over. We can be friends now.' The two men walked to the scene of the battle, the crossroads of their lives.

Clarence explained, 'I saw a film of it...' Gustav interrupted, 'So did I.' He'd seen the same footage on TV ten years earlier. Clarence pointed to a lamppost. 'There was a woman,' he stuttered. 'She fell out of the car, riddled with bullets. This is where I see her in my dreams. I still have nightmares about it,' Clarence said. Then Gustav said the words that changed everything. 'So do I.' Dumbfounded, Clarence said, 'There wasn't time to study the car. I was told to shoot anything that moved. So I shot it. I shot her,' he confessed. Then Gustav said the words that transformed Clarence's life forever. Slowly, methodically, Gustav replied, 'That's why I shot it too.'

Clarence was stunned. The guilt that he'd carried for 68 years, the memories that had chewed up his life for the last 15 of those years, he didn't bear alone. Both men had shot at that car. Both men had killed that woman. Once deadly enemies, they each found that the only person who could lift their burden of horror, guilt and trauma, was one another.

But that's not the end of the story. They found out who the woman was. Kathi Esser was 26. Her three sisters had all lost their husbands in the war. She worked as a clerk in a grocery shop. It seemed that one day she and her boss both snapped, got in the car and tried to escape the carnage of Cologne. Unfortunately for them, they drove into the crossroads between Clarence and Gustav's tanks. Kathi was buried in a mass grave 200 yards away. Sixty-eight years after her death, Clarence and Gustav each placed a yellow rose on her grave. Then they had tea with Kathi's family. One of Kathi's nieces said, 'You didn't kill Kathi. The people who started this war are the ones who killed Kathi.' Clarence's journey of atonement was over. He and Gustav kept in close touch until Gustav's death in 2017. Clarence sent a bouquet to the funeral, with the inscription, 'I will never forget you. Your brother in arms, Clarence.'

Clarence never stopped dreaming about Kathi. 'I don't wake up flailing any more, and I can sleep a full night,' he said in 2018, a year before he died, aged 98. 'I still see her in my dreams. I think I always will. I don't think she haunts me. It's different. It's not a nightmare anymore.'

The First and Second World Wars were different from almost every previous and subsequent modern war, because they largely involved not professional soldiers, but conscripted young men – many of them no more than teenagers. The tank is a fitting image of what it means to be a conscript – trapped in a situation that's not of your making, choosing or wanting. These people were scooped up out of their regular lives. Gustav's had been a simple existence. He was a farm boy from northern Germany. His family didn't have electricity, or a radio, or more than a few books. His big adventure was cycling to the railway line to watch the trains whistle by. He had no investment in the war. He had no grudge against Jews. He had no animosity towards America. The crime of war is that it takes two peaceable young men, Clarence and Gustav, with no reason to meet – and makes them deadly enemies. It's true that the intensity of war gave each of their lives an urgency, an importance and a sense of solidarity with their comrades that they probably never came close to matching thereafter. It's also true that Clarence was celebrated as a hero for his achievements and courage that March day in Cologne.

But Clarence was having none of it. All he could think of was Kathi, that young woman who could take no more grief, no more suffering and no more fear, and who was tragically plunged into the centre of the battle, there to die at the hands of ally and enemy alike. And Clarence, despite his nightmares and despair, did comparatively well. By contrast, his commander, Captain Mason Salisbury, returned home from the war, graduated from law school, and become a lawyer at a big New York firm. One winter weekend, he stayed at his parents' mansion on Long Island, played tennis and dined with his family. The next morning his father found him slumped in a car in the garage. Mason Salisbury had taken his own life at 30. Losing so many friends in battle was too much for him to bear. Who wants to be a hero if that's what a hero's inner life is really like?

Here we have four people – Clarence, Gustav, Kathi and Mason. I want to suggest to you that their stories show us what Christianity and redemption mean in the face of the horror and devastation of war. Mason shows us what redemption doesn't mean. It doesn't mean victory, triumph and celebration, if those things are masks for inner turmoil, profound dislocation, emotional trauma and a conscience like a bomb crater.

Kathi shows us who Christ is. Christ is the one who goes into the place of enmity, carnage and horror, and who loses his life because of a battle he had no part in causing or continuing. Yet through his life and death, not straightaway, but finally, comes a reconciliation with mortality, guilt, bitterness and one another, by which the nightmare of war is over and the dream of new life emerges. Without Kathi, none of the good and beautiful parts of Clarence and Gustav's story would have come about. But for almost 70 years, neither Gustav nor Clarence knew who Kathi was. So with Christ: the fact that we don't know him or acknowledge him doesn't mean that, long after his death, he is not making beautiful the bombed-out cityscape of our lives.

Meanwhile, Clarence and Gustav show us the almost invisible work of the Holy Spirit. The Holy Spirit was working in that camera crew whose footage Gustav and Clarence both saw 50 years after it was shot. The Holy Spirit was working in the circumstances that led to both men seeing the film. The Holy Spirit was working in the grace that led Clarence to track down Gustav, and in the words of reconciliation and solidarity that bonded them together. The Holy Spirit was working in the generous hearts of Kathi's family that forgave the two guilty men and bonded the three households together in a moment of healing unimaginable 70 years before.

Remember that Kathi's death, and the guilt and horror that accompanied it, filled Clarence and Gustav's dreams for the rest of their lives. After their meeting with each other, and the solidarity they found, and their joint act of honouring Kathi, and the forgiveness they received from Kathi's family, those dreams didn't end – but they were no longer nightmares. Maybe that's the best we can hope for from the legacy of war. Two brave men, each trapped by the tank of their human predicament, each killed an innocent, non-combatant woman, and spent the rest of their lives scarred by the horror of what they'd done. No one wanted to know. Half the world wanted to call them heroes. Half wanted them just to forget about it. Until they met each other, and in each other found solidarity, respect, understanding, peace.

Kathi's broken body became a blessing that brought reconciliation and overcame the dividing wall of hostility. That's how Christianity works. We can call the meeting of Clarence and Gustav and Kathi's family beautiful, tender, generous, forgiving, hopeful, reconciling, life-giving. But we have a word that means all of those things and brings what these people went through to the heart of our lives and the throne of grace. That word is communion.

The power of the sermon lies in the moving nature of the story, and the thought that flickers through the listener's mind: 'Is that all he's going to do – tell the story?' And then to discover that this story isn't just a remarkable tale of the legacy of war. It's an invitation into the heart of God – not in good times, but in the worst times we can imagine. There's a dignity in letting the story of war speak, and letting the legacy of war be heard, before gently offering theological interpretation and reframing. That offering of space seeks to model the preacher's attitude in speaking of war: to stand in awe and gratitude for those like the four protagonists in this story, and to try to learn from what they went through.

The sermon below is different in one chief respect: it's not talking about the past, but the present. It was preached six weeks after the 2022 Russian invasion of Ukraine. The surprise here is that it turned out an exegetical sermon was the way to go. I went that route because there were so many unknown and unresolved things in play, an arm's length sermon like 'Somebody Else's Fight' just wouldn't do. You can't be an expert on a story that's changing all the time. But neither can you be silent. The sermon below is the result of wrestling with a text until that text yields the truth you need to express.

Thou preparest a table before me in the presence of mine enemies
Psalm 23
6 April 2022 at the 'Preaching in Perilous Times' conference

'Behold, I am sending you as sheep among wolves,' says Jesus, as he commissions the 72 disciples to be his representatives in Israel. In doing so, he coins what we could call the defining metaphor for what it means to be a follower of Jesus. In the words of the African American theologian Howard Thurman, Christianity's original and characteristic context is that of those with their backs against the wall. Ukraine is not a small country. But because of its renunciation of nuclear weapons and its heritage within the Soviet empire, its situation in the face of Russian invasion is that of a sheep surrounded by wolves – of one with its back against the wall.

I don't know if you ever get sent Jacqui Lawson e-cards. I'm grateful for those who remember me at Christmas, Easter and birthdays, but (leaving the music to one side) I hope it doesn't sound ungrateful to say I have some issues with the theology of these cards. There's invariably a cosy church snugly abiding in a village nestling before warm hearths, as a cheerful bird merrily brings a happy message down your chimney or through your front door. This is not a context the Bible understands. The Bible repeatedly portrays the people of God as beleaguered, under threat, oppressed, near despair. Nine times in the Bible we're given a picture of sheep in danger and God as the shepherd who is with them despite all. It comes up in Jeremiah, Ezekiel and Zechariah; in all four Gospels; and in 1 Peter. Most famously of all, it's the subject of Psalm 23. Now, just as it may surprise you to learn that 1 Corinthians 13 was not in fact written for weddings, it may be news to you that the twenty-third psalm was not actually composed for funerals. In fact, it may not be much of a stretch to say that the twenty-third psalm was composed for the Ukrainian experience of death, destruction, horror and fear in the face of Russian invasion.

We have many questions in the face of the horror of war and the shock of one European country invading another; something we regarded as unthinkable. Psalm 23 doesn't answer our questions. Instead, it transforms our context. It turns our fear into worship. I want to explore with you now the four things Psalm 23 has to tell us that offer to shape our imaginations as we contemplate, intercede for and respond to the plight of the Ukrainian people. I say four things, because Psalm 23 is arranged in seven parts as a chiasmus – that is to say, the first part corresponds with the seventh part, the second with the sixth, the third with the fifth, leaving the fourth part like the point of an arrow, the central message of the psalm, which the other six parts all support. So as I go through the four main themes I'll take the first and seventh together, then the second and sixth, then the third and fifth, and finally the fourth alone.

Let's start with parts one and seven. 'The Lord is my shepherd, I shall not want.' I want to suggest to you that these words are all we need to perceive the theological issues at the heart of this crisis. We're so used to Crimond being played unbelievably slowly and the words 'The Lord's my shepherd' and some of us have sung it so many times it's lost almost all power to move us. But look at it again. The Lord is my shepherd. No one else is. Not some strong man who tells a story of Making Russia Great Again, a story based on mythical origins, ancient entitlement, unjust deprivation, enemies within, failure of will, restoration of destiny, inevitable struggle, final conquest and endless glory. We've heard such a story before. It was the story of the Nuremburg rallies. It was the story that swept Donald Trump to the White House. It's not a new story. It was the story Karl Barth and Dietrich Bonhoeffer rejected when they said, 'The Lord is my führer.' Stalin made Russia great. OK, he killed 20 million or more people in doing so. There's bound to be casualties in a noble quest. That's destiny for you. Remember the chilling moment in the passion story when the crowd shouts, 'We have no king but Caesar.' Let me put it as clearly as I can: Vladimir Putin is telling a false story. The true story is the Lord is my shepherd.

And then, alongside that, just as crucially, 'I shall not want.' The myth that captivates our world is that we haven't got enough. Our lives are saturated with advertising. How do I get YouTube for free, how do I get WhatsApp for free, how do I get Facebook for free? Because my choices and messages are all getting swept up to enable the providers to have extensive data for advertising. If I go online and research an exotic fruit from Mauritius, you can be sure tomorrow somewhere I'll be getting the chance to book a holiday in Mauritius, buy travel books for Mauritius, meet attractive women from Mauritius. Advertising is based on the premise that we don't have enough. It finds your interests and wants and turns them into desperate and gnawing needs you can no longer resist. In what planetary universe does Russia need Ukraine? Look at the map! Russia is enormous. The size of the country defies comprehension. And now its leader thinks it doesn't have enough! Are you serious? How much conflict and war is based on the myth of 'not enough'? 'Not enough' is the basis of our insecurity. Martin Luther said the thief and the robber are heretics, because they propound the false gospel that there isn't enough for you and for me, so I must have yours. What does the psalm say? 'I shall not want.' With God, there is always enough, and always will be. In its first line Psalm 23 goes right to the heart of the invasion of Ukraine.

When we look at the end of the psalm, we see 'goodness and mercy shall follow me'. This is so many kinds of wonderful. Who is pursuing Ukrainians now, so that four million have already left the country? In the psalm, it's goodness and mercy doing the hounding. You can't escape goodness and mercy. They'll get you in the end. 'All the days of my life'. This is a forever thing. It doesn't run out. See the myth of scarcity again. God is not going to run out on us. Putin presents his war as a necessary thing because there's so much evil, and only a strong man like him can overcome it. But God says you will be beset, pursued, surrounded by goodness and mercy. Remember Hitler and his longing for *Lebensraum*. He claimed Germans needed living space. They were running out of room. What does the psalm say? 'I shall dwell in the house of the Lord my whole life long.' You will never be short of space. You will always have a home in God. Don't give in to the rhetoric of scarcity. In God there's always more than enough. The invasion of Ukraine is based on a lie – not just a historical lie, not just a cultural and religious lie, but fundamentally a theological lie.

Now for the second part, coupled with the sixth part. 'He makes me lie down in green pastures; he leads me beside still waters.' Let's go back to the fundamental setting of the psalm, and of the Bible in general. There's a tension running through the Old Testament between Israel as a settled, agrarian people, following the cycle of the seasons in the Promised Land, and the children of God as a wandering pastoral people, accompanied by sheep who went with them wherever they wandered. The failures of Israel mostly came during the agrarian period, where the temptations of the land took them away from dependence on God. Psalm 23 unequivocally assumes that Israel is a wandering people. Being a refugee is not an absurd, egregious departure from the norm. It's not that unusual. Here we have no abiding city. None of us get to stay put very long. 'My ancestors farmed this plot for centuries' is always liable to become a form of idolatry. The good shepherd leads the sheep to where they can find food and drink. The food and drink don't always come to them.

And it's when we flip across to section six that we realize this part is fundamentally about food and drink. 'You prepare a table before me in the presence of my enemies.' This is how you show wealth in the Middle East. In the West you display power by having a magnificent mansion, a huge area of parkland around it, and a large limousine resting on the gravel drive, which you can scarcely see because of the iron gates that keep people out. In the Middle East, you show abundance by inviting everyone to a massive banquet where there's way too much food. The good shepherd gives the sheep all the food they need. Then the good shepherd has a banquet for the whole village. (Note, by the way, that preparing food is a female role in biblical times, so God preparing a table is showing a female face of God.) And again, this is a telling moment. God doesn't address enemies by destroying them with greater force. God invites them to behold a banquet where there's more than enough – enough for them too – and poses them the question, 'Do you insist on continuing with the carnage deriving from your assumption of scarcity, or will you come and join this table of abundance?' The now-controversial Bishop George Bell stood up in the House of Lords in 1944 and told the nation that if Britain continued with its carpet-bombing of German cities, it would soon become no better than the Nazis and lose its moral right to win the war. People were so furious that it meant he never became Archbishop of Canterbury. But he was following the logic of Psalm 23: are we allowing ourselves to descend into the scarcity of enmity, or are we preparing a table of abundance that all can join?

Turning to parts three and six, we're faced with the question of where, in the end, we put our trust. In what lies our security? These are words that challenge us. The Lord has a rod and a staff. The rod is like an axe – an aggressive instrument that can be directed at an attacker. The staff is where we get a bishop's crozier today – it's a tool for picking up a branch or hooking in a leg to release a sheep from a tight ledge or deep thicket. In other words, the Lord can protect us and the Lord can rescue us. But there are two other ways we trust in the Lord. 'He leads me in the paths of righteousness.' The Lord is indeed a leader. There are many ways we can go, and not all of them lead to still waters and green pastures. God beckons us. We can't pretend we don't know the good places to go. Which path leads to love, joy, peace, patience and kindness? Which path leads us to the hungry, the stranger, the sick, the prisoner? Which path leads to justice, mercy and humility? Paul, Matthew and Micah, and many others, give us plenty of indications of where God is beckoning.

But the fundamental form of trust is beyond protection, rescue and direction. 'You are with me.' This is the revelation at the heart of the whole Bible. You are with me. That was what Moses discovered at the burning bush. That was what Isaiah discovered in the Servant Songs. That was what Shadrach discovered in the fiery furnace. That was what Mary of Nazareth discovered at the Annunciation. That was what Mary Magdalene discovered in the garden. That was what the disciples discovered on the day of Pentecost. Every single one of these people had their backs to the wall. They could all identify with the people of Ukraine right now.

Which brings us to the central part, to which the whole psalm is directed, 'Even though I walk through the valley of the shadow of death, I fear no evil.' We all live fragile lives in the face of our own mortality. We act in solidarity together, providing healthcare and support, to postpone death, take away isolation, understand fear. War reverses all that. It hastens death. It dismantles solidarity. It destroys trust. It actively seeks the precise things we spend our whole lives trying to establish. Which is why it's so horrific. It's not just the violence, the anger, the perpetual danger. It's the way war undermines and reverses the deepest principles of social existence. It's the worship of death.

The central words of the psalm proclaim, 'I'm here too.' God says, even in the valley of the shadow of death, There's no escaping me. I'm here when the hands of two civilians buried in the rubble of a destroyed building meet, and squeeze, and thus find hope. I'm here when a father waves off his whole family on a train and wonders, as he turns towards the conflict, if they'll ever see him again. I'm here when a tank rumbles over a bridge and a cowering family hiding under the bridge wonder if they can hang on long enough for the tank to pass. I fear no evil. War is the hell of being separated from God, of dwelling only amid horror and destruction and the shattering cacophony of explosive death. I fear no evil, because this is not the last chapter of the book, and I know how the story ends, and it's not with rocket-launchers or 40 miles of tanks. It's with the things that populate this psalm: goodness and mercy, overflowing hospitality, abundant provision, safe home, the companionship of God.

One hundred years ago, nearly to the day, my grandparents, in their early twenties, left Kyiv, fleeing the evil of Stalin. They didn't flee their Ukrainian homeland together. They doubted they'd ever see each other again. By different routes they made their way by 1926 to Berlin. There they married and had three children. They found goodness and mercy, but they also found the valley of the shadow of death: they fled the evil of Hitler in 1938. They were led to still waters and green pastures in the UK. There, their daughter, my mother, met a man and married him and had four children, two of whom died, but two of whom survived. The second of those two surviving children was me.

We read Psalm 23 today because we believe that Jesus is the shepherd it describes. Jesus is the one who, in the feeding of the 5,000, leads us to green pastures. Jesus is the one who, at Cana, makes God's abundance out of our scarcity. Jesus is the one who, on Maundy Thursday, prepares a table in the face of his enemies. Jesus is the one who, on Good Friday, walks through the valley of the shadow of death. Jesus is the one who, on the mount of Ascension, promises goodness and mercy will follow us all our days.

In all these ways, we read Psalm 23 because it tells us the story of Jesus. We read it because it gives us the context for the heresies that characterize the invasion of Ukraine. But I read Psalm 23 because it is my story, the story of my family's search for green pasture and freedom from fear. This is a story so much bigger, so much deeper, so much longer than the story of Putin and the story of war. This is our story. This is our context. Our eternal context. We read Psalm 23 because it is the story of forever.

This is the first sermon in the book in which I've spoken about my family. There are two ways to do this. You can make your own family story a passing illustration in a sermon that seems to be about faraway things, adding poignancy and immediacy – as I do here. Or you can preach a whole sermon about your own story, perhaps on Mothering Sunday, or if it connects with a Scripture passage helpfully. What you can't do is do so very often. A sermon is about God, not about you. It's certainly not a therapy session. But one lesson I learned early in ministry is that if you don't tell the congregation about yourself and your family, they'll make things up. People need to know you're a human being. So used sparingly, family content is healthy. What's almost never healthy is to talk about your partner or children. If you praise them, you're boasting. If you ridicule them, you're humiliating them; and they may never forgive you.

5

Preaching about Disability

St Martin-in-the-Fields held its first conference on Theology and Disability in partnership with Inclusive Church in 2012, and has continued annually since, going online during the pandemic. Being involved has been informative, moving and profoundly educational; being asked to preach on the subject has been a wonderful challenge.

One of the questions raised is, should all preaching about disability be done by those with lived experience of disability? The conference makes a big play of the phrase, 'Nothing about us without us is for us.' Hence its uniqueness as the only such event where the great majority of contributions are from those with lived experience. My response to this is, never say never. It's a liberating move to say that the disability community has within itself everything it needs for its own theological reflection. And it's certainly provocative to shift the balance of power toward those often excluded or obscured. But to say that the only people who can speak about this are those with lived experience is to downplay the benefit of offering the wider church the opportunity to enjoy the wisdom and insight of the perspective of those without personal experience of disability.

The vital thing is to speak from an appreciation of abundance and asset, rather than from an assumption of deficit and scarcity. The problem with many gospel healing stories is that they tend to be read as treating what today would be termed disability (ripe for understanding), as if it were illness (ripe for healing). But the gospel healing stories are not the only texts that have a bearing on disability. Indeed, a good test for the preacher and exegete is to take a passage not generally regarded as part of the disability canon and read it through the lens of disability. That is what the two sermons in this chapter seek to do. Both were preached on what at St Martin's is known as Disability Weekend, at the Sunday Eucharist following the Saturday conference. In each case the title of the conference plays a role in the sermon, but the sermon is principally designed to reclaim the Bible for disability by taking two Old Testament passages that might not be regarded as having anything to offer if disability were treated as an 'issue' and letting them speak to disability treated as a perspective.

Still calling from the edge
Job 38.1–7, 34–41
17 October 2021

When I was growing up, there was only one purpose in my parents inviting relatives or friends round for dinner. I wasn't a great conversationalist and I quickly realized that the adults were allowed to ask the children questions like 'What are you taking for your exams?' or 'What do you think you'd like to be when you grow up?', but children were not allowed to ask adults questions back, like 'When do you think you're ever going to get a pay rise?', 'Isn't it about time you faced the fact you drink too much?' or 'How long do you seriously think that obviously fragile marriage of yours is going to last?' I'd realized as a child that a lot of socializing is actually a game, but when you're a child you haven't been completely let into what the rules are. So I regarded the food part of the evening as a prologue to the time when my father would say, 'I wonder if we might play a game.' Looking back, I suspect my father was the same as me, and preferred a game that called itself a game to a game that didn't.

We mostly used to play acting games, like Adverbs and Charades. There was always a lot of sending people out of the room, which was really an excuse for a covert second helping of dessert. But one game we never played, more difficult than any of those acting games, which in fact I only discovered later in life, is called Questions. I came across Questions in Tom Stoppard's 1966 play *Rosencrantz and Guildenstern are Dead*, which follows the exploits of two minor characters in Shakespeare's *Hamlet*. In Stoppard's play, Rosencrantz and Guildenstern pass the time by playing Questions. Their dialogue is a dazzling to-and-fro of catching each other out. It's like verbal tennis, except every utterance must be a question. If you hesitate, change the subject or say something that isn't a question, you lose a point – and there's an elaborate scoring system, in which three points make a game and three games make a match. You also can't ask an existential question, like 'What is life?' or a rhetorical question, like 'How long must I endure this tiresome game?' or a question that largely repeats a previous question.

When it's played well, as by Rosencrantz and Guildenstern in the play, it's amazing to watch, because you need both to suspend your desire to say something that isn't a question and try to keep up with the rapid-fire interchange of counter questions. So:

> Why did you come to church today?
> *What would you have me do instead?*

What are your favourite things to do on Sundays?
What would you recommend?
What did you like doing when you were a child?
What does childhood have to do with adult life?
Why don't you like to think about difficult things?
Would you like me only to enjoy the things you enjoy?

Then the interchange might stop, because the last question could be accused of being existential, rhetorical or changing the subject, or all three. But keeping going for eight questions is pretty rare.

The serious issue behind the apparently trivial game of Questions is this. Is answering a question with another question simply an evasion of any genuine dialogue, even to the point of hostility and exasperation – or could it instead be the joint entry of two conversation partners into a deep mystery? Imagine you took away the penalty for hesitation and gave each other all the time you needed. Then keep the playfulness, but take away the element of competition. Then take away the cleverness, and turn it into a project of each player asking a deeper question on the same trajectory as the previous one. Now you've turned an idle party game into a conversation you may remember for the rest of your life.

You've also gone to the heart of the book of Job. Job loses everything and what he doesn't know is that the reader is waiting to see if he will curse God. Job's friends assume the issue is a moral one and that Job's losses are a result of him having done something wrong. But eventually Job dismisses them, realizing that his dispute is with God alone. Job rails against God and reels off a list of quite reasonable questions that he demands that God answer. In chapter 38 and 39, of which we heard two parts this morning, God begins to respond. But God's response is not what we're anticipating. There isn't a big reveal that explains why things have turned out so badly for Job. Instead, God unfurls an overwhelming list of questions.

God's long speech covers 20 areas of the natural world and in each case, God asks whether Job is capable of comprehending or conceiving of the ways of each of these creatures or phenomena. The speech covers earth, sea, morning, the underworld, light, snow, storm, rain, stars, clouds, the lion, raven, ibex, wild ass, ox, ostrich, horse, hawk and falcon. The effect is twofold. Job finds himself no longer furious but awestruck, humbled by his tiny place in a colossal universe of immense complexity and deft design. Meanwhile, his situation is transformed from a problem into a mystery. A problem is a straightforward deficit like a breakage or a malfunction that you can simply fix and return to how it should be; a mystery is something unique and wondrous, which absorbs the whole of your intellect, emotion, aptitude and experience, and which you can only enter, after which your heart and soul will never be the same again. Before God's speech in chapters 38 and 39, Job is saying 'Why won't you fix this problem?' After this speech, Job is saying, 'Take me with you into this mystery.'

Over the last 24 hours, our community has been hosting the annual conference on Theology and Disability, with the theme '(Still) Calling from the Edge'. It's the tenth conference and the second to be held online. Participants in the ten conferences, several hundred people in total, come from extraordinarily diverse backgrounds and have lived experience of a wide range of disability. But as far as I've discovered, through conversations with many of those involved, participants have two things in common. They have experience and gifts that church and society have seldom understood, rarely honoured and frequently suppressed. And they have questions that challenge the location from which theology has often been done and the subjects that theology conventionally addresses. In other words, they're looking for receptivity and belonging in church and society and they're drawing us all into deeper relationship with God.

I want to pause for a moment and reflect on three possible meanings of the phrase, 'calling from the edge'. One is to say, 'Hello, look over here, will you, there's some of us on the edge, neglected, sometimes scorned and invariably forgotten by everyone else.' One weekend a year in our community we turn everyone's attention to a group of people who have a lot to say and whose wisdom and perspective is too often excluded. That's the first meaning, and it's not untrue, but it's far from the whole truth of what's going on in this phrase.

A second meaning is to say, 'Anyone who sings the Magnificat, which speaks of God in Christ exalting the humble and meek, anyone who reads Matthew 25, which talks of meeting Christ in those experiencing disadvantage, anyone who reads the Beatitudes, which say "Blessed are you who mourn," and anyone who knows the story of St Martin, who gave his cloak to a man in desperate trouble who was later revealed to him to be Christ, knows that the edge, rather than the centre, is where the kingdom of God is to be found. So calling from the edge is calling for a renewal of church and society to be reshaped along kingdom lines, a call to turn the world upside-down – and those who are on the edge already are calling others to join them.'

That's getting closer to the truth. But a third meaning is to realize that calling is another word for vocation. What calling from the edge means above all is the discovery that those who live with disability have a particular vocation; and it's only when they get together, and only when the questions they are asking take centre stage, and only when they are seen for once for what they uniquely are – precious, honoured and loved in God's sight – and not for what they are judged to be not, can that true vocation, by which God is renewing the earth and inaugurating the kingdom, truly be discovered and embodied and lived out as a blessing to everyone. For each of us discovers our vocation when, often with the help of others, we reflect on who we uniquely are, what we alone have experienced, how wondrously we're made, and discover what we can be and do and say that only we can be and do and say. And the catch is that God has chosen not to bring the kingdom without us but through us – so if the kingdom is to be all God calls it to be, we must respond to our calling and play our role in realizing it on earth as in heaven.

Perhaps every disabled person has experienced others regarding them as 'that annoying person who keeps asking us to change things or keeps needing us to adapt so they can participate or belong.' In other words, almost every person with a disability is accustomed to being seen as one who asks questions that invite others to live in a bigger, more complex, but more wonderful world. Which brings us back to chapters 38 and 39 of the book of Job. What we discover in the book of Job is that the one who asks questions that invite others to live in a bigger, more complex, but more wonderful world is called God. God is so annoying. God keeps calling from the edge, to say, 'Is your world, is your church, big enough and complex enough to accommodate me? Only if you listen to my questions and allow yourself to be humbled and inspired by the universe which my questions point to will your life be as wondrous as I made it to be.'

And that brings us back, finally, to the game of Questions we explored earlier and the transformation in the way we play it. This is a challenge for everyone, those with named disabilities and those with hidden, unnamed ones. Are the questions disability asks about God going to be like Rosencrantz and Guildenstern questions, combative, annoying, impossible to stay with because someone always loses patience or can't respond? Or are we all going to allow ourselves to be drawn into a rather slower, less abrasive, more absorbing shared pondering, where each contribution invites a further question, more profound, far-reaching and awe-inspiring than the one before? Job had a sequence of quite legitimate, entirely appropriate and very urgent questions. Yet in return, God gave him not answers, not solutions, but a torrent of further questions. Those questions were not defensive, not evasive, not hesitant. They were expansive, humbling and inspiring. They led Job to transformation, wonder and worship. They do the same to us.

In as unthreatening a way as possible, this sermon sets out to make both wide-ranging and subtle changes to the way the conversation about theology and disability has historically tended to take place. The first change is to move from anger and lament to a tender dialogue of mutual respect and curiosity. This mimics the shift in Job from a book about plausible explanations for his painful and perilous situation to a profound dialogue between him and God. By making this about the book of Job and about a Tom Stoppard play I try to find permission to say something as a critical friend about the tone in which the disability conversation is often conducted – a tone whose acerbic character can scare off others who fear they'll say the wrong thing and never be forgiven. The second change is from a problem to be solved to a mystery to be entered. This is a theme I've written about elsewhere, but again, here it's an important insight about how to and how not to read the book of Job and how to and how not to approach the theology of disability. It's taken for granted at a conference that those who experience disability present a gift to be cherished rather than represent a problem to be fixed – but the opportunity of a sermon is to find new and compelling ways to make the same point, in this case not simply from conviction but from exegesis. The third change is to shift the conversation from one in which neglected yet insightful people with disabilities call from the margins to self-satisfied and unthinking Christians who are slow to hear, to one in which the person with disabilities is directly, personally and transformatively addressed by God. That's the work of the section that plays with different meanings of the conference title.

Here are some guidelines on preaching about disability.

1. Avoid 'us and them' language. The whole point is to incorporate the experience of those with disabilities into that of the Church as a whole. This can't avoid some uncomfortable moments, as all recognize the resistances and the barriers and the apparently insurmountable scriptural passages that seem to other those with disabilities. But the preacher has to choose their words very carefully – words that chart a helpful path rather than replicate old dichotomies or clumsy forms of expression.
2. If you're not a person with disabilities, ask someone who is to read your sermon and suggest any necessary alterations before you preach it.
3. Don't assume a passage of Scripture has nothing to say about disability. The creativity and discovery begin when you open your heart to what the Holy Spirit is saying that you hadn't heard previously.
4. Make sure you're genuinely addressing what is being revealed about

God, rather than simply replicating what one part of the church wants to say to another. While a good guideline for any sermon, it's a particular consideration on this subject.
5. If you're not a person with disabilities, ask yourself if you're the right person to be preaching this sermon. You may well be, but you may well not be the best judge of the answer. Find someone who's better placed to answer the question and be obedient to the answer they give you.
6. Remember that preaching is fundamentally about sharing good news, good news definitively articulated in the Bible. There may be all kinds of things to say about reasonable adjustments and changing attitudes, but they may be better suited to a lecture or seminar than to a sermon. A sermon is about revelation for all, not communication of information, however important, from one group to another.

While the first sermon engaged with the heart of the Job passage, as God responds to Job's legitimate questions with a torrent of overwhelming questions, the sermon below rather more boldly seeks to trace disability through a passage that's conventionally read in a very different way – as an example of how Israel's God works through a Gentile. Crucial to the method of the sermon is not to try too hard – that is, not assuming that finding insight about disability in the Old Testament is difficult, but relaxing and expecting the Holy Spirit to disclose something at every step. This is about reclaiming the Bible for those with disabilities – a task that can be modelled by those with or without disabilities. This second sermon seeks to embody the guidelines offered above, most especially the commitment to hear what God is saying here and now to these people in this building – to each of us, preacher and listener alike. The key to the sermon is surprise: it's a surprise that Isaiah is describing God working through a Gentile, and it's a surprise that the language employed to do so has such a bearing on disability.

Riches hidden in secret places
Isaiah 45.1–7
18 October 2020

One comedy strand that's taken on a life of its own in recent years and just keeps on giving is 'Overheard in Waitrose', a Twitter account that shares deprivations only the rich can truly understand. Among my recent favourites is, 'Darling, do we need parmesan for both houses?' There's also joy to be found in, 'Daddy, does Lego have a silent T, like merlot?' Some may identify with 'Mummy, will we have to sell some of the holiday homes now that we have left the EU?' Or there's the unique, 'Well I don't understand how you can't have organic courgettes. What is this? East Berlin?'

The trouble comes when you swap the hardships of the privileged for the more intense deprivations of the dispossessed. That's precisely what happens when Judah is carried away into exile in the sixth century BC. Quickly it exchanges Waitrose for the soup kitchen. And yet what it discovers in the midst of its enforced humility is a bigger God and a closer God, a wider range of friends, and a new understanding of its own capacities. I want today, on what we might call Disability Sunday, to suggest that we can reimagine disability in a similar way. If we stop assuming that everything in ourselves and others that can be termed a disability is Babylon aching to get to Jerusalem, a soup kitchen longing to get to Waitrose, and start considering what insights we might only find in Babylon, we're close to transforming our own and our society's perception of disability, and at the same time getting closer to what the gospel is really about.

I want to read with you one of the four most significant pieces of literature associated with Israel's sojourn in Babylon. Isaiah 45 is a sensational moment of revelation, not just in the Old Testament, but in the whole religious history of the world. I'm going to explain that bold claim, but I'm not going to dwell long on what Isaiah 45 meant in the sixth century BC. I want to focus on what Isaiah 45 means in the context of disability today. I'm going to suggest that there are ten features of this passage that we could call a manifesto of what God is saying to society, church and each one of us about disability today.

Here's number one. It's a single word: Cyrus. Why is that sensational? Cyrus was a Persian king. When this was written, he was poised to invade Babylon. In other words, Israel's destroyer was about to be destroyed by an invader from further east. But unlike Babylon, Persia was glad to see Judah's exiles return home. The point is, and this is what makes this verse so crucial in the Old Testament, Israel's saviour was to be *someone from another race, nation and religion.* Which means that God was the God not just of Israel, but of the whole world. A humble Israel was discovering a bigger God. What this means for us is that God works in myriad ways and through a kaleidoscope of people. You may think your body doesn't have the features of a West End dancer or your mind doesn't have the steadiness of a chess champion. God doesn't care. God used Cyrus. God can use you.

Here's number two. Again, a single word: anointed. This is even more sensational when you realize what the word is in Hebrew. *Meshiak*:

Messiah. Messiah is the one who Israel began to long for, to anticipate as the transformative agent who would bring an end to oppression and humiliation and inaugurate peace and prosperity. You realize the significance when you translate it into Greek: Christ. Isaiah is calling Cyrus the Christ. Christ came from nowhere, and his greatest act was when he was deprived of the use of his hands and feet. Now, it's fashionable in biblical scholarship to say that Isaiah had no idea there would one day be a man called Jesus of Nazareth. But even if you accept that, what was Isaiah certainly referring to? Saul, David, Solomon, the great kings of Israel 400 years before. Isaiah is tacking Cyrus onto the back end of that list. That's plenty sensational, even if you don't accept the reference to Jesus. And what does that mean for us? It means that when the Holy Spirit wants to work through you, you are anointed to be part of the great line of those who've been agents of liberation for God's people. You may not think you fill the profile to be God's anointed. Well, it's not up to you. Stop pushing the Holy Spirit's anointing grace away. God had a role for Cyrus. God has a role for you.

Here's number three. 'Whose right hand I have grasped.' This was clearly not written during a pandemic. But feel the force of the image. Imagine yourself before an easel, painting. If you're like me, that's a daunting prospect. The fact is, your right hand isn't fantastically gifted at painting. Or drawing. Or any of it. But imagine the Holy Spirit taking your right hand and causing you to make fabulous marks on the canvas, to do things beyond your imagination, to astound yourself with the wonders you could do in each other's power. That's how the Holy Spirit works through disability. Take my hand, precious Lord. You may not even have a right hand. The Holy Spirit will find a way. There are plenty of people who paint better with their feet than I can with my right hand. 'Whose right hand I have grasped.' These are words that say life isn't about becoming brilliant at everything; it's about learning to let the Holy Spirit to work through you, however you're wired up, however strong or weak in body, mind or spirit you may feel. God grasped the hand of Cyrus. Let God grasp yours.

Here's number four. 'I will go before you.' Thirty-five years ago, I met a young priest with a Northern Irish accent. I asked how he'd ended up in Sheffield. He said when he'd been small, he'd been involved in the Troubles and had lost a member of his family and connected with the Corrymeela Community in County Antrim. Eventually, he'd fled Ulster and tried to make a new life in England. When he went forward for ordination, he met with the director of ordinands. The director said to him, 'I know who you are. I'm a member of the Corrymeela Community. Years ago, we were sent a story about a young boy mixed up in the Troubles. I've been praying for that young boy ever since. And now – here you are.'

'I will go before you.' The Holy Spirit went out ahead of that young man and prepared a way for him. You may feel your limbs don't work, your neurodiversity is a mystery, you have challenges visible and invisible. Isaiah is telling you that God will go ahead of you. God went ahead of Cyrus. God is saying, 'I will go before you.'

Here's number five. 'I will level the mountains, I will break in pieces the doors of bronze and cut through the bars of iron.' Who says there's no disability audit in the book of the prophet Isaiah? This is saying you'll be able to go the 500 miles from Babylon to Jerusalem in a wheelchair. The mountains will be turned into accessible ramps and the valleys will have lifts available. But there's also something profound here about being in prison. Doors of bronze and bars of iron. Israel felt it was in a cage. Whether that was a cage of its physical or mental condition, or a cage the society of the time put Israel in, who knows. If you feel you're in a cage, God is saying, 'I will set you free.'

We're halfway through our manifesto, and we've only read two verses of Isaiah 45. Here's my favourite: number six. 'I will give you the treasures of darkness and riches hidden in secret places.' I'm not quite sure what this meant for Cyrus, since he had enough treasure for a lifetime, wherever he kept it. But just behold what it means for you. Answer me this: Do you have treasure? Do you have riches? Are they hidden? For all the negative things you've had said to you, all the remarks that have diminished your expectations or made you feel you had nothing to bring to the table, is there still a candle burning in a part of your soul that says, 'If they only knew'? Here's the question: Is your treasure concealed in darkness? Are your riches hidden in secret places? Have you let anyone get to know you well enough to know where the secret treasure lies? Have you allowed God to get to know you well enough? Are you as inhibited by false modesty as you are by others' disdain? I believe God has already given you everything you need to respond to the call being placed upon your heart. But you've got to get it out of the cavern, shift it from the back of the larder. Now's the time.

Here's number seven. 'I, the Lord, the God of Israel, call you by your name ... I surname you.' I wonder if there's a name that no one else knows. You were given a name at birth. You were given a nickname at school. You were given a surname. Maybe that changed at some stage. God is saying, 'I know your real name. The name no one else knows. And I'm giving you a surname, because you're directly related to me.' Names can have negative associations. But if you're precious, honoured and loved, you have a new name. A new name doesn't make you a new person. But it can identify the person you always were that was longing to get out from behind a label or a stereotype. God is calling you by that new name, right now.

So to number eight. 'For the sake of my servant Jacob, and Israel my chosen.' In other words, this isn't fundamentally about you. I'm not calling you because I feel sorry for you or because I've tried everyone else. I'm not calling you because I want you to be my pride and joy above everyone else. This is about all God's people. They can't flourish unless they receive what only you can give. They're inhibited to the extent you're not able, allowed, prepared or willing to give it. If you had the only kidney that could save a dialysis patient's life, you'd give it like a shot. Your treasure hidden in darkness is like that kidney. Unless your light shines, the world will remain to that degree in the shadows of night. Let it shine, not for your sake but for everyone's.

Number nine. 'Though you do not know me.' Cyrus clearly didn't know the God of Israel. But do we? Yes, of course we know about creation, Israel, Jesus, the church and the life to come. But we still assume God wants only the strong, the wise, the beautiful, the resourceful, the faithful. Do we really believe the Holy Spirit is aching to work through people as fragile and humble as us? There are numerous obstacles in the way of disabled people finding their voice and singing their song. But sometimes the biggest obstacle is our own self-doubt, our own misgivings. God knows you. Do you want to know God in return?

And finally, number ten. By this time, we should be shaking with expectation. 'So that they may know, from the rising of the sun and from the west, that there is no one besides me.' This is all about God. This is all about worship. This is all about the whole world being reconciled to God and enjoying God forever. This is about glory. This isn't a sideshow, a subplot of a more significant story. God is saying, 'I am wholly invested in this story, and utterly absorbed in your part in it.' There's nothing more important than this.

Isaiah 45 was sensational when it was written 2,500 years ago. It was an earthquake whose tremors make us shudder today. But there's another earthquake just as significant. And its tremors shake not just the church, not just society, but heaven and earth combined. Can you feel them shaking your heart? I hope so. Because God's got a job for you to do. As big as Cyrus. Just for you. Even you. Especially you.

This is a sermon about disability. But it's not really a sermon about disability. It's a sermon about providence and vocation. It's for everyone who longs to play a role in God's realm and yet feels inadequate and unprepared and has to be reminded that this story is about God and not about us and that God will find a way whether we cooperate or not, so we might as well cooperate and enjoy it. And that means everybody. One of the ways to make it for everybody is to make a sudden shift from us to God, a shift that coincides with and legitimizes the shift from those with disabilities to everyone. It's a sermon that seeks to model what it means to go from deficit to asset, from scarcity to abundance. It's designed to bring a tear to the eye, but also to bring more power to the elbow.

Preachers have the opportunity to change people's lives by transforming the way they think and feel about themselves and about God. You don't sit down and think, 'How am I going to change people's lives?' Instead, you take the insights that the theme or passage present and then hone your words so they take maximum effect in people's imaginations, consciences and souls. You don't have to shout, you don't have to exaggerate, become sentimental or manipulative: you simply have to stay with an insight until it turns into revelation. You don't have to do all the work: the listeners will be more satisfied, and will remember more deeply, if you let them do some of the work for themselves. But you do have to trust the process and, often, perhaps every time, allow the Holy Spirit to turn your faltering 'Who am I?' into a resolute 'Send me.'

PART 2

Seasons

I

Preaching on Advent Sunday

Advent is awash with resonances – and they're not all the same. On the one hand, there's the traditional emphasis on eschatology, with the four Sundays of Advent associated with the Four Last Things – death, judgement, heaven and hell. (Does anyone really preach on hell on the Sunday before Christmas?) On the other hand, Advent becomes a synonym for Christmas and carol services take over from early December. In between are two compromise approaches. The Revised Common Lectionary offers two Sundays on John the Baptist and one on Mary and/or Joseph. The John the Baptist stories are appropriate if we see him as the forerunner, but are challenging if we're trying to fit him into a linear time sequence in which the nativity comes at the end. The more general approach is the theme of preparation. The advantage of this is that it fits the two poles of Advent – the first, past, coming of Christ in Bethlehem and the second, future coming of Christ on the last day. The weakness of talking about preparation is how easy it becomes to slide into platitudes about being prepared.

My approach is to make the most of the four last things on Advent Sunday, which is far enough away from Christmas not to need too much tinsel, and which gathers an array of musical opportunities. If you can stretch to an Advent carol service in the evening, you have two opportunities to explore the great themes of time and eternity, judgement and mercy, death and beyond, existence and essence. This is the Sunday to go for the broadest canvas imaginable and address the largest questions in your congregation's imagination – and your own. Then you can relax and let Christmas begin without getting into a fight about it.

There's a major problem at Advent, sometimes picked up in the Sundays prior, that you're not going to solve: the New Testament was written by people who in general had a high expectation that the last day was going to come soon. It didn't. You can try to evade the problem by saying that a lot of speculation focused on the destruction of Jerusalem in AD 70, but that's a diversion into fruitless historical speculation. You can't hope to do much more than acknowledge the issue and move on – unless you want to confront it head on with a sermon about what would be gained and lost if God did bring the world to an end. In the sermon below I do attempt to take the issue on, in a slightly different way.

People love a preacher if that preacher speaks about the questions they've always had but never felt comfortable raising in a church setting. The preacher doesn't have to resolve all the anomalies of the Christian faith, but must face them honestly and offer some path through them. The truth, after all, is supposed to set us free. A church is so much more energized and honest if it's a place where the difficult things are talked about rather than suppressed or evaded. A congregation doesn't expect its preacher to have read all the commentaries or studied with the great philosophers – but it does expect its preacher to have been to the bottom of the pond of faith and doubt and faced the most challenging questions and to have something to show for it. Otherwise why be trained for the ministry? Advent Sunday, like Easter Day, is a day for demonstrating the joy that lies at the end of the struggle.

The sermon below uses a technique I like to employ, perhaps because I was a student of history before I started on theology. It embraces the questions of time and eternity within a large historical sweep, thus relativising some questions and highlighting others. It's designed to convey confidence ('Don't worry, I've got this') in territory many might shy away from. Out of that confidence one particular insight emerges, and that insight then twists round to a profoundly theological conclusion.

The end of the world
Advent Sunday
30 November 2014

Let me tell you a story with five dimensions. It's a story about the end of the world. What we now call the first century AD was a time of fervid expectation of the end of all things. Jesus came into a culture where a lot of people were awaiting God's sudden engulfing of history. Jesus' use of the term 'Son of Man' was engaging that expectation, because it was a code term that cited the book of Daniel. Some of the imagery around the crucifixion – the darkness, the storm, the earthquake, the raising of the dead – is part of the same imagery.

As you may be aware, the world didn't end in the first century. Some people say that Jesus was just wrong. Others that the destruction of Jerusalem in AD 70 and the scattering of the Jewish people was an end of the world of a kind. Others say it's all a metaphor. That unresolved question leads to part two of our story, which begins 300 years later. In the year 312, Emperor Constantine converted to Christianity. To many

Christians this seemed like the end of the world – in a good way. God had finally taken hold of history, Christians were no longer persecuted – indeed, they were in charge. Heaven had come to earth. All didn't turn out as rosy as first hoped, but for many, perhaps most Western Christians for much of the 17 centuries since then, the end of the world had completely changed its character. Whereas for the early church the end of the world was the dreaded thing that might be about to happen, for the Constantinian church the end of the world was a good thing that had already happened.

Let's move to chapter three, which we might call the less upbeat time after the fall of the Roman Empire in the fifth century and for another thousand or more years after that. Here the sense of future foreboding returned, but what changed was that the end of the world was not so much a sudden, cosmic event as a concluding, largely personal event. It was less about heaven coming to earth and more about a vast judgement scene where all kinds of people were sent to everlasting bliss or eternal torment. If you look above the west door of a Romanesque or Gothic cathedral, you get the message pretty quickly, and half the fun is seeing the popes and abbots and bishops heading downstairs while the weary and heavy-laden float upstairs. The end of the world isn't an interruption any longer, but more of a fair and reasonable completion of a story, where the bad get punished and the good vindicated.

But two things change as we transition from part three to part four. One is that between the seventeenth and the nineteenth century, there took place what's usually known as the turn to the subject. In other words, instead of looking to God as the reference point for all things, people increasingly looked to human beings. That didn't necessarily mean they stopped believing in God; but it did mean that God's action in history came to be seen more as arbitrary intervention and less as something normal and obvious. The other thing that changed was that from around the middle of the nineteenth century, people gradually stopped believing in hell. Tabloid newspapers still screamed that notorious criminals should rot in hell, but in general when a person was facing their own death, they were less worried that they would roast in eternal torment than that they would simply be wiped out into a white space of oblivion.

So in part four of our story, the judgement scene of the Gothic cathedral no longer makes any sense. Let me take you to the playground of your primary school, or at least mine, circa 1972. You're having a wild old time, totally absorbed in tennis-ball soccer or forty-forty, and then the dinner lady, or lunchtime play supervisor as she should probably be known, rings an old ship's bell to summon you back to the classroom.

You find this action deeply disappointing, unreasonable and tragic, and resent it to the core of your soul. In the part four version of the end of the world, God is an arbitrary, unreasonable dinner lady calling time on human existence for no legitimate reason and Jesus' prognostications are an embarrassing intrusion of far-fetched language into the self-absorbed world of modernity. Despite the horror of two world wars, people still held on to the assumption that science and civilization could iron out the glitches in existence and bringing the world to an end was as egregious and pointless a waste as calling time on a primary school lunch break.

And so to part five, which is the last 40 or 50 years. Here we have a completely new dimension. The end of the world is something we don't resent God for doing to us; it's become something we fear doing to ourselves. When I was growing up it was the nuclear threat: I recall the day in 1980 when Ronald Reagan was elected. I really thought nuclear war had become more than likely. No sooner was the Cold War over, than the ecological threat became widely understood. If we weren't going to destroy ourselves suddenly with bombs, we were going to do it slowly with greenhouse gases. The end of the world – a mysterious prophecy of Jesus, a fulfilment in Constantine, a dread in the Middle Ages, an arbitrary intrusion in modernity – has become, today, a punishment for all our industrial sins and an unprecedented challenge to turnaround management.

What are we to make of these five dimensions of the end of the world? Well, in a word – they're all wrong. They're wrong because they all see time in a linear way – like a journey from A to B – and it looks like a guillotine comes down before we reach B, either because God doesn't want us to reach B, or because we wipe ourselves out before we get there. But time isn't like that. I wonder if you've ever seen a large funnel-shaped vortex, which looks like a game or a challenge but turns out to be a fundraiser. You launch a 2-pence piece into it as if setting off a battling top, and the coin goes round and round and round, gathering pace and gradually descending into the vortex. It's mesmerising to watch the coin more or less maintain its trajectory without descending too much, and eventually sink into the throat of the funnel where usually it goes round and round at least 20 times before disappearing.

For Christians, time is like that. We're all being drawn inexorably towards the end, like a speck of metal toward a magnet or a coin into a vortex. The end of the world isn't a random moment when an arbitrary God, in a fit of petulance, loses patience with the world and sends everyone upstairs to bed without their dinner. The end of the world is where God started. The purpose of creation was to lay the foundations and set out the ingredients for the end of the world. As soon as God involved us in the story, it was guaranteed the story wouldn't entirely go as God would have wanted or expected. But God always wanted us to be part of the story despite that. And that's why we were always going to need an end of the world to draw together all the good parts and redeem all the bad parts and make a true and wondrous world in which we could be God's companion forever. Jesus is God showing us the purpose of creation and the cost of our waywardness. But fundamentally, Jesus is God showing us what that end of the world will be like. Jesus is the end of the world.

This means we evaluate everything backwards. We see what place it takes in the end of the world, and we estimate its significance today accordingly. A cup of coffee and a tender hand on the shoulder offered to a colleague who's having a hard day may seem an inefficient use of time to a work-study consultant, but it looks like the end of the world. A desk-off in which two colleagues fight about the tidiness of a shared office may seem vital at the time, but it doesn't belong in the end of the world. A weary afternoon spent at the bedside of a dying relative may seem hopeless and miserable at the time, but at the end of the world we'll see how it's an icon of how God abides with us. If you're in a quandary about how to live your life or you're facing a crossroads of truth or virtue, ask yourself the backwards question: does this belong in the end of the world – or is it something I'm trying hastily to squeeze in before the dinner lady rings the bell?

In all the examples I've given, notice the ambiguity about the word 'end'. Sometimes it means conclusion, like the words 'the end' in the last frame of a film or book. But sometimes it means goal or purpose, as in the phrase 'the end justifies the means.' If we're to understand the end of the world, we need to take our eyes off the conclusion of the world's story and look more closely at the purpose of the world's existence. The more aware we are of the purpose of the world's existence, the less worried we need to be about the conclusion of the world's story. Of course we care about nuclear catastrophe and ecological degradation. But the answer to these questions lies not in averting a conclusion to the world's story; it lies in clarifying the purpose of the world's existence.

And that's why Advent is all about the second coming of Jesus. When we sing 'Lo he comes with clouds descending', we're not celebrating a correct prediction of the timing of the world's conclusion, or even hoping that on judgement day we'll be going upstairs rather than downstairs. We're saying that in Jesus, God has shown us what the world was created for. It was created for perfect relationship between God and humanity, human beings with one another and humankind with the whole created order. And in Jesus we see all these things made flesh. The astonishing thing about creation is that, rather than skip straight to the end of the world, God has given us time to shape and colour and influence and inflect what the end of the world will finally be like. Because the end of the world will be made up of stray elements of this world – the cast-offs, the remnants, the pieces left on the floor when the sewing machine of our driven existence has done its work. Jesus became one of those cast-offs to show us how God makes the end of the world out of what we in this world reject and tread down.

And so our Advent faith is not that we know the day or the hour, but that we understand the purpose of all things. We know that the end of the world is real, but we need not fear it. We need not fear it because we have already seen it. The end of the world is Jesus.

The sermon in fact makes three moves, but in such a way that they all feel like one move. It argues that time is not linear but more like a vortex (a shorter sermon could simply summarize the first half of the sermon in one paragraph); that the end of the world is more about purpose than climax; and that in Jesus, God has shown us that purpose. It certainly takes on the anomaly of the world not ending in the first century – but it does so in the only way I know how, to place it in a transformed context. It's an example of starting off as an Advent sermon and ending up as a Christmas sermon, because it begins with eschatology and ends with incarnation. Which demonstrates that the themes of Advent and Christmas don't need to be at odds with one another.

Here are some guidelines for preaching on Advent Sunday.

1. Don't be an Advent bore. Don't criticize congregation members or the rest of the world for celebrating Christmas early. Enjoy the fact the world is rejoicing in a Christian festival – the incarnation, the utter commitment of God to us, the entire presence of God with us. Way too many clergy and preachers spend Advent telling everyone else off for focusing on Christmas. It would be hilarious if it weren't so tragic.
2. Try to claim Advent Sunday for the great eschatological themes of time, judgement, death and eternal life. If you can have a thorough Advent Sunday facing the toughest issues about existence, you've done much better than achieve a lame Advent muttering about preparation.
3. Don't pummel people with technical language like eschatological. Focus on the biggest questions of life: why is there something rather than nothing, is there a reality beyond this one, what within this reality might tell us about the other one, is the other one enormously bigger/longer/deeper than this one, what becomes of us when we die,

and so on. Not everyone who comes to church has a clear and consistent faith – possibly the minority – but everyone lives in a world where almost no one wants to address these questions and watches football instead. Make your church one where you face these questions together.

If the sermon above addresses these guidelines from a cerebral point of view, the sermon below does so more from an emotional point of view. Some sermons are about heart and head, others major on one or the other. You can never leave the head entirely behind. To be a truly transformational sermon you need to address the gut also – the place deeper and more visceral than the heart where the real decisions are made and real faith resides.

Advent is often described as a time of waiting, and the sermon below addresses waiting as an experience of profound discomfort, of longing for consolation or resolution. There's waiting when you've got plenty else to be getting along with – and there's waiting where you can't think about anything else, as some people experience, for example, when hoping and trying to conceive a child. This sermon engages with the latter kind. Just as you win the love of your congregation for addressing the biggest questions, you win the trust of your congregation by handling this emotional territory with a steady hand. If you get this right, people will say, 'I thought you were talking just to me.'

Never mind the width
Isaiah 64.1–9
29 November 2015

Have you ever been hungry? You start by feeling that you could really do with a bit of something, maybe a snack. But before long, if you've got no way of finding a mouthful or a whole meal, you begin to feel your own fragility: your stomach aches, your concentration begins to waver. It starts to be difficult to do ordinary things, so you begin to seek distractions – something absorbing that takes your attention away and enables you to lose yourself. You doubt your own judgement. You realize you're becoming selfish, because you're so mesmerised by your own desperation that you can't consider the needs of anyone else. When, finally, you do find food, it can be that the yearning, and the ache for the pain to go away, is so great that you don't truly enjoy it or savour its taste or texture. Greedily, you wolf it down because your body has taken over and the rest of you has been elbowed aside. Hunger has drained all the joy and you're left with raw, voracious compulsion.

We don't want to see ourselves like this. It's not just the physical discomfort. It's the discovery that we can be so needy, so selfish, so consumed by one thing to the exclusion of all else. We certainly don't want anyone else to see us like this – to witness the narrow, precarious, craven creature we can be. What a loss of dignity.

Hunger is the most basic of our human needs and desires. But more often, it's a metaphor for other longings that can take over our life. I wonder if you know, for example, what it's like to yearn to have a life partner. Your life has good and rewarding things in it, but deep down you just profoundly want to matter to another creature, to have a commitment and a relationship to build your life around, to shape meaning out of the rhythms and texture of your days and the movements and achings of your heart; and perhaps most of all to make something beautiful together to leave as a legacy on planet earth and feel that your life has been at least somewhat fruitful.

But year follows year and there's no genuine sign of your being in any potentially permanent relationship. Your plans for your career and your financial planning, which had always been provisional, begin to take on an unexpected air of permanence. You come to wonder if anyone will ever find you attractive, if maybe you're hanging out in the wrong places, or if you're just being too choosy. Before you know it, the waiting takes a grip over your mind and soul and becomes as convulsive as hunger. Your internal radar can't help flashing sirens when it picks up nearby people with vibrant marriages, designer children and imagined happiness; and you find yourself avoiding conversation with them and withdrawing from their company, lest your need and grief turn into sharp words, inappropriate tears and blinding self-pity. You don't want other people to see you like this. You can't bear to see yourself like this.

Of course, these are only among the most intense of many profound yearnings that can't be assuaged by material comfort or professional accomplishment. Look to your left; look to your right: you're likely to see someone who's waiting; been waiting a long time.

Not long ago I sat down with a young man called Jeff who'd lost his beloved and only sister in a tragic accident. What made the tragedy so poignant was that Andrew, the man responsible for the accident, was a close friend of both Jeff and his sister. Even worse, Andrew's own brother had also died in the same accident. The four friends had been travelling together. It would have been great in many ways if Jeff and Andrew could have sat down together and talked through the events of that day and shared their grief and loss. But Jeff told me he just couldn't do that. 'I know I should and I know I must, but I'm sorry, I just can't bring myself to forgive him. I know in my head he's hurting for his brother as much as I am for my sister, but he's not missing my sister like I do. No one is. No one knows how important she was to me. I just can't forgive him, and I just can't face him.' I asked, 'D'you think one day you will?' Jeff said, 'I know one day I've got to, because this hatred is just eating me up and I can't think about anything else. Until I can forgive, I won't be able to start living again. But I'm not there yet – nothing like there yet. And I think it's going to be a while.'

All waiting is a kind of hunger. All hunger is a kind of waiting. You can fill up your life with good and worthwhile things, genuine and valuable tasks, absorbing and deserving projects, admirable and interesting people; but suddenly, you get moments when you see with piercing clarity that it's all a distraction, all a way of making you so busy that you don't need to think about the one thing you desire above all else, and long for with your whole being, and need like a hungry hole in your stomach. You can deal with waiting through distraction, through busy-ness and fluster and hurry and entertainment; but when all your distractions have expired, the waiting's still there for you, gnawing at your soul like a hungry dog growling and pawing at the back door.

Back in the days when it was common to go to a haberdasher and ask for yards of cloth for sewing or dressmaking into trousers or skirts or outer garments, people would imitate the proverbial salesperson and say, 'Never mind the quality – feel the width!' In other words, 'Who cares whether the material comes from the very best fabric? See how much there is of it, for such a bargain price!' It's a parable for what we do to our lives to hide ourselves from the depths of our struggles and sadness and pain. 'Never mind our deepest desires – see how easy it is to occupy ourselves with our trivial ones! Don't distress yourself about the things that really matter – see how quickly you can get your hands on the things that don't!' It's perfectly possible to turn your whole life into a distraction, a whole enterprise of feeling the width. Maybe that's what you're doing right now.

The church has a season for helping us set aside our distractions and get profoundly in touch with the powerlessness of waiting. It's called Advent. In Advent we dismantle our elaborate defences, and, for a few weeks, or days, or moments, face up squarely to our deepest yearnings, our unresolved longings and our rawest needs. But Advent is also about a confidence deeper than our needs, a hope more far-reaching than our desires, a future more comprehensive than our most poignant yearnings.

In our self-protection we habitually say to ourselves, to one another, and even to God, 'Never mind the quality, feel the width. Let's just make ourselves busy and perhaps we'll forget about it.' In Advent, God says to us, 'Never mind the width. Your life isn't about quantity of activity or length of days. Let go of the width. Feel the depth.'

The answer to the agony of waiting isn't width. It's depth. Right now, in this Advent moment, feel the depth of your life, and look into the deep heart of God.

Advent says, 'Yes, you're hungry. Yes, you long for fulfilment and resolution and completion and consummation. Yes, you're aching all over, yes, if you stopped your incessant activity and paused for one second to look in the mirror you'd be sobbing with disappointed dreams and deflated desires and unmet longings and dashed aspirations. Yes, life hasn't turned out as you trusted it would, yes, it feels like everyone else has it easier than you, yes, it's sometimes impossible to find the patience to keep going, yes, you feel that if you admitted your grief for one moment it would crush you and incapacitate you and disable you from functioning in any respectable and grown-up and self-effacing way.' Advent goes to the bottom of our waiting.

But Advent doesn't stop there. Advent goes under and around our waiting. Advent also says, gently, cherishingly and tenderly, 'No. No, this isn't the way the story ends. No, God isn't ignoring you or punishing you. No, this isn't God's last word on the matter. No, God hasn't finished with you. No, this groaning, this aching, this longing won't be your eternal condition. God came in Christ to be with you, to groan with your groan, to ache with your ache, to yearn with your yearning. God in Christ suffered on the cross to show you a yearning that's greater even than your yearning, a grief that's greater even than your grief, a longing that's greater even than your longing. A longing for you. Christ rose from the dead to show you how the story ends, that all your pain and agony and tears will be taken up into glory, that all your sadness will be made beautiful and all your waiting will be rewarded. Christ ascended into heaven to show you that you'll spend eternity with God, that your hunger will be met in God's banquet, that everything you long for will be exceeded and overwhelmed in the glory of the presence of God, and that when you see the marks on Christ's hands and the Father's broken heart you'll finally realize how achingly, convulsively hungry God has always been for you.'

Just for this moment in Advent, dare to feel the depth. Never mind the width. If you're tired of waiting, go deeper. Feel the deep texture of life. Eternal life isn't an infinitely *extended* version of what we have now: it's a *deeper* version of what we have now. If you want a glimpse of eternal life, even amid the sadness and the longing of waiting, go deeper.

Remember all those people you were envious of who seemed to have everything you didn't have? Go deeper and see who they really are, and what they truly long for, and feel your envy begin to melt into compassion. Go deeper into your fears and come out of the bottom of them and let your hatred become hope. Go deeper into your loneliness and make a companion of the truth you find there. Feel the wonder of your createdness, sense the unlikely mystery of your being here at all. And receive all the rest as a bonus, a gift, a blessing.

Advent isn't an escape. It's an encounter with the time that is deeper than our time, a time we call eternal life. It's a discovery of a longing that's deeper than our longing, the longing we call God's waiting for us. It's an experience deep down and through the bottom of our experience, a place where grief is no longer isolating but companionable, where alienating hurt becomes tender wisdom, where unfulfilled longing becomes the sculpting of a greater hole for grace.

It's hard to do Advent all year round. It's almost easier to be left alone in our waiting. But just this once, this Advent, take the risk on God that God's taken on you. Feel the quality. Feel the depth. Go deeper and keep digging. Keep digging until you find you've dug deep into the heart of God. And there discover a real hunger, the deepest hunger of them all: God's hunger – for you.

One of the most common and most painful pitfalls of sermons is the tendency to portray Christians as better than others – to play into our desire to get ahead of others and to use God and faith as a way of making us better or giving us a vantage point from which we can look down on others. This sermon seeks to bypass all that and bring us face to face with our own struggles, and to see those struggles as a stimulus to come face to face with God. It turns on a very simple distinction between breadth and depth. Having established how facile a solution breadth is, it offers depth as a different way to engage our grief and sadness, and through them to find God. But in a move I make often, it's not content to remain there, but instead turns our struggle into an insight into the character and nature of God, who struggles to reach us. Thus, what starts close to self-pity ends up as worship. The result is a sermon that engages profoundly with our most uncomfortable reality and makes it the place of encounter with the living God. Which is what the Bible does over and over again, and what a good sermon should do.

2

Preaching in Advent Season

Advent season is really two Sundays, because Advent Sunday, which we've already considered, is a unique day for considering the last things, and the fourth Sunday in Advent is another unique Sunday for considering the mystery of the incarnation, focusing directly on Jesus' virginal conception, or at least on the joint divine and human role in his conception.

There are two related themes that characterize these two Sundays and the two sermons I offer in this chapter address one each. The first is the delay of Christ's second coming, which is a continuation from the theme of Advent Sunday, but this time in a more reproachful tone of voice – engaging with a sense of disappointment, even betrayal, that Christianity hasn't turned out to be what it claims to be. The second is a similar lament in the mouth of John the Baptist. John the Baptist is a very difficult subject for a sermon, because all the preacher's instincts are to talk about Jesus, and John is not Jesus. The most straightforward answer is to address what he was looking for from Jesus, and recognize that it's very much what we are looking for from Jesus; and to assess the ways in which John is happy with what Jesus is giving, or if he – and we – are missing something vital.

I dislike the phrase 'teaching sermon'. It assumes a relationship of preacher as instructor and the humble faithful as needing information and formation. I believe the Holy Spirit has been at work in the listeners' lives since those lives began, and so the preacher's role is to provoke the response of Jacob: 'Surely God is in this place, though I never knew it.' The sermon below shows how much theological ground you can cover through this approach, without ever having to say, 'I'm now going to tell you about heaven,' still less, 'Let's move on to realized eschatology.' The sermon also challenges the distinction between an exegetical and a theological sermon, because it's both. By exploring 2 Peter, it reclaims for the congregation a part of the New Testament that preachers seldom dare to tread. But, as often in preaching and invariably in Advent, what the preacher is doing is to elucidate how what the author of 2 Peter is addressing is exactly what we today are worrying about.

What's new about the sermon is that rather than go along with the general air of dissatisfaction about the delay of Christ's second coming, the sermon offers constructive arguments about what would actually be lost, and thus takes on the abiding sense in church and society that God owes us something and hasn't paid up. This pervading attitude of entitlement exists as much in congregations as in those who stay away; the difference often being that congregations treat it as a family secret we politely refrain from mentioning. Leaving aside the simple fact that if Christ had returned in the first century we would never have been born, there are, in fact, strong arguments why we might affirm the 'delayed Parousia', but they're so seldom aired that Advent in general and a sermon on 2 Peter in particular offers an excellent moment to air them. But lest they prove daunting as a sermon subject, they're tucked into a sermon that's begun and ended as a meditation on the nature of personal attention – which turns out to be a description of having God's attention. The secret of addressing such weighty theological arguments is to maintain a lightness of touch that roots complex issues in everyday experiences.

The hastening that waits
2 Peter 3.8–15a
10 December 2017

'I know you're in a hurry.' I wonder if you've ever said that, asking for a person's attention, when it's clear they're rushing to something else. And you could simply say, 'Don't worry, we can talk about it later, I'll send you an email, it's not urgent,' and permanently or temporarily fade into the background of their life. But sometimes you don't, something urges you to press on despite their haste, to delay their urgency, with a question only they can answer or a fact that you really need them to know. Maybe what you're really saying is, 'I need to know that I'm more important than this thing you're rushing to.'

That's the spirit of Advent: a pause to reflect on what the rush is, what it is that's hastening on, and how to relate to it. The Second Letter of Peter, from which we've just read, is all about these questions. It's full of florid and graphic language about the fire of judgement, but its questions are as important today as when they were written. These are the questions: What is heaven? Why doesn't it come straightaway? And how should we act in the meantime? You could call those the Advent questions. I want to spend a moment pondering them together.

What is heaven? Second Peter calls heaven 'a home for righteousness.' The popular notion of heaven is of a secluded other place, an ethereal realm that gathers souls to itself, a disembodied paradise that shares no correspondences with earthly existence: in short, a place we go to but where we don't do a whole lot. The New Testament for the most part portrays heaven rather differently. It sees heaven as creation renewed. The universe was created for God to dwell with humankind, and heaven is that full, uninhibited, uncomplicated dwelling of God with humankind amid a renewed creation; it is the installing of reconciled human relationships in a restored pattern of created well-being. To put it succinctly: we don't go to heaven – heaven comes to earth. There's no rapture. Creation isn't ultimately jettisoned as a useful but dispensable prototype. Heaven is the fulfilment of all God's intentions for creation.

And the way heaven comes about is that it's constructed backwards. Heaven isn't all brand new and shiny, like a whole new creation from scratch. The kingdom of God is made up of two ingredients: God's original intention for our flourishing; and God's painstaking reintegration of the rejected, neglected and ignored elements back into the story. In other words, heaven is the vindication of all the good that's been lost and trodden down, and the transformation of all the bad that has distorted its created purpose. In short, heaven is a mixture of God's design and the redemption of all that went astray. If we want to imagine heaven, we don't need to picture clouds and harps and wings. We must simply envision what it would be like if all in history that has been wasted, ruined, lost or excluded were brought back into the story and allowed to flourish. Jesus' ministry embodied and inaugurated the kingdom of God because it did both of these things: it depicted and modelled heavenly relationships and it reintegrated those who were rejected and lost.

So that's what heaven is: the renewal of creation brought about by the reincorporation of the wasted and the cast aside. And that's why Jesus' resurrection is the epitome of heaven: because his crucifixion was the most horrendous waste of God's most sublime purpose, and the resurrection shows how even that can be reintegrated into the story. The resurrection is the perfect heavenly moment.

So, on to the second Advent question: why doesn't heaven just come straightaway? It's a question that becomes more than a theoretical question in the face of horrendous human experiences like the Syrian civil war or indescribable crimes and suffering like the Holocaust. Why does God let the agony continue if heaven is available?

I believe the reason is that when time comes to a stop there's something lost as well as something gained. The something that's lost is all the good that there's been in the world in the 2,000 years since the Ascension of Christ. We've noted that heaven works retrospectively: it restores all that's been lost and vindicates all that's been trodden down. But heaven also highly exalts all that's been faithful and cherishes everything that's been genuinely hopeful. In simple terms, heaven doesn't create new life: it restores the life that's already been created, healing the wounds and mending the flaws.

Pause for a moment and dwell on what would be lost if there were no new life: not just the joy and fulfilment and wonder of bringing new creatures into being, but the renewal and replenishment and enrichment of existence. There's no question that the prospects for retrieval of what's been lost in the neglect, rejection and oppression of so much of humankind and the wider creation is beyond enumeration; but if heaven is truly everlasting, a point will surely come when the joy of restoration will seem insufficient without the dynamism of new beginnings. That's what's lost in moving from creation to new creation.

It's also true to say that while profound suffering, pain, distress and evil undoubtedly display the worst in human nature in particular and creation in general, they can also elicit the best in human character and created virtue. I'm not suggesting that God creates or permits evil in order to construct a vale of soul-making. I'm pointing out that, if God hastened forward the last day and the infusion of heaven on earth, these outstanding moments and qualities in human courage and selflessness would never surface. Some of the best, perhaps the very best, dimensions of human nature come to light in the face of adversity. Abolish adversity and they would never come to light. Just as in the body, pain can be distressing but it usually serves a purpose, drawing attention to something that needs urgently to be addressed, so adversity in life becomes the opportunity that brings to the fore gifts, talents and merits that would otherwise have no outlet.

So that's the answer to our second Advent question. We don't get heaven straightaway because there's a real joy in making new things and because even the worst adversity can yet have some silver linings. But what about the third question: How should we act, given that the end of all things has been promised, and could come any time, but has not yet come?

Well, here's the interesting point. When we talk about the continued creation of the good and the new, and the paradox that adversity can elicit qualities that benign existence suppresses, we're more or less looking at a definition of church. The church is a community where the Holy Spirit continues to bring forth new life, and empowers people to face adversity with dignity, solidarity and hope. Think for a moment about how the story of the church ends. I think there are two contrasting reasons that the church's story might one day have run its course. In the first scenario, the whole earth has turned to the God of Jesus Christ in faith and hope and love. There's nothing left for the church to do. In the alternative and diametrically opposite scenario, there remains not one single believer, no, not one. There's not a single Christian left in the world.

In the first scenario, the church would have fulfilled its destiny both in breadth and in depth, in evangelism and discipleship, in witness and holiness, and arrived, like Pilgrim in John Bunyan's story, at the celestial gates. It would be a celebration of the fruitfulness of the gospel in the soil of the human soul. In the second rather gloomier outcome, the outstretched fingers of God would have become utterly loose from the receiving hand of humankind, and there'd be no golden thread, no inner meaning of history, no willing vehicle for God's grace amid a turbulent and fervid world, and there'd be no further reason to postpone the full disclosure and completion of God's original purpose. We seem about equidistant from either scenario right now.

And into this fascinating historical situation comes this intriguing phrase from Second Peter. It talks about 'waiting for and hastening the coming of the day of God'. On the face of it, the phrase sounds absurd. How can you wait for something you're at the same time hastening? It sounds like an oxymoron, a contradiction in terms. But you only need to think for a few moments about the crises of your life to see how helpful and accurate the phrase is. You're sitting in intensive care by the side of your loved one, and you want the doctors to be frantic and busy, but you know deep down that only time will heal. You've just had a terrible relationship breakup, and you desperately want to do something to take the pain away and make it better, but again, deep inside, you know that only time will help you come to terms with it. You see a report of an earthquake on the TV, and you want agencies to rush aid to the situation, but you know it's going to take years for the country seriously to recover.

The hastening that waits. I wonder if that's a description of your life. I wonder if that's an apt definition of love. I wonder if that's a suitable self-understanding for the church – perhaps especially, this church. It's what we're doing together right now: pausing to wait on God in the midst of all our urgency. It's certainly a phrase that sums up the season of Advent: the hastening that waits.

Second Peter goes on to offer us another interesting injunction: 'While you're waiting for new heavens and a new earth, strive to be found by him at peace.' Again, it sounds like an oxymoron: if you're striving, how can you at the same time be at peace? But maybe striving to be at peace is the same as the hastening that waits: it's a perfect summary of our lives before God, in all its paradox and purpose. If it was just striving, there'd be no faith and you'd be impossible to live with; if it was complete peace, you'd be in heaven already and no earthly use.

I want to take you back to where we started, with one person saying to another, 'I know you're in a hurry.' 'I know you're hastening, but I'd like you to wait.' I'd like you to imagine the two conversation partners as you and God. We've spent a few moments reflecting on how much we want God to bring heaven, but also on some very good reasons why heaven hasn't come just yet. Advent is a time for the hastening that waits. But ponder this: who's talking to whom? Is God the one that's hastening, while you say, 'Wait a moment, will you? I've got some questions, some requests, and some things to tell you.' Or is it the other way round: you're the one hastening and God taps you on the arm and says, 'Could I have a moment? In the midst of all your striving, can you and I find some peace?'

Maybe what you're both saying is, 'I need to know that I'm more important than this thing you're rushing to.'

It's a very old technique, but one I enjoy using – taking a short phrase from the Scripture reading and playing with it till its multiple dimensions are fully enjoyed. When I lived in the United States, I became much more attuned to the practice of giving a sermon a title. I found this a good discipline (just as it is for an undergraduate essay) to ensure I stuck rigorously to the argument; but also a way of lodging the key phrase in the congregation's mind before, during and after the sermon. In this case, 'The hastening that waits' is just such an intriguing phrase – indeed, one so resonant that it has been used to sum up Karl Barth's theological ethics.[1]

Here are some guidelines on preaching in Advent season.

1. While the pressure to include Christmas carols in a service two or three weeks before Christmas may be strong, and efforts to insist on Advent music likely to be counterproductive, there's almost never a corresponding pressure to preach about Christmas before Christmas Eve, so it's perfectly possible to have a Christmas feel to the liturgy and music while sticking to the lectionary readings for preaching.
2. There's a primal quality to the themes of Advent – death, most obviously, but also the nature of heaven, the experience of disappointment, the suspicion that Christianity has not lived up to its billing. Sermons in Advent should address these issues head on: the mood of quiet but

---

[1] Nigel Biggar, *The Hastening that Waits: Karl Barth's Ethics* (Oxford: Clarendon Press, 1993).

undaunted trust conveys as much as the words themselves about what it means to be a Christian in the face of disillusion and sadness.
3. The entitled assumption that we each consented to be born after signing a contract that God would give us peace, security, health and plenty is extraordinarily widespread and needs to be countered with a gentle reminder that there was never such a contract, and that our existence is pure grace. While engaging with and understanding people's disappointments about life and faith, the preacher's job is not to amplify them, but to offer wider framing and use them as opportunities to enter more fully into understanding God's disappointments.
4. You don't have to apologize for the absence of Christ's second coming in the first century, like a train operator explaining why a service is not running because of a strike and offering vouchers for another day. We can read the Gospels as suggesting the world is a problem for us and God to fix, but much better to read them as proposing the world is a playground for us and God to enjoy. In the end, eagerness for Christ's second coming is a lack of confidence in the sufficiency of his first.

The sermon below is about John the Baptist. If even Jesus had difficulty explaining what John represented, we shouldn't feel too bad that we struggle too. The tendency is to turn John into the Old Testament in human form – rugged, sharp edges, scary at times, full of wrath, pointing to Jesus, ultimately incomplete. Besides being a caricature of the Old Testament, this doesn't focus on the parts of John most fruitful for preaching. Among the more propitious directions are questions like, if John was calling people to faith before the ministry, death and resurrection of Jesus had yet happened, what exactly was that faith? If John was antagonistic and polarizing, are there circumstances in which the church should be so too? How important is it that the gospel writers saw John as fulfilling scriptural hopes for Elijah to return? What does it mean for the least in God's realm to be greater than John?

But the central question John the Baptist raises is the one addressed in the sermon below: if Jesus inaugurates God's realm, how come things don't look and feel any different – and in particular, what am I doing in prison? It's pretty much the central question in Christianity, from a pastoral point of view: if Jesus changes everything, why is everything the same? This sermon, from my time in the United States, engages with that very pressing sense of disappointment.

It's working
Isaiah 35.1–10, Matthew 11.2–11
12 December 2010, Duke University Chapel

Around ten years ago, when I was the pastor of a neighbourhood church in England, I got a call from a woman in distress. She said, 'Pastor, my house is haunted. Can you come and do an exorcism?' Now, you may be aware that one thing I don't possess is adrenaline. I'm not the kind of pastor who gets a crisis call, jumps through the window of a waiting patrol car, starts up the siren and tosses a flashing light on the roof, and then heads into danger while a screech of the tires announces, 'Lights, camera, ministry.'

But I try to take people seriously, maybe more seriously than they take themselves, especially when they're in distress. So a day or two later I visited the woman, and we sat together on her sofa as I explained that Jesus, in his death and resurrection, had overcome the power of evil, and that the way we embody Jesus' victory is through baptism. But baptism doesn't always give us freedom from fear. So I was inviting her to join me as I visited each room in the house, sprinkled the waters of baptism and prayed for deliverance from fear. And that's exactly what we did. Fifteen minutes later, when we'd entered and prayed and sprinkled in each room, we returned to the sofa in the sitting room. The woman looked at me with disappointment in her face. 'Is that it?' she said. 'I could have done that.'

She was a bit more honest and direct than most of us, but my guess is that almost everyone here will have felt like that about Christianity at some stage or other. What does it all amount to? A mysterious man long ago, who did and said interesting things and got buried for it. A whole bunch of people trying to follow him, or somehow use him as a route to immortality, and as often as not falling out with each other or turning it all into a power grab or a form of imperialism or patriarchy or division. A story of aspiration, illusion, fragility and failure. Maybe that's how you feel right now. 'Is that Christianity? Is that it? That's no big deal. I could have done that. I could make that up, easy.'

And the feeling is multiplied and focused when you've actually given your life to it and put yourself in personal danger because of it. We all know that the cynic is the failed romantic. You don't hate if you haven't first loved. You don't feel let down if you weren't first built up. That's where John the Baptist got to. He'd proclaimed Jesus. He'd done the whole camel's-hair-coat and locusts-and-wild-honey diet and call-to-repent thing. He'd thrown his entire life into preparing the way for Jesus. And now he'd been tossed into prison. And he finds himself thinking, 'Jesus, are you for real? Is this it, or are we going to see some action? When do we get the baptising-with-the-Holy-Spirit-and-unquenchable-fire routine? Hey? Bring it on! I don't want to be pushy, but, really, now would be a great time.'

To put John's question into contemporary language, we might say, 'Hey, Jesus, why're you hanging out with the people who don't matter and not being more strategic? It seems Pilate's still running Jerusalem, Herod's still in charge in his palace and the Jewish authorities have still got the temple and the practice of the law all buttoned up. It feels like you haven't got the head or the heart for tackling the systemic issues. You've not even set foot in Jerusalem yet. Are you the one who is to come or is it time we were looking for someone else?' It's important to feel the force of John's question. He's basically right, and most of us for most of the centuries that have followed have wondered about the same things. When it comes to constructing a messiah, Jesus just doesn't look the part.

You can imagine John, in the loneliness of his prison cell, pondering the shortcomings of Jesus. Jesus was from Nazareth – that's another name for nowhere. Jesus lived a humble life and his disciples were a mixture of common people and formerly notorious sinners. Hardly movers and shakers. Jesus was constantly in controversy and was destined for rejection and suffering. This isn't exactly baptizing with the Holy Spirit and unquenchable fire. Jesus looks and sounds too much like the ordinary, the mundane, the downright failure to be a messiah.

Are you John? Are you in a physical or mental or emotional place where the kingdom is very hard to see? Are you in prison right now? Do you feel duped, let down, disillusioned by Jesus? Have you lost the joy? Are you privately furious with Jesus because you believed he changed everything, but everything seems too much like it always was? Have you given your heart and soul to Jesus and now find yourself asking, 'Are you the one who is to come, or should we be looking for someone else?'

Listen to Jesus' answer. 'The blind receive their sight, the lame walk, the lepers are cleansed, the deaf hear, the dead are raised, and the poor have good news brought to them.' At first reading it sounds like a catalogue of the kind of things we read in the Bible and grabs our attention no more than a table attendant reeling off a list of the specials in a restaurant when we've been to the restaurant before and we know the specials are always the same. But we need to look closely at each of these six statements. Jesus is announcing salvation in three dimensions.

First, he's saying that the salvation he's bringing reaches every aspect of human experience. It overcomes disability, by addressing blindness and deafness; it overcomes sickness, by cleansing leprosy; it overcomes alienation, by bringing hope and joy to the poor; and it overcomes death, by the power of resurrection. We'd express the part about disability differently today, but the point is the same: Jesus is gently saying to John, this may not be lightning and fire and revolution and judgement, but it's a comprehensive wave of healing on every level of existence. And healing is the heart of the kingdom.

Second, Jesus offers a succinct summary of everything that has already taken place in the first 10 chapters of Matthew's Gospel. The blind received their sight when Jesus touched the eyes of two blind men in chapter 9. The lame walked when Jesus both forgave the sins of the paralysed man and told him to stand up, earlier in chapter 9. The leper was cleansed when Jesus stretched out his hand and touched a kneeling leper in chapter 8. The deaf man was healed when Jesus cast out a demon, again in chapter 9. The dead were raised when Jesus took the hand of the daughter of the leader of the synagogue, again in chapter 9. The poor had good news brought to them repeatedly, but most of all when Jesus began the Sermon on the Mount with the words, 'Blessed are the poor in spirit: for theirs is the kingdom of heaven.' Jesus is gently saying to John, 'These are not just words, they're things I've already done.'

And third, Jesus refers John to the promises and hopes of Israel. His words echo several places in Isaiah, including chapters 26, 29, 42 and 61, but especially chapter 35, our Old Testament reading for today, made familiar by its role in Handel's 'Messiah': 'Then the eyes of the blind shall be opened, and the ears of the deaf unstopped; then the lame shall leap like a deer, and the tongue of the speechless sing for joy.' Jesus is gently saying to John, 'All the promises of the Scriptures are finding their yes in me.' And more than that, because added to Isaiah's hope are two new dimensions, the curing of the incurable illness of leprosy and the overcoming of the final enemy, death. Jesus' salvation is no let-down, no betrayal, no disillusioning anti-climax: it is comprehensive, already fully under way and beyond hopes and expectations.

But the trouble is, for John the Baptist, it still doesn't feel like it. Like the woman who asked me for a dramatic exorcism and said, 'I could've done that,' John's not impressed.

In the satirical Monty Python film, *Life of Brian*, set in first-century Judea, the opposition to the Romans is hopelessly split. The People's Front of Judea is at loggerheads with the Judean People's Front, the Judean Popular People's Front, the Campaign for a Free Galilee, and the Popular Front of Judea. One of these splinter groups has a secret meeting where a vigilante soldier asks, 'What have the Romans ever done for us?' One by one, his fellow freedom-fighters grudgingly acknowledge a host of benefits the Romans have indeed brought. But Reg, their leader, remains unconvinced. He finally demands, 'All right ... all right ... but apart from better sanitation and medicine and education and irrigation and public health and roads and a freshwater system and baths and public order ... what *have* the Romans done for *us*?' To which the reply comes, 'Brought peace.' Reg has no answer to that. And John the Baptist has no answer when Jesus describes what salvation means and how it has come with him.

Around 15 years ago, I attended a conference about the renewal of the Christian faith. All the speakers came from big churches with famous ministries. Every one of them was miserable. They were full of complaints about what was wrong with the church and the world. All the speakers were cross with the world because it had strayed so far from the church. But when they spoke about the church they seemed just as cross with that too. So the argument about the world needing to be more like the church didn't sound quite so convincing. And then, after four or five of these dismal addresses, one pastor got up and simply said, 'I don't know about you guys, but at my church, we're having a great time. Strangers are finding faith, relationships are being healed, people are dying in such a way that fills everyone with gratitude and the glory of God, beautiful new friendships are being made, the Holy Spirit is surprising us and Jesus just keeps showing up.' And I thought, 'I want to be in his church. In fact, I want to believe in his God. He seems to be having all the fun. He doesn't seem to be anxiously counting numbers of members or size of endowment or targets for diversity. He seems to be enjoying the kingdom, whatever the outcomes. The other guys seem to be so caught up in believing exactly the right things and living totally unimpeachable lives and being righteously furious with all the bad people that they seem to have lost the joy altogether.'

I still want to be in that pastor's church. I want Duke Chapel to be like that. Sure, we all have wilderness times of heart or head. We all have John the Baptist times in prisons of our own or others' making, which make us wonder if Jesus is for real or if he was just a well-intentioned guy who was misunderstood. But those are the times we desperately need to look at our church, not to see perfect doctrine or squeaky-clean ethics, but to see what Jesus described and what that pastor was enjoying. Strangers finding faith, relationships being healed, people dying in such a way that fills everyone with gratitude and the glory of God, beautiful new friendships being made, the Holy Spirit surprising us and Jesus just keeping on showing up.

Several years ago, about 9 months after I came to Duke Chapel, a worshipper who comes about once a month greeted me in the narthex. There's always a lot of people around after the Sunday worship service and there's never time to say very much to each other. I often wonder if I've fully understood what someone's just told me and whether they've actually had a chuckle in their cheek or a tear in their eye. This person simply took my hand, looked at me seriously and said, 'It's working.' What did it mean? It was such an enigmatic remark. I pondered it for a long time. But then I thought about John's question to Jesus. 'Are you for real, or should we be expecting a different kind of kingdom?' And I remembered that pastor years ago who was enjoying himself. I reflected on the life of Duke Chapel and thought, 'People are finding their voice in faith. People are forging unusual and brave friendships. People are facing their own powerlessness and being filled with the Holy Spirit to take risks of patience, courage and hope. People are feeling their hearts on fire as the good news is sung and spoken and lived. People are meeting Christ in the stranger and entertaining angels unawares. Relationships are being healed and people are discovering ways to be with the socially disadvantaged and those of other faiths. It's working. This *is* for real. This is beautiful. This is joy.'

Jesus and John both knew they were going to be executed pretty soon. Neither was interested in an escapist, cotton-wool gospel. But one of them saw through his circumstances to the vision of God. This sense of peace and beauty and joy isn't about material comfort or tangible success. It's about being in the groove of the Spirit. It's about being with the grain of the saints. It's about consistently finding yourself where Jesus shows up. It's about knowing that where you are may not be classy, may not be prestigious, may not be noticed by the great and the good, may have no relation to paid employment of career prospects or a sense of achievement; but it's something much deeper, much more important, much more permanent. And that's dancing in the rhythm of the kingdom, singing the song in God's heart, glimpsing the dawn of salvation, breathing in the glory of God's art.

Can you see that beauty? Can you feel the peace and purpose of Christ's coming kingdom? If you can, then others will see you, as I saw that pastor all those years ago, and rediscover the joy. They'll feel their heart lighter than before and sense their lungs filling with hope. And they'll turn to one another and whisper, quietly but confidently, 'It's working.'

The sermons in this chapter have used three stories from my own experience. I try in my sermons to get a balance in the stories I use. Some are from fiction – novels or films. Some are from real life – newspapers, websites, non-fiction books. Some are from things people told me – their own experiences or events in the lives of third parties. And some are from my own history – of people I've encountered, adventures I've had, or things that have happened to me.

The riskiest area is people I've encountered. Two of the stories above meet that description. In one case, I've changed almost all the pertinent details and kept only the direct speech. My test of this is whether the person themselves wouldn't be sure if the original story involved them and would be most likely to conclude that it wasn't. If they can't recognize themselves in it, others won't. In the other case, the details are pretty accurate, but the chances of the person ever reading this book (or hearing the original sermon), or of anyone who'd heard the sermon or read the book meeting this person, are minutely small. I'm not so fastidious as to insist on gaining a person's consent in every single circumstance, such as this one, when the passage of time is so great and possibility of making a connection to the original person so small. But the ideal is when I can ask the person in question for permission to use their story and my request gains a thoughtful reply. I've never had someone say no; and sometimes they have told me being quoted has proved a deeply moving experience for them.

The third story in the sermon above is about a national event that many others attended. It's possible that others' memories of the event are different from mine: that the other speakers weren't as miserable as I recalled, for example. The point here is that I'm telling the story with integrity. I'm not making up a story and telling it as if it were true, or changing the details of an actual event so it fits the argument in which I'm inserting it. I'm a big believer in changing ancillary facts in order to anonymize the protagonist; but I don't believe in changing stories to suit what you want to say. How can a congregation trust you if you're presenting as fact something that never happened? To do so undermines the whole practice of preaching – not just your own, but everyone else's too.

3

Preaching Before Christmas

The Sunday before Christmas is my favourite Sunday of the year to preach. It has everything – the raw panic and overwhelming joy of Mary and Joseph's respective annunciations, the profound theological exploration densely packed into the Luke and Matthew readings, all in the context of the heightened awareness and expectation of the approaching Christmas festival. I'm offering three sermons in this chapter to seek to bring the reader's enthusiasm to the same level as mine.

You have ruined my life
Matthew 1.18–25
22 December 2013

Around a dozen years ago there was a miniseries on TV called *Best of Both Worlds*. Diane is a flight attendant who makes regular flights from Stansted to Bologna. On one flight she meets Mark, a handsome Italian architect. No reason not to live happily ever after; except it turns out that Diane is already cheerfully married to restaurant manager Martin and has a young son, Jack. But architect Mark is serious about Diane, and his whole Italian family loves her. Diane realizes if she's to keep Mark she has to marry him, so in no time she finds herself with two husbands. This requires a fair bit of subterfuge, and all her best efforts to pass off one husband or another as a close gay friend eventually come to grief. The final scene of the story takes place outside a restaurant in the pouring rain. The rain epitomizes the torrential tide of reality that smashes into each character's life when the truth finally emerges. A furious and heartbroken Mark shakes his head as his body quivers in disbelief before the woman he still loves but to whom he's just realized he's not legally married. Sensing the lost hopes, family humiliation and profound betrayal crashing down upon him, he yells, 'You have ruined my life.'

The story may be a little far-fetched, but the final line certainly isn't. We invest our hearts and souls, and often our finances and reputations too, in fragile people, dubious property, precarious careers and dangerous whims. When another person lets us down, we call it betrayal; when a money deal lets us down, we call it a swindle; when the economy lets us down, we call it bad luck; when we let ourselves down, we don't know what to call it. But what the poignant tale of the flight attendant, the architect and the restaurateur illustrates is that each character takes for granted that other people are objects we move around on our chessboard in order to achieve a fulfilled life. There are rules, and bigamy is clearly playing outside the rules – but everyone assumes they are entitled to a successful, comfortable, well-regarded existence, and that someone who takes it away from them has taken away an inalienable right. If a daughter emails and says, 'Dad, they say I plagiarized my essays, they're throwing me out of college,' that existence may be in jeopardy; if a police officer knocks at the door and begins a sentence with the words, 'Madam, we have reason to believe there are category A drugs in this house', that existence may be in deep trouble; if a phone rings and a familiar but distressed voice says, 'There's been a car accident – it's bad – it's terrible', that existence may be changed beyond recognition. The successful, comfortable, well-regarded existence is gone, and angry, devastated people are yelling, 'You've ruined my life.'

And that's where the Christmas story begins. Joseph thinks he's got this whole thing sorted. He comes from a distinguished family – he can trace his lineage back to King David. That's as good as it gets. He's got a nice little carpentry business and he cuts a fine figure in the Nazareth chamber of commerce. He's been matched up with a fine young woman from across the village and the betrothal is all done and dusted. But then Mary says, 'Joseph, you need to know something. I'm pregnant.' The successful, comfortable, well-regarded existence is suddenly gone. Gone without trace. Gone without chance of recovery. And we can almost hear Joseph yelling at Mary, 'You've ruined my life.' Joseph had a life planned out like a wooden statue chiselled in his carpenter's workshop. And Mary's walked right up and snapped an arm off. The statue's beyond repair. Don't insult Joseph by talking about glue, by saying all those statues in Rome have missing limbs. Don't try to make it better. It's a life-changing catastrophe. Joseph knows he's not the father – but you think anyone else is going to believe that? He's like that Italian architect raging at Diane in the pouring rain, sensing the lost hopes, family humiliation and profound betrayal crashing down upon him, and shouting at the woman he still loves, 'You've ruined my life.'

This is how God's stories begin. Out of a place of shame, of fear, of betrayal, of anger. God calls people whose lives are a mess. Jacob's life is ruined by rivalry, deception and cowardice. But God makes him the man from whom all Israel is descended. Jacob's son Joseph has his technicolour dream coat, but his life is ruined by his own bombast and his brothers' envy, and later again by Potiphar's wife's lust and deceit. But God makes him the man to save Israel from famine. Moses is saved from the Nile by Pharaoh's daughter, yet his life is ruined when he kills an Egyptian to defend a Hebrew slave. But God raises him up to lead his people through the Red Sea to freedom. It's no different in the New Testament. Practically everyone Jesus encounters has a ruined life: parents whose children are close to death, people who've lost their sanity or place in society through leprosy or demon possession, people who've fallen into disreputable professions like prostitution or tax extortion. And the most poignant conversations Jesus has are with people like Nicodemus, who realizes that if he follows his soul and becomes a disciple of Jesus, he too will be ruined.

And once we leave the shores of the Bible and go out into the rough sea of the church's history, we see the same pattern. Think about John Newton, whose life was ruined when he was forced to join the Navy. After trying to abscond, he was given eight dozen lashes and reduced to the lowest rank. He considered murdering the captain or committing suicide. Eventually, he was left marooned in West Africa. Even the ship that took him back to England two years later very nearly sank. His life was ruined a hundred ways. Yet God raised him up to become, in time, a leading advocate of the abolition of slavery and author of the hymn 'Amazing Grace'. Somehow it seems that in the moment of shame and loss and betrayal and humiliation, God's wondrous work takes root. In the ugliness and dirt and rejection of the manger, God's spark of renewal is born.

But there's more to it than that. If we go back to the story of flight attendant Diane and angry, betrayed architect Mark, it's nice to think that, even as he stands in the pouring rain feeling like his life is ruined, God might yet have a future for Mark. But what's a bit more challenging to grasp is that in the story God might be suspiciously like Diane. I'm not suggesting God is a secret bigamist. But I am saying that when we stand outside a restaurant in the pouring rain yelling, 'You've ruined my life,' as often as not the one we're yelling at is God.

There's a story about a letter that was found from a person in public life to his brother. In the letter he's talking about his son who is doing well in his studies. He looked set for a military career, which could well be followed by a spell in politics and a settled family life to make his father proud. But the letter says this promising boy has gone astray. He seems to have joined some kind of a sect, and he's refusing to join the army because he says he won't fight, and he doesn't want to marry because there's things more important than having a family; and all his values have been turned upside down. The letter is an archaeological find from the third century. It's written by a Roman senator. He's talking about his son's conversion to Christianity.

Before I came to St Martin's, I spent seven years working with students at an American university. One year I was asked to give a talk to the entering class. I was asked to say a bit about the work of the chapel and the campus ministers from all the different denominations. I said, 'We're all different but we've got one thing in common: we're here to ruin your life.' All the other pep talks told the students how to follow their dreams and how many facilities and support services there were to help them construct a successful, comfortable, well-regarded existence. I thought I should be honest and acknowledge that if that's what they were looking for, faith would ruin their life. I wasn't invited back.

There's a sense in which God is just like Diane. We want to use God to be another object we move around our chessboard in our attempt to construct a successful, comfortable, well-regarded existence. But God's having none of it. God spoils our plans, disrupts our expectations and turns our tidily organized world upside down. Matthew's account tells us that Joseph resolved to divorce Mary quietly, but that then an angel appeared to him in a dream and told him that Mary's child had been conceived by the Holy Spirit and would be the saviour. What we're not told is how Joseph replied. Can you really imagine Joseph said, 'OK, that's all right then – you had me worried for a moment there – right you are, carry on'? I very much doubt it. My guess is he said, 'That's all very well – but *you've still ruined my life.*' My guess is, for most people here, your existence would have been a whole lot simpler, tidier and more comfortable if God hadn't come into your life. You know what it means to be Joseph. You know what it means to be architect Mark. You know what it means to stand in the pouring rain and stare at God and say, 'You ruined my life.'

But this brings us face to face with the heart of the gospel. God may be uncomfortably like Diane. But so are we. Because what we struggle to understand and what we need the Bible to show us every day is this: *we've ruined God's life.* God had it all sorted, just as much as Joseph in his tidy carpenter's workshop. God had made the sun, moon and stars. God had made human beings and the whole creation. God the architect had everything organized, just like Italian Mark had his world constructed around Diane. But then we ruined it. We wrecked God's whole big idea. We were right at the epicentre of God's dream, and we shattered it. And we wonder if God must be thinking, every moment of every day, why did I ever get involved with humanity? What have human beings ever brought me but trouble? God must look at us with deep, sad eyes, and say, 'You've ruined my life.'

It's true, we have. But what does God do? God could sulk, could flip, could lash out, could destroy. But God still loves us. And so this ghastly reality, this humiliation, betrayal, shame and waste, becomes the point from which salvation arises. The God who could deal with us by remote control, the God who could love us from afar, the God that could keep us at arm's length – that God is ruined, lost, over. But see what happens. Instead we get God with us, Immanuel, God who fills our wombs and blows open our dreams, God who walks into our existence and shakes us into life. We ruined God's life, so God can no longer love us by remote control, from afar, at arm's length. God ruins our life, so we can no longer love God by remote control, from afar, at arm's length.

We all have to make Joseph's journey. We all have to stop thinking of ourselves as architect Mark in the story and realize we're Diane. We all start the story by shaking our fists at God and saying, 'You've ruined my life.' But we all have to realize that we've ruined God's life. And it's out of the ruins of God's life that our salvation comes. And it's out of the ruins of our lives that we discover that a ruined life isn't the end of our story with God: it's the beginning.

The key to this sermon is the urgency, the almost breathless hurry in which the argument unfolds. Unlike many illustrations from a TV programme, this one the congregation is unlikely to remember: the art is not to tell the whole story, but succinctly to build up to the point where the crucial line (again, the title of the sermon) has maximum impact. Then that line becomes a prism that can be turned round and light shed in various creative directions. Once again, the rhetorical device is that we enter deeply into Joseph's story and identify with him, until the rug is pulled and we suddenly see everything from God's point of view. Hence the sermon works on an emotional and theological level at the same time and the pace enables the ending to come as a surprise even if the point it's making isn't new.

Here are some guidelines for preaching before Christmas.

1. Along with Holy Week and Easter, this is perhaps the most emotionally charged Sunday of the year. Make the most of it.
2. The gospel texts are richly textured: you may not want to flick through a few commentaries every week, but this week you'll need them to appreciate all that's going on.
3. Unlike some Sundays, the narrative material is well-known to the con-

gregation so you can employ humour and dramatic silences for the listeners to do some of the work for themselves.
4. This is practically the first sermon of Christmas, so don't be reluctant to make it more or less a Christmas sermon.
5. The epic – grand scale, broad canvas – and the lyric – intimate and personal – are seldom so intertwined as in these stories, so your sermon would do well to be the same.

The following sermon reduces the annunciation to its most elemental form: the partnership between God's Holy Spirit and a human body. Which creates the chance to talk about the human body, our attitude to it – and God's. I was so moved by a sermon my former colleague preached at a wedding, entitled 'This is my body', that I picked up the same theme and applied it to the annunciation. This sermon requires a very particular, tender, gentle tone of voice. Each person in the congregation should feel like you're addressing them alone. You may want to announce at some stage in the service that people will be available to speak with anyone especially touched by a sermon like this; it certainly addresses issues that run deep in many people's experiences.

This is my body, given for you
Matthew 1.18–25
22 December 2019

I wonder how you feel about your body. Maybe you live with perpetual pain, or old age is making every joint creak. Perhaps you have a physical disability. It could be you spend an hour a day applying makeup, drying your hair, using preparations to enhance your appearance. Or possibly you live with shame, about carrying too much weight, about scars you try to hide, secrets you want no one to know, hurts you tremble to name. We spend enormous amounts of time thinking about our own and one another's bodies. They harbour some of our deepest and often unresolved feelings.

There are two days in the Christian year when we think especially about the significance of the human body. The first is Easter Day, when we discover our bodies are not just for now, but forever, not just for earth, but for heaven. The second is Christmas Day, when we realize that God regards our bodies so highly as to take on our human flesh in Jesus. These are the two central moments in our year: God entering life and overcoming death.

Given these two high watermarks of the Christian understanding of the body, you might be surprised that the history of Christian reflection on the body is so troubled and confused. I want today to look at why this is so, and to suggest how the story of Mary conceiving a child through the Holy Spirit can redeem so much of this pain and grief. I want to explore three reasons why, despite the fundamental affirmation of Christmas and Easter, the body has been such a difficult subject for Christians.

The first is fear. The body makes you do things your mind would rather you didn't do. The body makes you greedy for more, because that little bit of salt in the caramel or gin on the tongue makes you long for a second, a fifth, a forty-third helping. The body makes you lust for touch, taste, sight, for fulfilment of desires and indulgence of feelings, in the face of what your conscience or forbearance tells you. The body makes you tired, lazy and inclined towards comfort, even when your mind says you need to be thoughtful, alert or helpful. In such ways our bodies seem to be beyond our control. So we seek to bring them to heel, through denial, discipline, training, habits, practices, distractions – all of which work sometimes, but none of which suppress the bodily wants that present themselves as a tsunami of needs. Schooling the body never entirely works; those who set and uphold wise rules for others invariably fail to keep them themselves, resulting in hypocrisy and humiliation.

But fear isn't the only reason for the body being so problematic for the church. The second reason is hurt. The body has been the principal site of the domination of the powerful over the weak throughout history. Slavery names the way the body of a person is made to fulfil the wants and needs of a master – a person who has somehow gained control and dominance over them. Assault names the physical imposition of one person's body over another's, to express physical supremacy, sexual gratification or mental ascendancy. Torture names the way a person uses control over another's body to inflict agony, demonstrate power or extract information. Such experiences have been known to perhaps the majority of the world's population throughout history. They yield physical wounds and mental scars that many can never erase. Sadly, like every exercise of power, the church and its representatives have sometimes not just suffered such things but perpetrated them.

There's also a third dimension inhibiting Christian understanding of the body, besides fear and hurt, and that's neglect. For much, perhaps most of Christian history, the body has been treated like some kind of undercarriage that supports us on earth but won't be needed in heaven; like the boosters that fall away from a rocket, leaving only the mind or soul or both. Sometimes this has led people to believe it didn't matter what they do with their own bodies or anyone else's, since the body doesn't really matter one way or the other. Sometimes it has led people towards a harsh rejection of the body, as an encumbrance they'd be better off without. Licence and abstinence both risk a pernicious separation between our bodies and the rest of us. This gives us no positive way to think about how we can live well or apply our physical selves for good.

When we look to the account in today's gospel of the young Mary conceiving a child by the power of the Holy Spirit, we can see how each of these troubled interpretations tells its own version of the story. The view of the body through a lens of fear sees sex as dangerously full of lust, desire and wilfulness, and affirms that Jesus was born, as John's Gospel puts it, 'not of blood or of the will of the flesh or of the will of man, but of God.' The hurt perspective perceives the story with profound suspicion, noting that no mention is made in Matthew of Mary giving consent or indeed having any agency at all, and thus replicating and even validating a pattern where powerful people, invariably men, inflict their will, frequently bodily, on vulnerable people, often women. Meanwhile, the neglect version is one in which Jesus came to bring a spiritual message, and so the human role in conception was appropriately minimal.

When you add in the post-Enlightenment scepticism about how it was possible to conceive a child without a conventional meeting of sperm and egg, then you begin to realize why the so-called doctrine of the virgin birth has become perhaps the least popular of the stories associated with Jesus. But I want to suggest a different way of reading the story.

One of the greatest insights I've learned in studying the New Testament is to understand that references to Mary, mother of Jesus, are often ways of talking about Israel. Mary is the embodiment of Israel at its best: faithful, obedient, willing, devoted. She is, in her way, the one who perfectly keeps the covenant with God that Israel is portrayed in the Old Testament as having painfully broken. The conception of Jesus through Mary and the Holy Spirit is a way of saying Jesus is utterly human and Jesus is at the same time utterly God. But it's also saying that Jesus is utterly Israel. In other words, God hasn't given up on the covenant with Israel: Jesus is the fulfilment of that covenant. He's a Jew – his mother is Jewish. But he's also God, because he is conceived by the Holy Spirit. He's the complete embodiment of everything the Old Testament longed for – the total harmony of God and Israel.

See the significance of Mary fully participating in the birth of Jesus.

In this moment we find revealed the purpose of the human body. Given how terribly the human body, particularly the vulnerable and often female or juvenile body has so often been treated, it's completely understandable that many people feel it's compounding the misery for anyone to presume to tell them what their body is for. When you've been cruelly maltreated, of course you want to know no one will ever be able to do that to you or anyone else again and that the perpetrators will be brought to justice. But the boldness of Christianity isn't just about keeping people safe from harm, important as that is. It's also about joyfully discovering what our lives are actually for. Mary discovers what her life is for and her discovery is a discovery for all of us.

Remember when Abraham was told what Israel was for. In Genesis 12, God says that through Israel, all the peoples of the earth would find a blessing. Now here in Matthew 1, Mary is told she's to be a channel for the way the Holy Spirit will bless the world. The name for that blessing is Jesus, which we discover means Immanuel: God is with us. What Mary discovers is that she exists to be a channel of the Holy Spirit. What we discover is that *we* exist to be a channel of the Holy Spirit. That's what our bodies are for.

See how liberating this claim is. We have a constant voice inside us telling us that our bodies aren't good enough. We don't have the right shape, height, strength, fitness, beauty. At the same time, we have constant voices *outside* us telling us that our bodies have to experience particular things to be fulfilled: the best coffee, the most exotic travel, the most comfortable sofa, the wildest sex, the experience of childbirth, the liveliest dancing, the most terrifying bungee jump. But hard as it may be, we don't have to listen to those voices. Because we've discovered through Mary what our bodies are really for.

Our bodies are for conceiving, nurturing and giving birth to the way the Holy Spirit blesses the world. How liberating to know we won't finally be accountable for whether we ate that dietary additive or experienced the rush of being a gifted surfer! We'll be held to account for precisely this: 'Did you allow your body to be a channel of the grace of God's Holy Spirit?' Before you say, or do something, ask yourself, 'Is this expressing my desire to let the Holy Spirit work through me?' See how it's not about being clever or fit or wealthy or talented: it's simply about letting God work through you.

That means letting God's grace be seen in your smile, to make strangers feel appreciated and welcome. It means letting God's Spirit be channelled through your touch, when you draw close to a person the world has shunned. It means letting God's gentleness be felt in your words, when you speak a difficult truth to a person who isn't ready to hear it. It means putting your body between another and danger, like John Crilly, who three weeks ago confronted Usman Khan on London Bridge, despite believing his antagonist was wearing a live suicide belt. It means letting your wounds become a channel not of bitterness but of grace and glory.

I don't think I know anyone who doesn't have a hang-up about their body. The likelihood is, Mary did too. But she discovered her body wasn't fundamentally a place of fear, hurt or neglect. She believed her body was made to give birth to the work of the Holy Spirit. So is mine. So is yours.

You might want to finish a sermon like this with an extended period of silence rather than leap straight into music or the creed. You need to anticipate that your sermon may have a profound effect on the listener and not in false humility be taken by surprise if it does. A sermon like this expects to leave an impression. Ask yourself, 'What would be a good outcome from preaching a sermon like this?' – and prepare accordingly.

The following sermon takes a different approach from the following two. It's truly exegetical – but not in the way the practice is generally performed. It's a sermon that arises from looking closely at the structure of the annunciation passage, and perceiving the three moves that take place in that structure. You can only preach a sermon like this if you're committed to plan out your whole sermon before committing a single word to paper or screen.

How can this be?
Luke 1.26–38
20 December 2020

The history of the calendar makes for interesting reading. Julius Caesar introduced the practice of marking 1 January as the beginning of the year. But in the Middle Ages, people marked 25 March as New Year's Day. Why? Because that was nine months before Christmas, the feast of the Annunciation, the day when, as recorded in today's Gospel, the angel Gabriel visited Mary and brought her the news that she was to be the mother of Jesus, the Son of God. In 1582, Pope Gregory XIII introduced the Gregorian calendar, which corrected the discrepancies in the old Julian calendar, and reverted to 1 January as New Year's Day. But Britain and its colonies, then including what became the United States, didn't swap to the Gregorian calendar until 1752, and it was only then that 25 March stopped being celebrated as New Year's Day.

I want to explore why marking 25 March as the start of the year, and in that sense the most significant day of the year, was actually quite a good idea, and why Gabriel's conversation with Mary in Bethlehem ranks alongside Mary Magdalene's conversation with the risen Jesus in the garden on Easter Day as perhaps the two most significant conversations of all time.

Let's start by looking at what I'm going to call the three dimensions of human existence. Each dimension is awesome and glorious – but at the same time circumscribed and inhibited.

Dimension one is that we're alive. We breathe, we can move, we can feel, and explore, and discover. We can grow and develop and stretch and act. Throughout the pandemic we've been deeply aware of what we can't do, but there's still an astonishing number of things we *can* do – things we mostly take for granted unless we're injured or disabled – and even then, there's still an indescribable number of things we can still do. We're alive. Yes, we're alive – but we're still creatures: we're still limited in time. The course of our life is threescore years and ten – sometimes more, sometimes less – but, in the light of eternity, the blink of an eye. Meanwhile, we're also limited in space. There are a hundred million stars in the galaxy and a hundred million galaxies in the universe. And we're limited to just this one planet and only a tiny square yard of that. So as much as we're alive, we're limited by time and space.

Dimension two of human existence is that we're not alone. We have each other. We have people, of myriad different sizes and shapes, characters and aptitudes, longings and lovings. We also have other creatures, puppy dogs and tarantulas, leopards and butterflies, in a glorious array of colour, form, movement and energy. We can make relationships, make friends, make adventures, make love, make new life, make home. Together we can work, party, journey, play. There's almost nothing in the world we can do that the word 'together' doesn't make twice as good. But this, too has a shadow side. There's a poison at large which distorts relationship, undermines trust, introduces envy, diverts attention, misconstrues kindness, destroys love. It's much more damaging than coronavirus, and much more infectious. We can try to eradicate it, through effort, legislation, control or training; but it always sneaks back in. We don't like the old-fashioned word 'sin'. But whatever we call it, it inhibits the second dimension – relationship.

Dimension three of existence is understanding. We learn. We know. We think and experiment and hypothesize and conclude. We research and unearth and test and investigate. We listen and ponder and weigh and connect. We translate, interpret, communicate and increase. This knowledge is in many ways a greater power than our bodily strength, or even our solidarity in relationship. It's what most marks us out from other creatures. But again, it's incomplete. Socrates was the wisest man in Athens because he knew he knew nothing. We know so much – but don't know so much more. We have knowledge, but less often understand what we know. We are limited in what we can imagine, let alone realize, let alone bring into existence.

So these are the three features of our human existence. We're alive – but we're limited by time and space. We make relationship – but such connection is infiltrated by sin. We know – but there's so little we really know.

Hang on, you may be thinking, what happened to 25 March? What happened to Gabriel's conversation with Mary? Why was it so important?

Well, if we look closely at this epic conversation, we can see how it's divided into three parts. Gabriel speaks and Mary replies – not once, not twice, but three times. And what I want you to see is how each of these interactions maps onto the three dimensions of human existence I've just outlined. Let's take them one at a time.

Here's the first interaction. The angel Gabriel is sent by God to a town in Galilee called Nazareth, to a virgin whose name is Mary. And Gabriel says, 'Greetings, favoured one! The Lord is with you.' But Mary is much perplexed by his words and ponders what sort of greeting this might be. This may not seem like much of an interaction. Gabriel says only seven words and Mary isn't recorded as saying anything at all. She is just perplexed and ponders. But look at what's happened in the light of what we've been exploring about human existence. We're alive, but we're limited by time and space. See how the angel Gabriel overcomes those two limitations and arrives from the God of eternity and everywhere to Mary in her particular time and her particular place, Nazareth, in Galilee. In an instant, the first human limitation is dismantled, transcended, displaced.

Let's look at the second interaction. The angel says, 'Don't be afraid, Mary, for you have found favour with God. You will conceive and bear a son, Jesus. He will be called the Son of the Most High. He will reign over the house of Jacob forever, and of his kingdom there will be no end.' Mary is quick to spot the fatal flaw: 'How can this be, since I am a virgin?' See how this discussion is all about the second dimension of human existence – relationship. Gabriel is saying that God has overcome your distance from glory; your son will be God's son too; your son will be of the line of Jacob and of the line of the great king David. In other words, he will restore the great connection between Israel and God that was disrupted in the exile 500 years ago. Yes, Mary, you're quick to see what relationship can't do, how relationship can't automatically create life, overcome division, outflank alienation. But you're about to see how God can overcome even our human separation. Just you see.

Then there's one more interaction. Remember that the third dimension of human existence we explored just now was understanding. With that perspective, listen to this third interaction. Gabriel says, 'The Holy Spirit will come upon you, and overshadow you. Your child will be holy; he will be called Son of God. And now, your relative Elizabeth in her old age has also conceived a son; and is in her sixth month. Nothing is impossible with God.' Mary says, 'Here am I, the servant of the Lord; let it be with me according to your word.' And there's nothing left to say. What Gabriel overcomes is the limitation of Mary's understanding. Gabriel explains how Mary will conceive, recognizes this will be a unique child, and helps Mary grasp the astonishing revelation by pointing to what has already happened to Elizabeth. Finally, Gabriel utters the words that clear out the limits of all human understanding; 'Nothing is impossible with God.' Game, set and match. Mary says, 'You have transcended my limits of time and space; you have transformed my limits of broken relationship; now you have transported me to the presence of God and opened the eyes of my understanding. All I can say is, let me live in this wondrous new reality you have opened out before me.'

It's sometimes said that Jesus is conceived the very moment Mary says, 'Let it be with me according to your word.' Because our creaturely limitation of time and space, our sinful limitation of broken relationship, and our imaginative limitation of understanding name the ways we're alienated from God; and Mary's words are the moment all three dimensions of that alienation are set aside, and we and God are together like never before. Jesus represents the full companionship of God and humanity, and Mary's words are the moment the word becomes flesh, at least in the tiniest form, and the companionship of God and us, for which the whole universe was created, and which is so deeply inhibited by the three dimensions of our flawed nature, finally at this moment comes into being.

So yes, this is just about the most important conversation that ever took place. And yes, it makes sense to make 25 March, the traditional date of Jesus' conception, the moment of the utter cooperation of humanity with God, New Year's Day, so that we might forever recall how God overcame our limitations and turned our alienation into glory.

We stand today, in the midst of the pandemic, overwhelmed by limitation, which has inhibited our flourishing, our livelihood and our ability to imagine anything beyond a return to how life used to be. But this story lifts us out of every limitation into everlasting joy, companionship and understanding, crystallizing on a simple question and a gentle, conclusive answer. How can this be? Nothing is impossible with God.

The exegesis as usually understood takes place several paragraphs into the sermon, but the paragraphs that precede it depend entirely upon it and correspond with each dimension of it. If you're going to claim to talk about the three dimensions of human existence in three paragraphs, you're going to have to choose your words very carefully: in this case the words are chosen to correspond to the exchange between Gabriel and Mary expounded later. It looks like the passage is being fitted into a structure provided by the sweeping claims about human existence; but in fact, it's the other way around, made much the more interesting by being presented this way.

One motif I often use, perhaps too often, is to rate a moment in the Bible against some kind of notional scale of significance: thus, I here talk about Mary and Gabriel's conversation as one of the two most important in history. The superlative captures the congregation's attention but has to be used adroitly to ensure there is no suspicion of exaggeration. The interesting material about the calendar is introduced to provide a backdrop to the superlative claim, and to provide a chatty introduction to a theologically weighty sermon. Again, you can do a lot of theological work with almost any congregation provided you couch it in accessible language and highlight the personal dimensions of what is being said.

4

Preaching at Christmas

There are two rather different moments for preaching at Christmas. The obvious one is on Christmas Eve or on Christmas Day, where people are happy to pause to consider the claims of the Christian faith, whether they're a weekly churchgoer or paying an annual visit. The other is at a carol service, either for the whole community or a particular part of it, where the appetite is for a homily and too many words on the Word quickly leads to diminishing returns: a brief sermon is part of the covenant of hospitality.

Here are some guidelines for preaching at Christmas.

1. For a short carol service homily, you need a compelling image or story. You only need one. It can be an image from the Christmas story or completely outside it; about a gift or something very different. It can be a story related to Christmas or something analogous, for example from a newspaper about a baby born outside during a war. Just stick with the one image or story and dig into it for everything it can yield.
2. For a longer Christmas sermon, there are broadly three ways you can go: a depth of engagement with the various elements and characters of the Christmas story is most suited to the Luke 2 reading, and offers the chance for humour and contemporary analogies.
3. A reflection on Christmas itself, maybe including gift giving and the awkwardness of getting it wrong. This is more suited to a homily, or a service where the traditional readings play a smaller role.
4. A reflection on the cosmic dimensions of the incarnation. This is a better fit for John's prologue. There's no inherent reason why a sermon on the prologue need be especially cerebral or mysterious.
5. You're likely to be preaching to a greater proportion of strangers who will be well aware of the shortcomings of the church over the centuries and today; shortcomings you can only subtly dismantle, but would do well to touch on.
6. The best way to build trust is to offer some self-deprecating humour and some recognition of what the church has got so badly wrong, together with a recognition of the profound search for truth we all share.

7. You absolutely must not tell people what is wrong with the way they celebrate Christmas or give any impression that churchgoers are superior to those who come seldom or never. But you may wish to offer an invitation to an enquirers' course before the service ends.

This chapter offers a sermon and a homily, beginning with the longer form. The Christmas Eve service in which it was preached is simple: some choral and some congregational carols, and three or four Scripture readings covering the familiar story in Matthew and Luke's Gospels. The majority of those present won't know the preacher, so trust needs to be built up quickly in order then to break through to the simple, direct truth.

On Earth as it is in Heaven
John 1.1–14
24 December 2019, St Martin-in-the-Fields

When you sit down to try and think about what to get your friends, family and colleagues for Christmas, you realize that there's always one person who is impossible to buy a present for, because they don't really have interests, or their interests are so obscure you have no idea what will please them. Then there's the person it's easy to get a present for, because they seem to love everything, and so long as it's handmade or natural fibre or recycled, they're bound to whoop and squeal on opening it. Then there's the person who is pretty fixated on just one thing and, while that seems limiting, once you hit the sweet spot you can be pretty sure you can keep on hitting it.

I know one such person, quite a small person, who won't eat much for breakfast but will eat a boiled egg. So one year I got her an eggcup. The next year I got her a fancier eggcup. Then, deciding it was time for a change, I thought I'd explore an egg-timer. Not one of those tick-tock ones that've been superseded by stopwatches on an iPhone. No, I wanted to find an hourglass, which of course wasn't an hourglass exactly, but could pass sand through a tiny gap for as long as it takes from dropping a raw egg into boiling water till it's soft boiled.

It turns out that whatever your poison, Amazon, eBay or the High Street, such a thing is incredibly hard to come by. Making a glass wide enough to hold a weight of sand but narrow enough to let through just one grain at a time is a highly skilled operation. And I've no idea just whose job it is to count the grains of sand individually to reach exactly the right number for a soft-boiled egg. Then of course we might disagree on what texture a soft-boiled egg has. No doubt it boils faster at altitude.

But what I do know, because her mother told me, was that when finally I did track down a real hourglass egg-timer, I hit the jackpot, because this young lady spent Christmas Day pleading with her parents to lay aside the new cappuccino machine and the turkey and just boil an egg instead, over and over again, because she was mesmerized by the grains of sand sliding through the aperture in the hourglass. Then she would turn it over and religiously wait for every grain of sand to pass through before overturning it again. She loved trying to guess when the last grain would drop. There was no end to the pleasure she took in it.

I want to ponder with you the significance of that aperture, and the hourglass that surrounds it. Imagine for a moment, if it's not too overwhelming, the whole activity of the world, all the bustle and life of human beings, all the wonder of creation, all the micro level of amoeba and electrons, all the macro levels of stars and space and galaxies – and then stretch that colossal breadth of reality back 14.8 billion years to the beginning of time, and if you're still going stretch it forward to the end of time, whether that's less than 14.8 billion years or maybe a whole lot more. I want you to think of that as all the sand at the bottom of the hourglass. You may well say, that's a mighty big hourglass, too big for a soft-boiled egg – and you'd be right. But encapsulate it all there, nestling at the bottom of the glass.

And then I want you to turn your attention to the top of the glass, the part that, because of gravity, is empty, so empty you can see through it from one side to the other. I'm going to give a name to that part of the glass. We can look down at the sands of time at the bottom of the glass and we can call that reality. The top of the glass has a different name. It's called heaven. It's empty not just because of gravity but because we don't exactly know what's there. But what I'm going to suggest to you is that it's a lot larger than the bottom of the glass. That's a mind-boggling statement, because the bottom of the glass is vast beyond description. But I want you to imagine the top of the glass as even bigger.

Now, ponder with me the aperture that joins the top and the bottom of the glass together. The first thing that strikes you is that it looks absolutely tiny. The second thing you realize is that it's somehow, astonishingly, able to bear the whole weight of the top of the hourglass without cracking. The third thing you wonder is how on earth everything that's currently in the bottom half could ever get through this tiny aperture and reach the other half.

Stop there for a moment, because that's the crucial point. Listen to the language very carefully. *How* on *earth* could everything get through to the other part – the heaven part? And here's your answer. At one moment in history, one person emerged who was totally part of the bottom half and totally part of the top half. Just contemplate that aperture for a second. That aperture is utterly of the same substance with the bottom half and of the same material as the top half. And yet it's utterly unique, because there's nothing else like it at the top or at the bottom.

That aperture represents what Christians believe Jesus is. Jesus is that tiny moment in history that connects time to eternity, reality to heaven, now to forever. He is completely part of time, reality and now; but at the same instant he's completely part of eternity, heaven and forever. And more than anything else he is the aperture, the route, the causeway from now to forever, from earth to heaven, from time to eternity.

See how this is what the Christmas story is telling us. The full range of humanity, from underclass shepherds struggling on zero hours contracts and facing the unforgiving reality of universal credit to affluent kings, citizens of nowhere, with their heads in the stars. The full dimensions of existence, from the lowly earth of the manger to the ethereal skies above Bethlehem. The full range of experience, from the terror and humiliation of an unexpected pregnancy and the horror of Herod's massacre to the joy and gladness of gold, frankincense and myrrh. The story sums up in the language of its time everything we mean by reality, all 14.8 billion years of it across the whole universe, in its ordinariness, depth, texture, fragility and wonder.

And then three things happen. An aperture appears. This tiny baby, this delicate, swaddled new-born child defies description, because, like the aperture above the bottom half of the hourglass, this one being encapsulates the whole of the glass – and indeed makes us for the first time realize it is an hourglass, and we've been looking at only the bottom half of it. This is the second thing: in the light of this birth we discover that the whole of existence is contained in the bottom half of the glass, and that there's this whole colossal upper glass called heaven that all the splendours of existence can't come near to and can never reach – or *could* never reach if it wasn't for this astonishing possibility, the appearance of a causeway, route, aperture that leads us from one to the other, time to eternity, earth to heaven.

And then a third thing happens. Not perhaps suddenly, but gradually, as the Gospels tell the rest of the astonishing story. What happens is that the whole almighty hourglass is tipped over by 180 degrees, *turned upside down*, and now the full panoply of time and existence is on top, weighing down on the tiny aperture that is Jesus. That's what happens in the rest of the gospel story. The full weight of existence, and most painfully, the aspects of existence that are hurtful, cruel and wrong, weighs on the shoulders of the one who opens a way from time to eternity. That's what culminates in the cross. It must be hell for Jesus to carry all that weight. In the resurrection, the aperture becomes unblocked and now we can pass through Christ to heaven, a glass indescribably more wonderful than the other glass. It's like the gravity that held us down in the lower glass and the minuteness of the aperture that looked impossible to traverse have been transformed by the upside-down 180-degree transformation of God's kingdom, and now we're drawn towards forever just as surely as once we were locked in time.

That's the wonder of Christmas, the mystery of the gospel and the joy of Jesus. And what we're doing right now, as we gather this holy night to worship and celebrate this story, this upside-down glory, this reverse of gravity, is like my young friend, leaving aside for a moment the presents, the anxiety, the hubbub of the season, and become mesmerized by the hourglass, the aperture and the absorbing sight of tiny granules of existence passing through the full humanity and utter divinity of Jesus. It's like we've blocked everything else out. Nothing else matters.

Well, let me tell you a secret – the secret of Christmas. Nothing else does.

The sermon rests on the image of the hourglass. The hourglass has three main features – the bottom, the top and the aperture between them. The big reveal in the sermon is that Jesus is the aperture and that Christmas is the decisive moment that links the top and bottom, or heaven and earth. It's a memorable and simple image.

But it needs more than this image to shape the sermon. The other decisive element in the sermon is the child. The child enables the preacher to do a number of things that overcome any difficulty in building trust and landing the basic concept. The first element of trust is that the preacher understands Christmas from both an adult and a child's point of view. This isn't a preacher who's going to tell the congregation off for forgetting the true meaning of Christmas: the preacher understands the difficulty of getting the right present and the different ways a child can engage with presents. The child in question was in fact a neurodiverse child, but it's not necessary to say that – there are enough hints for anyone who's alert, but the point is to allow the listener to appreciate the hourglass with the fascination of the child. Once the structure is in place and the hourglass image is fully and compellingly grasped, a surprising amount of information can be put into the structure without the sermon feeling heavy. By the end we are wide-eyed in wonder at the gift of God in Christmas, just as a child is wide-eyed in wonder kneeling beside a Christmas tree to open a present. The conclusion has come a long way from the anxiety and burden of present-buying and preparation to a true sense of worship.

The sermon below is what I mean by a homily that's ideal for a carol service for the community, assuming no prior knowledge but nonetheless expounding the John 1 passage succinctly.

The tangent
14 December 2021

When I was at school, we used to have curious long, thin poisonous implements known as pencils. There was always someone in the class who licked them and got a grey tongue; and you wondered, if they missed school next day, whether it was serious. You started with a regular pencil called HB, and then they got finer and finer, starting with H1 down to H plenty. They were good for writing, but when the compass and the protractor came out, I started to get nervous. Not just because the compass was literally lethal, or because the protractor sounded like a kind of venomous snake, but because anything that involved drawing sent me to the bottom of the class. I could do the lines OK, but the circles had me stumped.

But while the activity of drawing made me feel a failure, the philosophy of mathematics interested me from the very beginning. In particular, I continued to reflect on the notion of the tangent. I struggled to draw it, but it was easy enough to imagine a circle being just kissed by a line as it touched its circumference while heading elsewhere.

What fascinated me was, if you were to focus in on the point of intersection, like a microscope burrowing down to the tiniest degree, and if the pencil were the maximum possible H number, so its line was almost invisibly precise, would there be a single point of contact between the circle and the line? Because your regular HB line usually ran across the HB line of the circle and it wasn't really a tangent at all, more a line across a circle with a significant overlap – at least under a microscope. To be a genuine tangent it needs to have just one point of contact, where the line kisses the circle.

Only much later did I realize that this fascination with the precision of a tangent was an insight into Christmas. Imagine us – imagine existence on the grandest dimensions imaginable – as a circle. What happens at Christmas is that that finite circle comes into contact with a line that goes on forever. We could call that line God. Existence is the circle and God is the line. And there's just one tiny point where the circle meets the line. That point is Jesus. Jesus is the point, the tiny point, that's completely circle and completely line. Jesus is the moment God gently kisses humankind.

Jesus comes as a tiny new-born baby. That somehow emphasizes the point I was trying to imagine in my juvenile geometrical imagination: that minuscule, single point where the line and the circle meet. And here's the thing. There could have been just the circle, on its own, with no tangent: existence, but existence without meaning. And there could have been just the line, going on forever, with no circle: God, but God with no connection to existence. Both, put like that, would have been a terrible tragedy: an eternal waste, a literally pointless reality.

But here's the wonder of Christmas: it lies in the tiniest of all human creatures, a new-born baby. Here's the moment where time and eternity, earthly existence and ethereal essence, humanity and God meet; and gently kiss. It's the tiniest, most easily missed, and most fragile moment. But it's the point. It is, literally, the point. It's the point of everything.

The homily only lasts four minutes, but covers a lot of ground simply by speaking about the implements of compass, pencil and paper. No need for a long grounding in the politics of first-century Palestine or the disasters of the contemporary Christmas table. A homily like this should be sufficiently satisfying to stay in the imagination of regular and occasional churchgoer alike for quite some time.

5

Preaching in Epiphany

Epiphany, like the magi, is laden with gifts. The stories closely associated with the season – the visit of the wise men, the baptism of Christ, the wedding at Cana, the call of the first disciples, the Nazareth Manifesto sermon in the synagogue, and Simeon and Anna's encounter with the baby Jesus in the temple at Candlemas – are all brimming with texture and resonance and begging to be preached upon.

What all these stories have in common is the theme of revelation and the feeling of new beginnings. There are a lot of firsts in this season. Whereas John the Baptist in Advent engages with failed hopes and lost dreams, the season of Epiphany is much more upbeat and full of expectation. In this chapter, I take three sermons: a homily on Epiphany itself, a sermon on the baptism of Christ and a sermon on Jesus' inaugural sermon at Nazareth.

Epiphany itself is often submerged in re-entry after Christmas, but can be rescued, for example by holding an Epiphany carol service later in the season – and should be, because it's a chance to reflect on a passage, Matthew 2.1–12, that seldom gets covered in appropriate detail at Christmas. There's so much to say about the balance between human quest (in perhaps science, or through other faiths) and divine revelation, and about the nature of the Gentile inclusion in the Jewish covenant. Here, I focus on the simple contrast between the two towns mentioned in the story and their significance today – with the backdrop of a modern parable.

Bethlehem and Jerusalem
Matthew 2.1–12
8 January 2023

George Orwell's 1945 novel *Animal Farm* tells the story of Manor Farm, neglected by its alcoholic owner, Mr Jones. Two young pigs, Napoleon and Snowball, drive Mr Jones off the farm and assume control. Snowball introduces literacy programmes and a windmill, but this leads to conflict with Napoleon, whose dogs drive Snowball away, leaving Napoleon in supreme command. Napoleon re-narrates the story of the revolution as one in which he alone brought freedom, and ruthlessly purges any animals alleged still to be loyal to Snowball. Napoleon resists reforms that will bring greater prosperity to the farm, while selling the faithful old horse Boxer to the knacker's yard in return for whisky for himself. The slogans of the revolution are all changed. 'Four legs good, two legs bad,' becomes 'Four legs good, two legs better.' The egalitarianism of the original revolt is subverted by the slogan 'All animals are equal, but some animals are more equal than others'. The name changes back from Animal Farm to Manor Farm. In the final scene of the novel, the pigs invite the neighbouring human farmers over for dinner, and when the animals outside look in on the pigs and men, they can't tell which is which.

The novel is devastating on two levels. Most obviously, it's a parody of the Russian Revolution, the battle for ascendancy between Trotsky and Stalin, and Stalin's creation of a travesty of the state for which Marx and Lenin planned and dreamed. Orwell struggled to get the book published during the Second World War, because of the close alliance with and widespread admiration for Stalin at the time. But on a deeper level, *Animal Farm* is a savage critique of any attempt to make the world better by changing the regime. It's a modern parable of the Fall, in which good intentions and abundant resources turn into violence, enmity, lies and hypocrisy.

The story of the magi coming from the east to worship the new-born king may seem a long way from *Animal Farm*, but you could say it's the same story in just 12 verses. There are two ironies at work in this story – a poignant one and a painful one. The poignant irony is that, like *Animal Farm*, this is indeed a story of a revolution. The magi discern through their stargazing that there's regime change afoot in heaven and earth. There's a new king born – not one who's just going to unseat the local potentates in the Holy Land, but one who's going to turn upside-down all earthly notions of power and authority. But despite the star apparently telling them otherwise, the magi assume that the new kind of king is going to be born where the old kind of king hangs out: Jerusalem. Herod may be a puppet ruler, installed by the Romans in a misguided attempt to offer some kind of legitimacy for their occupation of the Holy Land, but he's still a king, and he's living in a city that outstretched every other city in the region by a country mile.

But Jerusalem is not where Jesus is to be born. Jesus is born in Bethlehem. Being born in Bethlehem demonstrates two strands of God's logic. The first is fulfilment. Jesus meets the hopes of Israel. Bethlehem is mentioned in Micah as the place from which a new transformative leader will come; it's also the town from which the great King David came. The second is God's upside-down kingdom: a lowly girl gives birth to God's son, she does so in a stable, lowly shepherds are the first to worship, faraway kings perceive what no one on hand could grasp. So the poignant irony of this story is that, even guided by a star, the magi were so hard-wired to assume that real power, leadership, royalty and authority belong in Jerusalem, that they couldn't understand the ways of God revealed in the little town of Bethlehem. But we, the readers, can see what they can't see. There's a pantomime dimension to the magi story, where we already know Jesus has been born in Bethlehem and we're shouting, 'He's behind you!' to the magi as their camels stroll past Bethlehem and head on to Jerusalem. This is how irony works – we the readers, or audience, can see what the main players can't see.

But there's also a painful irony in the story. I recall a number of Christmas cards with, on the front, five utterly simple, but memorably smug words, 'Wise men still seek him.' We find a similar, but more congenial sentiment expressed in the carol 'O little town of Bethlehem' in the words, 'Where meek souls will receive him, still the dear Christ enters in.' Both notions convey the word 'still'. Both make the point that the Christmas story can be as alive today as 2,000 years ago. But that cuts both ways. The mistakes of the Christmas story can be as alive today as the successes. Which brings us to the painful irony in the magi story: Christians still stroll on to Jerusalem rather than stop at Bethlehem.

It's there in the temptation story: the tempter shows Jesus all the kingdoms of the world and their splendour, and he says to him, 'All these I will give you, if you will fall down and worship me.' The point is the same: look how you can overlook real people, real life, real relationships, by going straight to Jerusalem and bypassing Bethlehem. The church has done this countless times over the centuries: been so tempted to be close to the centres of worldly power, so keen thereby to gain opportunity for its ventures and influence over the affairs of state, that it's missed Bethlehem in its fixation on Jerusalem.

This is where *Animal Farm* becomes so painful. Think again about the early days of the animals' revolt, when the revolution brought real change, humans were displaced from the seat of domination, and the goods of the farm were distributed abundantly and evenly. Then think about the last line of the book: 'The creatures outside looked from pig to man, and from man to pig, and from pig to man again; but already it was impossible to say which was which.' The revolution has created no more than a new version of oppression, and it isn't even new – it's more or less the same as the regime with which the story began.

This isn't simply a matter of ethics, that we think we should be with the movers and shakers and the powerful and strong; it's about theology – it's about the assumption that God dwells in places of power and that the more powerful we are, the closer we can get to God's providence and purposes. The story of the magi dispels that false notion. God dwells in the obscure, forgotten, neglected, shadowy little town of Bethlehem. The emptiness, lies and fragility of Jerusalem are exposed by Herod's furious panic and violent impulse to exterminate the threat to his throne. By contrast, Bethlehem, though short of inns, becomes literally the centre of the universe, where heavenly angels, hardy shepherds and discerning magi all gather.

Animal Farm is a prophetic challenge to us every time we make ourselves out to be better than others, every time we naively assume merely changing those in charge makes for real change, every time we confuse good use of power with our exercising that power ourselves. But the story of the magi is an even deeper challenge. It shows us how much our exasperated failure to encounter God derives from looking in the wrong place, how much our notion of power is a long way from God's, and how we can get so close to the stable, somewhere so very right, but end up at Herod's court, somewhere so very wrong.

I wonder where Bethlehem is for you today. And how much time you're wasting trying to reach Jerusalem instead.

I generally make a distinction between an ethics sermon, which is chiefly about us, and a theology sermon, which is chiefly about God. A common caricature is that the former is about preachers visiting their prejudices upon and exerting inappropriate power over their congregations, while the latter is too heavenly minded to be any earthly use. As a rule, I eschew the former and seek most often to offer the latter. Sermons should be about God, not us. But in some cases you can hope to achieve both – and this is one such case. It's a simple distinction – we assume Jesus is in Jerusalem, but he turns out to be in Bethlehem – but it's one with significant theological and ethical ramifications, and this homily highlights them. I call it a homily because it makes one simple point, without extending it or complexifying it or adding any extra dimension to it. But it's such a memorable and applicable point, it's well worth making just as it is.

Turning now to the baptism of Christ, we find perhaps the definitive occasion when the preacher needs to explore both Old Testament and gospel passages together. In general, I dislike the game of 'See how I can weave together aspects of all three readings', which is fine for esoteric parties but generally empties a sermon of any rhetorical power. The sermon that says, 'I've run out of things to say about the gospel so for the last couple of minutes I'm going to turn to the epistle' I dislike even more. It's rare that speaking about more than one reading genuinely sharpens the edge of a sermon. But the baptism of Christ is invariably one of those rare occasions. Because it's impossible to understand the many mysteries of this event – why did it happen at all, why was John involved, why at the Jordan, what do the words spoken mean, why the dove – without reference to the key texts from Isaiah that undergird the story.

My Beloved
Isaiah 43.1–7, Luke 3.15–17, 21–2
9 *January* 2022

Every good story is based around a broadly threefold structure. There's the setting of the scene, during which you identify an anomaly, an obstacle or a quandary; there's the overcoming of that obstacle, by the power of detection, the receipt of new information, the muscle of a superior strength, or the disclosure of a secret; and finally, there's the new reality on the other side of the crisis. To be a good story it needs either the mystery to be intriguing, or the resolution to be absorbing. It's a great story if it manages both. The heart of most stories relates to the gradual or sudden revelation of what constitutes the mystery.

Take the 2020 Netflix series *Bridgerton*, set in the high society of Regency London. It starts out as a remix of *Pride and Prejudice*, with the two highly eligible main characters obviously attracted to one another, but standing aloof from any emotional association for reasons yet to be disclosed. Daphne cannot lower herself to the demeaning process of making herself marketable to a lofty suitor – a pride that makes her reluctant to acknowledge her longing for Simon. Simon's true motives are more complex and unveiling them becomes the true subject of the drama. Drawn to Daphne as he undoubtedly is, there's something preventing him from acknowledging his love. When forced to give a reason, he says he's incapable of having children. It never feels like a satisfactory explanation. We're simply drawn deeper into the mystery. Simon's unwillingness to risk conceiving a child curses his relationship with Daphne even after they marry. Gradually, however, we discover Simon's oppressive upbringing at the hands of his demanding and ice-cold father. At last, when close to despair, Daphne happens upon a collection of letters Simon wrote to his father when still a child, all in immaculate handwriting, all expressing profound love and an insatiable desire to please – and all rejected, in most cases, unopened. Finally, Daphne understands what is at the root of all the pain and grief. Simon cannot bear to impose on a child the suffering he experienced himself. All is understood, all is forgiven, all is transformed. The story ends with the birth of their first child, the living representation of reconciliation and hope.

I want you to think of the Old Testament as a story of this kind. The scene is this: Israel settles in the Promised Land, having been rescued from slavery and given a covenant. The problem that arises is this: Israel can't stay faithful to the covenant. The obstacle to be overcome is this: Israel finds itself in exile in Babylon, 500 miles to the east. The surface question is, how on earth is Israel going to get back home? The deeper question is, how are Israel and God to be reconciled?

The difference between the Old Testament and *Bridgerton* is that the TV series follows a conventional pattern of scene-setting, problem, obstacle, resolution and happy ever after – whereas the Bible is a much more complex assortment of angles on the same story and detours from it. So you really need a guide to direct you to the key parts of the Old Testament. The good news is that we do have such a guide. It's called the New Testament; specifically, the Gospels. The Gospels are saturated with quotations from the Old Testament, and these quotations point to what the authors regard as the key moments in the Old Testament story. But just as the New Testament is a guide to the Old, so is the Old Testament to the New. One of the most crucial passages in the Old Testament, in fact, arguably the most crucial passage in the whole of the Old Testament for understanding the Gospels, comes in the first seven verses of Isaiah 43.

These seven verses are so arranged that the first verse mirrors the seventh, the second mirrors the sixth, and the third the fifth. What these pairs of verses give us is a miniature version of the whole Old Testament story. We begin and end with creation. God calls us by name and creates us for glory: think of this as the creation of the universe, but also as your creation as a human being, with a purpose to reflect God's glory and answer God's call. Then, after creation, the next great event is the exodus from Egypt: note the words about passing through the waters and the sense of being formed as a nation. Then the third great event is the return from exile: we don't even know if this had taken place when Isaiah's words were written, but it clearly had before someone collected a host of writings together and called it the Bible. Those are the three great events in the Old Testament and woven through them is the language of God's promises: I call you by name, I am with you, I am your Saviour, I made you for my glory. All this is the language of covenant. The covenant between God and Israel is the consistent theme that unites the three great Old Testament events.

Think of these three pairs of verses as like a plinth that holds up the statue of the middle verse, verse 4. Verse 4 is the secret at the heart of the Old Testament. Imagine it like Simon's childhood letters to his father in *Bridgerton*. When Daphne discovers and reads Simon's letters home, all is revealed and everything finally makes sense, and she loves him like never before, and understands and forgives all the confusion of the preceding episodes. Isaiah 43 verse 4 is like that. It's the moment when everything in the Bible, for the first time, makes sense. Here are the most revealing and perhaps the most important words in Scripture: 'You are precious in my sight, and honoured, and I love you.' Here's the whole reason for creation, the whole purpose of the exodus, the whole agony of the exile. God's whole life is shaped to be with Israel.

I want now to shift our focus from 2,500 years ago in Babylon to today. What does it mean to baptize Esme today? It means to hear God saying these very same words to her that God says to Israel in exile. You are precious, honoured and loved. Words at the heart of the Old Testament. Words at the heart of the Bible. Words at the heart of the universe. Let's look at those three words to see what they are truly telling us, and truly saying to Esme.

We'll start with 'precious'. Precious means something of infinite value. It means I don't know whether to put it on the mantelpiece in the centre of the room where everyone can see it and admire it, or whether to hide it in many layers of velvet cladding so it can never get broken, and lodge it in the deepest vault of the safest bank so no one can ever steal it. That's how precious you are. Precious means intricate, deftly and finely woven or crafted, with a design that would need a microscope fully to enjoy, with a subtlety and delicacy beyond the skill or imagination of any but the most accomplished artisan. Precious means unique, inimitable, astonishing; it means I would give up everything else just for this.

Now let's turn to honoured. Honoured means respected, cherished, even revered. More subtly it means, 'I understand you are not me; you have your own rhythm, identity, metabolism, style, history. The point of our relationship is not to make you a pawn of my ambitions, a clone of me, an agent of my desires. It is for you to become all that you are called to be, as I become all that I am called to be. Honoured means I cherish you. I don't seek to change you, use you, become you. I enjoy you for the wonder that you are. I treasure the privilege of being in relationship with you.'

The third and last word is loved. Loved means a movement of the heart and an act of the will. It means something is moving in me, beyond my thought, decision or resolve, that draws me to you, regardless of your virtue, or even reciprocation. I interpret your actions in the best light, I light up with life in your presence, I'm overjoyed at the very thought of you. But love also means sheer determination and selfless resilience. I change your nappy however smelly it is, I stay in touch with you however little you seem to value it, I stretch out my hand to pull you out of the swirling torrent even though we've never previously met.

And here's the thing. We need all three words. You might think the third word contains the other two, but the truth is … it doesn't. Think of a domestic argument where one party says, 'But I love you.' The other party says, 'If you love me but don't honour me, it's not the love I want.' Think of the minority-ethnic employee who is told, 'You're a precious part of this organization,' but privately thinks, 'You don't honour my traditions, you don't love me, you just need my skills and are glad my being here helps you tick some boxes.' Think about the war veteran who comes back from the Remembrance Day parade and thinks, 'Yes, you honoured me today, but the rest of the year you're ashamed of the war I fought in. I'm not precious, I'm an embarrassment; I'm not loved, I'm kept out of sight, because my life-altering injuries don't support the victorious story you want to tell.'

Precious, honoured and loved. We need all three words. Not loved without being honoured. Not honoured without being precious. Not precious without being loved. These three words are at the epicentre of the Old Testament.

Now look what happens when the adult Jesus makes his appearance in Luke's Gospel at the start of his ministry. Heaven is opened: in other words, we're about to discover who God really is. A voice from the cloud speaks. 'You are my Son, the Beloved; with you I am well pleased.' In other words: you are precious, honoured and loved. The love God has for Israel – the key to the whole Old Testament – is now fulfilled in Jesus.

And that's reflected in what happens when we baptize Esme today. Baptism is God saying to her, 'You are precious, honoured and loved.' All three. It's what Esme's parents say to her every day. It's the fruit of baptism and the most wonderful gift. You are precious, honoured and loved. It's the secret of everything. God created the world and came among us in Christ and will be with us forever, because God's whole being is devoted to saying, 'You are precious, honoured and loved.' It's what we want to say to each other. It's what we long to hear a community say to us. It's the gospel of Jesus Christ. And it's revealed in Jesus' baptism. And ours.

The whole sermon seeks to crystallize complexity in simplicity and distil the whole of Christianity into three words. The surprise is that these words come not from the New Testament but from the Old. The reflection on *Bridgerton* both offers a structure within which to place the three great Old Testament events, which form the structure of Isaiah 43, and introduces the mood of a love story with a transformative moment at its heart – which sets up the focus on the key verse, Isaiah 43.4. But the heart of the sermon is the joy of the three compelling words and the recognition of their insufficiency alone, but their abundance together. The fact that there was an actual baptism at the service presents an opportunity to bring the generalities down to a concrete level.

Here are some guidelines on preaching in Epiphany season.

1. Remember 'new' is a compelling word in advertising, because it contains hope and beginning and discovery. Epiphany should feel like that. Your sermons in Epiphany season should start with that mood as a default. While New Year resolutions don't always last long, they tie in well with Epiphany and baptism of Christ themes.
2. More, perhaps, than any other liturgical season, there's a consistent thread through all the Sundays of Epiphany – that of unfurling revelation. It's appropriate to refer to the other Sundays to the extent it helps you affirm that theme.
3. The baptism of Christ is one of the great preaching Sundays of the year because it combines a crucial gospel story with the hint of discovery, since it's not as well-thumbed as Christmas and Easter. Make the most of the occasion. It can also have the feeling of 'everyone's now back after Christmas and New Year', so it can have a reunion feel too.
4. There's something extraordinarily comprehensive about several of the stories of this season. They lend themselves to an approach of 'everything that matters is in this passage', which is an attractive and infectious way to approach a sermon. Let that comprehensiveness fill your imagination and find ways to convey it to your people.

Jesus' first sermon at Nazareth is such a favourite for a progressive congregation that it almost matches Matthew 25's account of 'when did I see you hungry' in the pantheon of standard social-action texts. Which makes it especially difficult to preach on, since there's an underlying assumption that the congregation already know that the preacher will affirm this church's outreach projects and castigate other churches for their imperviousness to the suffering of their neighbours. So you have to find a new angle in order to feel the power and awe of this moment in Luke's Gospel. This is what the following sermon tries to do.

The whole Gospel
Luke 4.14–21
23 January 2022

I'm terrible at taking verbal instructions. I must have sat in a hundred chemistry lessons where the teacher told us what to do with a Bunsen burner and a test tube; and the rest was totally lost on me. I just couldn't take the information in. I never finished an experiment in my whole time at school. Likewise, directions. You have no idea what a difference Google Maps has made to me. It was useless stopping to ask for directions, because as soon as someone said, 'You turn left at the post office and then it's the second on the right,' they might as well have been talking Urdu. And writing it all down isn't always the answer. Last week I made an apple dessert, and even followed a recipe; but it was already in the oven before I realized I hadn't put any fat in the topping. And don't start me on shopping lists. I never come back with everything I planned to buy.

I'm sure a psychologist could tell me what syndrome I have. But I'm not sure it really needs a psychologist. I think my brain simply retains certain kinds of information better than others. If you asked me what the usual Leeds or Liverpool line-ups were in the early seventies, or which year Richard Nixon resigned as president, I could tell you.

Now, all this is harmless. We each have to find workarounds for our deficiencies in life. But the point is, when it comes to Christianity, we all have parts we're likely to forget. And that would be pretty harmless too, if it weren't that there's often a pattern to those things we forget. Those who tell us the things we tend to forget about Christianity aren't called psychologists; they're called prophets. A prophet points out the things we tend to forget because it suits us to ignore or suppress them. We ignore or suppress them because they address parts of our lives we'd like not to dwell on, or highlight people in our community or issues in the world we'd rather avoid.

Let me give an example. It's not my example – it's from the American writer Wendell Berry. He describes what it was like 200 years ago in the American South, when a slave-owner would sit in church with his slaves seated behind him. The slave-owner believed that his believing slaves would go to heaven; but he nonetheless felt justified in keeping them in slavery on earth. How was this done? It was done by insisting that Christianity is not a prescription of how to live on earth, but of how to go to heaven. Christianity is all about what God will one day do, and not at all about what we must do today. Berry suggests that this is the root of the aversion to addressing issues like the climate emergency in the same part of the world today; it begins in the sociological imperative not to question the institution of slavery, and the consequent requirement to reorganize Christianity to take out all the parts that might put it under scrutiny. Southern landowners forgot parts of their religion just as readily as I forgot the instructions for my chemistry experiments. Indeed, Berry goes on to say that the whole insistence on the separation of church and state comes from the fear that prophetic preachers would seek to legislate the demands of the gospel to love neighbours and resist oppression.

Which brings us to Luke chapter 4. Each of the gospels has a programmatic moment near the beginning that sets out the whole gospel. Mark has the parable of the sower. John has the wedding at Cana. Matthew has the Beatitudes. Luke has this moment in Nazareth. He portrays Jesus in his childhood synagogue on the sabbath, being given the opportunity to choose his signal text for his whole ministry. You can see him working his way through the great scroll of Isaiah, all the way to chapter 61. And what he gives, as surely as any chemistry teacher, as any Google Map, as any shopping list, are the four things we mustn't forget when it comes to remembering whom the gospel is for. He's giving us the whole gospel, in a way we can't forget, or wriggle out of, or ignore.

So here are the four categories. Number one, the gospel is good news for the poor. Poor means, in any room where the decisions are made, the people who aren't in that room. Poor means any who have to go without, so those they love and care for can have a little. Poor means all who, whenever they get paid, find someone creams off a big percentage and they're left with not enough. Poor means those who, when Jesus calls, have nothing to leave behind, so they can come straightaway. Poor means all who have nothing but each other. Poor means those from whom the most evocative words in our language – home, belonging, dignity, respect, safety, trust, love – have been taken away. Good news means, *you're going to get those words back*.

Number two, the gospel means release for the captives. Captivity is prison. Prison means loss of control. Prison means shut in by a door that only opens from the outside. Prison means not knowing how long till that door opens, if it ever will. Prison means shame, it means exclusion, it means punishment, it means being hidden out of sight, it means not being allowed to move very far, it means violence, it means fear, it means isolation, it means powerlessness. Prison means your life is in someone else's hands, and they get to choose when you eat, if you sleep, if you exercise. Prison means your life is not your own. Release means *you get your life back*.

Number three, the gospel means recovery of sight to the blind. Today we don't read this as suggesting disability is a deficit. We don't define ourselves by the one thing we're perceived to lack. But what we still experience today is social exclusion by discriminatory judgement. Exclusion means overlooked for resources or opportunities for which you're perfectly well qualified. Exclusion means humiliated because you're perceived to be different. Exclusion means not seen when you're in the room, not counted because you don't matter, not wanted because you don't belong, not trusted because you're not understood. Recovery means *being heard, seen, cherished, wanted.*

Number four, the gospel means letting the oppressed go free. Oppressed means living every day under threat of someone's anger, tiptoeing around someone's violence, vulnerable to someone's exploitation, constantly at risk of being attacked, robbed, hurt, used, tormented. The first category means being at risk because of what you lack, the second means impoverished because of constraint, the third means vilified because of what you are: this category means subject to the whim of somebody else, manipulated by someone more powerful, at risk from those who could destroy you any moment. Oppressed means facing cruelty, danger and injustice at every turn. Going free means *having the devil taken off your back.*

Notice how in the gospel Jesus goes on to become each of the categories he's talking about. Homeless in Bethlehem, Egypt and around Galilee, he's poor. Arrested in Gethsemane, he's in prison. Cast out of Jerusalem, he's excluded. Nailed to a cross, he's oppressed. Jesus isn't just talking about Isaiah 61; he's living it.

What Jesus is describing and embodying is salvation. Salvation means two things. It means shedding impoverishment, imprisonment, discrimination and oppression. And it means embracing belonging, liberty, love and hope. The danger with salvation is that we do what I used to do with my chemistry experiments: we focus on the Bunsen burner and the test tube – and forget the rest. When Jesus spoke about impoverishment, incarceration, exclusion and oppression, it's almost certain that those listening to him assumed he was talking about one thing: the occupation of their land by the Romans. These were people whose identity, solidarity and prosperity were being destroyed by Roman occupation as surely as the Channel Islanders' lives were destroyed by Nazi occupation or Black people's lives were destroyed by apartheid. When Jesus spoke of the year of the Lord's favour, people thought of the jubilee year, when land was restored to its original owners. They thought, he's saying the land's coming back to us. Of course they thought, just get rid of the Romans and all will be fine. Like people thought, just get rid of Saddam Hussein in Iraq, or just remove Communism from Russia.

But shedding our chains is only half of salvation. The other half is embracing restored relationships. Fighting injustice is half the story; modelling justice is the other half. All of us are like me with my apple pudding: we're all inclined to leave an ingredient or two out. Or maybe half the recipe. Don't forget the slave owners in the American South found a way to leave out the earthly part of the gospel altogether. This is why the most radical and powerful word Jesus says in Nazareth is one I haven't yet mentioned: 'Today.' 'Today' shakes us out of our desire to park this for another time, our tendency to intellectualize and theorize and prevaricate and never get to the moment of truth. No one's much bothered about what Jesus is saying – until he says, 'Today.' If you think about it, every sermon is opening the Bible and looking up at the congregation and saying, 'Today.'

You may be familiar with the Ignatian practice of the Examen. The Examen is where you sit down quietly at the end of the day and review all its events, recalling your feelings about each one, noting what hurt, if you got it wrong, when God has been present to you and where the Holy Spirit was drawing you towards life. I'd like you to think of Jesus' words in Nazareth as a morning version of the Examen. Imagine praying, each morning, like this:

- Show me where your children are poor. Awaken me to where I impoverish others. Visit me in the place of my own poverty.
- Show me where your children are imprisoned. Awaken me to how I incarcerate others. Visit me in the ways I am in prison.
- Show me where your children suffer discrimination. Awaken me to when I exclude others. Visit me in my own experience of rejection.
- Show me where your children are oppressed. Awaken me to how I dominate others. Visit me in my own place of fear.

And then at the end, instead of saying Amen, you say, 'Today.' That's your agenda for today. For every day. Because we're all prone to leave one part of salvation out. Which is why we need not just to make a list, but to live that list: a list that celebrates the good news that Jesus hasn't left us out – so we must leave no one out either.

This sermon embodies several of my favourite tropes. It's comprehensive: it offers four scriptural categories that translate into a checklist for daily devotion. It's Christological: halfway through it points out that in offering these four categories (or finding them in Isaiah), Jesus is outlining the shape of his own ministry. It's reflexive: rather than pointing the finger at oppressors, it highlights our own complicity and failure. It's both personal and political. And it's theologically interesting, in that the Wendell Berry insight is a genuinely fascinating and original reflection on some deep-seated (but baffling to outsiders) attitudes in the United States today.

The sermon starts with some self-deprecating humour. It's often an effective beginning to the sermon, so long as it doesn't introduce distracting elements and genuinely sets up the argument – in this case, the checklist. The humour is helpful because it's a serious and searing sermon, and the humour prevents it becoming overly solemn and sententious. Humour is often a sign the preacher is a little scared of the congregation and wants to buy sympathy or suspend judgement by feeding the beast with a one-liner or amusing anecdote. But the preacher needs to assume the congregation is thirsty for truth that addresses its deepest questions and yearnings, and humour's true role is to make that truth easier to hear and set the congregation up for that truth's power and surprise. Humour that's employed to win favour distracts from the sermon to the preacher. It needs to be a catalyst, not a detour.

6

Preaching in Lent

The subtlety of Lent is that it's really three seasons. There's the initial emphasis on discipline, fasting and holiness; there's the subsequent emergence of the wilderness as a time of confusion and paradoxical discovery; and there's the turn to the cross and the cost of discipleship. In between, if you're in the UK, is the somewhat anomalous Mothering Sunday, which you ignore at your peril. (I once did a broadcast on Mothering Sunday that began with a woman speaking about childlessness and another woman speaking about bringing up a multiply disabled child who died before turning 4. I got a letter berating me for oppressing happy mothers with this dismal tale of woe that ruined what Mothering Sunday was about. So much for trying to integrate Mothering Sunday into Lent.) In addition, Lent 5, formerly known as Passion Sunday, has a unique character all its own, that somehow combines Lent, Holy Week and Easter, especially when the reading is the raising of Lazarus. And Palm Sunday is in many ways the most spectacular Sunday of the year, transcending Lent almost altogether.

So while Lent seems like a single season, it's actually several, with only the second and third Sundays significantly resembling one another. The major preaching opportunities, besides Passion Sunday, are Ash Wednesday, best suited to a homily, and Lent 1, a moment for a programmatic look at sin and repentance. So in this chapter, I offer an Ash Wednesday homily and two Lent 1 sermons.

Ash Wednesday is a day for a homily because a service is often squeezed into a gap in the working day, but also because the major event is the ashing, and the address should point to that rather than elsewhere. Here's a homily that seeks to express the essence of Ash Wednesday while calling us to deeper discipleship.

God's secret
Matthew 6.1–6, 16–18
5 March 2014

The seventeenth-century French philosopher, mathematician and physicist Blaise Pascal is famous for many things – but perhaps most of all for a bet, or what he called a wager. He took seriously three pressing truths about our lives. One, that it's impossible to know for certain if the God of Jesus Christ is truly at large. Two, that if that God is at large, that God is wondrous beyond description, gracious beyond measure and generous beyond imagining. Three, that choosing whether or not to believe in that God is not something one can delay indefinitely or even at all; one must say yes or no, and live accordingly and, even more significantly, die accordingly.

Pascal suggests there are two straightforward options. You can wager that God exists – or does not. But here's the crucial part. Pascal says, simply consider your happiness: 'Let us weigh the gain and the loss in wagering that God is. Let us estimate these two chances. If you gain, you gain all; if you lose, you lose nothing. Wager, then, without hesitation that God is.' In other words, if it turns out that God does exist, you've gained eternal life and unlimited glory; if, by contrast, you turn out to be wrong, and there's no God, what have you lost but a little bit of pleasure and luxury, which don't stand for much in the light of eternity and pretty soon, through death, you were going to lose anyway?

Keep that argument in mind as we look together at what Jesus says in Matthew chapter 6 about practising discipleship. He talks about three things: giving alms, praying and fasting. You could say one, charity, is about relating to others; the next, prayer, is about relating to God; while the third, fasting, is about relating to ourselves.

But what Jesus' words show us, and the reason they're so painful to hear, is that it's more than possible to be a Christian in a way that doesn't truly take up Pascal's wager. It's possible to act in such a way that's nominally about seeking eternal glory, but essentially guaranteeing you get plenty of earthly glory, or what Pascal calls pleasure and luxury, at the same time.

Giving alms is, in theory, about seeking the good of the person in need, a person who could be you, a person in whom you see the face of Christ. But, as Jesus points out, if you give to charity with a trumpet voluntary blaring out to all the world how magnanimous and beneficent you are, you aren't really doing it for the benefit of the needy person – you're playing to the gallery and doing it for your own acclaim. You've backed the wrong side of Pascal's wager.

Likewise, prayer is, in theory, about an intimate and personal interaction between you and God. But, as Jesus points out, there's a host of ways in which you can so construct things that you're not really talking to God at all, but again playing to the gallery and seeking to gain prestige and regard for being such a pious and dutiful person. You've sold the glory of communion with God for the cheap and transitory currency of impressing other people. You've backed the wrong side of Pascal's wager.

Again, fasting is, ideally, the way you discipline your desires so you can learn to feed on God alone, and not greedily be at the mercy of whatever tempting morsel crosses your path. But, as Jesus points out, it's all too common to put on a hangdog expression and make sure everyone knows how much you're suffering and sacrificing, to the point where it's no longer about your resisting temptation and feeding on God alone but much more about you getting the credit for being holy, dedicated, selfless and strong. Once again, you've backed the wrong side of Pascal's wager.

It seems that to be truly holy, truly to back the right side of Pascal's wager, truly to live your life in the light and expectation of the eternal life that's given to us through Christ's resurrection, you've got to be able to keep a secret. Think about that for a moment. Why do we find it so hard to keep a secret? We find it hard because we're intoxicated by the pleasure of divulging fascinating information, seeing the awe and laughter and shock and surprise on people's faces, and receiving the acclaim that comes from being regarded as a person of knowledge, excitement and intrigue. Breaking a secret comes about when we value the unstable esteem of our audience more highly than we treasure the well-being of our confidante. It's the same dynamic as we saw with backing the wrong side of Pascal's wager – in our anxiety about where true joy is to be found, we'll settle for the easiest joy available and closest to hand.

Truly to have faith in God requires us to be able to keep a secret. To give money away, but to keep secret when, how and what we give. We must learn to enjoy others benefitting from what we give, without relying on them to say thank you or third parties to applaud us. To pray, but to keep secret when, how and what we pray. We must so deepen our relationship with God that we find joy not in our prayers being answered, still less in others admiring our piety, but simply in being held in God's heart. To fast, but to keep secret when and how we fast. We must so fill the space left empty by fasting with the joys usually kept at bay by our greed, that others don't pity or praise us but envy how alive we are.

And all those secrets are part of a larger, more profound, more personal and more uncomfortable secret. And that secret is this. We don't know if all our charity, all our prayer, all our fasting, all our faith, hope and love – if all of it is in vain. We don't know for certain. It's all a wager. That's a big secret – a secret we're very reluctant to share with anybody.

But what inspires us to make that wager, and keep that secret, is an even bigger wager, and an even bigger secret. God doesn't know if investing every sinew of creation, every drop of Christ's blood, every ounce of the Spirit's passion, will ever result in our showing any love, truth or joy in return. God's whole investment in us, despite our folly, failure and fragility, is the greatest wager of them all. Is it wise? Probably not. Are we likely to get better? I doubt it. Is God's wager based on a sober estimate of our goodness? Sadly, no. But God goes ahead anyway. That's the greatest secret of them all. And when we give, when we pray, when we fast, we're saying that we've got a bit of a sense of that secret, and how wondrous and gracious and awesome that secret is. And we realize, and recall, and resolve, 'Of course I'll wager all I have on God. Because God has already wagered everything on me.'

The nature of a homily is not the length, but the focus on one single point and the relentless driving home of that point with humour, illustration and rhetoric. The facile remark 'Sermonettes make Christianettes' absurdly implies that somehow one grows in discipleship according to the length of sermon one hears. All the sermons in this book could be reduced in length if that were what the context required. A homily requires the preacher to focus down on to the precise point and not waste a single word. Some congregations much prefer homilies to sermons, and if sermon writers lack the discipline of weighing every insight as to whether it belongs in the whole argument, you can understand why.

The First Sunday in Lent risks the most formulaic sermon of any Sunday of the year, because most often the gospel reading is of the temptation of Christ in the wilderness, whose threefold form lends itself to a ponderously predictable threefold presentation by the preacher. The secret is to find a way to present temptation, sin and the wilderness in a way that doesn't simply lock into this existing and tired pattern. In the two sermons that follow, I suggest two ways to do this: one by following the plot of a novel about renewal; the other by turning to the Old Testament lesson, one that looks enormously into Christian history and theology, but is underexamined in many churches.

Lent 1 is obviously about personal repentance. The key is to put that in wider social and theological context. But you need to start very personally and directly. Which is what the following sermon does.

Clear out
Matthew 4.1–11
5 March 2017

You've moved to London, and it's a long way from the town you know best. Time flies, and it's been a couple of years since you visited the community that really shaped you. But something comes up and it turns out you're going to spend a little while back where you used to belong. And you can't not go and see that one person, who knows you so well and loves you despite all, and from whom you tend to shy away because they're like a refiner's fire that burns away the dross and leaves you with no way to hide the truth. But you've been away a couple of years, you're a lot more worldly wise now, you're not going to be seen through as easily as in the old days, so you're off guard.

And the conversation starts simply and straightforwardly. 'What've you been up to?' There's lots of things to say to that. 'What're you working on?' That's a bit harder, because you know it's a two-edged question. It doesn't just mean 'What's keeping you busy?' – it really means, 'What's the part of you that's being tested, what are you learning, what's not working, and where are you having to grow through your mistakes?' But you blunder on, taking the question at face value, and offer up quite a few things, taking refuge in the quantity, and hoping the number of different activities will prevent the conversation settling on any single one of them. 'That's a lot of things,' says your refiner's fire. 'Which is the one that really matters?'

Oh dear. You've dug yourself right down into the place where you can't escape, like being buried in sand at the seaside when only your face and arms are still visible. You can't lie to a question like that. It's too obvious. Your whole jokey manner and casual charm has completely failed. Something drew you into this conversation. You could have avoided it altogether. Part of you wanted this. But most of you, for a very long time, has been running away from it. 'Hmm?' says the refiner's fire, pointing out, wordlessly, that you haven't answered the question. 'Actually,' you say, 'since you put it that way, none of the things I've mentioned is the one that really matters.' And at this point you lower your eyes, and look at the floor, because the truth is, you feel shame. Shame that your life is so full of padding and the real quality is so deeply buried inside. Shame that so quickly, so suddenly, this person who knows you rather too well and understands life rather too acutely has got to the heart of it all in about five minutes. And then, rather surprising yourself, you utter a sentence that begins, 'The one that really matters is…'

And you begin to regain a bit of your composure, and your self-respect, because you've said something good, and true, and in its way rather beautiful, and it turns out you're not a superficial ass after all, you're actually perceptive and full of self-knowledge and even wisdom, now you mention it. And you think, maybe the refiner's fire isn't so scary, so humiliating. Maybe we're on a level. But the refiner's fire hasn't finished with you yet. There's another question. 'So, if that's the one thing that really matters, why aren't you filling your whole time with that?' And in an instant, you know you could give a hundred answers, but each of them would be foolish and empty and cowardly and thin, and would make it even worse than it is, because they'd all be true, but they'd all illustrate the one thing you don't want to say, which is that your life is an elaborate organized conspiracy to avoid the one thing that really matters. And only the refiner's fire can really see that. Which is maybe why you've been away these few years. And why you feel so naked and embarrassed and yet inspired and repentant now. Because you've just got a glimpse of what it's like to lose the whole world and gain your own soul. And you're feeling exactly the way you should be feeling on the first Sunday of Lent.

Anne Tyler's novel *Saint Maybe* tells the story of how three young children find themselves orphans and how their 19-year-old and rather self-absorbed uncle, Ian, in an extraordinary assumption of guilt, holds himself responsible for their parents' deaths. Ian immediately leaves college and over the next 20 years takes it upon himself, without resentment or bitterness, to set aside the plans he had for his own life and instead give all his time to bringing up his dead brother's three children. It's not an easy ride, but, in losing the world, he gains his own soul. By the time the children are leaving home, the different family responsibilities are wearing him out and he finds himself overwhelmed by the muddle and untidiness. At this moment, in walks Rita, a strident, 20-something, self-styled clutter counsellor. Rita vigorously and unsentimentally throws out 90% of the contents of Ian's fridge, along with half of the attic, basement, and almost every other room. With unerring perception, she recognizes the exhaustion of the lingering memories and unmade decisions represented by every item of clutter. To everyone's surprise, Ian falls in love with and marries Rita. Maybe it's because she returns him to the simplicity of the one thing that really matters – the simplicity that led him to do such a radical thing when he was an apparently carefree 19-year-old all those years before.

Right at the beginning of his ministry, immediately after his baptism, Jesus goes out into the wilderness for 40 days to discover what really matters. And in his imagination, he's surrounded by three kinds of clutter.

The first kind of clutter is the desire for comfort. Anyone who says they don't share a desire for comfort is lying. When you're wearing painful shoes and you change into well-fitting ones, it feels great. When you're sleeping five to a room with only an abrasive blanket and no heating and you move into a carpeted en suite double with ironed 100% cotton sheets and central heating you feel like a million dollars. When you've gone days without any proper food and someone provides a hot, nourishing and tasty dinner, you feel like a different person.

But notice there are two kinds of comfort. There's the kind that's a means to an end – that gives you good rest, nice furnishings, healthy food, undemanding company and a sabbath from the tension of the world, all so that you can be ready for action like a boxer re-entering the ring after a break or a racing car returning to the track with fresh tyres. And there's another kind that's an end in itself, that seeks a home, furnishings, electric gadgets, relaxing surroundings, accumulated possessions, luxurious travel, all to attain a kind of perfection of ease, security and well-being, as if one could elevate to a nirvana of peace through physical satisfaction alone. How much time, energy and imagination do we spend seeking such a dream? 'Command these stones to become loaves of bread,' says the tempter to Jesus. 'Live the dream.'

The second kind of clutter is the longing for attention. 'Look at me,' we say, when we're five years old, taking the big slide down into the swimming pool. 'Look at me,' we say, when we're a little older, ensuring our Facebook friends or Instagram recipients know what a fabulous and stylish time we're having at a show or a party. 'Look at me,' we say, when we feel we've done all the work and got none of the credit, when we've done something truly selfless and not been rewarded, when we've said something clever and no one laughed so we insist on saying it again.

What is the cult of celebrity if not an attempt to gauge worth by fame, love by popularity, value by visibility? When we don't know if what we are or who we are matters, we can take solace in the fact that everyone's talking about us, everyone knows our name, we got zillions of likes and everything transferable about us has been forwarded to all the inboxes on the planet. But isn't this anxious, even insatiable greed to be seen a way of not acknowledging our true self-worth? 'Throw yourself down,' says the tempter to Jesus. 'Then everyone will look at you, and your acrobatic angel friends doing stunts with you. Then you'll know you really matter. You'll go viral.'

The third kind of clutter is the craving for control. I remember a woman saying to me about her rather emotionally unintelligent husband, 'He's one of those men who likes to be in charge of things. I don't think he wants his organization to achieve anything in particular, he just wants to be the one who decides what everyone gets paid and how all the desks are arranged. He thinks I'm wasting my life because I work with people whose problems I can't make better. He wants to see results, count outcomes, achieve change. Sometimes I worry he only wanted to have children so he could make them turn out as he wanted.'

It feels like every advert offers us greater control: remote control over our technology, effortless control over our car, painless control over our calorie intake, intricate control over our stress levels. We're being promised a life that can be operated from a control panel, without the need for, or distraction of, untidy relationships. The tempter shows Jesus all the kingdoms of the world and their splendour and says, 'All these I will give you.' You can have the whole planet under your control, just like that.

This is what a good job, a secure household, a successful education and a steady record of good health offer: comfort, attention and control. You could call them the three central aspirations of our culture. They're not, in themselves, bad things. They and their pursuit take up enormous quantities of our lives. But today, at the start of Lent, we see them for what they are: clutter. Clutter that crowds out our lives and means that when we sit down in front of the refiner's fire and face the question, 'Which is the one that really matters?', we find our head drop, and a quiet realization reach us: 'None of the above.' Comfort is a detour on the way to joy. Attention is a distraction on the road to love. Power is a diversion on the way to truth.

When God became a human being in Jesus Christ, God hired Rita the clutter counsellor and cleared out all that didn't really matter – the comfort, the attention, the control. Jesus took up a path that had naught for his comfort, a life that was almost all spent far from people's attention, and a way that renounced control. He went against all the aspirations of our culture. He spent all his time on the one thing that really mattered: us. Today, at the beginning of Lent, we come before the refiner's fire, we confront these two questions: 'What's the one that really matters?' and 'So why aren't you filling your whole time with that?' And we call for Rita the clutter counsellor, clear out all that doesn't really matter and humbly but seriously resolve to spend our time on the one thing that really does matter. I wonder what that is.

There are two ways to grab the attention of the congregation from the outset. The direct way is to zone in on existential reality, in such a manner that creates a breathless identification from the listener, eager, almost desperate to see how the journey ends. The other is to tell a compelling story, from literature or life, that draws the listener in and makes everything else disappear.

This sermon does both. The risk is in the jump from one to the other. But what's gained is a great deal of material that can amplify the rest of the sermon by repeated reincorporation of key elements, which gives the rest of the sermon both an intensity and a lightness of touch that many Lent 1 sermons lack. The sermon employs, as found elsewhere in this book, my favourite tactic of seeming to end on a satisfying note of ethical closure before expanding to embrace a truly theological frame of reference, by showing how this is in fact not fundamentally about us, but about God's purpose in Christ. But given it's a Lent 1 sermon, it has to end on a note of personal challenge.

Here are some guidelines for preaching in Lent.

1. Ensure your sermon is truly theological – about God – and not just a self-help manual for a more disciplined or healthy life.
2. Engage honestly and deeply with what makes us resist the overtures of God. Don't make discipleship out to be easier than it is. If Lent isn't about sacrifice it isn't Lent, and if sacrifice is easy it isn't sacrifice.
3. Give people space to name and face their wilderness – its lostness and its confusion and its bewilderment. Don't resolve everything so tidily that the humanity disappears. Few people need a kick up the backside. Almost everyone needs reminding of the glory that may require sacrifice to attain.
4. The heart of the Bible is that out of our despair and abandonment Christ brings resurrection and hope. This is your basic template for a Lenten sermon.
5. Lent retains a popular-level culture of making sacrifices and trying harder. The preacher's job is to set this in a wider theological frame and make it an opportunity to grow deeper and closer to God.

Lent can get very granular and focused on tiny details of discipline and devotion. There are alternatives to talking about temptation and giving things up. You can go to the heart of a theological divide that has led many faithful Christians to take a depressing course. It doesn't have to be done by criticizing those Christians. It can be done by going back to the foundational text that overshadows so much Christian theology. That's what the following sermon seeks to do.

'Both Sides Now'
Genesis 2.4b–9, 15–end
20 February 2022

I recall a night when I was 19. I was living in a community of maybe 25 people and, after supper, one of the household got out a guitar and sang some folk songs. The one I remember was 'Both Sides Now'. Joni Mitchell wrote the song in 1967 as her first marriage was disintegrating. She was sitting on a plane, contemplating what clouds look like from the ground compared to from above. Once she'd seen clouds as castles in the air; but now they only block the sun. Once she'd seen love as how you feel when every fairy tale comes real; but now it's love's illusions she recalls. The song epitomized my mixed emotions at the time. The community was a beautiful experience of companionship, coming right after I'd lost my mother to a long and cruel illness. Yet despite the prayer and gentleness of that community, something was wrong. Years later, the founder would end up in prison for what had happened there. Both sides now. The intensity of the contrast was so strong that I bolted out before the end of the song. I couldn't deal with the strength of diverging emotions.

The story told in Genesis chapters 2 and 3 could be called Both Sides Now. It's a story of how everything was created in wonder and joy, and how it now exists in tension and conflict. I want to reflect on the story with you this morning to explore what it's really saying. Because I believe that what it's saying goes to the heart of each of our lives, and the heart of what it means to be a Christian. But first, I want briefly to note what it's not saying.

One commentator calls this the best-known and most-misunderstood story in the Bible. Let me quickly mention a few things the story's not saying. It's not a scientific account of how the world began; instead, it's a parable. It's not an overarching story that casts its shadow over the whole Bible; in fact, only a handful of passages in the rest of the Bible refer to it. It's not an account of a historical event known as the Fall, or the origin of evil. The Old Testament doesn't deal with theoretical issues like evil, sin or death: it's more interested in practical responses. It's not about any hierarchical relationship between man and woman. The creation of Adam refers to the beginning of human life; the creation of Eve is the moment man and woman become different and complementary. There's no hint here of one being superior to the other. And it's not about sex. You can get all Freudian about the serpent if you like, but there's nothing in this story to connect sex with sin. Those are all misreadings of the story. So what would a true reading of the story say?

Let's go back to Joni Mitchell. Let's look at life, for a moment, from both sides now. On one side we have wonder and joy. We have myriad stars and galaxies in the universe. We have the minuscule miracle of microbes and minute organisms. We have expansive adventure, glorious beauty, spectacular vistas, fascinating details. On top of that we have human invention – technology, transport, music, art, sport, society. It never ends. On the other side we have three challenges. Challenge one is human fragility: resources run out, our bodies are limited, good things don't endure. Challenge two is evil: people sometimes genuinely mean each other harm, destroy rather than cultivate, pervert rather than enjoy. Challenge three is death: our lives end. It's baffling that there can be all this action, adventure, aliveness and animation, and it suddenly comes to a stop; but it does. The story of Genesis 2 and 3 is about what we do in the face of these three challenges. Forget the antiquated language and the misguided associations of this story. This story is even more relevant today than when it was written. Let's see how.

I want to look with you at the established strategies for dealing with the challenges of limitation, evil and death. I reckon there are three. They're all touched on in this story, and they're all very much alive today. I want to explore each of them with you. The first is knowledge. The whole quest for human knowledge is the seeking of a second opinion. We dwell in a mysterious and wondrous world: we want to find out for ourselves what makes it tick. Like investigative journalists, we're suspicious of conventional answers and stride around in long raincoats, jamming our foot in the door and scrutinizing company accounts to discover secrets not yet disclosed. Last summer I read a remarkable book about astrophysics that was full of claims about what physics has taught us about the origin, nature and destiny of the universe. But all I could think of was how little we still know about the things we most care about. The serpent tempts the woman and the man to eat of the tree of knowledge. They do eat. They do gain knowledge. But on the things that matter most, they're still in the dark.

Here's the second strategy: mastery. We use the expression 'control freak' to describe a person whose efforts to have everything in life under their command prove counterproductive: seeking to control antagonizes others, takes away the joy of surprise, and ultimately proves futile, because important things, like fragility, evil and death, can't finally be controlled, and other things, like love and laughter, are ruined by control. Consider the management-speak term 'futureproof'. Of course you should design projects so they don't become obsolete in a few years' time: but futureproofing promises more than that – it suggests control over the future, the removal of risk, surprise, accident, even luck. Everyone from a 2-year-old child to a 69-year-old Russian president is liable to throw a tantrum when they discover there are things they can't control. But the key to life doesn't lie in amassing more and more control: it lies in working out how to live when things aren't in your control. In this story God gives humanity the animals to be helpers and companions – but there's no mention of mastery over them or the earth. The attempt to dominate destroys not just nature but humanity: perhaps it's only in the age of the climate emergency that we're finally realizing that.

And here's the third strategy: escape. The story is about the false idea that humanity's freedom lies in escaping from God and ends with Adam and Eve departing the garden for a harsher, sadder life elsewhere. Norah Jones sang the words, 'Come away with me in the night.' She spoke of walking together on a cloudy day, through fields 'where the yellow grass grows knee-high.' It's a dream a lot of people had during the pandemic – to escape to a place where there was no sickness, no isolation, no fear; just for a few days, a day even. Our lives become ever more ones of escape – through an Xbox of perpetual gaming, through the fantasy our phone will bring excitement and diversion, through altering our consciousness, through movies or celebrity melodramas. But eventually we must return to the unfinished business we were trying to escape from; it doesn't go away, however far or fast we run.

At this point we need to acknowledge a sober truth. Christianity has often been used as a totalizing form of knowledge. It has frequently been employed as a form of mastery and control. It has repeatedly been treated as a method of escape. But this story doesn't commend any of these understandings of Christianity.

This story goes to the very heart of what faith is all about: trust. There's something more enduring than knowledge, more profound than control, more honest than escape: and that's trust. As this story shows, trust is the most challenging thing in the universe to establish and the easiest and quickest to destroy. But it's the most powerful thing in all creation. Have you ever seen high-flying acrobats in the circus? Letting go of their trapeze, 150 feet in the air, sometimes without a net, and gripping each other's wrists just when you thought they were bound to fall? Imagine the trust that takes. But trust makes other astonishing things possible. It's incredible that a 747 jet gets off the ground; but what's really extraordinary is that 500 people entrust their lives to the pilot. It's remarkable that a surgeon can correct a problem in the heart or the brain; but it couldn't happen if the patient didn't say, 'I trust you to hold my life in your hands.'

In this story God gives humanity purpose, permission and prohibition.

The purpose is this: care for the garden. The permission is this: you can do whatever you like. The prohibition is this: there's one tree you can't eat from. The story's a tragedy because, in the face of indescribable abundance, humanity focuses on scarcity. Granted the dazzling plenitude of the whole garden, humanity fixates on the one thing it can't have. It then, through its obsession with knowledge, mastery and escape, tries to make sufficiency out of that one tree.

But here's the good news. God takes that other precious tree, the tree of life. And God comes into the garden in Jesus. And Jesus climbs the tree of life, and from himself on that tree gives us abundant food, his body and blood, that feeds us abundantly for evermore. And when we gather at Christ's table, we enact our trust that God's abundance transforms our scarcity, that we will one day inhabit the garden of abundance with God forever.

In the meantime, our purpose is to live God's abundance and not shrink into our own scarcity. Every occasion when we realize our quest for knowledge is a displacement of our need for relationship, every time we admit our impulse to control is a poor substitute for trust, every moment we accept our tendency to seek escape is a diversion from our true walk of faith, we revisit this story and rediscover what it's really about. Fragility, evil and death are real and they circumscribe our lives. But because of this story, we need never let their threat of scarcity obscure God's overwhelming abundance. We realize that the only way to live is not through knowledge, mastery or escape – the strategies of scarcity – but through trust in God's abundance.

We've looked at life from both sides now. It's scarcity's illusions we recall. We trust instead in the everlasting abundance of God.

While this sermon contains a good deal of theoretical assertion – that our human project is directed toward knowledge, control and escape – its heart is in the wistful mood established at the beginning, by citing a very famous song that most listeners will know. The secret is to maintain this wistfulness throughout and demonstrate that God's abundance arises through that wistfulness, not as a giant escape from it. The term trust emerges as the alternative to the three doomed human strivings. Popular songs have an immense power to epitomize and sustain a mood or tone, and I use them quite often – twice in this sermon, in fact. Very occasionally, if a single line is salient in providing the hinge of the sermon by having two possible meanings, I'll sing that line. But that's not a device to be used often – no more than once or twice a year.

You can't go through Lent just saying it's tough but we'll find a way to get by, or even that it was tough for Jesus and we should follow him, suspending our questions of where and why. At some stage, you have to go to the heart of Christian theology and explore what the fundamental choice-points are; and sometimes that means acknowledging that profound mistakes go a long way back. At that point you can't just say there's a problem – you have to point out a more fruitful way. Which is a lot for one sermon. But when a passage is as significant for the tradition as Genesis 3, you owe it to your listeners to try.

7

Preaching at Easter

Like Christmas, there are two occasions for preaching at Easter. The most obvious is the Easter mid-morning celebration, which, along with Christmas, would normally provide the occasion for your two big sermons of the year. Like Christmas, there may well be a good number of new faces, so the emphasis has to be outward-facing and accessible.

But there are also contexts where a homily is required, notably an evening vigil on Holy Saturday or a dawn service on Easter morning. So in this chapter I offer one example of each.

Here are some guidelines for preaching at Easter.

1. However much you may wish your Easter congregation had been with you through the rigours of Holy Week, there are likely to be several, perhaps a majority, that haven't, so don't set up your whole sermon as a sequel to whatever you've said or done in the preceding days.
2. Few congregations are likely to be preoccupied with the precise details of how a dead body came alive, how grave clothes were folded, or how a stone rolled away. The point is, what does it mean? Likewise, if the Turin shroud were proved to be genuine, it wouldn't on its own mean anything; the preacher's job is to show how the resurrection of Jesus means everything.
3. There are broadly two approaches to Easter preaching: the first stays close to the circumstances of Jesus and Mary in the garden, or whichever gospel account you follow.
4. The second takes a wide canvas, perhaps as wide as Genesis to the maps – or creation to the last day, and going as deep as the collapse into oblivion or nothingness and as high as exaltation with God forever.
5. You need to make a choice whether you want to go with the traditional language of victory and conquest. That certainly sits with the ancient imagery of Christus victor. But it assumes a complex arrangement by which Jesus departs from his fully human character and takes on some other task, a tussle with death or the devil, which he wins off stage. That buys uncomfortably into a notion that Jesus comes among

us primarily to fix our human problem. Which makes his coming a detour in light of our scarcity rather than the fruit of God's eternal abundant purpose. Much better to find language that Jesus' resurrection demonstrates that God's purpose to be with us will not finally be thwarted, even by our death or our resistance to that purpose.
6. A homily, as ever, turns on a single idea. The best Easter sermons are extended homilies.

An Easter Day congregation is divided between the exhausted, who've laboured through the vigil of Maundy Thursday and the grief of Good Friday, and may have spent Holy Saturday cleaning the church or preparing flowers, and the carefree, who've skipped the rigours of Holy Week and have just shown up for the candy on Easter Day. An Easter Day sermon needs to speak to both. Which isn't so difficult when you recall that resurrection has no power if it doesn't come out of agony, but also more mundanely that any congregation on any Sunday will be a mixture of the joyful and the miserable, and every sermon needs to touch both realities.

This sermon conveys the feeling and theology of Easter as elementally as I know how.

Resurrection in nine words
John 20.11–18
1 April 2018

Resurrection is a breathtaking mystery. It's also the epicentre of the Christian faith. It's something to be discovered, believed and lived. It's an idle tale if it simply remains a technical event: if it's real, it's a cosmic transformation. It's not something to agree with in your head. It's not even something to believe in your heart. It's something to know in your gut. I want to walk you through what it means to know resurrection in your gut, know it so deeply that you're beyond historical exploration or existential anxiety. I want to show you resurrection in nine words: nine words that take us from despair to hope, from death to life, from darkness to light.

The first three words are all terrifying words. This is the first: gone. Mary Magdalene comes to the tomb on the first day of the week. And what does she find? The body of Jesus is gone. If ever insult was added to injury. That's the first sensation of bereavement, loss, grief: he's gone. Early one morning, my father came into my bedroom after several days of keeping vigil at my mother's bedside. And as soon as I heard his hand on the door, I knew what was coming, although I couldn't yet comprehend it. 'Samuel,' he said, very slowly. 'She's gone.' Gone. Gone where? Who knows. Gone away? Yes, although her body is there in the bed. Gone. It's so final, ultimate, irrevocable. So unyielding, uncompromising, ruthless. My mother was called Ruth. I remember thinking, looking at her lifeless body, that we were now Ruthless. Because we had no Ruth. You resort to humour like that because you can't take in the full reality. Gone. You don't get any choice in it, it happens by some outside force. Gone. Mary Magdalene feels that outside force. Jesus is gone. What an unforgiving word.

And then comes the second word: over. Once you've begun to apprehend the first word, this second word dawns on you. Over. You start to look back on all the things that once were but are no more. Mary recalls the tenderness of Jesus' voice. The way she felt when she was with him, like she didn't want the day to ever end, like this was a conversation that went to the heart of her soul. It's over. The way he walked, with that curious bend at the shoulder. The way his hair parted. The way he laughed. Over. No more laughter. Once it seemed the laughter would never stop, like a joke that kept on getting funnier every time you told it. She thought about the people whose lives he touched, the children he healed, the song he put in people's hearts. She remembered the times with the Twelve, when they all felt as close as a group of people can ever feel to one another, honest and faithful and courageous and true. Over. Over and gone. Lost and gone. Over and done. Do you stay in that place till the reality sinks in? Or do you ever really accept that reality? Mary stares into the darkness of the tomb. It's over. Jesus, and that whole Jesus thing, that turning the world upside-down together. Over.

But there's a third word that's even worse. Gone is about the present – he's not here. Over is about the past. It's finished. But there's an even more terrifying word that's about the future: never. Jesus was many things: but he made possible a whole lot more. Jesus said many things: but the things he made you think were even more amazing. Jesus did many things: but already he'd started to get people to do similar things and together they were set to do even greater things. But would those things take shape, be realized, come to pass? Never. If 'gone' takes the life out of a body and 'over' snatches the memories away, 'never' robs us of all hope. Never. It's like a boxing match where gone knocks the stuffing out of you, over brings you down to the canvas, and never goes beyond all mercy and kicks you out of the ring. 'It's not going to happen', says never. 'Whatever silver lining or small consolation you're holding onto, it's a fantasy.' Never. Brutal, cruel, final.

Those three words tell us where Mary Magdalene is at the beginning of our story. The fact that she's searching in vain for Jesus' body only makes her pathos more acute, more pitiful, more agonizing to watch. I wonder if you've ever wanted to stop a person doing something fruitless, like chase a ball into the water when you know it's already gone too far out to retrieve, or pursue a relationship that is never going to be mutual, or shake a dead body when there's not a shred of life to be retained – but you realize the person has to go through this pointless effort for a painful length of time until they can face the truth. That's where Mary is early on Easter morning.

But here's the fourth word. Here. It doesn't add up: Jesus is here. He's in front of her. It's like a scene from a pantomime. Her body is facing the tomb but her head turns behind her to Jesus. Then her body turns to Jesus but her head turns to the tomb. And her words are spoken in both directions, as if her head and body are going in opposite directions. It's supposed to be funny. Because how else to communicate the wonder of this moment? Here. Jesus is here. I though he was gone. But he's here.

And quickly there's another word: now. It's the central word of the nine words of resurrection. Now. Remember at the tomb of Lazarus, Martha said, 'I know that he will rise again in the resurrection on the last day.' But Jesus is saying, 'No – now. Not on the last day. Now. Here. Now. Not something you can postpone till you've thought about it. Not something you can tuck away and re-examine when you've recalled all your scepticism and misgivings. Now. What in the world could possibly be more important or take your gaze away from this moment: now. This is it.' Creation gave us life on earth. But that's a long time ago. On the last day we'll be given eternal life with God. But that's a long time away. This is now. This is creation and the last day all rolled into one. This is time collapsed into one moment, one man, one woman, in a garden, God in Christ, Israel in Mary, here, now. This is the whole Bible, the whole of eternity in one face-to-face encounter: now.

And here's the word that goes with here and now: new. Is anything really new? Even a tiny baby – surely it's just the recycled DNA of its parents? I remember my cynical philosophy professor saying, 'There's no such thing as originality: originality is just forgetting where you read it.' Is there anything so naive as a middle-aged couple starting out on a new relationship, convincing themselves that they won't make all the same mistakes as they did before? Is there really such a thing as new? Well, Mary discovers, yes, there is. A person who died in agony two days previously, standing utterly alive and thrillingly real, in front of her, with hands she can grasp and a face she can kiss. That's new. A world made new. A life made new. A dream made new. Oh yes. So true it makes you shake your head with incomprehension and wonder. Oh yes. This is new. For sure this is new.

That's what takes place when Mary meets the risen Jesus. Gone – over – never turn into here – now – new. It's the biggest transformation in world history. But there's more. Look at the last words in the story. Mary turns her own experience into a message to tell to the disciples: she knows straightaway that this isn't something strange that was about her, it's something astonishing that's about the whole world. And this is the first word of what happens as she tells her story: again. Feel the tremor that goes through your body when you recognize the force of that word: again. You thought it was gone, over, never. But it's again. That's the resurrection: it's both new and again. It's creation repeated and the last day anticipated: new and again. Like a hug with your best friend, like your favourite holiday destination, like the most exquisite dessert you know how to cook: new and again. The best two words in the language and even better together.

But there's another word: always. It ends up being the last thing Jesus says to the disciples: always. 'I'll be with you always.' It seemed each hope was blocked; now every single one is open: always. It seemed the truth was gone, over, never: but it's turned into always. Always and again. A repetition, but a non-identical repetition: everlasting and ever-new. This is now how it will always be. Death will no longer be the perpetual curse in every hope. Regret need no longer be the lingering poison in every memory. Always. Forgiveness isn't going to be withdrawn. Everlasting life isn't going to be curtailed. Read my lips, says Jesus to Mary and Mary to the disciples. Read my lips: always.

And there's only one word left, and maybe we've got so much resurrection we almost don't need it. But it's a crucial word because it takes the tiny episode of Mary meeting Jesus and puts it on a canvas that makes us realize this is the story of eternity, the story of God seeking humanity from before the beginning of time until the end of all things, the story of humanity finally seeking God in return. The word is forever. Mary's agony of gone, over, never is our insight into the grief of God at our indifference and inertia in the face of eternal love. Mary's agony, deep and crucifying as it is, lasts two nights: God's agony lasts as long as time. But there's something longer, wider and bigger than time: and that's forever. Mary sees the risen Jesus and she passes from time to forever. She discovers what is longer than everlasting, truer than always, beyond permanent. She's looking straight into the heart of forever.

You can't rationally explain grief. We're told it's better to have loved and lost than never to have loved at all. But here's what they don't tell you: only just. You can't rationally explain faith, except to say, it's the astonishing change, the wondrous hope, the indescribable peace that begins in your gut and spreads, perhaps slowly, to your head and your heart and your hands, when you realize the three terrible words, gone, over, never, have been engulfed by the six tremendous words, here, now, new, again, always, forever. We have a word for the moment that happens. We call it Easter. Happy Easter: here, now, new, again, always, forever.

Notice how much of this sermon is a balance between building trust with the listener and taking the listener beyond the conventional realm of discourse into profoundly personal, visceral, existential territory. The power of the sermon lies in the extent to which so much emotion can be crystallized into a single word. It's the ability of the preacher to coin a word that combines the drama and tragedy and transformation of the Easter story with the strongest and deepest experiences in the listener's life. By the end of the sermon, the listener should feel that these nine words not only cover all that matters in Christianity, but all that matters in the world and in the listener's own life.

The sermon wins the trust of the listener by its evident understanding of the depth of human experience and the profound emotions that go with it. No attempt is made to say, 'I recognize that the Church has often been cruel, manipulative, criminal and oppressive.' Instead, the preacher cuts through the hubbub of opinion, comment and chatter and gets straight into the real stuff of faith – the territory of gone, over, never, and their more positive companions here, now, new, again, always, forever.

The homily below seeks to retain the simplicity of the sermon above, but rather than go for the full emotional experience, uses gentle humour and intriguing paradox to make its point.

Letting go
John 20.11–18
4 April 2010

I began to learn classical Greek at the age of 12. I wish I could say it was out of devotion to reading the New Testament in its original language. But the truth is, it was part of a long, arduous, carefully orchestrated and ultimately successful campaign to avoid taking physics and chemistry. The first Greek word I learned was the first person singular present tense indicative verb *luo*. I quickly discovered it means 'I loose'. You learn it on day one of the Greek class because it's a short, regular verb that's easy to conjugate. It's a particularly useful verb for those who are in the habit of tying up oxen or releasing mules. Now, as a 12-year-old boy from a small town, I didn't have a lot of life experience to bring to sentences like 'I would have loosed the oxen' or 'They are going to loose the donkeys,' let alone 'I would have loosed,' 'I used to loose' and 'I was going to have loosed.'

But then comes the great day when you first pick up a copy of the New Testament in its original Greek. And then you enter a new world. You read the end of the raising of Lazarus story and, as Lazarus comes out of the tomb, Jesus says, 'Unbind him and let him go.' And we see this word *luo* means 'Unbind him.' Turns out it's useful for more than oxen. You read the sonorous words of Ephesians, 'He has broken down the dividing wall of hostility' and discover the word for 'broken down' is our little friend *luo*. You look at the description of Jesus in the book of Revelation and see 'Him who loves us and freed us from our sins by his blood' – there's *luo* again, freeing us from our sins. And in a passage from Acts often read on Easter Day, Peter says, 'God raised Jesus up, having freed him from death, because it was impossible for him to be held in its power' – and there is *luo* yet again, in the freeing from death.

So little *luo* gets to make an appearance at all of these and plenty of other moments in the New Testament. And what all these moments have in common is that each one of them paints a picture of resurrection. Resurrection is the defeat of death, the reconciling of hostile parties, the raising from the tomb, the healing of the sick, the restoration of the outcast and the forgiveness of sins. *Luo* starts off meaning loosing donkeys but ends up meaning all of these things.

And when we get to this most precious Easter moment of all, the meeting of Mary Magdalene with Jesus in the garden, this little and apparently insignificant word *luo* gives us a clue to one of the mysteries of the story. Why, when Mary finally recognizes Jesus, does Jesus say, 'Do not hold on to me' – or in the older translations, 'Do not cling to me' – or in the famous Latin translation, '*Noli me tangere*'? The answer lies in that little word *luo*. Because resurrection means letting go. Jesus looses us from the threat of death, Jesus looses us from sickness, exile, estrangement and sin. What his ambitions are for oxen and donkeys we never fully discover, but Jesus sure has a lot of use for that little word *luo*. Jesus is in the loosing business. That's the message of Easter. Jesus looses us, he makes us soar, he sets us free, he lets us run, he makes us fly, he lets us live, he sets us on our feet again.

And our response to the good news of Easter is to learn to let go. To let go of our own sin, in the first place. To permit God in Christ to forgive us and heal us. To allow ourselves to be defined not by the dreadful things we've done but by the wondrous things God has done. And in letting go of our own sin to let go of sins done to us. Not to cling on to resentment and bitterness, but to recognize how those who have hurt us have participated in a realm of damage that preceded them and will outlast them and is largely not of their making, and to make a fundamental choice to see ourselves not as a victim but as a child of grace.

And in letting go of our bitterness to let go of our life. Not to cling so tightly on to our life that all we can think about is how we keep it longer or extend it further, but to let go of our life so that we allow God to take it, use it, play with it and enjoy it wherever and however and for as long or as short as God wants to. And in letting go of our life to let go of one another's lives, that we face the loss and death of those we love not with the vice-like grip of possession and denial but with gentleness and gratitude and mercy and compassion. And part of that is about forgiving God for taking these precious people away from us.

Do not cling to me, says Jesus, because I have come to loose you – I have come to let you go. This is half of the good news of Easter. God looses us, forgives us and sets us free to live with him forever, unburdened by our hurts and failures in this life. But the other half of the good news of Easter is that God is wholly committed to us, to each one of us, to the whole creation, and that God keeps every promise to restore us to life and be our companion forever.

In the end, the good news of the Christian gospel lies in the paradox of that tiny word *luo*. On the one hand our deepest delight is that God sets us free. On the other hand our strongest hope is that God never lets us go. Today we find the strength to let go of all that stands between us and eternal life, content and elated in the good news that God never lets us go. God looses us; but never lets us go.

Like many homilies, this kids the listener by pretending to be about something idle, obscure and of little account – but gradually that tiny something becomes practically everything. Unlike most of the sermons in this book, it ends on a note of ambiguity. But it's a tantalizing and enticing ambiguity, consistent with the ambivalence of theology about how God both frees us yet remains our companion.

8

Preaching in Easter Season

Lent is a season of 40 days; Easter is a season of 50 days. Lent is miserable; Easter is joyful. But somehow, it's easier to keep up the solemnity of Lent through a whole season than the effervescence of Easter. That makes Easter the most challenging, yet the most important season for preaching.

The greatest help comes in the New Testament texts themselves. You can revert to the Acts reading if you like, but the collection of texts from Matthew, Luke and John that pepper the Easter season are worthy of the scrutiny that almost annual attention gives them. The reason the texts remain so compelling is that, as I discuss in the first sermon below, they're asking the same questions in the first century that we're asking today. Did it happen? Was it really physical? What difference does it make? These are among the most important questions in all Christian faith, so they deserve to be faced and addressed each year. And addressing them shouldn't be like Jacob wrestling with the angel – a lengthy struggle that ends as more or less a draw; it should be like going to the mountain top and seeing the Promised Land. Indeed, this is the secret of Easter preaching: your congregation starts like the disciples on the Emmaus Road, stood still, looking sad; it finishes like those same disciples realizing they felt their hearts on fire as Jesus talked with them and explained the Scriptures to them.

Easter is about transformation. At Christmas, God deeply meets us where we are; at Easter, God takes us from despair to joy. The Christian faith you're nurturing in your people needs both dimensions. One parishioner said to me on the way out of church one Easter morning, 'Where's the room for doubt?' (having just sung 'No more we doubt thee'). I said, 'It's Easter Day! We've got 51 other Sundays for doubt.' The sermons for Easter season can by all means start with doubt, but this is a season for reasoned and passionate articulation of the truth of resurrection and the difference it makes.

I'd call the following sermon a typical sermon for Easter season, because it looks methodically at the three main objections to the resurrection but frames them in a topical context – one that enriches the debate about resurrection and offers some new vocabulary to express it.

The new normal
Luke 24.36–48
18 April 2021

A year ago, on 1 April 2020, the African American poet and activist Sonya Renee Taylor wrote these words in an Instagram post.

> We will not go back to normal. Normal never was. Our pre-corona existence was never normal other than we normalized greed, inequity, exhaustion, depletion, extraction, disconnection, confusion, rage, hoarding, hate and lack. We should not long to return, my friends. We are being given the opportunity to stitch a new garment. One that fits all of humanity and nature.

No more than a week or two into the pandemic, Taylor had realized how deeply this experience was already shaking our sense of what constitutes normal.

I want to suggest to you that a year into the pandemic, we're perhaps better placed to think about Jesus' resurrection than at any time for a century or more. The reason is that there's scarcely a person in this country, let alone world, whose life hasn't been profoundly affected by the virus and its fallout. It's shaken our confidence about what we previously took for granted. From the perspective of April 2021, we can look back on the last century as a sustained effort to gain mastery over all the unpredictable and hitherto uncontrollable aspects of our natural environment, such that what we called normal became increasingly subject to our decision and definition.

See how that confident sense of being in control of the normal came to determine how we've come to read the story of Jesus' resurrection. 'Normal' comes to mean the way things turn out when I'm in control and things go according to my plan. It's a view that sincerely believes I'm the centre of the world, I'm the centre of history, everything's evaluated by how it fits in with my sense of my life. Let's look at the resurrection of Jesus through those lenses.

The straightforward approach is, it just didn't happen. Why? Because resurrection is something that can't happen. Can't happen biologically: the body's dead. Can't happen historically: never happened before or since. Anyone who calls Christians dogmatic hasn't spoken to many hardened atheists lately. So what's this story doing in Luke's Gospel, about Jesus appearing and eating fish? It's just made up, apparently. Even though it's remarkably similar to the story in John's Gospel, and it seems unlikely the one author knew the other? Yup. Like most dogmatism, this view needs a bit of imagination. So how do you account for the greatest evidence for Jesus' resurrection, that a group of dispirited disciples suddenly turned into a dynamic posse of evangelists changing hearts and changing the world? Wish fulfilment. They couldn't deal with Jesus' death, so they hallucinated or pretended he'd risen. Even to the point of martyrdom? Seriously? And generations after them, up to this day? I think we've got to do better than wish fulfilment.

Now, I'm not mocking the hard-line atheist position here. Because all of us, at some time, or most of the time, have looked at the resurrection stories and thought, 'How'd he do that?' Which is why so many Christians for so long have been open to having it both ways. By this I mean we get to keep our sense of the normal – people don't rise from the dead, silly – but we're happy to acknowledge that something special happened that Easter Day 2,000 years ago. Let's have a closer look at that statement, 'something special happened'. This is what leads to the assertion that Jesus rose spiritually. We usually think of this as coming out of a worldview that says, 'People back in those days didn't grasp science and history like we do, but they clearly felt Jesus with them in some way: it couldn't have been physical so it must have been spiritual.' Now take a look at the part of Luke chapter 24 we've just read together. Jesus says, 'Why do you doubt? Touch me. I'm not a ghost. What ghost has flesh and bones? Give me something to eat. Look at my hands. Look at my feet.' Here's the point of the story. Luke is writing a story precisely for the benefit of those who tend towards a spiritual view of Jesus' resurrection – to tell them they're wrong. Let's drop the superiority complex that says we're so much cleverer than those uneducated first-century disciples and that we get to control the sense of what's normal. This story shows us the same arguments were alive and kicking from the very beginning. Luke says Jesus isn't a spirit and Jesus isn't a body that wasn't really dead come back to life. He's physically resurrected. Luke rules out having it both ways. It's physical resurrection or no resurrection at all as far as he's concerned.

There's actually a third way to wriggle out of what Luke's telling us. We've talked about 'I'm telling you it didn't happen' and about 'I guess something happened, but only spiritually.' The third option is, 'Maybe it did happen; but it doesn't matter or make any difference.' This is the other argument Luke's account sets out to demolish. Let me walk you through how he does it.

Jesus refers to 'Everything written about me in the law, the prophets and the psalms' – what together we'd call the Old Testament – and how it's now been fulfilled. Now this needs a bit of explanation. The Old Testament centres on the covenant God makes with Moses on Mount Sinai. Everything before it, like the creation and the exodus from slavery in Egypt, prepares for it and everything afterwards, especially the entry into the Promised Land, the emergence of the kings and the building of the temple, derived from it. When Israel went into exile, they lost land, king and temple. When they returned two generations later, they got back the land and rebuilt the temple – but they didn't have their own king. So thereafter they were looking for a new king, the messiah, to restore the covenant with God and control over the land. The confusion over Jesus' crucifixion is that his followers took him to be this new king and were dismayed that he was so conclusively rejected and humiliated. So Jesus is teaching his disciples to reread the Scriptures: to recognize a God who suffers with, is rejected by, and yet is restored among the people. It's all there, but it requires Israel to read its story a different way. Jesus gives the Old Testament back to the disciples as a book they now realize was all about him.

Then Jesus says some more revolutionary words. 'Proclaim this to all nations.' We're so used to words like 'nations' in the Bible and in worship songs we miss the significance of what's going on here. Remember all that smiting that bothered you so much in the Old Testament? That was because Israel was a tiny nation surrounded by threatening neighbours. The nations were always on the point of destroying Israel, even a couple of chapters after being on the end of an old-fashioned massacre. Assyria and then Babylon smote big time, destroying the northern kingdom for good and casting the southern kingdom into exile. The nation of Rome was occupying the Holy Land as this conversation was taking place. The nations were scary, hostile and predatory. Jesus says this good news is for them too. That's almost inconceivable. The risen Jesus is asking the disciples to turn round thousands of years of history and create something beyond endemic enmity. Something called church. It's unthinkable.

But the coup de grâce is yet to come. I once witnessed a person come back from the dead. Not a resurrection miracle, but a feat of modern medicine. A parishioner took a huge overdose. Hours later he woke up, his stomach on fire. He was rushed to hospital. I held his hand as he lost consciousness. The next morning, I was called back to the hospital. I said, 'But he must be dead.' They said, 'We gave him a new liver.' I said, 'He's not going to like that.' I wasn't wrong. I was with him when he woke up. He was volcanic with rage. Think about when the disciples saw Jesus. Last time they'd seen him, they'd fled, denied or betrayed. They must have thought he'd be mad as hell. 'Errr, look, Jesus, about what happened in Gethsemane. I know it doesn't look good on the video...' What does Jesus say? 'Peace.' Now again, we're so used to the word 'peace' that we think it belongs to Woodstock, John Lennon and flower power. But see what the word means here. Jesus has been through the most significant event in universal history. The first thing he says afterwards has got to be pretty significant. 'Peace' isn't a way of saying, 'Here's a joint, take it easy, man.' It sums up everything Jesus has sought and achieved. And at the end what is the message he entrusts to his disciples to take to the nations? Forgiveness. Peace with God and neighbour. Peace be with you: now, be with each other. If I can, you can.

These are the ways Jesus demonstrates in this short episode the difference resurrection makes. Resurrection makes sense of the Bible. If God can raise Jesus from the dead, God can create the world, liberate the Hebrews, be in covenant with Moses, come among us in Christ, be with us forever. Resurrection turns enemies into fellow disciples. Jesus turns centuries of antagonism and slaughter into the promise of a future together. Resurrection embodies peace. Jesus restores those who deserted him: he offers each one of us a future bigger than our past.

So Luke's brief account of the appearance of Jesus to the disciples on Easter Day scuppers any attempt to assert our normal over God's normal, dismantles any effort to have it both ways and demolishes any bid to pretend the resurrection doesn't matter. There's only one option left to us. Let's say Jesus' resurrection really does matter – that it's actually the most important thing that ever happened. What then?

Again, the clue's in the story. Notice this line: 'While in their joy they were ... still wondering.' A lot of people at St Martin's over the last year have done the Being With course together. The main part of each session is responding to four wonderings. In the final session of the course one of the wonderings is this: 'I wonder, if you could change one thing about the world, what it would be.' In the course I was in last autumn, one of our beloved congregation members gave a response I'll never forget. She said, 'I'd abolish the whole notion of normal.' I sensed her comment came from a childhood of being regarded as different, and an adulthood devoted to helping those dismissed as different to discover true pride and belonging.

I was captivated by her idea of abolishing the normal. Until I read the words of Sonya Renee Taylor – 'We will not go back to normal. Normal never was. ... We are being given the opportunity to stitch a new garment.' And then I realized Taylor's words were not just about the pandemic. They were about the resurrection. The resurrection is God's invitation to enter a new normal. To set aside the old normal that says it couldn't happen or doesn't matter. To allow ourselves to be stitched by the Holy Spirit into a new garment. To allow our imaginations to be captivated by peace, our bodies transfigured by forgiveness, our whole beings somersaulted into joy.

Jesus comes among us and says, 'Don't be afraid. Touch me. Read the Scriptures with me. Wonder with me. Eat with me. Be sent by me. This is more real than anything you once thought was real. Welcome to the new normal. Welcome to resurrection.'

The difficulty when you're conveying a message your congregation already knows, and doing so several times over the course of six weeks, is in making that message vivid and thrilling. The simple rule is, if it's vivid and thrilling for you, it'll be so for your listeners; if it isn't, it won't be. So the real work is not in preparing a good sermon, but in immersing yourself in the imaginative world of resurrection – and perceiving its difference from the world around us. It's like passing from time to eternity. It requires naming your worst fears and allowing the Holy Spirit to transform them, one by one. It takes trust and hope; but the results are wonder and joy.

Here are some guidelines for preaching in Easter season.

1. Be more careful than usual about the use of stories to carry the sermon. It's hard for any story to come close to the wonder of Easter, and asking a personal or fictional narrative to bear so much weight risks reducing the resurrection, rather than amplifying it.
2. Let the gospel stories do the work. They're all sermons in themselves. They know our doubts; they share our confusion; they point to where the treasure lies.
3. The backdrop to almost any sermon in Easter season is that these are stories written by simple people from a primitive society, whereas we live in a sophisticated technological age of science; in short, we know better. A sermon can't just focus on the historical/scientific dimension – it has to engage with the emotional depth of the stories and the remarkable transformation brought about in the disciples.
4. The risen Lord is the crucified Lord: he bears the scars and shows the wounds. This isn't a matter of joy replacing sorrow, it's about joy outlasting sorrow. You don't want to be preaching sermons that make your grieving or hurting congregation members avoid church for this season because you're not touching on their distress. You need to incorporate that dimension of distress as you explore resurrection.

5. Don't ignore the Acts readings: after all, the obvious answer to the 'so what?' of Easter is church, and Acts is all about church. And some of those readings, for example Philip and the eunuch, are bursting with resonance for today.

The following sermon is more conventionally exegetical in style, but since the story is well known and easy to follow, it shouldn't be necessary for the listeners to be distracted by having to have the text in front of them. In a different way from the sermon above, it envelops the congregation's doubts and makes them the launchpad for the assertions the text suggests.

Making a meal of it
John 21.1–21
13 April 2022

Why does God make it so difficult? That's the question with which Thomas Aquinas starts his magisterial *Summa Theologiae*. Why doesn't God make it all clear to reason rather than resorting to revelation? Thomas says, if God relied on our reason, only the clever would get it, it would be hard work and there would be lots of mistakes. Jerome, the fourth-century translator of the Bible into Latin, said that God's self-revelation is 'a pool deep enough for scholars to swim in without ever touching the bottom and yet shallow enough for children to paddle in without ever drowning.' And the seventeenth-century French polymath Blaise Pascal said, 'In faith there is enough light for those who want to see, and enough shadow to blind those who don't.'

The account of the disciples' fishing expedition in John chapter 21 is a story of how revelation works, in discipleship, ministry and mission.

The disciples say to themselves, the resurrection is all very well, but surely it's time for food. They go fishing. There's a sadness about this trip; they're not with Jesus, as on many boat trips before and there's not many disciples left – only seven in fact. Bit of a survivors' photo. But seven is always an important number in the Bible. Seven is going to be enough. And the named disciples – Peter, Thomas and Nathanael – are precisely the three who have previous experience of having doubt transformed by Jesus: Peter denied, Thomas wanted physical proof, Nathanael thought nothing good could come out of Galilee. Touchingly, all the disciples with one accord say to Peter, 'We're going with you.' The church has always had a cult of charismatic leaders. But look here: Peter's a charismatic leader who leads his people to failure. Nothing. In John 15, Jesus says, 'Without me you can do nothing.' And lo and behold, nothing is precisely what the disciples, under Peter's visionary leadership, achieve all night. Night tends to be a bad time in John. But failure becomes the moment of revelation. Remember that: failure isn't a sign that you're pathetic or that God hasn't blessed you. Failure is the moment of revelation: the moment you live God's dream, not your own.

It's fair to say the disciples are not the sharpest knives in the carving set. Jesus is on the shore, but they don't recognize him. Now the church tends to regard Jesus as either the perpetual judge or the source of utter affirmation. He doesn't say, 'You shouldn't be fishing,' nor does he say, 'On you go.' He says, 'Make one change: cast your net on the other side.' Well it works, big time. Way too many fish: 153 – maybe telling the early church that if Israel wasn't nibbling, try the nations. You're not useless; but it's obviously not working. No need for a new boat or new nets or new disciples. Make one change. Just a suggestion. That one change could change everything. It could be a revelation.

Now the Beloved Disciple says, 'It is the Lord!' Notice how we're not told whether the Beloved Disciple recognized Jesus on the shore or realized that the miracle could only have one cause. We constantly say, 'If I could just see Jesus, I'd get it.' Or, 'If I could just have a sign, I'd follow.' But look – in this story Peter does see Jesus and he does experience a miraculous sign – but he *still* doesn't get it. It's just like Easter morning. Peter enters the empty tomb, rummages among the grave clothes and yet is bewildered. The Beloved Disciple gets it. All the light for those who want to see, but enough shadow for those who don't or can't or won't.

Then Peter wraps a cloak around himself and dives into the sea. There are two things going on here. A naked man in the water obviously refers to baptism and takes us back to John chapter 1. But wrapping a towel around yourself takes us back to foot washing in John chapter 13. Foot washing and baptism are the two ways disciples in John are prepared for service. In different ways they're forms of death: baptism once and for all, foot washing regularly. Here they combine.

By now it's dawning on us that John chapter 21 is like a highlights package of the whole gospel. Just think – fish, sea, miracle, recognizing Jesus: if you're paying attention you realize we're back in John chapter 6, where all these things appear, and once Jesus turns out to have some bread ready for breakfast, we've got the full set, and we're clearly back in feeding of the 5,000 territory – another occasion when there was way more food than was needed. We're back to the place we started and we're recognizing it for the first time. That's revelation: when you come back to something or someone or somewhere and this time realize what, who or where they really are.

Take yourself back to chapter 18, where Peter warms himself by a charcoal fire before betraying Jesus three times. Imagine what Peter's thinking. He must get an almost allergic reaction to seeing a charcoal fire again. He's just had his biggest ever success as a fisherman and Jesus is straightaway taking him back to his place of failure. Each of us have a charcoal fire: something whose texture, smell and sound instantly reminds us of something horrendous, something miserable, something that makes us nervous and guilty and distraught. Jesus knows what that thing is for Peter, but Jesus turns that thing into good: a source of food and warmth for God's people. That's what our greatest sins are for: they're waiting to be turned into instruments of God's blessing.

Then Jesus takes the bread and gives it. I don't think I need to help you with that one. It's the penny-drop moment: it makes us realize that the whole of this scene has been a Eucharist. We gather together – seven, 70 or 700. We face our failure, whether our efforts were malign or just pathetic. We hear Jesus' words, which turn our scarcity into God's abundance. We respond in faith. We share food. And look at the next words – they're about Jesus' appearance to the disciples. We look across to Luke's Gospel, and its account of Jesus' appearance to the disciples at Emmaus, and we could simply copy and paste Luke's words – 'and he was made known to them in the breaking of the bread.' Revelation in failure: confession. Revelation in Jesus' words: readings and sermon. Revelation in baptism. Revelation in forgiveness: the peace. Revelation in the breaking of the bread: communion. Look in verse 10: there's even an offertory procession when the disciples bring Jesus some of the fish they've caught. There's probably notices and coffee if you look hard enough.

But we're not done yet. Jesus isn't done yet. The meal isn't the end of the Eucharist. There's some commissioning to do after breakfast. Just as we've discovered what mission, meeting God in the world, is about, through failure and God's activity beyond our comprehension, so we're about to find out what ministry, meeting God in one another, is about. This is one of the most poignant, truthful and human scenes in the gospels. Peter denied Jesus three times at a charcoal fire. Here he gets three chances to put things right. The key to the conversation is the difference between *philein*, to cherish, and *agapein*, to lay down one's life. Different kinds of love. Peter seems not to grasp the difference.

Jesus says, 'Peter, will you lay down your life for me?' Peter replies, 'You know that I cherish you.' Jesus says, 'Peter, will you lay down your life for me?' Peter says, 'You know that I cherish you.' Jesus says, 'Peter, do you cherish me?' Peter is exasperated that Jesus needs to ask a third time and reacts as if Jesus has mistrusted him. How could Jesus ever do that? Has Peter ever let him down? ... Then Peter replies, 'You know that I cherish you.' The irony is overwhelming. Peter thinks he's given the right answer. He's hurt that Jesus needs to ask. He's said he cherishes Jesus, which proved insufficient at the first charcoal fire, but what he hasn't said is that he'll lay down his life for Jesus, which is precisely what he didn't do first time round. And agonizingly he doesn't even realize what he hasn't said. The fact that he can't find the right word shows he hasn't learned his lesson. Why get so exercised over one little word? Sometimes one word is the wafer that contains the universe – or the mouthful that poisons the whole meal.

Can we ever trust and rely on a person again when they've not only let us down but haven't even learned their lesson? Turns out Jesus does. He does love, even though he knows. He works with what Peter's giving him, not what he'd like Peter to be giving him. He gives Peter his marching orders. 'Tend and feed my flock.' Remember Jesus isn't just the good shepherd. He's the lamb of God. Whenever a priest is called to a flock, that priest is not just called to imitate the shepherd – but to realize that one of the sheep will turn out to be Jesus. That's the fun of ministry: finding out which one. And then the final twist. Peter, who can't find the words to say, 'I'll lay down my life for you,' learns that he's going to lay his life down anyway, even if he tries to wriggle out a second time. Sometimes your finest moments in discipleship come when you don't realize what you're doing.

So here's discipleship. Discipleship isn't devoted following of Jesus: it's making pitiful misunderstandings and offering painfully inadequate responses and finding Jesus uses us anyway. And here's ministry. Ministry is discovering you're a flawed half-reconciled failure but, rather than indulgently pondering your inadequacy, instead getting on with offering food and oversight, since that's what Jesus has called you to do, and dwelling in the shadows of half-reconciliation and tentative discipleship; and somehow making a meal of it. And here's mission. Mission is working all night because you know you're God's gift to fishing and having nothing to show for it; and then having the faint streak of humility to take one piece of advice and finding the superabundance of God's glory all falling in your lap when you'd done nothing to achieve it.

And at this point we realize that this fishing story isn't just the shape of the Eucharist – it's the shape of the whole gospel. Jesus is with us. We try to survive on our own strength. We fail. Jesus appears to us. We don't recognize him. Jesus speaks to us. His words give abundant life. Jesus shares food with us. Jesus calls us to reconciliation. We half get it. Jesus points a way through suffering to glory. We fancy a different way. But in the end, he says, 'You're coming with me.'

This is John 21. You can skip the other chapters. The whole gospel, baptism and Eucharist, discipleship, ministry and mission, word and sacrament: it's all here. Swim in it without ever touching the bottom. Paddle in it without ever drowning. It's the dawn of faith. There's enough light for you to see. Just enough.

This sermon includes several of my favourite techniques. It's comprehensive: it demonstrates the shape of the Eucharist and goes on to reveal the shape of the whole gospel. In between, it offers a summary of discipleship, ministry and mission – being with God, the church and the world. It reincorporates: it begins with quotations from Jerome and Pascal and returns to them, now with new meaning, at the end. It highlights one simple takeaway – what's the one thing you could do differently – for those who like a direct application on which to reflect. It addresses the surface level of the story but sheds light on the rhetorical and intertextual power of the story. (By intertextual I mean the way this story amplifies and is amplified by other parts of the Scripture.) It has humour, but that humour comes by letting the story speak, rather than as an imposition or distraction. It leaves the listener feeling satisfied, inspired and understood.

Preaching is in some ways an artificial relationship. You talk to people through the week, in formal meeting, casual banter, quick correspondence, or heartfelt disclosure. Then for ten or 15 minutes you stand up and you talk non-stop without pausing for permission or checking for understanding. Since it's a construction, you can make the most of the role you're called to take up and step a little out of character and become a person who's just discovered the New Testament, who's astonished by its claims and who's overjoyed to share this startling news with your people. You don't cease to be a person of compassion and care, thoughtfulness and trained pastoral discipline. But each time you rise to preach, you also become a person who's beside themselves to tell your congregation something world-changing, life-changing, awesome and urgent. And never more so than when announcing what Easter is really about.

I include the sermon below because it's so much fun. Sometimes it's good to break out of your customary style and say something differently – and Easter is the best-of-all time to do this.

The Fingersmith
Luke 24.13–35
30 April 2017

Most of the stories of Jesus' resurrection are pretty untidy. There seem to be bits left out, or non sequiturs, or sudden disappearances where a clear record should be. The story of Jesus' appearance on the road to Emmaus is different. It's perfectly crafted. It begins with two isolated disciples discouraged and disconsolate on the road; it ends with the eleven disciples joyful and united in the upper room. It beautifully allows the two disciples to set out all the pieces of the jigsaw – the mighty words and deeds of the prophet, his shattering death, their longing for him to redeem the nation, and the confusing reports of the empty tomb and the news of the angels – before Jesus himself fits all those jigsaw pieces together by connecting his prophecy with his suffering, his own story with the Old Testament story, and his resurrection as the final completion of the picture.

The Emmaus story deftly and satisfyingly sets the word of Jesus' explanation alongside the sacrament of his taking, blessing, breaking and sharing the bread and then sees both as empowering the two disciples to be sent forth in mission as witnesses to God's glory. The account provides a mini gospel narrative: Jesus coming alongside us, being doubted, demonstrating his identity, being recognized and departing. The narrative provides a whole story of discipleship: from sorrow at the start, to sarcasm as the conversation begins, humiliation as the disciples are told how foolish they are, devotion as they urge Jesus to remain with them, hospitality as they share a meal, incandescent inspiration as they realize how their hearts were on fire, to headlong haste as they scuttle back to Jerusalem and untold joy as they share the good news. And the story depicts a straightforward model of church: meeting Jesus, understanding Scripture, recognizing God in suffering, joining communion, experiencing Easter, sharing faith. What Emmaus depicts about one Sunday, the church embodies every Sunday.

So the Emmaus story is about resurrection, revelation and response. But more than anything else, this story is about recognition. The power of the story resides in the profound irony that Jesus was walking with them, but they didn't know that it was Jesus. It makes you look rather more closely at everyone – at friends and strangers, at family members and people you scarcely know.

In one of Roald Dahl's short stories, the narrator has just bought a stylish and shiny BMW and is driving it up to London. He stops to pick up a hitchhiker. The hitchhiker looks like a rat and has grey teeth. Just like a rat, he has dark, quick, clever eyes and pointy ears. He's wearing a cloth cap, his jacket has vast pockets. Getting no answers to his questions, the narrator says he's a writer. His guest says he likes a trade that involves skill, because to get on in life you have to become proficient at something very difficult. Then, goaded by his guest, the narrator takes his brand-new BMW up to its maximum 129mph. But at that point he's mortified to hear the siren of a police car. Once the police motorbike has stopped, things don't go well. The policeman sidles up to the BMW as if preparing the driver for his execution.

The policeman lets his prey toast in the boiling oil he's cooked up for himself. Once he's recorded all the relevant details, he turns his attention to the passenger, whom he proposes to call as a witness. He asks the passenger his job, but the ratty-faced man lies and says his job is to carry cement up ladders, but that he's currently out of work.

The policeman concludes his enquiries in triumph. He's clearly looking forward to seeing the narrator in court and getting him locked up for a good stretch. After the police officer has gone, the narrator resumes the conversation with his passenger and asks why he lied to the policeman. The passenger equivocates. Then the narrator notices his passenger rolling himself a cigarette – an operation the man performs with incredible speed and dexterity. The hitchhiker highlights his extraordinary fingers, which he holds up and says are more agile than those of the finest pianist.

Then the story takes on a different shape. The hitchhiker holds up a leather belt and asks if the narrator recognizes it. With horror the narrator realizes it's his. He feels around the top of his trousers and discovers his belt is gone. In no time the narrator realizes his shoelaces, his watch, his driver's licence, a key ring with four keys on it, some pound notes, a few coins, a letter from his publishers, his diary, a stubby old pencil, a cigarette lighter and last of all, a beautiful old sapphire ring with pearls around it belonging to his wife – every single one of them begins to emerge like a string of sausages from the voluminous pocket of his passenger.

The narrator unmasks his passenger as a pickpocket. But the hitchhiker disagrees. He describes himself as a fingersmith. He says the words proudly, as if he were announcing he was the Archbishop of Canterbury. He warns the narrator he could remove his false teeth if he wanted to. The narrator retorts that he doesn't have false teeth. But the fingersmith is a step ahead: he replies that if he had they'd have been removed some time ago.

But then the fingersmith pulls off the coup de grâce. He triumphantly holds up the policeman's notebooks – and chuckles while saying he's never done an easier job. The narrator is in awe and shares his gratitude. 'It's always nice to be appreciated,' replies the fingersmith.

Like the Emmaus story, the story of the hitchhiker is one of recognition. Initially, the narrator's mind is intrigued by this ratty-faced man with grey teeth, whose eyes are dark and quick and clever, whose ears are slightly pointed at the top and whose jacket has enormous pockets. But when the police officer gets involved, it's no longer just an arm's-length mind-game. The narrator's heart is thumping as he faces loss of licence, loss of reputation, loss of money and quite possibly loss of liberty. The hitchhiker turns out to be his saviour, and the narrator's eyes are opened, and he recognizes a true fingersmith, who transforms everything when he produces the police officer's two pocketbooks, containing all the evidence against him.

Think about those three stages of recognition, because they're exactly the same three stages the disciples go through on the road to Emmaus. The first is about having an open mind. The disciples have to be cajoled into having an open mind – Jesus is pretty blunt with them and calls them fools. But perhaps the crucial thing is that Jesus hears them out. He doesn't interrupt them or say he knows what they're thinking. He stays tuned to the end of what they have to say. Then he tells the same story back to them in a revealing way.

The second dimension is having an open heart. 'Were not our hearts burning within us?' the two disciples say to one another. There's a difference between having an open mind and having an open heart. You can have one without the other. It's interesting the disciples only realize their burning hearts in retrospect. They're on edge. They could be in danger. They've been badly hurt. Their hearts are tender and protected. They thought they were just opening their minds. But it's gone beyond that.

And then, finally and conclusively, they have open eyes. I wonder whether their eyes really could have been opened without their minds and their hearts being opened first. So many research studies find that we see what we're looking to see. Because the two disciples could not comprehend their companion being Jesus, their eyes refused to see him beside them. The conversation and the meal together changed their heads and hearts, and only then could they see the nail marks in the hands of the one who broke bread and the face of the one who was crucified – their risen Lord.

Open minds, open hearts, open eyes. Three stages of resurrection faith. I wonder which is the important one for you. Maybe you struggle with information overload and it's hard to keep an open mind, to discover new things. Perhaps you've been deeply hurt, and you're reluctant to let your heart be open to burn with hope again. Or possibly there's truth or love or life staring you in the face and for some reason you just can't see it.

But the resurrection is this. Christ the fingersmith has stolen your thoughts, your feelings and your sight, and you can't get them back until you open your mind and heart and eyes to him. And when you do, you will no longer stand still, looking sad, but will feel your heart burning within you as he opens up his life to you.

I've changed the sermon from the original by turning almost all the direct quotations in the story to reported speech, to make it possible to publish. But what the sermon shows is that a light touch, an ear for humour, and a compelling conclusion can make for a memorable liturgical event.

9

Preaching at Ascension and Pentecost

Ascension and Pentecost actually refer to three moments, all distinct from one another. The first is joyful, if somewhat two-edged. The disciples say farewell to Jesus and Jesus returns to heaven. The second is bleak: the Sunday after Ascension is a neglected moment in the liturgical calendar when we can reflect on what it's like to feel Jesus has gone, but the Spirit has not yet come. It's a unique moment of isolation and sensing a deep aloneness. Then Pentecost is a festival of great joy, tempered by only one, rather incorrigible, thing: the fact that the church has often been such a poor – sometimes criminally woeful – witness to the coming of the Spirit on the fragile disciples.

The reason Ascension is two-edged is that while it marks the completion of Jesus' ministry among us, and is therefore an occasion for celebration, it must have been a second bereavement for the disciples, having lost him in the most agonizing way imaginable, then having received him back, to lose him again, albeit in less painful circumstances. Ascension is two-edged today because it's officially one of the four great festivals of the liturgical year but is so associated with the more far-fetched dimensions of the pre-modern world-view (a human body levitating up to a sky perceived to be identical with heaven), and more prosaically, it falls on a Thursday, that perhaps the majority of churchgoers ignore it altogether.

As for the Thursday, however much you may encourage your flock to be with you for a midweek festival, there's little you can do about it. You can say, 'You seem to manage it at Christmas, so why not at Ascension?' but be careful lest you show your ignorance of the dates of bank holidays, and even more so lest your people take the point and stop coming at Christmas. It leaves you with a straight choice on the Sunday after Ascension: either you simply transfer the celebration of Ascension to the Sunday, which is the pragmatic solution (after all, Luke's dating of 40 days cannot have been more than an estimate), or you ignore Ascension in favour of a searching examination of what it feels like to be without God, between Jesus' departure and the Spirit's arrival, and what to do about it. Both themes are hugely fruitful. I would recommend doing the former two years in three and the latter one year in three.

The sermon below touches on the modern problem of the notion of Jesus disappearing into the cloud. It suggests this is too small an issue to focus on, when there are much more significant dimensions of the story – and doctrine – to dwell on. It's a theologically rich sermon that might not be a good fit for all the congregations I've served. But all the congregations I've served have needed to get a sense of what the Ascension really means and why it became one of the four great festivals in the first place.

Reaching out
Luke 24.44–53
29 May 2022

When you move to a new part of the country, or to a new English-speaking country, there are always expressions you've never really been aware of that you first have to understand and eventually fetch up using. When I lived in Liverpool I was baffled by the expression 'made up' until eventually I realized it meant 'really happy'. In Newcastle, 'Why aye pet' is so much more vivid than just saying, 'Yes'. After four years on Tyneside, I didn't want to say 'Amen' at the end of the creed – I wanted to say, 'Why aye pet.' In the American South there's the term 'y'all' which means 'you' (plural) and is so useful I still find myself saying it and more often writing it. But one ubiquitous American expression I never got used to was the phrase 'reach out'.

'Reach out' isn't what it appears. It sounds like a dramatic movie moment in a storm, where the ship's sinking and, before the prow slips under the waves, a passenger reaches out from a lifeboat to rescue an escapee. But it's far more prosaic than that. If you had a meeting with someone a week ago and they promised to sort out a few things afterwards but you haven't heard from them and you send an email politely enquiring why not, you'll get a reply that starts 'Thank you for reaching out,' which is a customary way to acknowledge your message while quite possibly masking a passive aggressive way to say, 'I'll get to this in my own time, if you don't mind, and there's no need to rush me.'

'Reach out' began to be used in America from the seventies, after the Four Tops sang 'Reach out and touch' promising, 'I'll be there with the love that'll see you through.' Now it's become widespread as a synonym for 'make contact'. Those who loathe the expression and would prefer to say, 'Thank you for contacting me,' have to reckon with the fact that 'contact' only became a verb around a hundred years ago, having previously been simply a noun. That's how language evolves.

I want to reflect on this phrase in the light of Jesus' Ascension, which we celebrated on Thursday. Traditionally, Ascension is one of the four great festivals, along with Christmas, Easter and Pentecost. But it's become the poor relation. Why? Because two of the gospels don't mention it, while one only just does; because the accounts in Luke and Acts are short and the accounts don't agree on whether resurrection and ascension were on the same day or 40 days apart; because it's not clear why it matters; and perhaps most of all because the idea of Jesus being taken up into a cloud seems fanciful.

It helps a little if you realize that Elijah was taken up into a cloud and a double portion of his spirit fell upon Elisha, so Luke's story is clearly echoing this tradition when Jesus is taken on high and the Holy Spirit falls on the disciples. And it helps if you realize that 'cloud' is a way of saying 'God' – as when a voice speaks from the cloud at Jesus' baptism and transfiguration. But I think the real issue in our difficulty comprehending Jesus' Ascension is much more profound.

The real issue is that we tell the story of God and us the wrong way round. We assume the story is all about us and we're the centre of the story. The story goes something like this. Humanity was put at the centre of all things. We messed up. God called Israel to be the people with whom God brought salvation to the world. When that project faltered, God sent Jesus to deal with sin and death and bring forgiveness and everlasting life. Jesus sent the Spirit to be his permanent presence on earth to spread the gospel until the last day – when God will finally take sin, death, evil and suffering out of the picture forever.

In this version of the story, the Ascension doesn't have much of a place. It does answer the question of where Jesus went after the resurrection. But the real point is that, if Jesus came to save us by dying and rising, once that's done, tying up loose ends is neither here nor there. It hardly qualifies for a major festival.

But just look what happens when we turn the story round. Here's the story from God's point of view. God dwelt in the glory of eternity, utterly sufficient in three-personed unity. Out of fathomless love, God resolved to be defined by relationship: not just the inner relationship of the three persons with one another, but outer relationship. Humankind is the name for the partner in that relationship. God's life was shaped to be in relationship with humankind, first by Jesus being both fully of God and fully of humankind, and second by the creation of the universe as the setting for that relationship. Israel was chosen as the people amongst whom God was to come among us in Christ.

What we then get are two sets of key moments. I want you to imagine a pair of square brackets inside a pair of curved brackets. The first outer, curved bracket at the beginning of time is God's original decision never to be just content with the inner relations of the Trinity, but to resolve to be in relationship with a partner – humankind. The final outer curved bracket at the very end of time is the moment God turns that relationship from one with all the contingency and flaws and suffering and fragilities of being in time into a relationship that's forever: a moment we call heaven.

But inside those two curved brackets is a pair of square brackets. The opening square bracket is Christmas. Christmas isn't just the nativity of Jesus, it's the whole story of the coming of Jesus, most obviously the annunciation to Mary, which is how we describe Jesus' conception. This is the moment Jesus' earthly life, the full relationship between God and humankind for which the universe was created, begins. The closing square bracket is Jesus' Ascension. This is the moment Jesus' earthly life ends. In other words, Ascension is the flipside of Christmas – two ends of the same rope, as it were. And in the middle, between all those brackets, is the epicentre of God's story: Jesus' crucifixion and resurrection. The crucifixion plays out the logic of the first two brackets, that being with us whatever happened would stretch God's character and love and commitment to the very ultimate. The resurrection anticipates the logic of the last two brackets, that nothing can separate God from God, which we see played out in Christ's Ascension, and that nothing can separate us from God, which we see confirmed on the last day and the entry-point to heaven. That's what it means to see Good Friday and Easter Day as a microcosm of the whole history of everything.

In this version of the story, the Ascension is no longer just a quaint description of the conclusion of Jesus' ministry. It's one of the handful of key moments in the whole drama. Let's go back to the notion of reaching out. The reason 'reach out' is such an irritating phrase is because it sounds dramatic and magnanimous, but it's actually become mundane and commonplace. But if we restore the idea of reaching out as compelling and captivating, then we can see more precisely how together, Christmas and Ascension are exactly that – reaching out.

Imagine an ocean liner floating happily just a foot or two away from the quayside. The quayside, dry land, is like heaven, the state of being utterly permeated by God's eternal grace; the ocean liner is the universe – more precisely the earth. At Christmas, God's longing to be in relationship with us means God reaches out and, in Christ, becomes a true passenger on the ocean liner – still utterly God, but now fully dwelling on the liner, fully inhabited in humanity. Then at Ascension, humanity reaches out to heaven. Humanity reaches out from the ocean liner of timebound existence into the forever of God's eternal essence.

But here's the crucial part. At Christmas, because Christ is fully divine, we can trust that the whole character and heart of God is wrapped up in Jesus being among us. Jesus isn't a parcel delivery van, sent to drop off a gift called salvation then skedaddle back to heaven. Jesus is God completely invested in relationship with us, without reserve. Now, look what happens at Ascension: because Christ is fully human, we see that he represents and embodies every single one of us, every person that ever lived and ever will. When he reaches out to heaven and is embraced into the whole of the Trinity, *we are too*. Christmas means God forever belongs with us. *Ascension means we forever belong with God.* Christmas is God in Christ reaching out to us. *Ascension is us in Christ reaching out to God.* At Christmas, Jesus embarks on the central definitive embodiment of God's indelible relationship with us. At Ascension, Jesus *dis*embarks from that definitive moment and *brings us with him into the heart of God*. We could even say Ascension is more important than Christmas, because God being with us isn't much good if God sinks into the human predicament and never gets out. But at Ascension, we discover that God takes us up into forever and that changes everything – and I mean, *everything*.

Perhaps we shouldn't be so hard on the term 'reach out', even if it's just a florid way of saying 'contact'. Because 'contact' is a simple way of saying maintain or keep a relationship alive, and the good news of Christianity is that relationship, which starts in God and is extended to us and then embraces all creation, is what the whole of essence and existence are all about. And 'reach out' is a reminder that relationship sooner or later involves effort, challenge, courage, sacrifice and trust. Reaching out is a costly, risky form of contact. So every time we hear someone use the phrase 'reach out', rather than get irritated with the exaggeration and embellishment, we can be renewed in recognizing the dynamic heart of our faith.

And this is our faith, in two simple sentences. At Christmas the whole of God reached out into unbreakable and eternal relationship with us, whatever the cost to God; and at Ascension, the whole of humanity and all creation reached out into unbreakable and eternal relationship with God, whatever the reluctance from us. Why aye pet.

The theological work done by this sermon is hugely important, and challenging not just conceptually for the congregation, but in its implications for the whole of Christian theology. I have one friend whose standard sermon, albeit one first shaped among American young people, is, 'Get over yourself.' But the message of this sermon isn't so different: it's saying that theology has actually too often been anthropology – focused on humankind and its attempt to break out of its predicament – rather than genuine theology – about God and told from God's point of view. So rather than see Ascension Day as something to be a bit sheepish about, this sermon comes close to saying that it's the day that contains all the other great days of the year.

Here are some guidelines for preaching at Ascension and Pentecost.

1. Don't make jokes about a body disappearing out of the top of the painting with only the ankles and feet left visible. Humour can be a sign of embarrassment and your job as a preacher is to show the significance of Christ's Ascension, not to ridicule it. In this situation, humour is most likely a sign of your discomfort with the subject matter.
2. Get a sense of the shape of Christ's story. Ascension is the other half of Christmas. At Christmas he came down; at Ascension he went up. If we rejoice in the beginning of the story, we must recognize that the story must end in some way like this. But both the beginning and ending are part of a larger story – that of God's eternal choice not to be without us, and God's final act in fulfilling that choice eternally.
3. Preach both the joy of Ascension and the grief of the Sunday after Ascension – but not in the same sermon. The grief sermon is a day to uphold stubbornness, resilience, endurance, indomitability – but also to comprehend sadness, bereavement, confusion and despair. It's also an interesting day to reflect on retirement and in what sense Jesus retired.
4. The great theological question raised by the Ascension is not about levitation, but about why, if Jesus returned to heaven when he'd finished, is there so much still wrong with the world? This would make a good theme for a Sunday after Ascension sermon. (I try to address it in the second chapter of my book, *Humbler Faith, Bigger God*.)
5. Pentecost is an occasion when preaching a sermon closely tied to the text is likely to miss the full weight of the occasion. The story in Acts 2 is about a single time and place; Pentecost is really about every time and place. Your sermon really needs to be about either the work of the Holy Spirit in general or about the church.
6. The Holy Spirit is perhaps the most popularly misunderstood of all the principal doctrines of the church. I find John Calvin's description of the characteristic of the Holy Spirit the most succinct and helpful way of communicating what the Holy Spirit is and does – to make Christ present, given that Christ is human and in one place at a time, whereas the Spirit is not human and can be everywhere. I usually include some phrase along these lines in every Pentecost sermon.

7. Perhaps the most compelling Pentecost sermon is a vivid account of the work of the Holy Spirit today, in the church and beyond. There's nothing better than thrilling examples of how the Holy Spirit makes Christ present in familiar and unexpected settings. It deeply affirms a congregation that feels marginal and people the world ignores as the key setting for God's blessing.
8. Any account of the church in a Pentecost sermon must acknowledge a) that it is profoundly flawed and human in the most negative sense – and one should name some of its worst crimes, including the terrible harm its representatives have done to children – yet b) the fact that it is infused with the Holy Spirit and remains the principal and definitive channel through which God acts in the world. This is a tough task, but very necessary. Some congregation members deal with the church's failures by saying, 'That could never happen here' – a view that needs challenging on the grounds both of humility and realism. Others deal with the church's failure by internalizing faith and keeping church at arm's length. For these people, the message is, 'We need you.'
9. The simple message of Pentecost, which is worth repeating every year, is that the church started with 12 fearful people in a locked room, but the Holy Spirit changed the world through them. The Holy Spirit can change the world through us, even if we're 12 people in a cold and empty church.

The sermon below tries to bear these guidelines about Pentecost in mind. Like the Ascension sermon above, it starts with some unthreatening territory, in this case a TV show, before using the analogy of the ingredients of a meal, as a way of talking about what it takes to be church. One of the subtle messages of the sermon is that church is a verb and not just a noun; that is, to be church together is to use language and to repeat actions that shape us as a people over time – things you have to go on saying and doing, and aren't a static thing (or even a building), like the term church as a noun might imply. An analogy might be the word 'family' – which is technically a biological thing, but whose flourishing requires frequently repeated intentional actions and words shared by all members.

Ready, steady, Church
Acts 2.1–21
5 June 2022

The TV show *Ready Steady Cook*, which ran for 15 years and then had a brief revival a couple of years ago, challenged chefs to make a meal out of an assortment of inexpensive ingredients. The day of Pentecost, the birthday of the church, is an invitation to do the same with the church. The story from Acts gives us the ingredients. We've got people. OK, they're frightened, fragile and fallible, but that's the only kind of people the world contains, so let's not complain about the ingredients before we've even started. Then, we've got a challenge. Jesus has given the disciples the commission to share the gospel to the ends of the earth. Currently, the disciples are locked in an upper room and don't seem to fancy it. But see how in this story, the disciples start locked in an upper room in fear, and quickly move to the open square speaking to everyone. They start with nothing; they quickly have everything. They start with fear and isolation; in no time every stranger is their friend, and every foreign language is their native tongue.

Let's look at how the recipe works. Let's look at how to make a church. You start with people. That's already a lot. Because we're not alone. If we've been battered or bruised by church, rejected because of what we believe or who we are, chewed up and spat out because we trespassed into a power game, antagonized or alienated by something too clumsy or superficial to commit to, then we might well want to take our ball home and say faith is just a private thing. But if there's one thing the pandemic has taught all of us, it's gratitude for one another. We can think alone, we can regret alone, we can ponder and ruminate and resent alone. But if we actually want to do something in the world, we need to do it together.

Then the next ingredient is diversity. The *Ready Steady Cook* bag would be useless if it only included one kind of ingredient. Making a meal is about getting the best out of a variety of ingredients – not reducing everything to one ingredient. What happens in a healthy community is that everyone finds that the things about them that had elsewhere been seen as deficits are here discovered as assets. Elsewhere you were dismissed as shy; here you become a person who pays attention to detail and enjoys keeping records. Elsewhere you were dismissed as a wheelchair-user; here you're cherished as a teller of stories and a dreamer of dreams. Elsewhere you were marginalized as argumentative and a troublemaker; here you're admired as one who challenges oppression and directs the community's attention to the forgotten and neglected.

Billy Graham used to say, 'Don't join an ideal church: you'll spoil it.' The point is, there isn't an ideal church, like a template we have to live up to. There is no church other than the one made up of ordinary people. The motto is 'Strive to be the best church you can be – don't become a failed version of another church.' Each of you that makes up that community has your own story, your own strong and tender areas, your own imagination and ideas. The church that emerges will be a result of the people that constitute it. You can't make macaroni cheese out of meat and potatoes – but you can still make a great supper.

We live amid an argument raging about identity. Race, sexuality, gender, nationality – these identities, often taken as a threat and thus as the pretext for persecution and exclusion, are all about going back to find a true self, distinct from other people and other ways of being. But Ready Steady Church has a different notion of identity. It recognizes that there's an important conversation about where we're each coming from, not least to understand and address how frequently people can be ostracized and diminished. But the real conversation is not about where we're each separately coming from. It's about where we're together going. Christianity is impoverished if it's a story about where we're coming from. It gets mired in debates about sin and the fall and whether God intended it this way or whether we have ourselves to blame and if some are more to blame than others. Christianity is fundamentally a story about where we're going – a society that lasts forever, has a place for everybody, is shaped by truth and justice and peace, is about the flourishing of every living being, where suffering is no more. Any disagreement about that? Didn't think so.

The next ingredient is to get organized. To be fair, at this stage of the Acts of the Apostles it looks like you're just saying to the Holy Spirit, 'Let's go wherever you want to go.' But it doesn't take long before the apostles get organized. They have a giving campaign, and you may recall Ananias and Sapphira get in trouble because they don't make good on their pledge. They have a feeding programme, and Stephen and six other deacons are ordained to make sure it's done in the best possible way. Once you look around the room and say, 'It's just us – we'd better get busy,' you begin to realize the power of organization. We use the word 'organization' blandly, to mean a bunch of people that don't have the close relationships of an association nor the historic credibility and status of an institution. But an organization is, by definition, more than the sum of its parts. That's why it's created. An organization is a group of people who've got organized. They've called in some favours, used their contacts, drawn on their experience, sought extra training, pooled their skills, raised awareness, advertised widely, raised funds, experimented with their programme, started to envision the future and planned a critical path to get there. That's what organizing involves. It's about discovering that, few and isolated as you may feel, you can nonetheless develop power, through momentum, movement, management and muscle. It's an extraordinary moment when it dawns on you that you've got something, you've started something, there's a spirit in the air and people have hope in their hearts, and you've brought together strands of individuals and constituencies that wouldn't previously have met, known, understood or cared much about each other. That's what organizing can do.

I want to pause there because sometimes when you're working on a recipe, the mixture on the way tastes almost better than the finished product. When you're making apple cake and you've got the flour, sugar, milk and butter all mixed in and, before you add the apple and baking powder, the mixture's so good you almost deliberately leave parts out of the baking tin because you like licking the bowl afterwards. The feeling of working on a project together can be like that. It's like putting on a play or being in a sports team. But it can also be seductive. You can get such a depth of solidarity with shared jokes and mutual encouragement that it's impossible for anyone else to break in. Fun church isn't always the best church. Fun church can give security and dynamism and energy, but it can evoke envy and exclusion and entitlement if it doesn't remain permeable. We haven't finished the recipe yet.

Every church needs a healthy dose of humility. Just remember, people have been at this for 2,000 years. We may assume everyone before us got this totally wrong and we're going to get it totally right. But the chances of that are quite small. Yes, plenty of those people were manipulative, cruel and small-minded. But I'm guessing the large majority were well-intentioned, kind and generous. So it's probably time to set aside the idea that the world and the kingdom have all been waiting for us to show up. But humility cuts both ways. As the Americans say, 'Wear your own size.' In other words, don't wear clothes too big for you and pretend you're ten foot tall. But also, don't wear clothes too small for you. In every generation, the church faces fresh challenges, some of which it's never faced before, and that's how people who've been neglected or overlooked for generations finally get their moment, because theirs are the skills and experience that matter most now. Any church that says, 'This is the way we've always done it,' is really saying, 'We're going to go on doing it the same way regardless of whether it's working or not.' That's complacency and laziness masquerading as faithfulness. Don't do yourself down: you may be like a defender on the football pitch who finds herself in front of an open goal. Don't look round and say, 'But I'm not a striker' – just kick it in the net.

We've almost got the full recipe. We just need the most important part. And that is, to live in no power but the Spirit's power. It's the Spirit that decides what kind of a meal this is going to be. It's the Spirit that decides if this is going to be a sandwich under the bridge with those sleeping outside or a high mass in a crowded cathedral with the great and the good clustered around. It's the Spirit that decides if this is going to be a group of first-generation second-language children reading poems of freedom or a crowd of recovering addicts rejoicing that they've found dignity. It's the Spirit that decides if it's all the colours of the rainbow gathering round to proclaim joy or if it's a pensioner in a flat clinging on in bereavement and too stretched to fill the gas meter.

That's Ready Steady Church. That's all the ingredients. We've all been there when it didn't taste right, when it actually tasted terrible, when it tasted so bad we didn't want to taste it ever again. But we all know how it's supposed to taste. It's not about quantity. It's not about expense. It's not about how many are eating or how stylish the table is. This is how it tastes. It tastes of humble bread, bread of trust, bread of truth, bread of toil. And it tastes of wine – wine of sacrifice, wine of suffering, wine of beauty, wine of glory. Because there's only one church that matters, and it's not wealth, it's not size, it's not power, it's not numbers, it's not grandeur, it's not acclaim. It's a church that looks like Jesus. Jesus the tiny baby, dependent on others for life. Jesus the young child, longing to discuss truth in the temple. Jesus in the desert resisting temptation. Jesus in the synagogue proclaiming jubilee. Jesus saying blessed are the poor. Jesus embracing the outcast and the unloved. Jesus betrayed by his own, scorned by the powerful, forgiving his persecutors, raised from the dead.

God sends the Holy Spirit to give us everything we need to look like Jesus. Nothing more. And nothing less. Now. And forever. Amen.

A sermon like this obviously roams wider than the passage in question, and its list of ingredients – people, diversity, organization, humility, Holy Spirit – is clearly arbitrary. But it's not claiming to be the only way to talk about Pentecost or to offer a definitive list of the marks of the church. Instead, it's taking a subject many Christians have understandably deep misgivings about – whether they feel proud to be part of the worldwide church – and reigniting their enthusiasm and confidence in what they're doing. You can't do that without noting what the problems are, but you can't do that if you wallow too long in the negatives, either. You have to find a way to sweep the serious downsides up into a tide of a future-oriented can-do mindset, not by cheerleading but by a mixture of careful reason, apt illustration, gentle humour and confident proclamation. Which goes for pretty much any sermon.

PART 3

Texts

I

Preaching on Old Testament Narratives

This chapter and the next are the reason I wanted to write this book. When I studied theology, I had only a vague idea of what I was looking to find in the Old Testament. Since I'd already benefited greatly from the Greek I'd learned in helping my understanding of the New Testament, I resolved to learn Hebrew. But the classes were at 2pm and I kept falling asleep in them, so after a few weeks I changed to the introduction to Old Testament class. I regret I can't read Hebrew, but I'm grateful to my teacher Graeme Auld who, in lecturing about Judges, awakened my interest in Old Testament narrative. As it happened, I only studied the Old Testament for the few months left of that academic year. But those few lectures inspired me to do quite a bit more reading for myself and over 30 years in ministry my interest has continued to grow.

When I came as vicar to St Martin-in-the-Fields, it was not the practice to read the Old Testament lesson as part of the weekly parish Eucharist. I quickly persuaded my community to reinstate it. Since then, I may well have preached as many times on the Old Testament as on the New, almost defiantly seeking to woo my congregation over to seeing, as I like to put it, that the Old Testament is the gospel. The only sure way to persuade is example, so I sought to offer multiple examples that cumulatively demonstrated a number of things.

Chief among those things is that Jesus dwells in the Old Testament and the Spirit breathes through the Old Testament. Three factors prevent people perceiving this. The first is the assumption of deficit. Christians see that the Old Testament has numerous stories, but doesn't have Jesus, so in comparison to the New Testament, which is mercifully shorter and thankfully freer of smiting and wrath, it's characterized by what it doesn't have. Second, what I call the 'Nine Lessonization of the Old Testament' runs deep: like the service made famous by the Christmas Eve liturgy at King's College, Cambridge, the Old Testament is primarily understood as the source of prophecies and proof-texts of what comes to pass in the New, and is considered to have no validity aside from that function as a text-mine. Third, the commendable desire to avoid supersessionism (by which the church is taken to have replaced Israel) and cultural appropriation (which claims the Old Testament as Christian without acknowledging it belongs to the Jews, a danger some try to avoid by employing the term 'Hebrew Bible') has left many Christians with no facility for talking about the Old Testament in a theological way. The result of these three factors leaves many preachers as ignorant and suspicious of the Old Testament as their congregations.

I'm determined to reclaim the Old Testament from preacher and congregation alike. To do so requires the preacher to attend closely to the passage, grateful that the lectionary has chosen salient passages for us; to become familiar with the context and significance of the passage in the Old Testament and the Bible as a whole – which requires a commentary, or several, that seeks to read the Old Testament theologically, not just through the eyes of historical criticism; and to allow the truly theological dimensions to emerge, not by force, but through patience and perception.

The sermon below counters a common criticism of progressive-church preaching – that it insufficiently discusses sin. On the contrary, this sermon is almost entirely about sin, employing categories from patristic theology in creative ways to reinhabit arcane terms – idolatry and blasphemy – and put them to use in contemporary contexts.

The distance between us
Exodus 32.1–14
11 October 2020

'It didn't work out.' Those words must be one of the great euphemisms of our time. Translated, they mean, 'It came to a pretty sudden end. But I don't want to talk about why.' They take me back 35 years, to my first summer as a student. Friends were heading to radical projects abroad or promising internships in the City. But I was full of righteousness, so I went to the east end of London to work with homeless women. The women were fine; the problem was the nun in charge of the project. She was the original Sister of No Mercy. Everything I did was wrong. The washing up always had a stain, the carpet always had some dust I'd missed, the bill stubs I'd paid always had the paper clip attached the wrong way. It was an experience of being totally undermined and humiliated. I finally realized that what she wanted me to be was a compliant young Catholic woman, interested in becoming a nun – and I was none of those things. So I was permanently in the doghouse. When people asked me how my summer working with homeless people had gone, I said, 'It didn't work out.'

The tragedy is, a great many of us grow up with an image of God like that Sister of No Mercy. We're perpetually in the wrong. We can only conclude our face just doesn't fit. So when we hear the word 'sin' we associate it with feeling we can't possibly get it right. When we imagine God, we see a censorious tyrant like that micromanaging sister. What I want to do today is to explore how today's passage from Exodus leads us to think differently about God and consequently come to a different understanding of what sin means.

I want to take us back to the very beginning. Before there was anything – a universe, a Big Bang, let alone life – there was God. God is the name of what there was when there was nothing – in other words, when there was no existence, only essence. There was already plurality within God: that's what Trinity means. But God wanted there to be plurality *outside* God, not just within. This was because God is fundamentally relationship, and God wanted there to be relationship with other, not just with same. Relating to someone different from you has a quality unlike relating to someone the same. The word we use to describe God's relationship with other is Jesus. Jesus is the embodiment of God's original desire to be in relationship across difference. It's that desire that triggered the existence of the universe.

But relationship across difference is fraught with risk. I may misunderstand you and construe our relationship not as gift but as burden, thus turning grace into resentment. I may try to make relationship exclusive and envy anyone else you want to include. I may seek to use our relationship to gain some benefit beyond the relationship itself.

We could call all these dangers the Divine Risk. The divine risk is the possibility that humanity will forget that relationship with God is the reason for its existence and turn to other gods; and that it will fail to realize that all its other relationships – with self, one another and the creation – are opportunities to practise the joy of discovery, appreciation and growth as an echo of its relationship with God. That risk makes God's goodness and mercy vulnerable to the contagion of sin. Sin is the name of the poison that inserts itself into the distance between us and God and inhibits, dismantles or destroys all other relationship.

If we look at the story from Exodus 32, we recall that God has led the people by the hand of Moses out of slavery and given them manna in the wilderness, water from a rock and commandments to follow. But despite all of that, the people still feel a distance between them and both God and Moses. And into that distance they allow doubt, resentment, mistrust and manipulation to grow. How do we understand this phenomenon? What makes us fail to relate to God, one another and the creation, and allow poison to fill the distance between us?

Here's the beginning of an answer. One early theologian talks about enjoyment. When I enjoy you, I wholeheartedly embrace your wonder, difference, mystery and depth. I don't trigger a cautious reflex and scrutinize you at arm's length; nor do I try to make you like me: instead, I celebrate, glory and rejoice in you, different as you are. The difference and distance are a blessing. The alternative to enjoying someone is to use them. When I use someone or something, I make them an object in my larger project. Rather than enjoy you for your own sake, in all your particularity and uniqueness, I relate just to the parts of you I can use to advance my own schemes. If you're a spanner or an iPhone, using is exactly the right thing to do. But if you're a cousin or a co-worker, using is precisely the wrong thing to do. Difference and distance present a problem for me to overcome.

This distinction between using and enjoying is helpful because it helps us identify how we can aspire for all our relationships to grow from instrumental use to mutual enjoyment. But this distinction also enables us to understand what sin is. It shows us that there are broadly two kinds of sin. Either we use what we ought to enjoy, or we enjoy what we ought to use. I want to walk slowly through these alternatives.

Let's start with using what we ought to enjoy. Remember the third commandment, 'You shall not make wrongful use of the name of the Lord your God.' Think about what this commandment is referring to. You're having an argument – let's say you're haggling with a customer about the price of a shirt. The customer tries to get it down to ten pounds and you invoke the name of God and insist, 'I'm robbing myself if I let it go for less than 15.' A name is precious. When you're besotted with someone, their name appears everywhere – you can't stop mentioning it and pondering it. You wouldn't dream of using it as part of an unseemly haggle over the odd five quid. That would be to use what you should enjoy. When we appreciate that God took human form in Jesus, we realize that every time we use another person for our own purposes, most extremely in slavery, but most commonly by treating them as an object rather than a human being, we're likewise using what should be enjoyed. There's a collective name for all these kinds of failings. It's called blasphemy. Fraud, sexual assault and boasting are all forms of blasphemy, in this sense. Blasphemy is when we use what we should enjoy – when we forget that something is precious, honoured and loved, and turn it into a means to our own ends. That's half of sin.

The other half of sin is enjoying what we should use. It's mistaken and sentimental to think we should enjoy everything and use nothing. It's wrong to use other people and today we increasingly think it's wrong to use animals and much of the created world. But it's absolutely right to use a car, a door handle or a cricket bat. The trouble is, once we stop enjoying God, we quickly start enjoying things we should use and turning them into a kind of god. We make a god of our career, of how much we get paid, of how tidy our home is, of how many hits our recording has on YouTube. The collective name for these failings is idolatry. All forms of addiction are idolatry. Remember the second commandment: 'You shall not make for yourself an idol.' Idolatry is when we lose sight of the one who made us to respond in companionship and instead invest in other gods, often of our own making. It's the other half of sin.

Today's story from Exodus 32, about the people making and worshipping a golden calf, is an account of the two kinds of sin in narrative form. The people blaspheme by turning God's liberation into part of their own project of survival. Meanwhile, they commit idolatry by making their jewellery into an object of worship. It's a repeat of the Adam and Eve story, where the first couple blaspheme by eating the fruit that should be left on the tree and idolatrize by making the serpent, rather than God, their authority.

But the second half of today's story takes us back to the Sister of No Mercy. See how Moses has a full-on ding-dong with God. Here's what matters about this argument. God is not a distant, arbitrary, censorious judge, laying down irrational rules and making absurd demands. The God that is portrayed in this tussle with Moses is a God who is with us, alongside us, making and restoring relationship every hour of every day. Our relationship with God is in most respects like our other relationships: we're always in danger of using another person in our own project, and we're always liable to make some material thing more important than the relationship. We do just the same to God. It's called blasphemy and idolatry.

Making and restoring relationships is what life is all about. Relationships happen when two parties resolve to take a risk and say, 'The distance between us is an invitation not just to find surprising commonalities, but to explore our differences with wonder and delight.' Good relationships are ones where the parties enjoy their differences and the distance between them, even to the point of seeing setbacks and disagreements as part of the fun of a developing association. But the risk in every relationship is that the distance and difference between the parties will not lead through enjoyment to delight and discovery, but through attempts at use, will be regarded as threats to be controlled, avoided or destroyed.

Read this story of the golden calf carefully. Remember, this could have been the moment when God said of Israel, 'It didn't work out.' But instead, it became the event that taught Israel what relationship with God meant. God is not a judgemental Sister of No Mercy, looking to catch you out and humiliate you. God is our companion, who made us for the wonder and discovery of relationship. God comes into our relationships when difference turns to hostility, when distance triggers suspicion. The Holy Spirit constantly repairs and restores relationships that our mistrust and lack of imagination have allowed to fester and fail.

Every time you're tempted to say, 'It didn't work out,' remember that the name for what occupies the distance between us is Jesus. Jesus' are the arms that stretch to fill the gap between us and God and between us and one another – the gap that would otherwise be filled by the poison of suspicion, mistrust or hostility. Jesus embodies God's utter enjoyment of us, and our utter enjoyment of God. In him there is no use at all. He fills the distance between God and us with grace and truth, until we are utterly with God, and we enjoy one another forever.

I hope no one could listen to or read this sermon and retain views that Christians have nothing to learn from the Old Testament, that the Old Testament is all smiting and wrath and thus generally deplorable, or that there is no Jesus in the Old Testament. The listener may not immediately think, 'I now want to read the Old Testament all the way through for myself' – and might be wise not to do so. But I trust the listener will approach the text thereafter with anticipation and expectation, rather than suspicion and dread.

Here are some guidelines for preaching on Old Testament narrative.

1. Never underestimate intelligence; never overestimate knowledge. Any listener can quickly grasp the chief dynamics surrounding any given Old Testament passage; but don't assume they are aware of them already. I almost never say in a gospel sermon, 'You need to realize that Jesus started his ministry in Galilee and healed and taught and then later came to Jerusalem where he was killed.' I assume people know that. But I invariably say in an Old Testament sermon, 'Israel was formed by its time in the wilderness and felt a huge sense of completion building its life in the Promised Land; but centuries later it felt in exile in Babylon that it had lost everything – land, king and temple. Yet somehow God was closer to Israel in exile than ever in the Promised Land, and it was this experience that caused the Bible to be written.' You just can't assume any of that material is common knowledge to a congregation, raised no doubt on Adam and Eve, Noah, David and Goliath, and Daniel in the lions' den.

2. Don't assume preaching is about giving from your vast store of knowledge into the congregation's vast pool of ignorance. Don't be shy of a passage that makes no sense to you on first reading. That's what commentaries are for. Expect to be sharing with the congregation something you had little understanding of a week ago. See preaching as reporting discovery, not training by a seasoned expert.
3. Understand the profound transformation that happened to Israel/Judah in exile in Babylon, and read most Old Testament texts in the light of that transformation. For example, the story of Jonah changes if you see his exile as Israel's exile, and the story of Job changes if you see his torments as Israel's torments.
4. Likewise, always look for parallels of the Old Testament story and the New. For example, when the pot is broken in the hands of the potter in Jeremiah 18, and he makes a new pot from the same clay, be open to seeing that moment as a summary of the whole Bible, not just of the Old Testament. Likewise, when you read in Song of Songs 8, 'Set me as a seal upon your heart, as a seal upon your arm; for love is strong as death,' be open to seeing the last words as a summary of the whole Bible and the arm as Christ's arms on the cross. This is known technically as typological reading and early theologians offer some florid examples of the genre; but in principle it transforms our reading of the Old Testament.
5. Enjoy the narratives for what they are. Don't rush in with moralistic judgements about all the killing and don't take all the numbers literally; instead, relish the humour and reversal and exaggeration and character description. These are stories told over centuries and cherished in communities. They're not contemporary news reports. And you're a child gathered to hear them, not a representative of the Press Complaints Commission.

The following sermon is an example of the way I try to preach about Old Testament narratives. It's not an especially familiar passage, even to those who haven't been scared away from the Old Testament. But it turns out to be a vital account relating to crucial questions about God that transcend the Old–New Testament divide. I want a listener to come away from this sermon feeling like they've just discovered a whole new branch of their family and have many more relatives to meet and enjoy – that their Scriptures aren't just restricted to the 27 books of the New Testament but they just inherited 39 book of the Old.

The questions that matter
2 Samuel 7.1–14a
18 July 2021

A couple of years ago we started a tradition at St Martin's called Ask the Vicar. Originally, it gave children in the congregation a chance to have their questions heard and their searching cherished by the community. During lockdown it went online. Since we opened up again, it's become a TikTok phenomenon, with people all over the world joining in and sending in questions they long to be taken seriously. There seem to be two kinds of questions: those arising out of curiosity, like Is God fat? Or Why does God move in mysterious ways? And those rooted in profound heart-searching, like How can I trust God?

When we read the Bible, it's easy to forget that it was written by people who had the same questions we do. We can easily assume the Bible was written by people who were certain, and we, because we're flaky, further away, or far more sophisticated, are the ones who have the questions. But that's not how it works. If you take a passage like this morning's Old Testament reading, you can see it's an account of profound heart-searching about the most important questions of all: the ones that affect not only our own lives but the whole meaning of everything.

I bet you know the joke about a client who goes to see a lawyer. The client needs legal help. But he hasn't got much money. So he decides to check out the lawyer's terms before he goes any further. He says to the lawyer, 'What do you charge?' The lawyer replies, 'I charge £1,000 to answer three questions.' The client is surprised and troubled. He responds, 'Don't you think that's rather a lot of money to answer three questions?' The lawyer nods, 'Yes, it is.' Then she asks, 'What's your third question?'

Second Samuel chapter 7 is about three questions. This may look like a story from 3,000 years ago about a powerful king trying to legitimize his regime by building a grand temple to the God who underwrites his authority. But it's much more than that. The three questions that emerge in this passage are perhaps the three great questions of faith. One theologian even calls this passage 'the most crucial theological statement in the Old Testament.'[1] I want to look with you at the three questions this passage addresses to see how they resonate with our faith today.

---

1 Walter Brueggemann, *First and Second Samuel* (Louisville, KY: John Knox, 1990), p. 259.

The first question is, Where is God? That's the most obvious question that this story is about: *Where is God?* The two tablets of stone on which were written the Ten Commandments were a wedding ring for God and Israel. They were carried around in a heavy structure known as the ark of the covenant and wherever that ark was, Israel believed God was among them. David sees his stable period of kingship in the newly conquered city of Jerusalem, uniting the northern and southern tribes, as the perfect moment to make a grand and permanent home for the ark of the covenant, enthroning God and at the same time enshrining his own leadership.

But the prophet Nathan expresses ambivalence about the project. He points out that God, the Lord of heaven and earth, can't be contained in a building. God isn't a creature under our control and God's purposes are not exhausted by our needs. Nathan goes to the heart of the ambiguity of our human quest for God. On the one hand we want an answer to our questions about ultimate meaning, perpetual truth, final purpose – we want to know why there's a universe, how we came to be here, and whether it's all a cosmic accident. On the other hand, no sooner than we sense we're getting an answer to these timeless questions, we're trying to control that God, to limit that truth, to put it in a building, make it our creature for our use and purpose, no doubt developing merchandise and patenting the brand.

Where is God? God's not far away, located in a control room beyond the stars, manipulating a digitized array of levers and pulleys; neither is God in a box, strictly controlled by us, invoked to justify our every power-grab and assertion of will. To find God, we have to set aside all notions of control, that God is a device to hasten our desires, and all ideas of use, that God exists to fix the unresolved parts of our lives. God is utterly other than us – and yet, as Nathan says to David, God is with us wherever we go.

Here's the second question. What does God want? Here's a perpetual question: *What does God want from us?* David wants to build a temple for God. It doesn't seem at all clear from what Nathan's saying that that's what God wants. But David has a mindset that faithfulness is doing lots of things for God, and faithfulness for a rich and powerful king must mean doing very big things for God. Look at this mindset more carefully. One of the hardest things in life is being in a relationship, with a boss or family member or a romantic partner, where you can't fathom what the other party really wants. If you long to win their favour, you're going to end up in a habit of doing things or giving things or saying things somehow to mollify, placate or distract them. But all the time you're in a perpetual cycle of fear, confusion, bewilderment and guilt. This is how Sigmund Freud described religion. He saw it as a constant pattern of guilt and inadequate strategies to assuage that guilt. The trouble is, some religion *is* like that. It's about a faraway God with irrational demands that you can never meet – and a perpetual sense of failure for which you always feel guilty. David's gesture of building a temple is a political manoeuvre to shore up his regime. But on a faith level it looks very much like the grand, ultimate gesture that says, 'God, now I've done this, you can surely never take your favour away from me.' In other words, it's a form of bribery. These kinds of gestures aren't about a real relationship: they're about offsetting damage, given there *isn't* a real relationship. It's saying, 'I'm going to do so much for you that you can never reproach me, regardless of whether it's what you really want.'

But see how radical is what Nathan goes on to say. This is what makes this passage the theological crux of the Old Testament. In fact, the most vital thing is the word Nathan doesn't say. Nathan doesn't utter the word 'if.' Think about the covenant between God and Moses: it's dominated by the word 'if.' If you keep my commandments, you will prosper. The whole thing's conditional. If Israel keeps its side of the bargain, God says, 'I'll keep my side of the bargain.' 'If' is the tiny word that echoes all through the Old Testament to this point. Now just think for a moment about the power of that tiny word 'if' in your life. If you get a decent job and finally bring in enough money, I will love you and stay with you. If you pursue a certain form of education and training, I will help you pay for it. If your behaviour improves, I'll buy you a new phone. 'If' is a word that dominates lives; and a word that overshadows many lives of faith. Nathan abolishes 'if'. There's no 'if' in what God says to David through Nathan. Imagine a relationship that has no 'if'. Imagine a love that replaces the word 'if' with the word 'always'. What does God want? Not a series of conditional demands we struggle to fulfil. God wants to be with us always. No 'if': always.

So to the third question. *Can we lose God?* If God is with us, and what God wants is to be with us always, can something still go wrong? It's a very legitimate question. Inside each one of us there are two voices. One longs for things to turn out well. The other whispers, 'It can't last.' Recall your moment of greatest joy: was there a piercing terror that it would all be snatched away from you? Second Samuel is the zenith of Israel's power and faithfulness: it's the high watermark of the Old Testament. And yet it's written in the knowledge that years later it all disintegrated. How can we place our faith in God if we're beset by the fear that it won't last – that at the moment of our death we'll lose everything? Here, Nathan uses two words that answer our question. He says 'forever'. God's commitment to us is forever. It's not dependent on our behaviour, it's not dismantled by our mortality, it's not derailed by the changes and chances of this fleeting world. Then Nathan says, 'I will raise.'

This is where the Jewish and Christian reading of this story part company. The Jewish reading is that one day there'll be another David, a messiah, who will restore God's people and redeem the earth. The Christian reading is that there has already been such a person – that these words are fulfilled in Jesus. Jesus did experience the alienation of God's people and Jesus did experience the alienation of God. Everything that might jeopardize the word 'forever' was embedded in his passion and death. But God raised Jesus. That raising demonstrates the fact that we cannot lose God. God and forever aren't just two things it's nice to have: *they're the same thing*.

And this is the point where we realize the significance of the three questions that emerge in this passage. Where is God? What does God want? Can we ever lose God? I think it's fair to say they're the three questions that really matter – the most important questions of all, for the universe and for each of us personally. The answer to all three questions is one word: Jesus. *Where is God?* God is with us in the one who expresses and embodies everything God means to us and everything we mean to God. *What does God want?* God wants to be with us in Christ. God is not especially interested in us offering gifts or making sacrifices, if such acts express our suspicion that we don't know what God wants and are resorting to bribery instead. What God wants is our companionship in Christ. *Can we lose God?* It sometimes feels like it, and in the way we treated Jesus we went as far as we can imagine towards doing so; but God raised Jesus and showed us that nothing can finally separate us, so we can give up worrying.

The people we find in the Old Testament aren't faraway characters in arcane stories. They're seeking the deepest meaning in life and the truth about God, just as we are. They ask profound questions, just as we do. Just like Ask the Vicar questions, some are curious, and never find an answer; some arise from profound heart-searching. To be a Christian is to trust that those most profound questions have found their answer in Christ. The real challenge is not to ask the questions – but to live the answers.

The danger of this kind of sermon is the facile move that all the answers to all the questions in the world are the same. Hence the story of the Sunday school teacher's question to the class, 'What's small and furry and bushy-tailed?' to which the child responds, 'I know the answer's

Jesus, but it sounds like a squirrel to me.' To avoid this danger, you need to show you're aware of the complexity of the material you're dealing with. But if the answer really is Jesus, you should be glad to say so.

The following sermon is about a book in the Old Testament, Job, that's demanding for the preacher because it's lengthy and explaining all the nuances takes a long time. You have to find a way of leaving out some of the nuances and focusing on just the part that concerns you today, in this case the phrase, 'I know that my redeemer lives.' There's scarcely a more powerful and moving phrase in the whole Bible; yet you can dismantle it with a lugubrious sermon exploring whether the notion of a redeemer in Jewish law had any direct connection with the role Jesus plays in the New Testament. You need to step back and say, who is God for Job? And, where is Jesus in this story? And the rest falls into place.

The Spanish Inquisition
Job 19.23–27
6 November 2016

One of the most famous comedy sketches in the history of British television depicts two of the Monty Python team having an argument when one complains, 'I didn't expect a kind of Spanish Inquisition'; whereupon a fifteenth-century Spanish cardinal appears and announces, grandly, '*Nobody* expects the Spanish Inquisition!' The cardinal then enumerates the Inquisition's chief weapons, which are surprise, fear, ruthless efficiency, an almost fanatical devotion to the Pope; although he and his fellow cardinals keep forgetting what these weapons are and how many there are of them. They also produce incongruous methods of torture, including a dish-drying rack, soft cushions and, finally and notoriously, the comfy chair.

There are two things going on in the sketch: there's an outer story about ham-fisted inquisitors and their diabolical acting, amplified by catch phrases and ridiculous clothes; and there's an inner story about the sophisticated and ruthless methods of the historical Inquisition and its apparent absurdity translated into twentieth-century Britain, which together offer a riotous parody of extreme religion and the practice of torture. The juxtaposition of the two makes the sketch so hilarious that it's become a cult classic.

The biblical character Job didn't expect the Spanish Inquisition either. But the book of Job has the same structure as the celebrated Monty Python sketch. There's an outer folk tale about an innocent, God-fearing man. This man gets in the middle of a heavenly dispute between God and Satan, nobly refuses to curse God for the many disasters that befall him, and is consequently restored to a fortune greater than his original state. The message of this story is that human suffering comes about because God is allowing Satan to test humans to see what we're made of – to see if our faith survives when God no longer seems to be blessing us. But inside this story there's another, longer, much more complex and sophisticated account of Job's debate with his three friends, Eliphaz, Bildad and Zophar, which offers no explanation for Job's sufferings, eventually implies God's own grief over human travails, and in which Job seriously challenges God's purposes and ways while still remaining faithful.

What these outer and inner stories offer us is a microcosm of the Old Testament as a whole. On the outside is a story of Israel and God, where what we seem to get is a view that God has made a covenant with Israel and if Israel remains faithful, God will keep Israel in prosperity, and Israel's trials and struggles are due either to Israel's own unfaithfulness or to God's testing and refining of Israel's faith. On the inside is a much more searching and complex story, in which there's grief, setback and trouble, and it's not always clear whether these are tests or punishments, or if indeed God is at least as dismayed by them as Israel is, and where Israel regularly asks, 'Oh God, why?' and 'How long, O Lord, how long?' – but always within a deeper relationship of trust and hope.

These two stories, the outer and inner story, represent two ways to believe. The first is a kind of transaction. It says, more or less, I'm going to calculate that God's offering me a good deal, in which I provide earthly faithfulness and God offers eternal blessedness. God remains distant and unfathomable, and it's never clear what's really in it for God; but so long as I can train my desires, control my impatience and be content to leave a good few questions unanswered, I can call myself a believer. The second kind of faith, the inner story, is very different. It's more like a love that will not let you go. It's a regular, in some cases constant, debate and wondering and dialogue and pondering that lives with anomalies and paradoxes but still draws you in to a vortex of desire and a whirlwind of mystery. It's not simple or dull but it's always absorbing and vital. I wonder whether your faith most resembles the outer story of conviction, or the inner story of the whirlwind. Or perhaps it's a mixture of the two.

In both the outer and inner versions of his story, Job experiences three levels of suffering. First, he experiences catastrophic deprivation of property, tragic loss of loved ones and profound physical agony. Second, he finds himself totally isolated: not only does he have no court of appeal to resort to, no cosmic justice system from which to seek redress, but to compound that, he has no true companionship. It's true that his three friends sit with him for seven days and nights because they see his suffering is so great – but after that, they're mainly concerned to prove his arguments wrong, not genuinely to walk with him through the heart of darkness. And third, he's stripped of any ultimate hope, because it seems even God is against him, to the extent of having apparently colluded in his sufferings. If the Spanish Inquisition had the draining rack, the soft cushions and the comfy chair, Job experiences the agony of pain, the loneliness of utter isolation and the extinction of hope. Three levels of torture – a torture so extreme that it would almost be funny if it weren't so utterly tragic.

The poignancy of the book of Job is that, while his sufferings are portrayed with an almost cartoon extremity, these three kinds of suffering are something we can almost all relate to. We can all recall or imagine what it means to be in terrible pain, or know heart-wrenching bereavement, or lose all our money or possessions. We can all understand, or in some cases perhaps know all too well, the sense of profound isolation, even abandonment, that wondering if we really have any genuine friends and fear that deep down, we're alone in a cruel world. And we can all recognize that tremor that runs through our whole body when we feel, for moments or perhaps extended periods, that there's no hope, that even God must be against us, that our ultimate destiny is bleak. And if we haven't touched on such despair ourselves, we need only put ourselves in the shoes of the people of Syria right now.

And here's the wonder of the book of Job. Deep in the heart of the book, right at the centre of the inner wrestling and wondering and struggling and despairing, comes, like a shaft of light from heaven, these most extraordinary words. 'I know that my Redeemer lives, and that at the last he will stand upon the earth; and after my skin has been thus destroyed, then in my flesh I shall see God, whom I shall see on my side, and my eyes shall behold, and not another.' From the deepest, deepest place of agony come the truest, most wondrous and perhaps most inspiring words in the whole of Scripture.

What I want you to see is how succinctly and comprehensively these short sentences address the three levels of suffering that Job is experiencing. We saw that Job experienced grievous loss and horrendous pain. Here he proclaims, 'After my skin has been thus destroyed, then in my flesh I shall see God.' In other words, the utter destruction of his physical possessions, relationships and his very body is real and total: but he will see salvation, not in some disembodied ethereal paradise, but in his very flesh. This is a statement of the most profound faith that God will restore him in flesh and blood, that all that time and chance have whittled and snatched away will be returned with interest and transformed into beauty. 'In my flesh I shall see God': feel the force of that. It's a visceral, visible, vivid transformation. This isn't a metaphor: it's belief and trust in a salvation that takes earthly shape.

Then we saw Job undergo total isolation from justice and companionship. But this proclamation changes all that. 'I know that my Redeemer lives,' he says. The word 'redeemer' in the Old Testament usually refers to the next of kin, whose responsibility it is to buy out debts, rescue one from slavery or avenge a terrible crime. It's the lack of any such person that makes Job so isolated in this story. Hence the power of this ecstatic declaration: 'I know that my Redeemer lives.' Job declares that he has a redeemer after all, and that God is that redeemer. He goes on to say, 'In my flesh I shall see God, whom I shall see on my side.' In other words, for all the doubt and distrust that God was against him, or at least had left him alone to suffer and die, he realizes that when he sees God, God will be on his side, taking his cause, in solidarity with him till the end of time and beyond. He's had a glimpse of ultimate eternal reality and in that vision, God is right there, saying gently, 'I'm by your side.'

And last, we saw, as the third layer of suffering, Job's whole hope extinguished. Yet here he says, 'My eyes shall behold God, and not another.' You can take this two ways. Throughout the book of Job, there's plenty of conviction that God is in control, but a lot of hesitation about whether God's power is ultimately a benevolent force. But there's also a shadowy and malign character called Satan, and there's a lingering anxiety that maybe Satan, not God, will win the argument and have the last word. Here Job leaves us in no doubt. 'My eyes shall behold God, and not another.' In the end, after the whirlwind and confusion and mystery has subsided, there's just God.

It turns out that just about the whole of the good news of Christianity is in this short Old Testament declaration. There is hope and ultimate purpose. That hope is lodged in a personal redeemer. That redeemer is by our side forever. And we shall experience that salvation in our own earthly flesh. It's not a promise simply to take away pain and distress. It's a promise that God's redemption will offer companionship and solidarity that transcends suffering.

And this promise arises not in the calm detachment of the outer story but in the midst of the whirlwind and chaos of the inner turmoil. That makes it even more remarkable, and even more reliable. It's not a glib answer; it's an absorbed discovery.

You'd almost think we didn't need the New Testament. But see this one last thing. What Jesus does is to inhabit the story of Job. Jesus is the human being that experiences the agony of pain, the horror of abandonment and, on the cross, the total loss of hope. He is the Redeemer. He lives. At the last he will stand upon the earth. After our skin has been destroyed, then in our flesh we shall see him, and not another, on our side. In his incarnation, Jesus moves from the outer story of assurance to the inner story of dismay, to share our confusion and despair and take us with him to a place of trust and hope. He faces the ultimate inquisition. And he meets us on the other side of agony, where the two stories become one.

The secret of this sermon lies in the line, 'You'd almost think we didn't need the New Testament.' The rhetorical technique is both to layer on the significance and texture of what Job's story reveals and to do so in a light, accessible manner so that you feel you've finished and got everything you could possibly want ... only to find that Jesus adds a whole extra and transformative dimension on top of that. The Monty Python material isn't just there to provide an accessible and cheerful introduction to a sombre subject; it provides the mechanism by which the complexity of Job can be communicated digestibly in a single paragraph, and a leitmotif to which the sermon can return to restore its directness and accessibility.

It's a dense sermon, and there's plenty there – such as the three kinds of suffering – that a listener might not fully comprehend on first encounter; but that's not a problem because the structure of the sermon is clear enough that listeners always know where they are and can completely grasp the power of the revelation that comes when the powerful line from Job 19 is repeated. Thus, what could become a cerebral sermon about different approaches to suffering becomes an emotional sermon about meeting God face to face.

2

Preaching on Old Testament Poetry

I'm no expert in Hebrew poetry. But I'm determined not to leave Old Testament poetry to the experts. I'm very aware that there are preachers who take one look at the lectionary passages, glance briefly at the Old Testament reading, see it's full of words like 'behold', 'thus says the Lord', and 'quenched like a wick' and give it no further thought, as if it was put there simply to remind the preacher how complex and recondite the Old Testament is and that there are much richer pickings to be found elsewhere. To get past such a reaction takes time, patience and a certain degree of confidence – but all these are forms of trust: trust that the Holy Spirit will speak to your people, through these ancient words, today.

Isaiah is called the fifth gospel for a reason. It's not just that quotations from Second Isaiah litter the gospels, especially the passion narratives. It's that without understanding the transformation that takes place in Second Isaiah, you can't really grasp the significance of the transformation that takes place as the early disciples come to see the cross not as a disaster, but the closest humanity has ever got to seeing the heart of God. Sharing the wonders of these chapters, if not all of Old Testament poetry, is a gift preachers cannot withhold from their congregations.

The simplest route to get past the diffidence many listeners feel toward a passage that is not only from the book of smiting and wrath but is also not transparently comprehensible on first reading, is to talk in very personal terms: 'Israel felt it had lost ... Israel felt bereft ... yet Israel discovered...' You can supplement that with analogies to refugees and exiles in our own time, of which there are always many examples to hand. But eventually you have to get the listener absorbed into the pain and grief of exile and the mystery and wonder of revelation.

In the sermon below, I compare the situation of Israel in Babylon to the perception many have in the West of church decline. The point is not to suggest the two experiences are commensurable, but to highlight the feelings evoked and reactions induced as similar – and to employ discoveries about the former to inform attitudes toward the latter.

I am about to do a new thing
Isaiah 43.16–21
7 April 2019

I once was invited to address an annual meeting of a regional religious society. That meant before I got up to speak there was half an hour of the legal business of the organization to sit through. The chair received the secretary's report and once it had been digested, the chair said, 'I need to tell you that our secretary has decided that it is time to stand down, and that, after 8 years of loyal service, we shall be needing to look for a successor. Are there any nominations?' There were none. Then it was time for the treasurer's report. After the treasurer had shared the financial proceedings of the society, the chair rose to say, 'I need to tell you that our treasurer has decided that it is time to stand down, and that, after 15 years of loyal service, we shall be needing to look for a successor. Are there any nominations?' Again, there were none. Finally, it was time for the chair's report. Once that was done, the chair said the unforgettable words, 'I need to tell you that I too have decided that it is time to stand down … Are there any nominations?' I need hardly tell you that silence reigned in that village hall for the third time.

There's a widespread feeling that such a story is a parable for the condition of the church in this country today. In the face of a melancholy perception that the churches are being overtaken by changes in society, there seem to be three kinds of response. One is a lament that things aren't how they used to be. Sometimes it comes with a sense of entitlement, that people should go to church, that the nation should take faith more seriously, that this is supposed to be a Christian country. Other times there's just a longing for a notional bygone time when churches were always full, Sundays were dominated by Sunday Schools and Easter was about an empty tomb rather than a chocolate egg. A second response is one of frantic activity – an impulse to be constantly busy, as if the situation can be rectified through sheer determination and commitment. This implicitly assumes that the smaller footprint left by the churches on the nation's soul is the churches' fault and can be alleviated by more concerted efforts and successful marketing. A third response is a kind of taciturn denial, a turning inward to concentrate on maintaining traditions and revering old ways, be it in ethics, dogmatic denial of difference, or curmudgeonly attitudes that assume change and decline are the same word.

I want to suggest to you that what all these three responses have in common is an assumption that there was a time in the near or distant past when the churches got it right, and that by reasserting the known ways, the church can remind itself of its identity and restore its strength.

I want to turn now to today's reading from Isaiah chapter 43. Israel is in exile in Babylon. Everything is lost – the promised land, the king, the temple – and the key question is, has Israel lost absolutely everything, or does the covenant with God abide? In losing everything that identified it as Israel, has Israel also lost God? During this profound period of re-assessment of purpose and rediscovery of identity, Israel looked back at its history and came to understand both how in the exodus from Egypt and the receiving of the law at Mount Sinai, God had created this nation; and how the God who had done this was the same God that had created the world. Israel also traced the way that, since the time of Solomon, the nation had grown more and more faithless and had brought upon itself the destruction that finally came in the early sixth century BC. By pondering its history, Israel found food for repentance but also for hope.

And only in that context can we begin to grasp how extraordinary these words from Isaiah chapter 43 really are. They start in a very familiar way: 'Thus says the Lord, who makes a way in the sea, a path in the mighty waters, who brings out chariot and horse, army and warrior; they lie down, they cannot rise, they are extinguished, quenched like a wick.' Like many Old Testament prophecies, they don't just call God 'God', they locate God as the one who acted in history to bring Israel out of slavery in Egypt, through the waters of the Red Sea, to freedom and into covenant relationship forever. But now we get two lines that are almost unprecedented in the Old Testament. The first goes like this: 'Do not remember the former things, or consider the things of old.' Really? This seems to go against the whole of the Old Testament law. Because if you think of Deuteronomy, for example, probably the one word that occurs more than any other is the command to 'remember'. Israel's relationship with God is founded on gratitude – and gratitude is about remembering. But here Isaiah says, 'Do not remember.' 'Do not remember the former things, or consider the things of old.' Surely Isaiah can't be saying that Israel should go against everything they've been taught about how to remain faithful to God?

Well, yes and no. When it says, 'Do not remember' here, it means 'Do not so fix your thoughts that you can't see anything else; don't be so preoccupied with the great things God has done and the terrible things you have done that you leave no room for receiving further information.' It's not completely demolishing everything Israel has ever been taught. Imagine it this way. Suppose you had a very precious item of pottery and you're looking at it smashed on the floor into several pieces, too many to reassemble. And along comes somebody with another item of pottery for you, more delicate and more beautiful and more wonderful than the one whose demise you are pondering. No one's saying don't be sad about the first item of pottery: they're just saying, don't let your grief over that original item prevent you seeing this new and glorious gift coming your way. That's what God is saying to Israel through the mouth of the prophet Isaiah right here. Look what the next words are: 'I am about to do a new thing.'

Feel the force of these words. Take a deep breath and appreciate the wonder of what Isaiah is saying. Here's the point. I said earlier that every form of reaction to the condition of the church today seems to assume that somehow, some generations ago, the church got it right and that we need to try to recover that thing, whatever it was, and restore those great days. And that's just one way in which religion in general and Christianity in particular gets into the habit of assuming that its job is to hold on to the things of old as long and as hard as it can until, inevitably, we eventually have to let go. Our technology should be like it used to be, our sexual ethics should be like they used to be, our worship should get back to former language and our architecture should return to ancient ways. It's like the church is a permanent road sign pointing back in the direction we've come from, with no expectation or instruction or enjoyment of anything that lies ahead. We turn God into a big-sounding word that really means no more than 'Can we please go back to yesterday?' and heaven into a recreation of circumstances from an earlier chapter in our history.

But God says, 'I am about to do a new thing.' It turned out the new thing wasn't 100% different from the old thing. Last time, God created a dry path through the sea that divided *Egypt* and the promised land; this time, God is going to make a river through the desert that divided *Babylon* from the promised land. Isaiah is challenging Israel and saying, 'All that you know about God should be preparing you to recognize this new thing God is going to do. It's up to you: are you going to keep staring down at the broken pot and lamenting the shattered dream, or are you going to lift up your head and see this new gift and respond to it?'

Isaiah is challenging today's church in just the same way. Are we going to be so certain we know what church should be like, so determined to reconstruct something along the lines of yesteryear, so adamant in holding on to our notions of a past golden era that we can't see the new and precious gift God is offering us? Is a part of us cross because God was supposed to be our trump card in trying to turn back the clock and now God is proving an unreliable partner in reducing the world to what we can understand and control? 'I am about to do a new thing.' Are we secretly thinking we'd rather hang our heads in despair and pen poignant poems about exile than have to adapt to a God who is way out ahead of us and preparing a new future?

PREACHING ON OLD TESTAMENT POETRY

In the end we can't hide behind the church. The challenge is for each one of us, whatever our age or background, whether we are comfortable or struggling, happy or sad. Listen, listen this morning, deep in your heart, to these unsettling words from God: 'I am about to do a new thing.' Whatever the cause of the furrows on your brow, be it health or a relationship, work or finances, a life too full or an existence too empty, hear God saying to you right here, right now, 'I am about to do a new thing.' Maybe not *for* you: maybe *in* you. Be renewed in your faith in a God in whom the future is always bigger than the past. Praise the God who, as Ephesians tells us, 'By the power at work within us is able to accomplish abundantly far more than all we can ask or imagine.' This is not the end of the story of what God is doing with you and in you. God has only just begun. God says, 'I am about to do a new thing.' A new thing in you.

As so often, the role of the preacher is to take a weary, distracted and burdened congregation, open up the Scripture through analogy, insight, humour and rhetoric and draw the listener towards hope, healing and heaven. The technique is to set up a problem at the beginning of the sermon that the sermon, perhaps with the aid of what might seem like detours and side paths, resolves and transfigures. The problem isn't, 'What on earth do these obscure words mean?' The problem is more likely one that the preacher has already perceived the passage provides the solution to. And so, the skill is to set the sermon up in such a way that the congregation feels deeply the question to which the preacher is going to provide the answer (either connecting with long-held anxiety or aroused suddenly by new urgency). If the preacher doesn't set the problem up successfully, in a way that grasps the congregation's attention, it can still be an interesting and educational sermon but it sails past the congregation like a bird headed for a different destination.

Here are some guidelines for preaching on Old Testament poetry.

1. While simply exegeting the passage, with the aid of commentaries, may be satisfying for the listener who knows the passage and its context well, congregations in general want to be located in the text, and want to answer the question, 'So what?' So the real work is, once you've done your own exegesis, to set the sermon up with a question to which this passage gives a compelling answer.
2. Once you've worked out what that answer and question are, you can ransack your personal history and memory of stories, from friendly anecdote to gripping novel to half-remembered news account, to offer a mood, direction and structure to shape (and usually begin) your sermon.

3. If you can consult an exegete like Robert Alter, who understands and can make accessible the nuances of Hebrew poetry, so much the better – but don't get so excited by the discoveries of repetition and rhythm and wordplay that you lose sight of the argument you're advancing. Remember, you don't need to persuade your congregation that you're clever or have worked hard – you need to inspire them that the living God spoke through these words and is speaking through them today.
4. Always be looking for the larger theological frame of reference in which the passage may sit. That may be Christological, but not always; after all, you don't want your sermons to be formulaic and predictable. The sermon above doesn't go in that direction. But in almost every Old Testament passage, there are at least three layers of meaning: what it meant then, what it meant to the early church in the light of Jesus, and what it means today; and while it can be cumbersome to go through all of them every time, you should at least do so in your head before planning your sermon.
5. Be aware of the fact that most Old Testament poetry was written from the point of view of a persecuted minority, as was most of the New Testament. Be mindful of your social location and be eager to point out that today's ideal reader is the one hearing these words from a context like the one in which they were written; which, by the way, may well not be your own. Take the trouble to find people who have written from such contexts about this passage, or similar passages, and consider incorporating their perspectives or actual words into your sermon.

The following sermon turns to a passage and scriptural book preachers have often read moralistically but less often theologically. I include it to emphasize my point that the preacher should always be alert to the theological resonance of the words in the passage.

Does not wisdom call?
Proverbs 8.1, 22–31
7 February 2021

I want you to imagine you're setting up a radio station. The parameters are: it has to be largely spoken word, its listeners are looking for depth, and you have access to anyone in the world you want to contribute. I wonder how you'd go about it.

I'm guessing the first thing you'd look to offer would be information. Every day new things happen, discoveries are made and adventures are had. In an age of social media, anyone can now contribute to the hubbub of ideas, attitudes and reactions. But it's a minefield. If you focus on the flaws of a movement or individual, you're told it's fake news. If you portray issues from only one point of view, you're accused of bias. Yet if you don't find a way to organize information, the listener quickly gets information overload and can't bear it anymore. So we need more than just information. We need knowledge. Knowledge is information that's been digested and reflected upon. It's hard to be a genius without knowledge, but knowledge can't do much on its own. Right now, we say we follow the science. But medical science is telling us everyone should stay home, social science is telling us we can't function or flourish without interaction and economic science is telling us we can't live if we don't work.

So we need something more than just knowledge. And here we run into the ways knowledge has been transformed in recent decades. The technological and digital revolutions have created a cult of expertise. Expertise names the combination of skill in accessing information and aptitude for applying knowledge that makes an individual or institution head and shoulders above everyone else. A good deal of the populist revolt of the last decade has been triggered by resentment and rejection of experts. When a person goes against something you know in your bones, or is crucial to your identity, the fact that they're regarded as an expert just makes you more furious and alienated.

You could call information, knowledge and expertise the noun of your radio station: its bread and butter. But to be a good radio station you need another level, that questions, plays with and recalibrates what you're taking for granted. We could call that level the adjective. One of these kinds of subversion is perspective. Why does all this knowledge assume Europe is in the middle of the map? What makes it exclude neurodiversity as a legitimate way of engaging reality? Why is American or Australian or South African history assumed to begin when the white settlers started to arrive? Who decides that the only personal pronouns are he and she? Have you noticed how often 'blind' is used as a metaphor for wilful ignorance, and darkness is a metaphor for dangerous and backward, when sight-impaired and Black people are just as much a blessing to humankind as anyone else? Every time someone trips us up and exposes our prejudice in the language we use, we're reminded that we need to pass through a new threshold of insight to deepen how we think.

But there are other, less confrontational ways to challenge perspective. One is humour. Irony and satire, slapstick and surrealism – they're all ways to change the temperature and context of discussion. You can produce all kinds of data, opinion and perspective on the prevalence of guns in America and the high rate of schoolyard massacres, but you can cut through it all in no time if, like Sid Singh, you just say, 'President Trump wants to arm teachers, which is crazy, because if Donald Trump's teachers had been armed, we probably wouldn't ever have had to hear his opinions about teachers being armed.'

A further way to challenge perspective is to alter the medium. Poetry is like humour – it twists and exaggerates and turns upside-down, so you can no longer regard a fact as a given, or take a statement at face value. Music adds another dimension again – quickly, the mundane is transcended by the beautiful, the dull by the inspiring, the conventional by the transcendent. Now we've added the adjective of perspective to the noun of knowledge, we've nearly got a radio station.

The last dimension, which we could call the verb, is relationship. People speak of emotional intelligence when a person realizes they need to pay attention, not just to knowledge and information, but just as much to a person's past experience or their passionate investment in an issue. Others speak of cultural intelligence, when someone appreciates that a question can mean something very different as you move from one region or tribe to another. This is the journey from knowledge to understanding, and from understanding what something means for you, to appreciating what it means for someone else, which we call empathy. We've arrived at the holy grail of a radio station.

There's a word we give to the noun of knowledge subverted by the adjective of perspective issuing in the verb of relationship. That word is wisdom. Wisdom is the highest pinnacle of human aspiration, because it brings together all the different sources and kinds of discovery, experience and reflection. It sounds a bit grand to think a radio station is seeking wisdom: but that's what we're all searching for. The Old Testament gives an honoured place to wisdom. I'm often asked why I seldom use the term Hebrew Bible. The reason is I believe it keys into the false notion that what Jews believe is less than what Christians believe, being shorter and lacking Jesus. It also fails to recognize that the Old Testament and the Hebrew Bible aren't simply the same thing with different names. The Hebrew Bible has three parts – the *Torah*, or Law, the *Nevai'im*, or Prophets, and the *Ketuvim*, or Writings. The characteristic of that third section, the Writings, is wisdom. A characteristic part of the wisdom literature of the Old Testament is the book of Proverbs.

Through aphorism and poetry, Proverbs immerses us in a quest to achieve what our radio station was seeking – to bring together all three dimensions of encounter, knowledge, perspective and relationship –

and thus make wisdom. Wisdom is the way God's character is imprinted on existence and the way humanity comes close to comprehending the ways of God. Thus, in today's reading from Proverbs chapter 8, wisdom is present when God creates the world and shapes the way God connects the different parts of creation to one another. Paul riffs on this passage when he writes the first chapter of Colossians. But Proverbs 8 isn't simply an infusion of sober judgement, careful calculation and shrewd assessment. The last couple of verses speak of delight, playfulness and rejoicing. Wisdom isn't restricted to long-bearded analysis, multi-volumed scholarship or relentless, dispassionate scrutiny. Wisdom and joy are ultimately inextricable. Joy is based not on denial or fantasy, but on true understanding, and wisdom is grounded not in forbidding intelligence, but in enchanted wonder.

We all know the familiar narrative of the Bible – route one we might call it – where Adam and Eve sin, God calls Abraham, Jacob goes down to Egypt, Moses brings Israel out of slavery, kings build the temple, Israel falls from grace, and Jesus comes along to restore God's relationship with Israel and transform it into forgiveness and eternal life for the whole world. But Proverbs offers us an alternative perspective, what we might call route two. Here we see humanity's quest for perfection, not as a hubristic Tower of Babel, but as a worthy search for knowledge, perspective and relationship. Jesus comes into this story not as a rescuer from sin and death, but as the embodiment of wisdom. He is the place where the logic of God meets the highest aspiration of creation. He is the coming-together of our earthly existence and God's eternal essence. He is the heavenly word made worldly flesh.

See how different this understanding of Jesus as wisdom is when we turn to the character of Christianity – to the kind of programmes our radio station makes. Route one Christianity risks always being suspicious, keen to expose the hollowness behind every human endeavour. 'You built the Taj Mahal? But it's not Christian, so it's worthless.' 'You compiled the Grand Library of Baghdad in the eighth century, known as the House of Wisdom? Sorry, it was built on sand, because it's not dedicated to Christ.' Route two Christianity is rather different. It sees the Taj Mahal and the Grand Library as part of the great human quest for wisdom – a quest that Christians believe finds its consummation in Christ, the embodiment of wisdom.

Here's a secret: quite a bit of Proverbs is found in ancient Mesopotamian literature, dating back 1,500 years before Proverbs was compiled. See how significant that discovery is. For route one Christianity, it's a serious threat, because it suggests some of what Christians cherish about Jesus began as an insight from another faith. But for route two

Christianity, it's not a problem at all, because you're glad for all wisdom and you appreciate that wisdom accumulates knowledge, perspective and relationship from diverse sources. Steps on the way to wisdom aren't worthless, whoever makes them. They're actions of the Holy Spirit – ways Christ is present beyond the immediate comprehension of the church.

Here's the crucial point that transforms wisdom from accumulation to something much richer. The central line in the whole of Proverbs is, 'The fear of the Lord is the beginning of wisdom.' In other words, all wisdom is, in the end, a form of worship. As we pursue knowledge, refine perspective and cultivate relationship, we're seeking and recognizing truth: and when we find truth, our celebration of that truth is what we call worship. Wisdom isn't the end of all our searching: wisdom is what enables us truly to worship the one from whom all blessings flow.

We don't have to choose between route one and route two. Remember, they're both in the Bible, like different ways to get from here to eternity. But think about that radio station again. What kind of a message do we want to give to the world beyond the church? Maybe not, 'You're useless, you're sinners – you're doomed until you accept our perspective'? Maybe, 'We appreciate your knowledge, perspective and relationship, and it's enriching our notion of truth, of wisdom, and even of Jesus.' That's the wisdom to be found in the book of Proverbs. Jesus is the full embodiment of the wisdom of God that spans the ages and the fulfilment of the wisdom of the ages embodied in a human being. The only response to such wisdom is worship.

Very few preachers know the Old Testament so well that they never fall upon a passage and think, 'What on earth is that all about?' But preaching isn't the lazy repeating of information everybody already knows, or the rhythmic reminder of insights picked up years ago. Your preaching may be transformed by taking the risk of exploring parts of the Bible you'd left as undisturbed as a dodgy attic in a game of hide and seek. If you don't go to the end of the rainbow, you won't find the crock of gold. And if you do, you may start seeing rainbows everywhere.

3

Preaching on Miracles

Earlier when talking about the Ascension of Christ I suggested the best approach to the implausibility of a human body levitating into the cloud was to say, 'There's something far more significant going on here.' That tends to be my approach to preaching on miracles in general. That's partly because the gospel writers take the same view. When Jesus transforms water into wine at Cana, of course there's wonder at the miracle, but John is chiefly concerned with that story as the overview of the whole of Jesus' ministry, which is about turning the water of our earthly life into the wine of eternal life, about turning existence into essence. So the skill is to acknowledge the miracle, but to see beyond it, and direct the congregation's attention to what it truly signifies. What might seem a clear distinction between miracles and parables isn't as exact as we might think: the miracles aren't fundamentally about a scientific transformation, while the parables aren't fundamentally about moral instruction. It may need a preacher to point those things out.

You absolutely must not spend a sermon saying what the miracles aren't, could not be, cannot be supposed to have been. A sermon brings people face to face with God. You can't do that by saying what's wrong with the Bible, or its authors' worldview. Instead you say, 'Look how wonderful this is; let me show you through it something even more wonderful.'

There are broadly two kinds of miracles in the Gospels: ones where Jesus exercises authority over the created world, and those where he brings about transformation in the lives of individual people. Cana and the storm represent the first; the man born blind and Lazarus represent the second. In this chapter I'm going to look at one of each, starting with authority over creation.

That was just a practice
Luke 5.1–11
10 February 2019

I want you to imagine that you're having a bad day. Not the kind of bad day where you lose your keys, leave your phone on the bus, forget to post the red-letter bill payment and spill coffee all over your clothes the moment you get to work. I mean the kind of bad day when the frailty of existence all crowds in on you. Maybe right now you're at a stage in life where you have a lot of bad days, and you can't get out from under them. Or perhaps you're keeping tremendously busy and not having a moment to yourself precisely because you fear that, left alone, the dark mist will descend.

I'm going to suggest four things we think about on bad days, when our isolation and fear and anxiety surround us, and life seems very very tender. It's not an exhaustive list, but I suspect you'll recognize it. We think, 'I am small. I am weak. I don't have enough, not enough to be confident it won't run out. And it'll all be over soon.' Those are more or less the four fears that crowd in on us on our dark days. I am small: I don't make much difference in the world. I'm a failure, no one would notice if I was gone. I am weak: I'm powerless to change the world – I can't even make the changes I need to in my own life. I don't seem to have the skills and talents other people have. My body won't do what I want it to do and I always seem to be out of luck. I don't have enough: if things really turn against me, I don't have enough strength, resources or fall-back options to make it. And it'll all be over soon. I won't live that long, I can't bear to think about all of that and maybe I'll feel my life has been pointless and all the things I've got so obsessed or cross or passionate about will have turned to dust.

I'm not intending to depress you. I'm simply putting you in touch with a state of mind that for some people is an occasional glance into the abyss and for others is a regular state of affairs. I recall having a period of a couple of weeks some years ago where I had terrible headaches and couldn't sleep, night after night, and for that period I was in this dark place almost the whole time. It was very bleak.

The reason I'm describing this wilderness feeling is because it's the perfect state of mind in which to read the first 11 verses of Luke chapter 5. One thing you've always got to remember reading the gospels is that salvation and health are the same word in Greek. The beginning of Luke 5 is an account of salvation, but it might just as well be a description of health. Since early days, theologians have seen the references to the boat as indicating the church and mentions of the fish as suggesting the number of converts made by the first apostles. But today I want to focus on the personal aspects of this story and the way it maps onto the deepest anxieties we have about ourselves and our lives. I believe this story takes us the closest we can get to answers to our four most searching doubts about life and existence. So let's take the story in four stages.

Here's stage one. Jesus is standing by the Sea of Galilee. And then he sits in a boat and starts to teach. Many of you know me well enough by now to recognize that I'm practically useless standing up. I can't concentrate, I can't hold a conversation, I can't enter into someone's world standing up. All I can think about is, 'When do I get to sit down?' When I'm asked to speak at an event, one of the first questions I ask is, 'Will the audience be sitting down?' If not, I say I won't do it. Because I don't believe they'll really be listening. When you say to someone, 'Let's sit down,' you're changing the whole nature of the conversation – you're saying, this is going to take a while, I'm giving all my attention to you, let's speak seriously. In this story, Jesus sits down with us and says all those things with us: it's as if the whole of his ministry is contained in this moment. He didn't come among us to stand and look round the room for better options: he sat down with us. And because Jesus is sitting with us, we're invited into a whole bigger world. He's talking about eternity, not just now. He's talking about forever, not just today. He's talking about everywhere, not just here. He's talking about everyone, not just us. Go back to the dark fear we started with: 'I am small.' You may feel small sitting down with Jesus, but he's putting you in an immeasurably bigger world, in which all of a sudden, every single gesture, word and breath matters. He doesn't make you huge – he makes every tiny thing in you important. And so you're no longer small, because you've entered an enormously greater and more significant world. Sitting down with Jesus is like walking through a secret door into a walled garden – except a garden whose walls stretch forever. Jesus sits down and says, 'Come with me into an incalculably bigger world.'

Here's stage two. Jesus says to Peter, 'Go on then, show us that bigger world: put out into the deep water and let down your nets for a catch.' Everyone knows the expression 'setting up to fail'. It was first coined in 1969. It describes workplace bullying. The boss never stops interfering, or withholds a vital piece of information, or undermines the task. Jesus' words to Peter look like a classic case of giving a person an impossible project and then watching them experience humiliating disaster. Sigmund Freud thought the whole of religion was like this – God giving us impossible tasks and then reducing us to grovelling penitents when we fail to perform them. Recall the second anxiety with which we began: I am weak. Here we come to one of the most profound mysteries of the

Christian faith, a mystery perfectly expressed by St Paul in 1 Corinthians 15: he says in verse 10, 'I worked harder than any of them – though it was not I, but the grace of God that is with me.' This is the mystery of grace. We think we are doing something, but when it is inspired by the Lord, it is not us but the Holy Spirit that is doing it through us. We all crave independence and hate the idea that we're being influenced by some external force, but the best feeling in the whole world is to realize you can't do something but you're doing it anyway in the strength of the Holy Spirit. It's like Dumbo losing the feather yet suddenly being able to fly. It's the moment when you're with a person in great pain, or watching a person being attacked, and you have no idea what to say but the words just come. 'I don't know what came over me' can be a lame confession of guilt; but it can also be a glorious carnival of inspiration. Peter pauses and takes Jesus' instruction on trust – and lo and behold, what happens next is not Peter, but the grace of God that is with him. We say to ourselves, 'I am weak.' Jesus says to us, 'Not in your strength – but let the grace of the Holy Spirit work through you. That's a power that has no limit, a force that never runs out.' Remember Isaiah – 'those who wait for the Lord shall renew their strength, they shall mount up with wings like eagles, they shall run and not be weary, they shall walk and not faint.'

Here's stage three. Peter sees the colossal quantity of fish – so much that it's too much for the nets, too much for his one boat, and when the second boat comes alongside, almost too much for both boats together. Remember Oscar Wilde: 'There's only one thing worse than not getting what you want, and that's getting it.' Peter's fear is our fear: there won't be enough. Things will go wrong, the weather will change, people close to me will die or go away: I won't have enough money, strength, ability, support. It'll all unravel. I'll be alone, with nothing. But it turns out Peter has a very different kind of problem. It's not that he hasn't got enough: he's got way too much. He's overwhelmed. But he's not just overwhelmed by fish: he's overwhelmed because he has realized his imagination is way too small. Jesus has called him to live in a bigger world and has breathed through his actions so the Holy Spirit is at work in him. Now he's beginning to see the results, and nothing will ever be the same again. It's too much for him, and he falls to his knees and says, 'You've got the wrong guy. I'm just a fisherman, and I'm no saint. Just leave me alone. I'm out of my league here.' This is the defining crisis of Peter's life: will he let Jesus take him into a bigger world and let the Holy Spirit equip him with everything he needs? One thing's for certain – he'll never again be able to say, 'I don't have enough.'

But Jesus doesn't take no for an answer. Here's stage four. Before

Peter has even digested the full implications of this monumental catch of fish, Jesus is at him one more time, saying, 'Look here, sunshine, this is just a practice. From now on, it's not going to be fish, it's going to be people. You ain't seen nothing yet. You've just put your toe in the water.' Recognize the economic implications of Jesus' words. Peter has just landed an enormous catch – enough to raise a fortune, buy a bigger boat, retire from fishing and employ staff to do all the hard work while he watches satellite TV back in the office and goes to Capernaum Chamber of Commerce dinners. But Peter never sees the money. Before Peter has even sold his catch, Jesus summons him. 'Peter, you're going to have bigger fish to fry.' Jesus makes Peter's choice for him. Jesus has induced Peter to do an unbelievable thing – to find a massive catch where shortly before there'd been no fish at all. Now Peter realizes he's going to spend the rest of his life with Jesus doing unbelievable things. One day he'll look back and think, 'This was just the audition – the play was a whole other thing.'

Don't think you're the only one who goes into a quiet, dark place, for moments or weeks, and thinks, 'I'm small. I'm weak. I haven't got enough. I'll be gone soon.' Open your ears and your eyes and your heart to what Jesus says to Peter, and what Jesus says to you. Jesus comes to you, sits down with you and gently says, 'Come with me into a bigger world. Let the Holy Spirit work through you. God will give you far more than you will ever need. This is just the beginning.'

See how God transcends your fears. Listen to Christ saying these words to you this very moment. Hear the Holy Spirit whisper these words to the whole Church right here and right now. And get ready: because Christ is here and, in the power of the Holy Spirit, you are going to do unbelievable things.

A lot of preaching is about the preacher's attitude toward the text. I've heard a good few sermons where the preacher is like a tail-end batter facing a fast bowler with fear and trepidation, and the sermon is a narration of the preacher's feelings as the ball is bowled. 'This is a difficult text ... I'm not sure what we're to make of ... we live today in a different world ... Amen.' Whatever the preacher is thinking in preparing the sermon, the congregation doesn't need to hear it. The sermon should not show any sign of its preparation – doing so unhelpfully distracts attention from the text to the preacher.

In a sermon like this you're looking to expand the imagination and faith of the listener. There's plenty of illustrative and informative material, but it's a simple structure where you see four elements in the text and seek to communicate the full import of those four elements to the congregation.

But to maximize the impact, you set out those four elements as vividly as you can, so the exegesis is addressing a question to which the congregation by now eagerly, even desperately, wants or even needs an answer. This is how to turn a worthy but dull sermon into an existentially urgent one.

Here are some guidelines about preaching on miracles.

1. Imagine the excitement and astonishment of those participating in the story. Your sermon needs to capture that.
2. Never think, 'It's just another miracle story.' Every story in the gospels is there for a reason, and the preacher's job is to discern that reason and preach about that reason, more than about the story itself.
3. Do not dwell on the implausibility of the story. You can acknowledge it in a sentence or two, but do not make the sermon in any sense about that implausibility. Make the sermon about the transformation Jesus brings.
4. Do not apologize for the Bible. Perceive what it's really saying. The default for stories about the human body is that Israel was like a human body and the Romans were like the disease of that body. Your standard miracle – take the Gadarene swine – is about the evil being removed from the body/Israel. In the case of the Gadarene swine, the evangelists make it easy by calling the man Legion, an obvious gesture to the Roman armies, and by involving pigs, something no Jew would ever be associated with. The story is clearly about exorcising Rome out of Israel. That's not to say no miracle happened; just to say the larger context is the one to concentrate on.
5. Do acknowledge that today we don't see disability as an illness in need of healing, but as a form of difference to be understood and appreciated as a fertile location for perspectives on God and the world. But don't let that be a reason to ignore a miracle about removing disability.

Once you take these steps, miracles should become some of the most exciting stories on which to preach. The sermon below tries to capture that excitement. It's possible I use superlatives too often, as in the first sentence of the sermon. But the important part of the first paragraph lies in the last line, which promises a holistic vision of not just the story, but the gospel as a whole. I'm fond of the 'everything in just these few verses' model, because it combines theology and exegesis, because it seems to be exactly how the communities in which the gospels were written perceived things, and most of all because I find it inspiring and satisfying for my own faith.

The Gospel in miniature
Mark 5.21–43
27 June 2021

We've just read perhaps the most vivid story in the first gospel ever written. It's about two women: an adult who's healed of chronic sickness and a child who's raised from the dead. I want to read it closely with you now. That's an unusual thing to do, because almost no one reads it closely. Non-Christians don't read it, because it looks like a faraway fairy story that's got nothing to say to the twenty-first century. Liberal Christians don't read it, because it looks like it's saturated in a thought-world of miracles and negative assumptions about women. Conservative Christians don't read it, because it's not obviously about the way Jesus saves us by dying for our sins. So no one reads it. But we're going to read it now. I want you to open your heart to this story and discover how it offers us the whole gospel in miniature, to transform the lives and imaginations of secular, liberal and conservative alike. We're going to read it because it shows us the personal, social, political and theological transformation of the gospel, all in 23 verses.

Let's begin with the personal. It's a story about a girl who becomes seriously ill and is on the brink of death. Scroll back a couple of weeks. The sporting world comes to a halt when Danish footballer Christian Eriksen collapses during Denmark's opening game of the European Championship. The cameras don't know where to look – roving from the distraught teammates to the bewildered fans to the devastated wife to the stricken opponents. Everything that was so urgent moments ago – the game, the tournament, the glory and passion of international sport – has all disappeared. Only one thing matters. That's where Jairus is when this story begins. He's a proud man with a prestigious profile, but his life is in pieces because of his sick daughter. He's on his knees, pleading with Jesus to come. Jesus does come – yet he makes a detour. A woman touches his garment and he feels the power go out of him as she's healed. Her life is changed. Then Jesus arrives at Jairus' house and raises the girl to life. See what's happening here on a personal level: Jesus encounters desperation (from Jairus), humiliation (from the woman) and derision (from the mourners); and he transforms all three: desperation into celebration, humiliation into restoration, derision into amazement. The story is saying that Jesus is present among the desperate, the humiliated and the derided. It's also asking, 'Are you desperate? Are you humiliated? Are you derided? If so, that's where Jesus is present to you.' That's the personal power of this story. That would be plenty. But there are another three dimensions to this story.

Let's turn to the social dimension. Notice the differences in the two stories. Jairus comes to Jesus through the front door: he's named, he approaches Jesus standing, face to face, he's from the ruling class, he has a community, the synagogue, of which he's at the centre. The woman approaches Jesus from the back door: she doesn't dare look straight at him, she just touches the hem of his garment, she's from the underclass, the socially and ritually excluded; she has no community. She has four levels of exclusion: she's had a continual flow of blood for 12 years, she's been through the rigours of premodern medicine, she's parted with all her money, and she's worse than before she sought treatment. Jesus doesn't exploit her: he brings her healing, which comes free. That healing gives her everything she lacks: an honoured place in society. Do you think her touching the hem of Jesus' garment was a spontaneous act? I doubt it. I imagine her plotting for years to find an outdoor space, away from any village, with a big enough crowd to create distraction and a purposeful Jesus who couldn't possibly notice. When all was in place, she pounced. But he did notice.

The key to understanding the whole story lies in the two words that feature in each half. The first word is 'daughter'. When the word daughter refers to Jairus, it's a weak word, indicating the hole in this prominent man's armoury: he has everything, but he's brought to desperation by his daughter's sickness. When the same word, 'daughter', refers to the woman, it's a word of power, dignity and acceptance. The woman starts the story as an outcast. She ends it as a person Jesus himself calls daughter: she's literally part of the family of God. The other key word is 12. When it refers to Jairus' daughter, it means puberty, being of marriageable age, entering into adulthood. When it refers to the woman, it means dejection, suffering and years of exclusion. What the story is saying is that Jesus is bringing a social transformation: he raises Jairus from his knees and brings the woman in from her exclusion and there's a place for them both in the world he's bringing into being. That's the social power of this story. That and the personal level would seem more than plenty. But we're only halfway through.

Let's turn to the political dimension. Think again about the number 12. We've seen that here it's a code word for female maturity, linked to menstruation. But in the Bible as a whole, the number 12 is a code word for Israel. Twelve sons of Jacob, 12 tribes of Israel, 12 disciples of Jesus. This is a story about what Jesus has in mind for Israel. Look at Jairus, falling on Jesus' feet, begging for mercy. It's saying, *Israel is on its knees* – on its knees before God. Look at the woman, beset by a condition that makes her unclean. It's saying, *Israel has been rendered unclean* by the Roman occupation. And then, what happens to the woman?

She's made whole, healthy, pure – so Jesus' mission is to do the same for Israel. And what happens to Jairus' daughter? She's restored to life. And just look at the dialogue between Jesus and the mourners when he arrives at Jairus' house. Jesus says, 'Why are you making such a commotion and weeping? The child is not dead but asleep.' Now translate that into a political context. Jesus is saying, 'Israel's not dead – it's asleep.' Feel the power of those words, where you are right now. The church isn't dead; it's asleep. Your marriage, your relationship, isn't dead; it's asleep. Your career isn't dead; it's asleep. Your faith isn't dead; it's asleep. Jesus is saying, 'I've come to resurrect Israel.' Again, there are two dimensions to Jesus' ministry, brought out by the two females in the story. The story is saying, Israel's not dead, but asleep; Israel's not defiled – it's being restored. That's the political power of this story.

Now for the fourth dimension. I want to highlight the profound theological transformation this story communicates to us. Notice how it upends notions of purity – not just in the first century, but in the twenty-first. We're obsessed by not exposing ourselves to uncleanness – which today we might identify with coronavirus. Masks, hand-sanitizer, distancing: we can't say the first century was preoccupied with cleanliness and we're not. See how Jesus turns all this upside down. It's not that he catches impurity from the woman – instead, *she catches purity from him*. It's purity that's infectious, not impurity. Holiness is more infectious than the virus. Restoration is more infectious than exclusion. Jesus' incarnation doesn't soil the name of God by consorting with humanity: it exalts humanity by consorting with God.

Look at the way the story depicts a transformation in our standing before God. The woman at the start comes in fear and trembling. By the end she experiences peace and healing – or what the Bible more often calls *shalom* and salvation – in other words, perfect relationship horizontally with society and creation, and vertically with God. In between, the woman tells Jesus 'the whole truth'. Here's the transformation these words disclose: when God knows the whole truth about us, God responds not with judgement but with mercy – not with condemnation and rejection but with healing and restoration. One of the churches I served some years ago was quite Anglo Catholic and I quite often used to hear confessions. The priest who taught me to hear confessions gave me a lesson I've never forgotten. He said, 'People are very embarrassed to bare their soul. But I've almost always come away respecting and admiring them more, rather than less.' I didn't believe him at the time – but I've found it to be true. What the story of the woman shows us is that God already knows the truth about us, and what comes about when our truth comes face to face with God's truth is not judgement, but healing.

Now see how this story is fundamentally about the same thing that the gospel is fundamentally about – and that's the transformation of death by resurrection. The story of the woman is tucked inside the story of the girl because what the woman is going through is a kind of living death. The inside story is an honest realization that some states, in this case permanent pain, spiralling poverty, ostracism from community and perpetual humiliation, are like a living death. So Jesus healing the woman is a kind of this-life resurrection. But the fundamental form of resurrection is the one in the outside story, where Jesus raises the girl from death itself. The whole story is saying to us, if you're facing the horror of a living hell, or the grief of agonizing bereavement, or the reality of your own death, Jesus is turning your story into his story, turning your oblivion into his imagination, touching you across the greatest abyss of them all and never letting you go. And then see how Jesus makes this story his story. Like the woman, he becomes the outcast, made cursed by crucifixion. Like the girl, he rises from death. Our story becomes his and his story becomes ours. Feel the power of this personal, social, political and theological transformation. Has any story ever written said as much in just 450 words?

But there's one more thing. And it's not done with words. It has a technical name: intercalation. It means the way this story starts with Jairus' daughter, breaks off to the woman, then returns to Jairus' daughter. It's like a sandwich. Just as the words 'daughter' and '12' are the key to understanding this story, because they disclose that it's really a story about Israel, about purity and about restoration, so intercalation, the sandwich effect, is the key to understanding Mark's Gospel. The story of the woman and the girl is a smaller story about healing encased in a larger story about resurrection. Mark's whole Gospel is a smaller story about Israel enfolded in a larger story about God. The whole Bible is a smaller story about struggle, suffering and setback embraced by a larger story of revelation, restoration and resurrection. Mark's story intercalates us all between Jesus' resurrection, at the end of the Gospel, and Jesus' return, at the end of time. Mark's message is that in Christ, God enfolds our small story in a larger, comprehensive and eternal story.

The story of Jairus' daughter and the woman with continual bleeding is our story, because it's about our two perpetual questions: the smaller question of 'How can I belong in this life?' enfolded in the larger question, 'What will happen when I die?' The answers to those two questions have personal, social, political and theological dimensions. Which is why we read this story.

I've offered so many sermons in this book because in the end example is the best teacher. A sermon like this seeks to address the four main targets of preaching. First, the head: there are lots of interesting things to dwell on, from why people don't read the story to the significance of the number 12 to the significance of intercalation. Second, the gut – where real transformation takes place – which is reached by questions like, 'Are you desperate? Are you humiliated? Are you derided?' Third, the heart, in phrases designed to move, like 'God already knows the truth about us, and what comes about when our truth comes face to face with God's truth is not judgement, but healing.' Finally, the hand, in phrases like 'Your marriage ... isn't dead; it's asleep. Your career isn't dead; it's asleep,' which encourage action without being directive.

When I've planned a sermon, I go through the plan to check if I've addressed these four elements. I do the same when I read through a first draft of the completed sermon. If there isn't much for the hand, I don't worry: sermons are after all about theology rather than ethics, and certainly not about the latter in the absence of the former. My sermons almost always address the head, because they usually begin with something I find interesting, baffling or bewildering, and seek to understand or explain. What I check to be sure of is that they also address the gut. It's going deep into the gut and finding truth there that distinguishes a great sermon from a good one. Occasionally I judge that a sermon has enough without inserting something that could jar, for the gut has to arise naturally and can't be forced. But I want two-thirds of my sermons to address the gut and resolve the profound doubts and despair that linger there. If they do, they'll be deeply heard, remembered and be truly a form of worship.

4

Preaching on Parables

It's easy to say, 'Ooh, I love this parable.' But the problem with a parable is that it's like a joke. Describing, amplifying and extolling a joke invariably kills the joke. A joke is small and perfectly formed. It doesn't need your commentary. The danger with preaching on a parable is that it kills the parable.

The big mistake with parables is to treat them as if they were Aesop's fables. A congregation can be so familiar with a preacher treating a parable as an Aesop's fable – a succinct, pithy, moral tale with no particular theological dimension – that I often make a point of saying that this is not what parables are. The crucial thing to look for in a parable is its theological dimension. In almost every parable, finding the theological dimension transforms the power and significance of the story. Thus, in the parable of the merchant who sold everything he had to buy a field in which was a pearl, you can take the story as a moral tale and urge your congregation to set at naught all their commitments and possessions in order to follow Jesus. But, much more profoundly, you can perceive that God is the merchant who sets aside everything – the well-being of Christ – in order to find us. God is the merchant; we are the pearl. Now you have a very different kind of story. The skill of the preacher is to transform the listener's reading of every parable like that. Sometimes that transformation is the hinge of the sermon; sometimes you note it in passing while pursuing another main subject: either way, you're taking understanding of the parable to a different level.

The good news about preaching on parables is that there's no such thing as a definitive sermon about a parable. So it shouldn't be hard to preach several times about the same parable. The sermons in this chapter don't even try to be definitive: they offer examples of the diversity of direction in which a parable can take you. The first sermon is about work, a subject that occupies the mind of perhaps the majority of a congregation but is addressed by most preachers only seldom. Yet the question, 'What is the value of my daily work in the realm of God?' is surely a pressing question for every lay Christian.

God's work
Matthew 20.1–16
20 September 2020

I want to tell you about three people on my mind at the moment. The first is Derek. Derek has worked hard throughout his life. He didn't have the kind of parents who could dip into savings to buy his first home, or provide him with a car: everything he's got in life he has achieved himself. He's established in his profession. But the pandemic has reduced his work, and his income, considerably. In his thirties, he feels he's at a crossroads. He finds himself in the middle of the day asking, 'Am I really in the right line of business? Is this really how I want to live?'

The second person is Clare. Clare is starting her final year at university. University was supposed to be a wonderful adventure, where you studied something you loved, met interesting people, lived free of the constraints of work or home and got ready to change the world. But the pandemic has decimated that. She's alone a lot, everything has shifted online, there's no social life and no one seems to have a job in the line of work she thought she was headed for. She feels like she either has to follow her heart into impoverishment or seek security without joy.

The third person is Julia. Julia is 65. Her work has changed over the years, from factory floor to market stall, to call centre. While she doesn't feel ready to leave work, work seems to be leaving her. The trouble is, she's never not worked. She doesn't know who she is if her life isn't shaped around her work. The truth is, she's terrified. The future seems to be a long, empty channel, concluded by death.

What these three people have in common is that for each of them, work is the principal way they know who they are. But the pandemic has catalyzed and crystallized changes in society and themselves that make the future of their work very unclear. Derek's question is, 'Is this still working?' Clare's question is, 'What will work?' Julia's question is, 'Is there life without work?'

The pandemic has affected work in several ways. Straightaway, lockdown separated the world into those working harder than ever, who felt the intensity and affirmation but also the pressure and danger of being on the front line; those who reinvented their work from home, learning new technological skills and detaching work from 'going to work'; and those who were suddenly superfluous, put on furlough because the work they did was not workable amid the constraints of lockdown. More gradually, we're now realizing the economic effects of the pandemic mean widespread unemployment. Eventually we'll find out how many of these changes prove permanent.

It seems a good time to reflect together on what work is really all about, for Derek, Clare and Julia, and for millions like them. Work is the principal way we exercise our creativity, skill, energy and experience to some purposeful end. The creation story in Genesis sees work as part of the natural order: from the beginning, people tilled the garden and maintained it. It's not a bad thing that our identity is wrapped up in it. God works, too: the Bible is replete with images of God as composer, potter, metalworker, clothes maker, gardener, builder, farmer and shepherd.

But as well as being a gift, work is also a necessity. There are many constraints on life, and we toil to exist among them. Often we fail, and our enterprises must begin anew, or elsewhere. If we're not our own masters, we harness ourselves to another's project, for a short or long period, and in return we receive a reward – whether we call it wages, earnings, income or salary – and without that reward we couldn't live. Society measures status by our level of reward, but privilege is more about being able to find an ideal balance between reward and creativity, income and enjoyment, energy expended and satisfaction gained.

Yet beyond skill and reward, there's a less tangible third side of the triangle of work. It's the things Julia fears she'll miss most, and the elements Derek is beginning to realize he doesn't have. Most obviously that means other people – colleagues, clients, customers, the intimate confidences shared at the coffee machine and the buzz of activity on the shop floor. It entails a daily, weekly and annual routine. Most of all it refers to a sense of fitting in to a larger purpose, often called vocation, where you feel your small contribution is advancing a greater good, directly or indirectly.

You can only really call work good if it has all three of these dimensions. Even the worst work can have elements of the third – you can hate your job and be poorly paid, but still enjoy your colleagues and surroundings, which was sometimes Julia's experience. Likewise, you can feel you're using your skills and being decently remunerated but if that third element isn't there and you haven't got real colleagues or can't see the good you're doing, you're going to feel like Derek and think you need to make some changes. And you can imagine being Clare and focusing on the first and third, using your skills for noble ends with great people, and then suddenly feel there's no way to do that if the second element is missing and you can't pay the rent.

I want now to turn to today's parable of the workers in the vineyard with those considerations about work in mind. The landowner goes out early and finds workers for his vineyard and agrees with them a daily wage. Then he goes out on four further occasions – at 9, noon, 3 and 5.

Each time he hires more workers, but interestingly no wage is agreed on these last four occasions. At the end of the day the landowner gives the same wage to all the labourers, whatever time of day he hired them – even the ones who just worked an hour at the end of the day. The whole-day workers saunter up, expecting an improved deal – but they get the same as each of the other workers. Now, scholars tell us the sum involved was a generous daily wage. No one has been short-changed. But the whole-day workers don't see it like that. What at the start of the day was a blessing – a good day's pay – has now become an insult, because it's extended to people who have worked a fraction of the time they've worked.

Let's be clear about what the parable is really telling us. If we recognize that the 'day's wage' is a metaphor for salvation – for forgiveness and eternal life – then we lose the sense of irrationality and injustice and it all makes sense. Forgiveness and eternal life are sacred things, beyond precious. To be given such things is mind-blowing and wondrous. Yet in our insecurity, rather than cherish them, we look askance to our neighbours and immediately feel they're not enough. So straightaway we demand more. But it's absurd to ask for three helpings of forgiveness or four dollops of eternal life. We make ourselves ridiculous if we commodify such things. One is all we could possibly need.

But it's a very revealing episode. Because it shows how, within seconds of experiencing the grace of God, we subordinate it to our own petty purposes and turn it into a way we can get ahead of our peers. Rather than enjoy it for the limitless bliss it gives us, we use it as a weapon in a perpetual unwinnable project of one-upmanship. The parable shows how envy destroys us, by distracting us from the fabulous things we have. Envy captivates us with constant comparison. It erodes abundance and turns it into scarcity. It leaves us feeling not cherished, but hard-done-by.

Having seen what the parable reveals, let's now look back at what we've explored about work. Derek's a 1 and 2 person – he uses his skills and makes money, but he's lost the why. Clare's a 1 and 3 person: she's fixed on using skills and doing good, but can't see how to make any money. Julia's a 2 and 3 person: she's made friends and just enough money, but never really had a chance to develop skills and do satisfying work. The pandemic is a crisis for all three of them. Let's see what the parable reveals to each one.

In each case there's bad news as well as good news. For Derek, who's given up the quest for fulfilment in order to exercise his skills and gain a healthy income, the bad news of the parable is that you can never find true security through work – still less through money. It's a painful lesson, but you do well not to invest aspirations in work that it can never fulfil. The only lasting security is the promise of forgiveness and everlasting life, and no amount of work can yield that – it's called salvation and it's a priceless gift. The good news is, that gift is available to Derek, and to all of us, every day.

Clare, like Derek, realizes she's making a sacrifice. In her case she's sacrificing a secure and substantial income in order to use her skills to put the world to rights. The bad news for Clare is that, though she may be putting her conscience first in a commendable way, she'll never achieve righteousness through her work. She may well want to stop being part of the problem and live her life as part of the solution. But we're all part of the problem, and there's no line of work so noble that it's immune from selfishness, pride and envy. The good news is, she doesn't have to be righteous to find forgiveness and eternal life. In fact, she'll probably do a better job for the planet and all who dwell on it if her work is founded on humility and gratitude, than on striving to be perfect.

As for Julia, who thinks she's worked to earn a living but in fact realizes she's worked more to be with people and have their energy rub off on her, the bad news of the parable is that your work isn't your real work. The real work of life isn't gaining skills, making a living or even finding meaning. It's learning to be a human being. The whole-day labourers receive forgiveness and eternal life but it's no good to them because they haven't learned how corrosive and destructive is the power of envy. Being healed of envy is more vital to their security than any amount of earthly reward. The good news is, because she's had a lot of jobs and not defined herself by her trade or profession, Julia's probably the best placed of the three to face her new and biggest challenge – of being a human being when not defined by her work.

In heaven there isn't any work. There isn't anything to fix, heal or complete. So our strategy of using work to build an unassailable citadel of security, competence or righteousness will fail. And so will our tactic of looking to either side to check if we're ahead of everyone else, morally, financially or psychologically.

Ponder this phrase from Ephesians: we are God's work of art. The work that really matters is God's work: the work the Holy Spirit does to conform us to the image of God in Christ. Joy in life lies simply in not impeding that work. That work is as real and important for a disabled child, a stay-at-home parent, an unemployed labourer or a person with dementia. There's no joy in evaluating our just reward or comparing ourselves to those around us. Joy lies in this: allowing the Holy Spirit to make us into the image of Christ. That way, when finally we receive forgiveness and eternal life, we'll realize we've already been enjoying them for a long time.

In this sermon the transformational shift – from seeing the giving of the same wage as monstrously unfair to understanding the wage as forgiveness and eternal life, that is, salvation – isn't the main focus, but still merits a mention in the middle of the sermon.

Here are some guidelines for preaching on parables.

1. Keep it theological. These are not moral tales. (If they are, several of them are terrible.) Don't resort to 'Isn't God weird?', which offers the congregation nothing.
2. Relax and recognize that there are many ways to preach on almost every parable.
3. Most guides to the parables don't take you very far, but Kenneth Bailey is the surest guide out there. See especially his *Jesus Through Middle Eastern Eyes: Cultural Studies in the Gospels* (London: SPCK, 2008).
4. A story that resembles the parable in some respects is not necessarily the most helpful. There's a danger that it can lessen or distract from the trajectory of the parable. Quick illustrative remarks that illuminate moves in the parable are generally better.
5. Showing how the parable can be read in more than one way in a sermon can be helpful – but be sure to make it a sermon, not a New Testament lecture.
6. Parables make an impact and capture the imagination: your sermon should do the same.

The parable of the talents is an especially challenging parable. It's largely resolved by the theological move – Jesus is the talent God doesn't hide in heaven but takes to the 'market' of the world. This saves the parable from its problematic but frequent application in urging overstressed young people to stretch themselves to the utmost as a form of faithfulness. But it's still a challenging parable. I preached on this parable in my first few months at Duke Chapel, and of all my many sermons there it remained the one with which I was least happy. So 12 years later I revisited that sermon and reworked it into the one below, addressing what I felt were the weaknesses in the original. That's the advantage of keeping a record of written sermons.

What do you take me for?
Matthew 25.14–30
19 November 2017

There are two common assumptions about Christianity. One is that it's a theory about how things are – how things began and how the world goes round. The other is that it's basically a moral code. Those two assumptions are widely held by the church's cultured despisers; but they're actually quite common within the church too. One way they surface is in the way we read Jesus' parables.

If we consider the parable of the talents, which we've just read, it's common to read the story as if it were about the way the world goes round. Thus, the talents mean, well, talents – they refer to human abilities. Jesus is obviously talking about people with extraordinary abilities like you and me, and telling us not to be shy about changing the world in our image. Alternatively, if we read the parable as a moral tale, a kind of Aesop's fable, then the talents clearly mean money. Jesus is obviously saying, 'Money won't help you if you keep it under your bed. Go out and make more money. Gain all you can, save all you can, give all you can.' How wonderful to have a parable that tells us we're fabulously gifted and should make more money.

But Christianity isn't fundamentally about the way the world is and it isn't basically a moral code. It's about God, and about how Jesus shows us the character of God. And if we're to live with God forever, we're going to need to be ready to face God on judgement day. That's what this and the other two parables of Matthew chapter 25 – the ten bridesmaids and the sheep and the goats – are all about. Jesus is preparing us to face judgement.

The parable comes in four scenes. Scene 1 is before the man leaves for the journey. Scene 2 is what happens while he is away. Scene 3 is what happens when he gets back. And Scene 4 is what happens to the third slave.

The talents are not natural abilities or great wealth but the Holy Spirit. The Holy Spirit is the talent Jesus leaves the church for the time until he returns. This parable is not telling us how to come to terms with the fact that we're super-talented or super-rich. It's telling us that, in giving us the Holy Spirit, Jesus has left the church all the gifts it needs for the time between his first coming and his second and that, if we don't use those gifts, we'll be in trouble.

So in Scene 1 the disciples learn all they need to know. Jesus is soon going to go away, which seems like bad news; but he's entrusting them with everything that is his, which sounds like quite a lot. They are his slaves. To say we're Jesus' slaves means we belong wholly to Jesus, which is wonderful, fantastic news. It means human nature and destiny are God's problem, not ours. What a relief that is. It's not necessary to dwell too much on the significance of separating talents into five, two and one. Jesus doesn't give us more than we can cope with and it's not a competition. There's no suggestion that the slave with five talents is better or more important than the slave with two. And don't forget that a talent was a colossal sum, maybe a million pounds in our money. Even the slave with one talent had way more than enough.

For some reason, and this is a mystery, one slave didn't use the gift. That's the shock we get in Scene 2. We may say, 'Wasn't it lucky that the first two slaves got a healthy return on their investment – I wonder how they knew which brokers to deal with and whether the FTSE was looking promising each morning.' But not if we remember that these slaves have spent quite a lot of their lives with this master. How do we know that? Because the master is Jesus, and the slaves are the disciples, and this parable comes right at the very end of Jesus' ministry, by which time the disciples have seen the length and breadth and height and depth of what God has been doing in Jesus. The way they use their massive gifts from Jesus, in other words the Holy Spirit, is by doing the things Jesus did, spending time with the people he spent time with, breaking bread with notorious sinners and facing the criticism of the powerful. We know what standards of success Jesus lived by. So success for the disciples means success in imitating Jesus. The one who was given some of Jesus' gifts looked rather like Jesus. The one who was given a lot of Jesus' gifts looked a lot like Jesus.

Come Scene 3, when the master returns, we find that imitating Jesus was just what Jesus wanted. Jesus says, 'You spent a lot of time with me to learn how I do business. I gave you these gifts so you could do business the way I do business. And you have, with the same result. Well done.' But then it comes to light that the third slave, who was given all the gifts Jesus bestowed upon the church, just not the special gifts, has done nothing with them. Jesus is bewildered. 'You never realized that the Eucharist was a meal where all kinds of people could gather round my table, rich and poor, women and men, skilled and unskilled, academic stars and those with special educational needs, black, Hispanic, Chinese, Indian sub-continent, Arab, Caucasian, all of them bringing different things to the table and each receiving back the same?'

'I guess not.'

'You never realized that baptism was the moment when all your foolishness and pride, all your evil and malice, could be washed away and you could be incorporated into the way God is redeeming the world?'

'Nope.'

'You never realized that reading Scripture invites you into a constant discovery of God's character and a revelation of the way God has already redeemed the world?'

'Uh-uh.'

'You never realized that in prayer you could open your whole heart to God and find that God's whole heart is opened up to you?'

'Errr ... no.'

And now at last we can begin to make sense of Scene 4, with its celebrated wailing and gnashing of teeth. Can't you imagine Jesus' reaction to his disciple? 'I don't believe this! You spend three years with me traipsing round Palestine. You see the way I share food with the outcast and bring all around my table. You see the way I transform people and give them possibilities they never dreamed of. You see the way I fulfil all God's promises. You see the way I open out a way to the Father that makes eternal life possible to all people. And then I give you all the gifts you need to establish and sustain this life after I've gone. But you don't. And now I'm back, you're saying it's *my* fault. You've made up this story that I'm a cruel master who reaps where I haven't sown. What are you saying? You yourself have witnessed me sowing seed everywhere I've gone, offering every person I've met the opportunity to enter the kingdom of God. What do you take me for? You're making up a story that's the absolute opposite of the truth for which I have laid down my life, and you're using that story to justify your astonishing laziness. I've told you, I've shown you and I've empowered you, but you've blocked your ears, closed your eyes, folded your arms and made up a story about me to excuse it all.'

I've gone through the parable in detail because I've met so many people for whom this has become the most significant story in the whole Bible. They're people who are deeply aware of their own social advantage and look to the Bible to teach them how to use such privilege without feeling guilty all the time. Maybe you're one of them. If you are, I have news for you. This parable is not fundamentally about you. It's about Jesus. It's telling us that Jesus is not a cunning manipulator, who gives us mysterious talents and then lies in wait to see whether we fail to use them properly. No, Jesus is a boundlessly generous friend who goes away and gives us far more than we want or need to imitate him in his absence. If we assume he's a generous friend, we'll experience the miracle and abundance of life in the Spirit. If we take him for a cunning manipulator, we'll experience life as miserable scarcity.

So this is what the parable means for us. Jesus has told us and shown us everything he means by church and kingdom. The church is the way he works through the ministry of those who seek to follow him, and the kingdom is the way he works in spite of the indifference and rejection of the world and the many failures of the church. But, for the moment, Jesus is gone. Before he left, he empowered his church with all the gifts it needs to obey his teachings and imitate his ministry. What he wants us to do is to use the gifts he gives us, and if we do so we'll succeed in the only way that matters – we'll end up looking and living like him. But what we can't do is just neglect these wonderful gifts he's given us to shape church and kingdom. To justify doing so, we would have to make up some false story that either Jesus hadn't given us these gifts or that he'll reject us on some other grounds. Such a story is a lie. It is making Jesus into a monster. How could someone who'd seen Jesus lay down his life, heard his words, received his invitation, been empowered with his gifts and been sent forth into his kingdom, ever take him for a distant, cruel or merciless master? Jesus says in this parable, and says to us today, 'I've given you everything you need to walk in my ways until I return. I have told you, shown you and empowered you. Trust me and use what I have given you. I will never let you down. What do you take me for?'

But as I said, the parable isn't fundamentally about us. Every parable has more depth the closer you look at it. To get to the root of this parable you need to see Jesus not just as the master who gives us gifts and the slave who puts God's gifts to work, but as the talents themselves. For in sending Jesus, the Father didn't bury God's love for creation in a hole dug in the ground; instead, the Father took that love to market, to trade with it, to face the risks and sufferings and dangers of relationship and encounter. The five talents are, in the end, the incarnation – God risking everything to be with us. The five more talents are, in the end, Jesus' resurrection – the proof that we will be with God forever. Jesus' parables aren't Aesop's fables: they're showing us the heart of God.

In this sermon I play with the two interpretations I think are most legitimate – the talents are Jesus and the talents are the Holy Spirit – and play along with the second interpretation, holding back the first interpretation as the surprise addition to make the conclusion more compelling. That's what I mean by saying you structure a sermon to maximize its rhetorical impact. I don't regard rhetoric as a boo word. It's not something you can avoid – it's something you can do well or badly. The sermon implies the best Sunday to read the parable of the talents is the Sunday after Ascension, when Jesus has gone but the Spirit has not yet come.

I include the sermon below to demonstrate three things. First, the diversity of ways you can preach on a parable. Second, how to handle a parable that everyone thinks they know, but which actually points to something more fundamental than simply underwriting their existing self-justification. Third, how to preach using a lengthy novel without letting the complexities of the novel submerge the sermon.

The light we cannot see
Luke 18.9–14
23 October 2016

The Canadian literary critic Northrop Frye divides every story ever told into four kinds. There's comedy, where life's setbacks are only apparent, and a deeper order is restored by reversal and new information, resulting in peace and progress. There's romance, where grand figures, often with obscure origins, face daunting challenges, which often come in threes, and finally overcome them, in a rarefied and noble quest where no one ever seems to pay for their accommodation. Then there's tragedy, where great people, ignorantly or proudly, flout the laws of nature and fate, apparently without cost, until mighty justice is done and humility restored. Finally, there's irony, in its extreme form known as satire, where the audience or reader can see something the characters themselves can't see, and life's paradoxical lessons emerge in vivid and sometimes harsh ways.

We live in an ironic age. We're a culture of observers, who are sceptical of the grand adventures of romance or tragedy, cynical of the happy endings of comedy and reluctant to shift from our vantage-point of judgement, criticism, analysis and (more often than not) condemnation. And so we have to be very careful when we take up Jesus' parable of the Pharisee and the Tax Collector, because this is a profoundly ironic parable and the danger is that, since we are habitually ironic people, it will only confirm what we assume we already know. Here, we think, is a parable about righteousness. The Pharisee is the epitome of self-righteousness: 'God, I thank you that I am not like other people: thieves, rogues, adulterers, or even like this tax collector. I fast twice a week; I give a tenth of all my income.' What a fool, we say: righteousness doesn't work like that; you don't get to mark your own homework. What a ridiculous prayer, to list before God one's own accomplishments. It's not really a prayer at all, but a command to God to recognize an application form for the kingdom that is laden with all the due qualifications. The tax collector is the soul of humility: that's what God wants, our recognition that nothing in our hands we bring, simply to Christ's cross we cling. It's a straightforward critique of judgemental-ism. It gives us full licence to be judgemental about those we perceive to be judgemental.

Which is where the irony turns round to bite us. Because we end up saying, 'God, I thank you that I am not like other people: self-righteous, judgemental, or even like this Pharisee. I'm tolerant and inclusive; I only exclude those who exclude me.' And all of a sudden, we end up on the wrong side of the parable. It's circular. However hard we try, we never get to keep our ironic distance and end up on the right side of the story. We're skewered.

So how should we consider other people, particularly when we know their professions but not their characters; their appearances but not their stories?

The Pulitzer Prize-winning 2014 novel *All the Light We Cannot See* by Anthony Doerr is set in Europe during the Second World War. It contrasts two characters. Escaping from a disintegrating Paris is Marie-Laure. Marie-Laure cannot see. She began to lose her sight aged 11 and now, as a teenager, cannot see at all. In her life are two crucial figures. Her father Daniel is a locksmith, whose biggest goal in life is to give his motherless child a reason for living despite her fragile sight. He constructs models, first of their neighbourhood in Paris, then of the town of Saint-Malo on the northern coast of Brittany, to which they flee on the fall of Paris in 1940. Marie-Laure's great-uncle is Etienne, made agoraphobic by his experiences in the trenches of the First War, who has a love of ham radio. After Daniel is arrested, Marie-Laure, with remarkable courage, joins the resistance by fetching messages wrapped up in loaves of bread she has learnt to fetch from the boulangerie and passing them to her great-uncle who transmits them on his radio to the Allied forces preparing for their D-Day Normandy landings.

The second main character in the book is Werner. Werner is an orphan growing up in Hitler's Germany. What enables him to escape the horrors of Berlin as not much more than a child is his extraordinary gift for electrical engineering. He's more than capable of constructing his own radio and listens in to broadcasts from all over Europe. He's taken away to a special boarding school for boys who may have a genuine contribution to make to the Nazi war machine. From there he's sent around Europe, tracking down radio hams who're sending secret information to Germany's enemies and to the Resistance. Werner is contrasted with two characters. One is Frederick, his close friend at the boarding school, whose futile opposition to the cruel regime and absurd ideology of the school leads to his being beaten to the point of profound brain damage. The other is Reinhold, who uses his rank of sergeant major to track down precious jewels and deduces that the most precious stone in France has been placed in the elaborate model of Saint-Malo designed by Daniel for his daughter Marie-Laure. Reinhold is an example of a person who found a way to benefit from the Nazi regime but whose hubris and greed become a metaphor for what has overtaken Germany as a whole. The question is, will Werner find an alternative to the futile sacrifice of Frederick and the mercenary acquisitiveness of Reinhold?

Here we have, on the face of it, a righteous Pharisee and a sinful tax collector – a noble member of the French Resistance and a technocratic Nazi invader. The climax of the story is of course when their two narratives converge: Werner realizes that the transmissions he's picking up in Saint-Malo are from exactly the same broadcaster he enjoyed listening to as a child, scanning the radio waves across Europe; and we realize that broadcaster is Etienne, Marie-Laure's great uncle. Marie-Laure, distraught about her father's arrest and disappearance, is determined to use what life she has left to bring liberation to her people. Marie-Laure cannot see the light because she is blind; Werner cannot see the light because he's enmeshed in the Nazi war machine, so much so that the boy who sided with the martyr Frederick in boarding school has since been engaged in rooting out and killing those seeking to outflank the German army. For both Werner and Marie-Laure, the radio becomes the route to all the light they cannot see – and eventually to each other.

Whether the story of Werner and Marie-Laure unfolds as a tragedy, a romance or a comedy I'll leave for you to find out for yourself. What it does demonstrate is the multiple identities of the two main characters and how, when they come to meet one another, those identities are superseded by something deeper and truer and kinder. They're both trapped – Marie-Laure by her blindness, by her virtual orphanhood, by the Nazi occupation of France, made crueller by the nearness of the Allied liberators after D-Day; and Werner by his own orphanhood, the horrific nature of his education and the inevitability that his skills would be used by the Nazis for nefarious ends. But they're also both liberated – Marie-Laure by finding a way despite her isolation and disability to participate with great courage in the Resistance, Werner by transcending his military duty and Nazi ideology to realize the treasure he has met in Marie-Laure. Both are blind. But both turn out not to be defined by their blindness. Both come more deeply to see.

The novel *All the Light We Cannot See* and the meeting of Marie-Laure and Werner offers us a way to respond to the challenge of the parable of the Pharisee and the tax collector. If we respond to the parable by continuing to make judgements on virtual strangers from afar, we get swept into the vortex of the parable and end up subject to its condemnation. The constant danger of our perception of others' self-righteousness is that our sharp observation simply cultivates a self-righteousness of our own. By contrast, *All the Light We Cannot See* invites us to recognize how complex and textured our own narratives are, how elements of courage and kindness are interwoven with entrapment and complicity and impatient cowardice. And each person we meet is a mixture of such qualities, just like ourselves. Every single time we're tempted to condemn another's actions we must ask ourselves whether, in doing so, we're seeking to assure ourselves of our own righteousness, somehow to jump the queue and draw ourselves closer to God. But the truth is, there is no queue. Grace and mercy are not scarce rations doled out by a weary God to those who've worked hardest to deserve them or jumped the queue to snatch them from others' grasp. We have nothing to gain by the misadventure of others – only growth in wisdom, compassion and mercy.

The final irony of this parable is that the two characters are both wrong, and both right. The tax collector is wrong to collaborate with Israel's enemy, the Romans, by extorting money on their behalf. And the Pharisee is obviously wrong to gloat and compare and parade before God his self-designated superiority. But don't miss the fact that while the tax collector is right to recognize that God wants nothing but his unalloyed repentance, the Pharisee is also right to seek a holy life, of tithing and fasting and frequent prayer. The truth at the bottom of this parable is that the Pharisee and the tax collector need each other. Their tragedy lies not so much in their sins of collaboration and self-righteousness, but in their isolation from one another. In *All the Light We Cannot See*, Marie-Laure and Werner discover their salvation lies in one another. Their challenge is to overcome layers of fear and prejudice and judgement so as to make that encounter possible. That's our challenge too.

Church isn't a place where we identify and lambast Pharisees while searching out and applauding tax collectors: it's a community where we meet one another, learn the complexity and texture of one another's stories, wonder at the grace and mercy by which our paths have crossed, realize with gratitude that our salvation lies in one another, and turn together in humility to recognize, like never before, our need of God. When Werner, as a child before the war, first hears Etienne broadcasting on the radio, Etienne concludes his broadcast by saying, 'Open your eyes and see what you can with them before they close forever.' Perhaps what we're first called to see is the complexity and wonder of one another. God's message to both Pharisee and tax collector is, in the end, the same: if you can't recognize the gift of one another, you'll never enjoy the gift of me.

The premise of the sermon is that the novel contains at considerable length most of what the parable communicates in six short verses. But just as the parable helps us see the power of the novel, so the novel illuminates the message of the parable. The parable could end up becoming circular, with every exposition taking us deeper into self-justification; by turning to the novel, we turn away from ourselves long enough to see that the work the parable is actually doing is not fundamentally about us at all. On this occasion I resist revealing the end of the novel because it's not material to the purpose of the sermon. I hope a sermon like this will increase the listener's appreciation for both the novel and, more importantly, the parable.

5

Preaching on Paul

Paul is a divisive figure in the church. He wrote half the New Testament. Half the church thinks, 'He's my guy. He's got the answers. He tells us the whole gospel. In fact, so much so that we hardly need the four gospels themselves.' The other half thinks, 'He's sexist, anti-gay, focused on a limited view of atonement and bleak; and in any case, the other half love him, and they're full of prejudice, so there must be something seriously wrong with him.'

The result is, if mainstream preachers seldom touch on the Old Testament, they keep even further away from Paul. Except 1 Corinthians 13, of course – a good fit for weddings. And this is a tragedy, because Paul has so many gifts to give the church. While I've long been on a campaign to persuade more preachers to focus on the Old Testament, I can't claim I've upheld Paul with quite as much energy. But I include this chapter to demonstrate how a preacher who doesn't think line-by-line exposition with chase-the-reference entertainment is the best way to inspire a congregation and bring the listener face-to-face with the living God can still talk about Paul and make his letters the focus of serious preaching.

I'll acknowledge a certain proportion of my sermons fall into the category of 'What on earth does this phrase mean?' I like to think that's because I'm determined not to shy away from the difficult or daunting dimensions of Scripture or theology, a determination rewarded by listeners that express relief that finally a preacher has addressed something that's long bothered them. But I recognize it's quite an achievement both to bring a bewildering phrase into common currency and to make that phrase a point of inspiration and transformation – and I can't say I always pull that off. Sometimes succeeding in the first half is enough. But the larger goal is to convince the kinds of people I most often preach to that Paul is speaking good news to them and isn't a sinister agent planted in the New Testament to make them feel excluded.

In this sermon, I'm clearly wrestling with a confusing expression. But I hope I succeed in making it an encouraging one.

Hoping against hope
Romans 4.13–25
28 February 2021

Today's New Testament reading, from Paul's letter to the Romans, contains a phrase that would be curious if it weren't so familiar, and when scrutinized seems meaningless; but I want to suggest that it can become our watchword as we enter the next chapter of this seemingly interminable pandemic. Paul is describing how Abraham is the father of faith, because even though he and Sarah were past the age of having children, he trusted God's promise to make him the father of many nations. In Romans 4, Paul talks about how Abraham looked down at his aged body and considered his wife Sarah's apparent incapacity to bear a child. Then Paul coins this familiar but curious phrase. He says Abraham 'hoped against hope'.

What can this phrase possibly mean? Hope isn't a transitive verb – that is to say, it's not something you do to something or someone; it's something you just do without having an object. So you can't hope against something, least of all something else that's also called hope. You can imagine a film called *Hope against Hope* where the two main characters both have the surname Hope and are locked in a titanic battle over the custody of their children, or were the first sisters to compete in a professional boxing match against each other. But otherwise, the phrase doesn't make sense.

What I think the phrase puts before us is a contrast between two conventional ways to live – two philosophies of life – and what being a Christian actually entails. I want to outline for you those two rival philosophies and show how the phrase 'hope against hope' describes the path to which we're called.

Here's what you might call the prudent path. You invest your resources wisely. That means you make the most of education and emerge with good qualifications. Qualifications don't just constitute training – they're credentials that speak for your ability and application even to people who don't know you. You save. In other words, you realize jam tomorrow could be a lot greater and more necessary than jam today. You avoid risk. You know that life can bring the unexpected, but there's no sense in inviting trouble, so you don't make rash decisions or commit to flaky propositions. You keep fit, you maintain your CV, you cultivate friendships and acquaintances that could be useful to you. You don't get yourself involved with unstable people, unwise investments, unsustainable projects. You stay out of debt.

What you're actually doing is constructing a world where you don't need to hope, because you've largely got life under control. To hope is to be vulnerable, to have your destiny in someone else's hands, to be incapable of making things turn out all right and finding your whole existence mortgaged on the unlikely event that someone else will do so for you, by design or by accident. I remember driving a car in Turkey and seeing in my rear-view mirror an open-top truck that seemed to have people hanging off it. Then as I approached the brow of a hill, I realized the truck was moving out to overtake me. As it passed me, I saw it was crammed with about 60 children, some in the body and others hanging off the sides and cabin. But we were approaching the top of the hill and the truck driver couldn't possibly see the road ahead any better than I could. It was one of the craziest and most reckless things I've ever seen. Mercifully, as we traversed the hilltop it transpired that no car was coming towards us. But that moment was the opposite of everything the prudent story is working for. That truck driver put his life and the life of those 60 children and probably mine as well in mortal danger for no good reason. He had to hope. But he could and should have acted in such a way to make hope unnecessary. That would have been the prudent path.

Let's look at a rival philosophy. This says, it's all in the mind. Difficult days will come, whether you've prepared for them or not, and rather than invest all your energies in pretending you can avoid bad things, use your imagination and resilience to ensure those things don't bring you down. Don't dwell on how the past could have been different, don't tell a false story of the present that makes it all about you and don't take refuge in a fantasy about the future. It's broadly the philosophy of ancient Stoicism. The former slave Epictetus said, it's not what happens to you that counts, but how you respond to what happens. So long as we focus on keeping control of our reactions, he said, we're free. Nothing can defeat us. Stoicism is a route to maturity, because it teaches you to stop criticizing, blaming and accusing others, and look inside yourself to find peace.

But if you look more closely, Stoicism is another project to construct a world in which you don't need to hope. Not, this time, because you've got all possible events under control, but because you've got your reactions to events under control. I once met a man who told me he had no fear. He was in prison with a conviction for armed robbery and I'd asked him, 'Isn't it rather frightening to break into a bank and demand the staff hand over the cash? Aren't you expecting the police to arrive and shoot you?' He said, no, he wasn't frightened of anything. He later described to me his childhood, in which his only parent was an alcoholic, and during which he'd learned to take money out of his drunk father's pocket from the age of 4 to get food from the corner shop. I realized that this was a man who'd taught himself not only not to feel fear, but not to feel pretty much any other emotion. He'd taken a series of choices designed to make sure that he need not trust anybody. What I couldn't get him to acknowledge, despite the fact he was in a long-stay prison, was that this approach, however understandable, wasn't working out terribly well.

So here we have two approaches to what we could call limiting the damage that life can inflict on us. But in a curious way, they both constitute kinds of hope. The prudent method rests on the hope that if we play our cards wisely, we won't ever have to face something that's beyond our control. The Stoic method rests on the hope that if we can keep control of our emotions and reactions, nothing will prove too much for us. The trouble is, helpful guides as both of them are in many circumstances, neither of them finally works. We can't keep everything under control; and learning not to be subject to our immediate reactions doesn't stop us facing things that threaten our identity and existence. So we need another kind of hope.

It's exactly this other kind of hope that Paul is talking about in Romans 4. He says that Abraham and Sarah trusted God and entrusted themselves to God's future, despite knowing they couldn't have a child. They had to weigh in the balance their knowledge of reality and God's promise. They backed God's promise, and they had a child, Isaac. In just the same way, Paul says, we must weigh in the balance our knowledge of reality and our faith in the death and resurrection of Christ. We should choose faith, Paul says. The difference, besides Jesus being God's son, is that Abraham and Sarah were trusting in a promise of something that hadn't yet happened, whereas we are holding on to faith in something that has already happened.

By describing Abraham's forward-looking promise and our backward-looking faith, Paul is giving us two of the three constituents of hope. When we feel bewildered, overcome, distressed or terrified, these are our first two steps. We look back and say, God made the impossible possible. God created everything. God brought me into being. God preserved my life when it could have been lost and God brought into my life people and places and precious things. God raised Jesus from the dead. God made life out of dust. That's faith – faith that leads us to trust. Then we look forward and say, God has promised us such things as pass our understanding. God promises to be with us always. God says, 'I will be with you in the valley of the shadow of death.' God says, 'I will be with you to the end of time … and beyond time. I will be with you whatever comes next.' Faith in what God has done leads us to trust what God promises to do.

Those are the first two steps of hope: faith and promise. But there's one more word in Romans 4 that completes the vocabulary of hope. When we say the phrase 'hope against hope' it sounds really difficult, like we're straining with all the muscles in our neck taut, as if we're in agony, or pulling a rope with an impossible weight behind it. But that's not what hope is. Imagine you were a guerrilla fighter bent on exterminating and assassinating every member of a rival movement, and you had the blood of many people on your hands. And then you were taken by surprise and thrown to the ground, and you saw the leader of the rival movement, and you closed your eyes because you thought you were going to be killed. But instead of savagely slaughtering you, that leader spoke your name and said, 'You've got me wrong, and my followers wrong. I don't hate you. I'm the one that gave you life. I want you to start again, and live like me. Today your life really begins.' That's what happened to Paul on the Damascus Road. It's called grace. Grace is the third word in the vocabulary of hope. When Paul writes about grace, he knows what he's talking about. Grace ties together faith and promise, and says, 'It's all gift.'

So now we know what it means to hope against hope. Our lives are thronged with two conventional kinds of hope: prudence and Stoicism. Useful as they can be, ultimately, they both fail. What we each must discover is the grace of God – the unmerited, unsought love that makes all things and transforms all things and is the reason we're here at all. Through remembering the promise and trusting the faith we realize grace has been what this story is really about all along. It's time to set aside false hope and entrust our lives to the only true hope. That's what it means to hope against hope.

While this sermon plucks out three aspects of the passage in question, it's also taking the opportunity to highlight on a broad canvas the difference the gospel makes; so by the end the listener isn't thinking, 'I'm glad to say I now know a lot more about Paul (or Romans, or even hope)', but instead, 'I now see the difference between the conventional wisdom of the world and the grace of the gospel.' Understanding a passage of Scripture isn't an end in itself; it's a means to the end of coming face to face with yourself – and with God.

Here are some guidelines for preaching on Paul.

1. Acknowledge negative perceptions many people have about Paul, but don't dwell on them. Rather like Ascension and miracles discussed

in previous chapters, the general approach is, yes, there are obvious difficulties, but see how much more there is beyond those difficulties.
2. Paul doesn't give you the opportunity to preach on a narrative, which often comes most naturally. Instead, it's more like the approach to Old Testament poetry, where you're more inclined to pick out one, two or three key phrases and either fit them together in a structure or see how they answer a question that matters to your congregation.
3. Be open to just focusing on one phrase: it's not always necessary to expound the whole passage.
4. Don't apologize for Paul. If you haven't got anything positive to say about a phrase ('women should be silent in church') ignore it and get excited about something else he's saying. Better to preach inspiringly about one phrase than half-heartedly or inhibitedly about the whole passage.
5. Do occasionally step outside a particular passage and introduce your congregation to the great debates about Paul that are lively in the academy today. The point is not to show your vast learning, but to help your congregation understand that the core issues about Paul are up for discussion and that his letters are not a monolith you have to take or leave. But remember your sermon is about bringing good news, not just remixing tired perspectives on Paul.
6. Unlike the gospels, Paul is invariably commending the faith to his readers. Your sermons on Paul are therefore likely to have a more apologetic tone than your sermons on the Gospels.

The sermon below is like the first one above, in that it sets up the passage as the answer to a question the congregation is likely to be struggling with, which in this case is, 'what we're tempted to do when things aren't going our way.' It's more psychological and in this sense uses humour and close observation to embrace our human fragility. But in the end, it's a call to develop the trust to live truthful lives.

Treasure in clay jars
2 Corinthians 4.1–12
3 June 2018

There's a great tradition in the Church of England. Perhaps most of the clergy, about all of the retired clergy, and a disturbingly large number of the laity, at some stage toward the end of the week or over the weekend, fumble their way towards the letters page of the *Church Times*. Why they take on this self-imposed flagellation, it's hard to say. Because very quickly, however joyful and inspiring a week they've had, they discover that actually they had no idea how much there was to moan about. The *Church Times* tries to be different from the national daily papers. Without being trite or unctuously cheerful, it seeks to bring good and happy things happening all over the church to wider attention. But each week its letters page tells a different story. Correspondents far and wide leap to point out that things aren't so simple; in fact, everything's been very badly handled; the church has gone to the dogs and the world is approaching hell, transported by a simple handbasket; all the wrong kind of ideas are in fashion and some pretty second-rate people are in charge of everything; it's all a total disgrace, as I've written 43 times previously to point out. Why do people read such sad correspondence? Maybe to remind themselves that things aren't really as bad as all that, and to resolve to do their duty and get a life.

The great critic of Christianity, Friedrich Nietzsche, used to say that the problem with Christianity is that Christians don't look very redeemed. There's something inescapably glass-half-empty about much, perhaps most, of the church. Even though God in Christ has redeemed our past through forgiveness and created our future through everlasting life, we still find a way to say it was disappointing that the final hymn was a little bit flat or the youth group was a little boisterous or the bishops should have spoken out on the demise of saying grace at lunch in primary schools. The point about the redemptive power of the *Church Times* letters page is that when you're feeling miserable, the last thing you want is to see people who are cheerful, especially if you suspect it's a cheeriness that's superficial or just for show. Instead, what you want is to encounter people worse off than you, which alone makes you feel maybe things aren't that bad really and, after all, worse things happen at sea; or alternatively, people making an almighty fuss about something really quite trivial, which occasionally provokes you into ironically thinking, 'Maybe my issues aren't as momentous as they seem to me, and maybe someone else would think I was making a mountain out of a molehill too.'

The apostle Paul was a man of many gifts, but it's probably fair to say he wasn't blessed with a particularly large streak of irony. In Second Corinthians chapter 4 he's clearly having a tough spell in ministry. Don't let anyone tell you the Bible presents a fanciful, rose-tinted picture of the life of faith. Quite the contrary: Paul frequently lists the hardships of an apostle in such terms that he seems close to a nervous breakdown. But that only makes his reflections the more fascinating, because if it was simply a pathway to glory, we'd struggle to relate to it; but in reality, it's all too human. Paul succinctly describes exactly what we're tempted to do when things aren't going our way. He's talking about preaching the gospel, but what he's portraying pretty much goes for anything we started off doing conscientiously and with great enthusiasm, yet find isn't turning out as planned. He's got four manifestations. You may want to think of them in relation to your life of faith, or alternatively they may apply to your regular work or personal challenges.

Here's the first. You find yourself changing the message. Paul calls it 'falsifying God's word'. What he means is, telling people what you think they want to hear. One person calls it diplomacy, another calls it being a chameleon, another says it's being spineless. It doesn't usually happen overnight. In A. J. Cronin's 1937 novel *The Citadel*, a young doctor, Andrew Manson, arrives in a Welsh mining town and marries Christine, a local teacher. Having struggled with every sinew to improve the lives of his miners, once his research is published, he takes up a private practice in London, where he quickly makes easy money from idle patients and lazy surgeons. His wife no longer recognizes who he is. Manson has done exactly what Paul is describing: he's started giving his patients what they want, rather than what they need. Anyone who's been a pharmacist, a teacher, a pastor or a parent knows what that means. It's gaining the whole world but losing your soul. Paul's having none of it.

The second thing Paul talks about doing in the face of adversity is manipulation. When it comes to things that really matter to people, like health, or faith, or love, the line between charm and manipulation can be a very fine one. It can start with flattery, progress to a show of neediness, then flip to a tone of great authority, and then slip into ingratiating requests. What starts as an apology suddenly becomes a criticism; a compliment somersaults into a demand for money; you start by being sympathetic and quickly you're made to feel guilty. In no time you've said or done something you'd never normally do and, like a gambler pressing in more and more coins, you keep going, seeking to justify the mistake you can't believe you've made. Paul's an expert with words and emotions: such experts can be dangerous. Like a hypnotist, the manipulator has you under their spell. But Paul's having none of it. He wants the truth to stand on its own merits.

The next thing Paul mentions is the easiest way to come to terms with our own failure: blame the audience. If you're a stand-up comedian and no one laughs, you come off stage and say, 'They're so stuck-up – they've got no sense of humour.' If you're selling hot dogs on the street and no one's buying, you say, 'They don't know what's good for them.' If you're giving a lecture and everyone's yawning, you say, 'Imbeciles! I'm surrounded by fools!' The journey of humility is one that draws you to realize that maybe it's not all everyone else's fault. Not long ago I was at a party and three friends posed with fetching smiles and I was walking by and said, 'I'd be glad to take your picture.' So one handed me her phone and I just couldn't get a good image on the screen. First it was blank and then it only seemed to show a picture of me. Finally, after fits of giggles one of my friends had mercy on me and showed me how to reverse the lens so it actually showed the three people I was trying to take a picture of. The next day I was sent a picture taken by another photographer of three people convulsed in laughter at someone trying and failing to take a picture of them. That someone was me. The three people weren't to blame. The phone camera wasn't to blame. I was to blame. I've since become more accomplished at flipping the lens from selfie to regular and back. It's not that hard. That's what Paul's asking us to do. Don't blame others just because it's not going well for you.

And the fourth thing Paul highlights as our response to adversity is pointing to ourselves. Bad evangelism has, over the centuries, been a mixture of all four of these errors, but perhaps the worst is to try to turn people into versions of ourselves. A Greek myth tells of the hunter Narcissus, who was led by the goddess Nemesis to a pool, where he saw his own reflection and fell in love with it. He was so absorbed in his own image that he lost the will to live and stared at the pool until he died. It's possible to do just the same, whether proclaiming the gospel, leading an organization, playing in a sports team or waiting for a bus. You just say, 'This is all about me! I'm the centre of this amazing drama! Everyone's getting at me, why are you all looking at me, everyone has to listen to me.' Paul says, 'No, actually it's not about you. Get used to it. There are billions of us here. They all think it's about them too. Stop being so mesmerised by your own reflection.'

Four mistakes we're all in danger of making when things don't go our way. Four things we all tend to say when we feel like raining on someone else's parade. Lying. Manipulation. Blame. Narcissism.

Paul's insights apply to almost any walk of life. But what he's talking about specifically is how we commend our faith to others. And here's the biggest insight of all. Paul says, we think we're the best representatives of Christ when we're successful and stylish and convincing. That's why we're tempted to lie, manipulate, blame or switch to permanent selfie. But Paul says, actually, it's not like that. Think about a clay jar: a fragile item of pottery you'd carry a candle in. It breaks the first time you drop it or nudge it into a surface or plate. That's what we're like. What's important is not how robust we are, but the treasure we're carrying. And Paul talks about two kinds of treasure.

The first is the kind we glimpse but can't comprehend, that we know but seem somehow to forget: 'The light of the knowledge of the glory of God in the face of Jesus Christ.' The light – like a candle in a dark room that changes everything. The knowledge – this amazing discovery, like the news Mary Magdalene broke to the disciples when she said, 'I have seen the Lord!' The glory – the very presence of God, shimmering, and making us shiver with wonder. The face: all the truth of forever and everywhere utterly present in the face of this one person. That's the indescribable treasure: the light of the knowledge of the glory of God in the face of Jesus Christ.

But the second treasure is possibly even more amazing: it's in the two contradictory words, 'but not'. Once you cut out the excuses and the shortcuts and the denials, you find you're afflicted, perplexed, persecuted and struck down. Everything you wanted to avoid. But see the light of the glory of God in the face of these two words: *but not*. 'We are afflicted, *but not* crushed; perplexed, *but not* driven to despair; persecuted, *but not* forsaken; struck down, *but not* destroyed.' We get to share Christ's crucifixion: but only so we get to share his resurrection also.

You can hate Paul, you can be angry with Paul, you can try to ignore Paul. But in the end, he's telling us the truth. Stop lying, stop manipulating, stop blaming, stop making it all about you. Open your eyes and see the light; open your mind and receive the knowledge; open your heart and feel the glory; open your soul and behold the face. And revisit all your life's failures. Recognize you were afflicted, but not crushed; perplexed, but not driven to despair; persecuted, but not forsaken; struck down, but not destroyed. Let Jesus' death and resurrection take place in your own body. And see what the glory of God can do.

The sermon works hard to be relatable: there are short sentences, chatty observations, rapid disclosures, intriguing insights. It's all designed to persuade the congregation not only that the preacher gets our very human temptations to expand or distort the truth, but more importantly that Paul does. The setting of the scene takes three-quarters of the sermon, which may be too much. But in this case, naming the problem is a big part of the sermon's agenda. There are a couple of solutions and a call to faith and trust at the end, but perhaps the key work of the sermon is exposing sin (and not in the conventional places) rather than offering salvation.

The final sermon in this chapter takes a different approach. Following guideline 3 above, it's not really exegetical at all. I wrote it very quickly on hearing a close friend was facing a terminal diagnosis. I don't see any benefit in sharing with the congregation the reason why I'm preaching this sermon – why it matters so much to me. Instead, I offer a variety of contexts in which this message might be relevant, without highlighting any of them. I don't want to distract the congregation into thinking about me – I want them to reflect on their own context, past, present or future; for there can't be anyone who hasn't been there, isn't there or won't ever be there.

This is absolutely a gut sermon. Sometimes you have to manage your emotions when preaching a sermon like this. Showing undue emotion when preaching isn't an impressive form of passion – it's sucking the emotion away from the congregation and taking it all to yourself. It's fine to pause to collect yourself, but you need to read a sermon like this through enough times to be fully aware of where the quavering parts are and be ready for them, by reading them slowly, quietly or, if necessary, pausing till you regain your composure.

Eye of the storm
Galatians 1.11–24
9 June 2013

In March 1990, the Five Nations rugby union championship lay in the balance. Scotland and England had both won all their matches and England travelled to Edinburgh knowing that the winner would take the coveted Grand Slam. The game is remembered as perhaps the finest in Scottish rugby history. But the defining moment came before it started. The England players ran on to the field to a largely hostile reception. But the Scots' captain David Sole did something different. He led his team out at a stately walking pace. It was an iconic moment. It said, 'There's nothing you can throw at us we can't deal with. We're going to win this game, and we're going to walk right towards you, and we will not be overcome.' And that's exactly what happened. England threw everything at Scotland; but to no avail. And David Sole's walk became part of Scottish folklore.

Think about that walk for a moment. Take away the furore of the crowd. Take away the intimidation of a stronger and more vaunted opposition. Take away the reservation that sport is only a game and the suspicion that all this competitive energy is displaced from somewhere less tangible but more important. Just stay with the walk. Get into David Sole's mind. This is the defining moment of my life. In this case, a defining moment in my nation's cultural life. Somehow a cluster of events have brought it about that what happens in the next two hours will be my identity, my legacy, my single truth. And I'm walking slowly towards it. I'm entering the eye of the storm.

When Paul writes to the Galatians, he's talking about just such a moment. He's talking about the eye of a storm. The storm is this: Jesus has come into the world, but the world has received him not. Jesus has come to his own people, but his own people have comprehended him not. The leaders of those people have got the Romans to string Jesus up in a cursed and humiliating and agonizing death. They've taken the most beautiful gift and most gracious gesture and most loving treasure and dashed it to the ground, treading its remnants underfoot. And when Jesus rises from the dead and sends his Spirit to raise up disciples of Jew and Gentile to be his body, the storm isn't over. Fanatical vigilante leaders of the special people take it upon themselves to exterminate the disciples, eradicate the followers, destroy all who bear the name of the risen Lord. And in the eye of the storm is Paul, most fanatical of the chosen ones. And the Spirit is like David Sole. The Spirit walks straight towards Paul. The Spirit ignores the crowd, the hostility, the heritage, the rhetoric, the vitriol. The Spirit of God walks right into the eye of the storm and starts its work of transformation with Paul himself.

Nine months before David Sole's iconic walk, Tiananmen Square was filled with pro-democracy protestors. The government in Beijing cracked down and on 4 June 1989, troops cleared the square of the student-led demonstrations. Hundreds, perhaps thousands, of people met violent deaths. Twenty-four hours later the square was largely empty of protestors. On that day an enormous column of tanks was making its way down one of the avenues leading into the square when a lone protestor stood in front of the lead tank. In a gesture that's come to crystallize Tiananmen Square, the summer of '89 and the pro-democracy movement worldwide, the man walked slowly toward the tank. It was one of the defining moments of the twentieth century. No one ever identified who he was. But the whole world understood what that gesture meant. He was confronted by uncompromising, ruthless, single-minded, unswerving power. And he walked slowly, calmly towards it. He didn't deny it, dodge it, deceive it, escape it, work around it, give in to it. He walked towards it. He walked into the eye of the storm.

I wonder what that man's witness means to you. Take away the global attention. Take away the glamour of a primal confrontation. Just focus on the tank, the symbol of unstoppable, inevitable suppression, and this fragile man walking towards it. Just contemplate walking towards the eye of the storm.

I wonder if you're facing a storm right now. Maybe you're in a situation at work where everyone's under terrific pressure and there's unreasonable demands or illegal practices or exploitative expectations or exhausting responsibilities or burdensome duties or terrifying challenges. Perhaps you wake up at night, sweating, worrying, not knowing how to think straight, who to talk to, what to do first, how to see beyond your terror. Or it could be you're facing a crisis closer to home. You're facing an illness, and it's serious, maybe very serious, and may only get worse. Or a relationship or a plan on which much was staked is in the fire of agony or in the balance of indecision. Your life, or the joy in your life, or the well-being of someone you treasure, seems to hang by a thread. Maybe the moment isn't right now, the storm isn't exactly overhead – but you can see it coming. You know it's heading toward you. Maybe right this moment you realize you've actually seen it coming a long time. A long time.

And all your instincts are to dodge, to escape, to deny, to dive for cover, to find a way out, to run away. Of course they are. We're surrounded with gadgets and opportunities to fly away into distraction, into alternative realities, into fantasy, into thinking about anything but what's in front of us. Everything is telling us to avoid this moment, to close our eyes and wait for it to go away, to let it sort itself out, to go to sleep and discover it was all a bad dream, to invite an ethereal parent or fairy godmother to wish this moment away.

Could it possibly be that God is calling you on this occasion, gently and quietly, not to deny, flee, distract, pretend, but to walk slowly, purposely, intentionally, towards the eye of the storm? Of course, some dramas are best avoided, some wounds are not things to dwell on. But for each one of us, I believe there's a David Sole moment, a defining storm we're called to walk towards, a storm in which everything we are and are called to be comes together in a moment we can't avoid or deny. Maybe you're facing such a moment right now.

Given that it's against all our instincts, let's take a little inventory of what walking towards the storm would mean. Stand before that column of tanks for a moment and think about what it would mean to start gently walking towards them.

It would mean going into your bottomless fear, naming it, facing the worst thing that could happen, feeling the impact of that worst thing, and then trusting that God will meet you on the far side of your fear, so that you go through and beyond your fear and out the other side. That's courage. Trembling courage.

It would mean facing up to the unspeakable waste, the dream of what your life was supposed to be, the template for what you thought God had in store for you, the good things you thought you were entitled to hope for, the goals and prospects and options, and instead focusing on just this one thing you're walking towards as perhaps the only thing

God wants you to concentrate on right now, and believing that God will look after the rest. That's trust. Quavering trust.

It would mean entering into the convulsing grief, the loss, the fear of separation, of isolation, of being forgotten, of not mattering any more, of being snuffed out like a candle, of an ending not of your choosing, of it seeming to many or all as if you'd never been, of having no meaning to your life except as God makes for you, and believing that that's all that counts. That's faith. Shuddering faith.

It would mean accepting the prospect of harrowing pain, of physical, visceral hurt of uncertain duration, of unpredictable depth, of relentless intensity, with no protection except the everlasting arms, and believing those arms will never let you go. That's hope. Quaking hope.

Fear, waste, grief, pain. That's what it means to walk towards the storm. Courage, trust, faith, hope. That's what we look for in the defining moments of our lives.

This isn't the way our contemporary culture teaches us to address the storm. Our culture teaches us to fix the problem. If we can't fix the problem, learn better techniques, apply stronger systems, use more advanced technology. In other words, find a way to control the storm. We live in a culture that believes in controlling the storm – that imagines that one day every storm will be subject to our control. We live in a culture that has nothing to tell us about a storm we can't control – a culture that tries to manage storms so as to make virtues like courage, trust, faith and hope unnecessary.

But maybe that's precisely what you're facing today. A storm you can't control. At work. At home. In your body. In your mind. In what God's calling you to. A storm you can't fix. A storm you can't manage. A storm that is coming right towards you.

And what we see in Galatians is that God walks toward that storm – like the man in Tiananmen Square, walking toward the column of tanks, like David Sole walking purposefully, intentionally, onto the Murrayfield turf. Maybe you can't escape, maybe it's useless retreating into a fantasy world, maybe this is something that isn't going to go away by itself. Maybe it's time for a different approach. An approach of faith, and hope, and love. Maybe it's time to walk towards it. And maybe that means naming, entering and going through and beyond your bottomless fear, maybe it involves accepting, reckoning with and accounting for the unspeakable waste, maybe it includes feeling, shouldering and understanding the convulsing grief, maybe it requires living with, enduring and incurring the harrowing pain.

Why? Because God so loved the world that Jesus walked towards the eye of the storm. Jesus didn't deny, avoid or escape Jerusalem. Jesus walked towards Jerusalem, as if it were a field of combat or an oppressor's tank. And Jesus took up his cross and walked towards Golgotha, beyond trembling fear, in spite of criminal waste, amid echoing grief, embodying terrible pain. Jesus walked slowly, purposefully, intentionally, into the eye of the storm, because only through the storm would he find what he was truly looking for.

And what he was truly looking for was ... us. He kept his eyes on the prize – and the prize was us. When God went into the eye of the storm of hostility and rejection and distrust and fury to find Paul, it was because that's what God does. God walks toward the storm to meet us.

And that's why we walk toward the storm – in trust, in resolution, in hope. Because God's walking toward the storm too – from the other side. There's no fantasy or denial or escape in God. God knows the way to us lies via the cross. God is walking into the eye of the storm to meet us. We walk into the eye of the storm for one reason only. To meet God.

At one time or another, each one of us faces a moment when it's time for us to drop our fantasy and denial and escape, and ourselves walk towards the storm. Because it's in the eye of that storm that we shall finally, fully and forever meet God.

Preachers should always be preaching to themselves, though never exclusively. Sometimes, though, it's more evident than others. That's something neither to shy away from, nor to indulge in. It's just part of what we're called to do.

6

Preaching on the Epistle

By 'the Epistle' I mean that part of the New Testament that isn't the Gospels and isn't by Paul – that is, Acts, the letters by other people and Revelation. There's quite a diversity of literature here, often covering territory largely unvisited by the preacher. But one of the chief results of the style of preaching I'm commending in this book is to encourage listeners that there's nowhere in the Bible they should fear to go. Preaching should not make the congregation think, 'How wondrous is the Bible' but, 'How wondrous is God.' I see the Bible as a ladder the believer can kick away on coming face to face with the God of Jesus Christ – but a ladder the believer constantly returns to in order to replicate that encounter. It's not the only means of having this encounter – revelation can come generally though creation, personally through conversation or confrontation, studiously through reading or assimilating information, or directly through prayer and contemplation. But it's the definitive form of revelation, because it's the record of revelation to God's people made over centuries.

The advantage and disadvantage of preaching on the nether regions of the New Testament are the same: the passages are ones with which the congregation is likely to be less familiar. This carries the opportunity of discovery; it bears the burden of explanation and contextualising. It may also, for example in relation to some passages in Revelation, raise the discomfort of wondering what this passage is doing in the Bible at all, although the lectionary compilers have done an effective job of reducing such furrowed-brow moments to a minimum. But there's more gain than loss. It can be invigorating to preacher and congregation alike to fall upon a hitherto uncharted part of the Bible and find it too has the words of eternal life.

I've chosen two sermons on Hebrews for this chapter, both of which take the approach of engaging broadly with a question the text addresses specifically. The first explores the theme of priesthood.

The new and living Way
Hebrews 10.11–14, 19–25
18 November 2018

When I was in primary school, school was really only about one thing. That one thing was the football game we played at break time. One day, the ball got kicked onto the school roof by mistake. My friends and I faced the unthinkable prospect of 45 minutes' break time with no ball to entertain us. Can you imagine? Something had to be done. Various forms of human ladder were devised to provide access to the roof. But who was to be the person who actually climbed up and got on the roof? Who do you think? Me, of course. Only one person was that stupid. I got up easily enough, made my way across the flat roof, and tossed the ball down with a nonchalant air. Only then did it dawn on me that getting down from the roof was a very different matter. It was too far to jump, and the human ladder didn't look so appealing from the top down. I did the only sane and sensible thing there was to do. I burst into tears.

Only years later did I realize that this was my first experience of how it sometimes feels to be a priest. I'd emerged out of a crowd and done something on behalf of the people. That's what priests do. A priest then returns to the people to communicate the consequences of what has been seen and done. I hadn't quite mastered that second part. But I was only 8.

You can't really grasp the urgency of the scriptural debate about priesthood unless you can appreciate how unimaginable it was for my 8-year-old friends and me to face break time without a football. Then you transfer that existential yearning to the time of Solomon's temple. Long before, under Moses, Israel had received the Ten Commandments on two stone tablets and those tablets were carried around in a trestle known as the Ark of the Covenant. Israel came to understand that this represented the presence of God. First in a tent, then in a shrine, and eventually behind a huge curtain in the temple itself, Israel came to believe that prayers offered and sacrifices made would cancel out the sins that distanced the people from God and thus jeopardized the covenant.

Imagine how catastrophic it was, then, that the temple was destroyed and the Ark of the Covenant irretrievably lost in 585 BC. At the time, it was all part of the horror that drove the people into exile in Babylon. But its true significance emerged 50 years later, when Israel returned from exile and began to build a new temple. What was the point of having a temple if it had no Ark of the Covenant at the heart of it? How effective could prayers and sacrifices be if the embodiment of the covenant was not there? The fact that there was now nothing behind the huge curtain symbolized the confusion of the 500 years that preceded the coming of Christ. If there was no Ark and no stone tablets, was Israel still more or less in exile, cut off from God?

For the letter to the Hebrews, this is the situation Jesus walks into. The crucial detail is that, at the moment Jesus dies on the cross, the curtain of the temple is torn in two – in other words, the sense that God is behind a veil and unreachable is over. Jesus is the high priest who has not only torn apart the curtain, but in his sacrifice has brought an end to the history of sacrifices by finally restoring our covenant with God. 'By a single offering,' says the letter, Jesus 'has perfected for all time those who are sanctified.'

At this point, you can see why many people resist calling Christianity a religion, but instead regard Christianity as the end of religion. Because the repeated offering of sacrifices, apparently to appease, or at least to propitiate, a distant God, seems to epitomize most assumptions about what constitutes a religion – rites, rituals, sacred songs, holy men, special clothes, guilt, blood, built-in incompleteness, and a lot of smoke. Jesus brings an end to all of that, with a single offering that does away with the hokey cokey. So there's no need for the usual trappings of religion.

So why, we might then ask, are we gathered here this morning with rituals and robes and religious paraphernalia and priests? I thought we didn't need priests anymore, because Jesus has taken away all that stands between us and God?

You could say I'm the wrong person to answer this question, because as a priest I have a vested interest (boom-boom). But what Hebrews goes on to say in the last four verses of today's reading is that once Jesus' sacrifice has opened the way into the sanctuary for all of us, it's for all of us to do the three things that are still needed once our sins are washed away. The first is to 'approach with a true heart in full assurance of faith,' that is to say to worship, to pray, to share in the sacraments, to pierce through the ordinary to find the joy, to recognize the alive and beyond in the here and now, to overflow with gratitude and wonder and to look to the fount of every blessing for transformation of all that falls short of truth and glory. The second is to 'hold fast to the confession of our hope,' that is to say to grow in faith, to form one another in the habits of holiness, to study, question, explore and discover the riches of our tradition, the depth of Scripture, the mind and heart of God and the ways of discipleship. The third is to 'provoke one another to love and good deeds,' that is to say to compete in showing honour, to 'encourage one another', gently to hold one another to account, to be a reconciling presence in one another's lives and to be a community of character that offers an example of what God's grace can do.

Hebrews thus uses the same language as Paul in summing up the three responses to Christ's salvation: faith, hope and love. But Hebrews' description of these three qualities is so comprehensive that they together sum up ministry in the church, discipleship in the heart and mission in the world. In other words, the result of Christ giving up his body is the appearance of a new body, also called the body of Christ, more commonly called the church, characterized by faith, hope and love, and issuing in discipleship, ministry and mission.

All of which is saying that the church collectively is now a priest, mediating between God and the world. The church collectively now does what the Old Testament priesthood used to do. Hence Peter calls the church a priestly kingdom and a holy nation.

But I haven't yet explained why we still have people we call priests. The reason, I believe, is partly pragmatic and partly aspirational. The pragmatic reason is that the three activities Hebrews outlines in today's reading – sharing worship, building faith and expressing love – are so foundational that some people are set aside to ensure the church continues to practise them in healthy and wholehearted ways. Just as a park ranger is set aside to look after a national park, ensuring its precious flora and fauna flourish and are sustained, so a priest is set aside to look after the church, to ensure it inhabits its identity as Christ's body faithfully and fruitfully.

But the aspirational reason is that there's more to the notion of priest than simply offering sacrifices, and there always was. Just as Jesus turned water into wine, taking the ordinary stuff of the everyday and bringing out the glorious wonder of the eternal, so a priest is called to see the priceless potential in every person, situation or community, and perceive how to elevate that potential so it attains its full splendour. Thomas Aquinas famously said, 'Grace does not destroy nature, but perfects it.' If you're a priest, you're expecting that sentence to come true in every single conversation you have. Here's an argumentative teenager: maybe she's really longing to be given some responsibility to try out her big ideas. Here's a bunch of people eating a lunch together: maybe if we all find something to be grateful for and identify how this sharing of food can empower us to take courageous steps this afternoon, we can make this meal a Eucharist. Here's a person chopping wood: I wonder if his finished product will become a manger, a nest for grace, or a cross, that carries the troubles of many. Here's a hall table, where the household dumps its keys and notepads and groceries and wallets and mobile phones. Maybe if twice a day we offer a prayer for what lies on that table we can make it an altar, which lifts to heaven the ordinary and incorporates it in the way God is redeeming the world.

A month before my selection conference, I sat down with a close friend to think seriously about what being a priest really meant. I've never forgotten what she said. 'If you're not a priest now, theological college and ordination won't make you one.' Ouch. What she meant was, being a priest isn't being taken up into a cloudy netherworld of vestments, prayer books and angels. It's being practised in the presence of God, raising people in the faith and being a reconciling presence in the life of others. In that sense, of course, all of us can be priests. Because all of us can grow in the practice of the presence of God – all of us can develop the awe and tenderness and humility and wonder and gentleness that come from knowing God is at work in us and in others and in the world. All of us can encourage one another in faith and holiness. And all of us can be a reconciling presence in the life of those around us.

Most of all, all of us can become people who see through what is, to what is possible, who see through the ordinary to the glorious, who see beyond clumsy failure to true fulfilment. Jesus is the great high priest who did that for the whole world – who saw that sinners could become saints and earth could become heaven. He took away the curtain that separates now from forever. People of God, this is our call: to be a priestly kingdom that, in the midst of our now, lives God's forever.

I very seldom say, 'I'm now going to preach a sermon on priesthood.' To do so turns a sermon into a lecture. By saying, 'This passage is asking a question that's pretty important for this community, and offering some answers we can really learn from,' that transforms a ponderous list of worthy sentiments into a tantalizing experience of 'Guess what I've got in this box.' In short, it's a whole lot more engaging to listen to, and because the congregation have at least heard the passage, and may well have access to it in leaflet or whole-Bible form, it's a participative exercise too.

Here are some guidelines on preaching on the Epistle.

1. Don't waste energy on unearthing who wrote the passage, when and where. It may be significant, but belongs in the midst of the sermon while enhancing a crucial point, rather than at the start, as if you were introducing a guidebook. I recall as a student hearing my New Testament professor say, 'Paul's letter to the Hebrews isn't a letter, isn't by Paul, and isn't to the Hebrews.' It's funny and informative, but it belongs in a New Testament lecture and doesn't really belong in a sermon.

2. The point of preaching is not, 'This is what the passage says,' or even, 'This is what the passage means if you understand its context'; it's, 'Here is the truth about yourself, the world, existence and God, and through these words, here is eternal life.' Set the bar high. If the passage touches on an issue that's covered elsewhere in the Scripture or history of the church or theology, feel free to expand the conversation in those directions. This isn't an exam in which you need to show how much you can say about the passage. It's more like a reception where you have an opportunity to introduce the congregation to God.
3. When you preach regularly to the same congregation, there's more than one thing going on. You want every sermon to blow the listeners away and transport them to the throne of grace; but you're also building a relationship of trust, in which subtler messages are being conveyed, such as, 'You can trust me to raise difficult issues tenderly and thoughtfully'; 'You can assume that if I open up a gut-level question, I'll close it again carefully so you don't have to deal with it all by yourself'; 'You can expect that, if this sermon raises something for you that needs further exploration, I'll be available to listen and talk it through with you, however painful and unresolved it is.'
4. If we believe that God gives us everything we need, we don't have to experience that everything all at one go, but can receive it, more digestibly, over a period of time. Likewise, no single sermon has to do everything. Be content to cover one issue really well, rather than losing confidence and trying to cover too much. The sermon above covers priesthood, which doesn't exhaust the passage or everything there is to say about priesthood; but it's a more important subject than might first appear, so concentrate on doing a good job with that subject.
5. You don't have to be topical. A great amount of comment on current events is either inappropriate, because it's not grounded in theology or Scripture, unwise, because it's superseded by subsequent events, or unhelpful, because it substitutes the instant and immediate for the time-honoured and profound. Being a preacher doesn't give you wisdom or authority to speak at short notice on events whose significance or precise detail have yet to be disclosed. A congregation may enjoy a confirmation or amplification of its own response to a news story, but it might be better served by being asked to work harder and investigate something whose relevance might not be so apparent, but whose significance turns out to be much greater. You may be looking at an obscure passage of the New Testament, but that doesn't make it of less account than a fascinating but transitory event in the world at large. Sometimes you can set aside your prepared remarks for a response to

a major community, national or global event; but it's often wiser to keep to your script and begin the service with a short meditation on recent happenings that doesn't claim to be comprehensive.

The sermon below is about three kinds of faith. It's an ambitious sermon, because it divides church history into three sections and associates each with one kind of Christian conviction. I like making sweeping generalizations about historical periods, because finding succinct ways to characterize complex matters is a skill I've honed since student days. Every preacher has to adapt and employ their own predilections to the preaching task. The point is not the historical sweep but the identification of what being a believer really means today – and this passage provides an ideal pretext for doing that and a lens through which to do it.

Cloud of witnesses
Hebrews 11.29—12.2
14 August 2022

I want to tell you a story about what Christianity has meant over the last 2,000 years; but also about what it might mean to you and what it might mean to people in the future. What moves me to do so is our New Testament reading from the second half of chapter 11 of the Letter to the Hebrews.

This chapter switches the letter from what Christians believe to what they are to do about it. The first words of Hebrews are, 'Long ago God spoke to our ancestors.' Now in chapter 11, the letter says, 'Here's what our ancestors did in return.' What we get is a long list of people in the Old Testament and the Apocrypha who were righteous, who journeyed obediently and who endured suffering with courage and faithfulness.

What I want to explain is how, over the history of the church, Christians have read this chapter in different ways and how those different ways might have a bearing on the way we read it today. I'm going to distil those ways down to three.

Let's start with the way Hebrews chapter 11 was read around the time it was composed, probably around AD 65 (fascinatingly a few years before the Gospels were written), and in the 250 years after that. In this period, chapter 11's vivid, moving and in some ways even lurid account of what it can require to be a disciple was taken as a template for what it meant to live a Christian life. It's extremely clear what the difference is between a Christian and a non-Christian. Christians face persecution, if not constantly, then periodically, most obviously because they refuse to regard the emperor as the highest authority, and certainly don't honour and worship him as a god. In this period, Hebrews chapter 11 is like a national anthem, bonding Christians across the Mediterranean with a common story as a cloud of witnesses.

The phrase 'cloud of witnesses' refers to how, while Christians seem beleaguered and few in number on earth, they're joined with the communion of saints in heaven: their eternal destiny is assured, and thus they can withstand persecution, even torture, because they're part of a body, Christ's body, that experiences the cross knowing that the resurrection will follow. I'm going to call this way of reading Hebrews 11 *faith*, because that's what the text calls it. Christians are a kind of underground resistance movement, confident that their cause will ultimately prevail, prepared to withstand any amount of suffering in the meantime.

Now let's shift the context almost entirely to perhaps the majority of the last 2,000 years, beginning near the start of the fourth century, when Christianity begins to be the official religion of the Roman Empire, and continuing until perhaps the eighteenth century. Quite rapidly, the dangerous element in Christianity disappears. It's not that war ceases, but conflicts are not characterized by persecution of Christians. The major dangers Christians face are no longer enemies all around them, wanting their extermination; their enemies are the lurking temptations of sin, the abiding threats of suffering and evil, and the inevitable prospect of death, with the most terrifying question of all, that of whether they're heading for heaven or hell.

The drama of Hebrews chapter 11, with its litany of sufferings and persecutions, becomes meaningful only in particular circumstances. Most obviously, following the Reformation, Catholics, mainline Protestants and radical reformers did unspeakable things to one another over a period of around a hundred years, and many of those things belong comfortably within the Hebrews roll call. In addition, during the missionary period, it's fashionable to dwell on what terrible things imperialists did to the countries they invaded, but many horrendous things were done to the missionaries too, for example, the Jesuits who were tortured in Japan in the seventeenth century. But for the most part, Christianity becomes an interior matter. I'm going to call this era *belief*, because belief refers to a set of convictions about God and the world that sometimes seem detached from the realities of Christian action and Christian relationships on the ground.

And so to the third context, that of the last 300 years or so, sometimes known as modernity or, more recently, postmodernity. Modernity in this sense names a time of greater confidence and, to some degree, mastery of the conceptual, physical and symbolic world by comprehensive schemes of thought other than Christianity. Examples are the legacies of Charles Darwin, Isaac Newton, Sigmund Freud, Carl Jung and Karl Marx. Postmodernity refers to the loss of confidence in such overarching schemes of thought or the prospect of any satisfactory replacements emerging. Gradually over this period, and more rapidly in the last 50 years, Christianity has seemed to be not a threat, as in the early centuries, or the air people breathe, as in the subsequent era, but more of a cultural inheritance, cherished by some, resented by others, ignored by many.

What Christians have become used to is what's known as pluralism, the reality that their convictions are one among many, and that what they can't do is demand that people accept those convictions without question, as was once the case. There are Christians in the world who are persecuted by members of other faiths or, for example in China, by a regime that fears any rival power base. But for the most part, Christians today look at Hebrews chapter 11 and identify with a litany of people whose lives were animated by their perception of and relationship with God; this doesn't necessarily lead Christians today to distance themselves from their social circumstances too much. I'm going to call this era *trust*, because what Christians who read Hebrews 11 today have in common with the early Church is that they seek to shape their whole life around their understanding of God as revealed in Jesus Christ, and that requires a lot of trust.

So what we've seen is that the way we read Hebrews chapter 11 discloses three parallel approaches to who Christians think they are and how they understand their relationship with the rest of society and the world. The first approach, faith, sees things in adversarial terms, where we're always under attack but God eventually prevails. The second approach, belief, sees Christians in a natural and appropriate majority, and transfers the battleground to an internal wrestling with sin and suffering in the face of death and judgement. The third approach, trust, recognizes that Christianity dwells in a plural and diverse landscape of ideas and lifestyles, and yet seeks humbly to put its hand in the scarred hand of the crucified and risen Christ and face life's struggles with dignity and grace.

Here's the important point. While I've tidily characterized faith, belief and trust as belonging characteristically to different eras, the truth is they're all alive and well and among us right now. I suggest the three categories clarify how different people understand what being a Christian means today.

For some people, this is a time of faith. Like Extinction Rebellion activists blocking motorways, or Pakistani believers facing persecution in a society that associates Christianity with Western imperialism, there's direct continuity between us and the litany of Hebrews 11. We're living in a time just like the earliest followers of Jesus. This rouses passionate hearts and impels us to radical action, but it can fill us with self-righteousness and prevent us seeing the damage we're capable of doing when we're convinced we're right.

For others I've grouped under the term belief, the world of Hebrews 11 is somewhat remote. There remains a kind of Christian entitlement, a sense that this is a Christian country, and that Christians should be in the majority in it or at least in charge of it. The distance from the circumstances of the first century isn't a major problem, because Christianity is largely about personal convictions and a personal relationship with God. This approach offers confidence and assurance, but can be experienced as narrow, negative and judgemental. It also sometimes aligns with political views that seem to neglect issues of poverty and inequality.

For others again, trust is the operative word. Trust covers the tendency in institutions, including the church, to do terrible things and protect their own; the difficulty in founding your life on any principle or relationship given how fragile and flawed both can be; and the complexity of reconciling the world of the Bible with the workings of the modern world. Here Hebrews 11 is part of a variety of accounts, perhaps including some from secular and other faith traditions, that stir us to trust in God and shape our life in line with what endures forever, rather than what passes away. This offers maturity and balance, but may seem too ironic, too dispassionate, too detached to do justice to a text that speaks of people being stoned to death or raised from the grave.

Here's a different question. Is God's attitude to us one of faith, belief or trust? That question puts a whole different slant on Hebrews 11. Now it's not just a list of larger-than-life scriptural figures who shut the mouths of lions and were sawn in two. Now it's a description of Jesus. It was Jesus who walked by faith through the Jordan. It was Jesus who was taken to the cliff-edge in Nazareth yet walked calmly away. It was Jesus who made women receive their dead by resurrection. It was Jesus who was mocked, flogged and imprisoned. It was Jesus who wandered in deserts and on mountains. It was Jesus of whom the world was not worthy. Jesus, as our passage tells us, is pioneer (because he goes before us) and perfecter (because he comes after us and completes what we've left unfinished). It's Jesus who embodies God's faith in us – a Hebrews kind of faith, full of passionate and utter commitment. No arm's length social-conformity belief for Jesus.

We can beat ourselves up because we feel we should have the kind of faith that shuts the mouths of lions or is sawn in two. We can get cross with a bourgeois and compromised church that seems to have forgotten what such faith is like. We can idealize places in the world today where church really is about that kind of faith. But Christianity isn't fundamentally about our radical faith in God. It's about God's astonishing faith in us. Astonishing because when it comes to trust, no one would seriously trust us. And astonishing because even when we do begin to get it, we mostly kid ourselves that belief is an adequate response.

This is how to read Hebrews 11. Don't spend your energy feeling guilty you're not so brave or get defensive and dismiss these stories as distant or far-fetched. Allow yourself to be humbled, moved and inspired by the astonishing revelation of God's faith in us. And then gently, simply and tenderly allow yourself to trust God in return. It's not as dramatic as first-century faith. It's not as safe as comfortable belief. But it's what a real relationship is founded on. Through that trust allow yourself to be drawn into that great cloud of witnesses. Let the Holy Spirit weave you together with other people as diverse and complex and flawed and contrary as you.

Because one day, thousands of years in the future (as these celebrated characters in Hebrews are thousands in the past), someone will themselves be humbled, moved and inspired by that great cloud of witnesses. And tucked away in that cloud – lost in wonder, love and praise – will be you.

The weakness of this sermon is perhaps that it's too much biased towards the head, and not enough toward the heart and gut. I let those concerns pass in preaching it by assuming that, for members of a congregation, the question of what their Christian convictions amount to, and how that places them in relation to the rest of society, can never be just a cerebral matter. And I addressed those concerns by twisting the conclusion in a 'heart' manner by turning attention to the listener in the last sentence. But it's a worthwhile question. In addition to preaching, I make broadcasts, write journalistic articles and compose more lengthy books, and the variety helps me identify different genres and keep them separate. This sermon is a little close to a journal article. But that's the advantage of preaching to the same congregation over time: variety is the spice of preaching. While you want to retain a good deal of continuity from one sermon to the next, so the listener can relax and not wonder what's going on, you can also vary between sermons that veer more to the gut, like the final sermon in the previous chapter, or to the head, like this one.

PART 4

Contexts

I

Preaching at a Funeral

In this chapter I consider five contexts for preaching in the context of recent death. In order, they are (1) Recent, sudden death of a person I knew well, had worked with, and regarded as a friend; (2) Recent, sudden, horrifying and unspeakable death of an effervescent young person I didn't know but whose family had opened their lives to me in the weeks between the death and the funeral; (3) Recent, expected death of an elderly person I had known for a few years but never especially well; (4) Memorial service for a well-known journalist whom I hadn't known personally but whose broadcasts I remembered from decades past and whose relatives shared with me as we prepared the liturgy together; (5) Global figure I'd seen from afar at whose UK memorial service I was asked to preach as my church sits beside his country's High Commission.

A good funeral sermon is worth a dozen regular sermons. If life has been long, healthy and happy, you need interpretation and profound identification of what is of abiding significance. If a life has been less than all or indeed none of those things, you need serious help to find clarity, hope and truth amid the grief and dismay. A sermon that can name the pain, regret or hurt, and yet transcend it and elevate heart, soul and faith to something of eternal validity that would have never been without this person's life, however short or complex, can be an inestimable gift – not just to the chief mourners, but to everyone present.

Here are some guidelines for preaching at a funeral.

1. The purpose of the sermon is to express what the deceased showed us about God. We can't see the dead person any longer, but we can still come face to face with God, even – perhaps especially – in the face of profound loss. As preacher, you are not there to extol the virtues of the deceased, list her accomplishments or adventures, describe how special your own relationship with him was, or offer platitudes about how 'She'll always be in our hearts.' You're there to demonstrate how his life offers us a window into the heart of God. This is as true if she were a universally acclaimed saint or a widely despised sinner.

2. There are two kinds of funerals: those where the family wants you to tell the truth and those where it doesn't. The first can be cathartic and epic; the second can be very difficult and unsatisfactory: but good work can still be done. More than once I've had a family say, 'You introduced me to a man I never knew.' The remark sounds two-edged, but it's really saying, 'You helped me come to terms with the parts of my father's life I always struggled with.'
3. Brevity is golden. Even the best funeral sermon can be ruined by saying too much. Most of my funeral sermons are five minutes. Almost none are longer than ten. If other people want to talk about the person as a family man or a professional woman, so much the better – you can focus on your key role, to peer through the icon of this person's life to see God.
4. When a family has means and time, I often ask them to write their own obituary into the second and third page of the order of service. This achieves several things. a) It relieves you of having to recount a life story. b) It gives the family agency (powerlessness being the most pervasive form of grief). c) If there's an argument to be had about getting the story straight about the fourth spouse and the parentage of the fifth child, it doesn't need to involve you. d) It can make the order of service a suitable document to share with any who can't attend – like a slice of wedding cake used to be.
5. Remember you're not just talking to the front row. I once got an accurate account of my funeral sermon from a friend of the deceased's mistress, who, her identity unknown to the family for 12 years, was sitting anonymously in row 16. Yet her grief was as real as that of anyone else in the building. Sometimes members of the close family are so absorbed in the event they can't hear what you're saying; but the close friend who didn't know the family well is hanging on your every word.
6. I often share my sermon with a member of the close family before the day, inviting comment or correction, lest a wrong move or inaccurate fact betray the potential of the address unnecessarily. I still regret that while in the US I once mistakenly described an internist as a surgeon, which undermined the authority with which I spoke about the man's life and distracted from the rest of the service – and could so easily have been avoided if I'd had the foresight and humility to check with a family member.
7. If you're given the opportunity to choose a reading, choose one that especially resonates with the deceased – and ideally one you've never previously chosen for a funeral, or perhaps even preached on in any context before. I keep this rule even after over 30 years of preaching at funerals.

This sermon was preached after the recent, sudden death of a person I knew well, had worked with, and regarded as a friend. The challenge in these circumstances is not to make the sermon all about one's own grief but to offer a shape and direction so that others close to her can recognize and claim the portrayal and turn their grief into worship – not of her, but of God.

The jar and jug that never failed
1 Kings 17.8–16
27 September 2019, on the death of Alison Lyon

Like everyone here, I was horrified to hear of Ali's collapse and death. Yes, I remember a train journey during which she shared with me the 16 maladies that constantly threatened her. Yes, she was perhaps the most engaged person in her own death I have ever known. Yes, she fitted more into 60 years than most people fit into 90. But this is all too painful, too tragic, too sudden, too cruel. Like many of you, I've descended into tears when I look across to the pew where she would sit, now empty; when I've thought about the day next month I was planning to see her new house, a day that now stares back at me in the diary, forcing me to admit she is really gone; when I've thought about the last time I saw her, and her hair was blustery, her shirt was linen, her wink was playful, and her voice was as jaunty as ever – but we said no proper goodbye: as if a goodbye would have been any use. As if a goodbye would have been any use.

I was slow to understand, when I first met Ali, the day she interviewed me to be vicar of St Martin's, that she was a woman who had survived. She'd withstood countless setbacks. 'I will restore to you,' says the prophet Joel. 'I will restore to you the years that the swarming locust has eaten.' Ali knew all about the swarming locust. They were on first-name terms. The swarming locust infested her life, bringing damage, devastation, at times despair. But the prophet Joel was right. For every year the swarming locust ate, the Lord restored in plenty through Ali's ministry to us and to countless others. Out of adversity, Ali became a channel of the Holy Spirit. The fruit of the Spirit is love, joy, peace, patience, kindness, goodness, faithfulness, gentleness and self-control. Have you ever met someone who embodied that Spirit like Ali? 'Haw-haw-haw,' Ali would say, never being great at receiving a compliment. But it's true, Ali. The Spirit was working through you plain as day. We all got so used to it we can only see it now. 'Well, at least they say the Spirit's female,' Ali would say. 'And there's no record it's ever been ordained, which is more than can be said for half my friends,' she'd also say. 'I will restore the years,' says Joel. That's what Ali did. She restored our years.

Look with me for a moment at our passage from First Kings. The prophet Elijah doesn't go to Israel – he goes to Gentile territory, Zarephath. He doesn't go to an influential man – he goes to a poor widow. Elijah loves with God's heart. He goes to God's edge. The widow has a choice to make. She's only got a handful of meal in a jar and oil in a jug. Does she use it on making a little cake for Elijah, this complete stranger and foreigner, or does she keep it for herself and her son? She has no idea who Elijah is. All she knows is the famine is going to engulf them all. She decides to make the cake for the stranger. Great is her reward. The jar of meal was not emptied; neither did the jug of oil fail. Scarcity becomes abundance in a single act of generosity.

Behold how Ali had the same choice the widow of Zarephath had. Ali had so many maladies; a widow in a famine had nothing on her. Ali could have kept her morsel of bread to herself. But in a perfect eucharistic gesture, Ali gave up her jug and her jar, that they might become part of how God delivers each one of us from the famine of our lives. And for decades at St Martin's, and just as much in a host of communities and institutions elsewhere, that meal and that oil made the bread of life that never ran out – the bread of life in reconciliation, in communications, in governance, in consultancy, in creative arts, in drawing wisdom from groups of people and making them think they'd had the idea themselves. She laid down her life for the inspiration, restoration and transformation of the world. Who does that remind you of? Exactly. But we only realize it now she's not here.

In October 1996, the author Rumer Godden went on Desert Island Discs and talked about her life in India and as a novelist. When asked to name her luxury, she told this story of Elijah and the widow, and instead of the word 'jug' she used the old-fashioned word 'cruse'. She recalled that the cruse of oil never ran out. But Rumer Godden made a request: 'I want the cruse on my desert island to be perpetually replenished, not with oil, but with whisky.' It's exactly an Ali kind of a story: steeped in scriptural imagination, deeply playful, irresistibly subversive, soaked in faith and humour and resilience and fun.

That's Ali, right there. A woman whose years the swarming locust had eaten, but through whom the Holy Spirit moved to bring reconciliation and healing. A woman who could have kept her morsel of bread to herself but instead let it become the bread of life, which never ran out and never will. A woman who, like Christ, laid down her life that others might flourish. A woman whose faith was subversive, hilarious and generous to the last.

Ali lived at the heart and loved on the edge. When we enter the kingdom of God, and share the bread of life that never runs out, and have restored to us the years the swarming locust has eaten, what will we find, but the fruits of reconciliation, truth and healing? And we'll have a vision of a prophet, wearing colour-coordinated linen, with hair that still looks a bit blustery. And it'll dawn on us that we'd been given a key to the kingdom, and we'd had it in our midst, all these years. And we only realized it when it was snatched away. And that key was Ali Lyon.

The second sermon I hesitated before including because the circumstances were just so indescribably sad. This was the funeral after the recent sudden, horrifying and unspeakable death of an effervescent young woman I didn't know but whose family had opened their lives to me in the weeks between the death and the funeral.

Unlike most funeral sermons, which are about life in the light of death, a sermon like this has to confront the horror of death at its epicentre. Death in the fulness of youth; the death of a person who gave such life to others; death for no good reason, out of clumsiness and mischance, with a little culpable fecklessness on the part of others: all of these enhance and sharpen the horror. But the real horror is one that, even at a funeral, we mostly set aside, yet the coffin makes unavoidable: death itself – death that destroys, renders meaningless, robs and obliterates. On an occasion like this, preachers have to go to the very bottom of their own faith and find something to make the situation less appalling. For that reason, it's probably the most important sermon in the book.

To prepare a sermon like this is one of the most demanding, yet rewarding, things a preacher ever does. It's why you take up the mantle in the first place. If something in you doesn't say, 'Yes, I'm glad and honoured to do this; this is what all my training was for,' you may want to consider if you're in the right profession.

Love as strong as death
Song of Songs 8.6–7
15 June 2017, on the death of Sophie Neve

The almost indescribable dismay of Sophie's death leaves us with three questions that gnaw away at our soul as we contemplate the aching absence and searing wound of life without her. The first question is, How can someone so utterly overflowing with life be struck down by the heartless, cruel destruction of death? Sophie was a party. She was a person who embodied and provoked energy, laughter, creativity, fun, joy, a person of fire and wit and strength. This is the magic of life. Life is everywhere around us – in the power of a waterfall, the glory of a rainbow, the wonder of a sunrise. Sophie had that power, that glory, that wonder. If anyone felt a bit of an outsider, Sophie made friends with them and brought them into that circle of life. It is simply impossible to comprehend that such a force of life could be engulfed by death – that such an eternal flame could be snuffed out as quickly and utterly as a candle. How can death so comprehensively overcome life? The question leaves us numb and dizzy and in shock – a shock that's lasted more than a month now and must feel like it'll never end.

The second question is, How can a person so full of purpose and drive be cut off by death when her story was so evidently just beginning to take shape? Death dismantles meaning. Every attempt to speak of beauty, truth and goodness runs up against the poisonous, ruthless, unmerciful desolation of death. The harshness of the way death attacks purpose is that it doesn't just deprive us of Sophie's future, it threatens our understanding of her past. All her plans, hopes, dreams – all snatched away; and with them the joy of those who loved her and invested their identity in her. All her gift to search out the eccentric and deep people, to understand their story and truth: all taken. How can death rob life of all meaning? The question leaves us utterly bewildered.

The third question is, What do we do with all this surplus love, love we have for Sophie, love we have no idea where now to take? And what becomes of the love Sophie had for us? Sophie might just as well have said, 'Set me as a seal upon your heart.' A seal in the ancient world was a mark of identity; it's saying, 'When people see your heart, let them see my seal on it. May you have no identity other than in loving me.' It's a big ask. But Sophie didn't mind asking big. And right now, she's got what she wanted. Not one person here can imagine their life ever being the same again. She is that seal on your heart.

But what do you do with the grief, the loss, the agony, the sadness? I want to suggest that this is the most important question. The heart of the Christian faith lies right here: is love stronger than death? And the whole essence of faith rests in a one-word answer: yes. That's what the resurrection means. Yes: love is stronger than death. Maybe not a lot stronger – maybe not always evidently or tangibly stronger; but in the end it won't matter, painful as it is right now. Only one thing matters: love is stronger than death. If love is stronger than death, at the end of time there will be no death, only love. And in that love will be meaning and purpose, and out of love and meaning and purpose will come life – this time a life that will never end, because it has no rival.

Think about Sophie's name. Sophie. It's Greek. It means wisdom. Sophie's life was much, much too short. But sometimes there's as much wisdom in a short epigram as in a long treatise. Sophie's epigram was perhaps this: love *is* stronger than death, and in the end of time there will be no death, only love. And the meaning and purpose and life that seem so utterly lost today will one day be reconstructed out of that love. And that life will never end.

It's one thing preparing such a sermon. It's another to make sure you're in the right mental and emotional state to deliver it, with 300 desolate family members and friends present, most of whom had no regular connection with Christianity, searching for something onto which to cling. Such an event is so important you must shape your whole week or fortnight ensuring you'll be in the right space to lead it. And when you've preached such a sermon, you can't walk away from the family: you will be bonded to those to whom the event meant most for as long as they want you to be so.

The next sermon was delivered at a memorial service for a person whose funeral had taken place a short time before, but for whom a separate service was arranged to enable more people to attend. I did know the man and information about him was plentifully available. But he was a private, single, reserved person and perhaps very few knew him especially well. So the secret was both to identify a central characteristic – one that could be transformed into an insight into God's love – and to make the rhetorical shape of the sermon as true to his character as the words themselves.

Doughty Dudley
Psalm 1
16 March 2022, on the death of Dudley Green

When I think of Dudley Green, I keep coming back to the same word. It's an old-fashioned word, which comes from a family of similar words, all of which mean strong, formidable or thorough. The word is 'doughty'. It's the kind of word you find in accounts of the Second World War, used about infantrymen who hold out in a besieged house for a long time until reinforcements arrive, and do such things time and time again.

Dudley Green was doughty. As I think about the connotations of the word doughty, I think about a similar adjective, 'redoubtable', and a similar noun, 'redoubt'. A redoubt is a defensive fort placed outside a bigger fort or castle, a particular feature of the network of forts Sébastien Vauban built all over France in the seventeenth century. Redoubtable means strong and worthy of respect.

This constellation of meanings is the kind of thing that would especially appeal to Dudley. But I know that if I started to describe it, he would quickly pull me up and say something like, 'Sam, I think you may have missed that "doughty" is a word of Old German origin, whereas "redoubtable" is a French word. Whether they have a common root among the Indo-European languages I actually couldn't say.' And you'd look up and Dudley would have a glint in his eye, and that default smile he always kept, and you'd realize that what he was saying was, 'Young man, you have no idea what you're talking about,' but in the nicest possible way. And then you'd return to watching the cricket and he'd say, 'I feel a wicket coming,' or, 'I think they should put the spinner on,' and you realized Dudley brough the same powers of analysis and attention to detail to every part of his life. He was a scholar and a teacher. He was a lover of sport, but always in the sense that sport is a way of judging character. He was a believer; but always a scrutinizer.

The first of the psalms is a celebration of the one whose delight is in the law of the Lord. To the modern ear, that's a curious phrase. We tend to think delight is for beauty, whether human or in creation or in art. We furrow our brow at the idea that a person could take delight in the law, especially a law like Israel's law, with all those injunctions about sacrifices and which animals you can't eat. But that's to miss one important thing. We tend to hope that God is forgetful, busy and big picture, and we tend to put our trust in God's forgiveness as an absent-minded thing, where God is too distracted to notice our failures and cruelties. But delight in the law isn't about a sweeping benevolence. It's about a fierce attention to detail. To understand all is to forgive all. God forgives all because God understands all. God's love is a detailed love, which understands our actions and thoughts better than we do.

Dudley was a man of detail. Detail in memory, detail in judgement, detail in scrutiny, detail in research, detail in preparation. For Dudley, detail was a form of love. Detail is a form of close attention and close attention is the way Dudley expressed love. After all, to write a meticulous biography of Patrick Brontë is to devote yourself to a level of detailed attention few of us could rise to.

So when I think of Dudley as doughty, it's not because he was a physically strong man, but because he found strength in close attention, in memory, in dedicated service. When we meet in heaven, Dudley will say to me, 'Sam, I've been waiting to tell you. The German "doughty" and the French "redoubtable" both have their origin in the "safe stronghold", in the words, "God is our strength and refuge" at the beginning of Psalm 46. I fully intend to listen to the angels sing those words forever. I thought you'd want to know.' And he'll have a glint in his eye.

For Dudley's strength was that he put his destiny in the hands of one who paid detailed attention to him. And to all of us. Now, and forever.

You don't have to pretend you knew the person better than you did. Such dishonesty is tempting, but unnecessary – and an indication you're being drawn into making the sermon too much about you. You can include reference to yourself in an anecdote, but only in such a way that the real attention is on the person you're commemorating. You can be very brief, so long as you make each word count. The members of the congregation should be left thinking 'Yes!' and feeling like a better version of themselves.

The next sermon I preached at a memorial service for a well-known journalist whom I hadn't known personally but whose broadcasts I remembered from decades past and whose relatives shared with me as we prepared the liturgy together. This service was a public event, in that it drew many luminaries from the highest ranks of journalism and public life, and since his widow was an adept and active networker, people came from all walks of life to support her as well as to commemorate him. I decided to take a risk and preach what some would call a 'prophetic' sermon – that is, one that might ruffle a few feathers. But I was confident that those present would understand that what I was saying was designed to honour the deceased and make a bridge between his career and the gospel story, and was not intended to denounce or diminish anyone. And so it proved.

The truth will set you free
John 8.26–32
11 December 2019, on the death of Richard Lindley

There used to be a profession called journalism. Observe two words in that sentence. Have you ever noticed that journalism is an ism? Like socialism, Epicureanism, or ... Anglicanism. In other words, it's something that requires commitment and conviction, and involves loyalty and solidarity. Law, accountancy, politics – those aren't isms; but journalism is. Likewise, the word profession. It refers to a guild, a guild of members who have training, apprenticeship, standards, integrity and a desire to serve the public even at cost to their own comfort or freedom. There used to be a profession called journalism. There used to be a man called Richard Lindley.

The word profession and the discovery that journalism is an ism, a kind of faith, are ways of saying Richard Lindley was a person whom Aristotle would regard as a man of virtue. All the cardinal and theological virtues, justice, temperance, courage, prudence, faith, hope and love, fit Richard pretty well, but the one that stands out is courage. He talked about the fear of failure that spurred him on. Thomas Aquinas says an important thing about courage. He says that those who have no fear aren't courageous. Instead, courage means being afraid, but persisting anyway. That was Richard Lindley.

And what is it that took so much courage? Meeting a man like Saddam Hussein, yes. Facing horror in Bangladesh, yes. Being arrested in Angola, yes. Facing Alzheimer's – yes. But one thing above all requires courage, from a journalist and from all of us. What requires courage most of all is to tell the truth. What makes journalism an ism, a form of faith, what makes it a profession, a guild of honour, is this commitment above all: to tell the truth, come what may, whoever's embarrassed, or aggressive, or alienated, or wild with threats. You will know the truth, and the truth will set you free. That is the Hippocratic Oath of Journalism. That was the creed of Richard Lindley.

The Christian faith is that there is truth, and that truth became flesh in Jesus, and the world is allergic to the truth, and so Jesus was crucified; but truth can't be suppressed, so Jesus rose from the dead and the Spirit came to empower Jesus' followers to spread truth into all the world. That Christianity, in the minds of many, ceased to be synonymous with truth is a great tragedy. That people beyond the church speak the truth anyway is part of the way God redeems the world, despite the failures of the church. One person who spoke the truth in such a way was called Richard Lindley.

Eight months ago in this church, a bunch of asylum seekers played the disciples, city slickers played the Sanhedrin and a New York mogul played Pontius Pilate, as the congregation of St Martin's enacted the passion of Jesus, as it does every Palm Sunday. At his trial, standing before Pontius Pilate, Jesus said, 'For this I came into the world, to testify to the truth.' Pilate replied, from exactly where I'm standing now, in a broad New York accent, 'What is truth?' ... And everyone thought, 'You don't know, do you? You've got so mixed up with lies, manipulation and distortion, that you actually have no idea.' In the first century AD, those who spoke the truth to people who controlled resources and information were called prophets. Today such people are called journalists.

There used to be a profession called journalism. Today, we're led by people who don't know what truth is. Journalism is becoming an adjunct of marketing, governed by algorithms. Real journalists, who believe the truth will set you free, are becoming so rare they're better described as prophets. We've gathered to honour Richard Lindley, journalist. Only now do we realize he was a prophet. And his faithful, dangerous, countercultural, courageous message was this: the truth will set you free. Free indeed.

The journalist Andrew Marr, writing in *The Spectator*, described these words as, 'That modern rarity, a properly fiery sermon,' and, noting that the service took place on the day before the General Election, suggested that the preacher 'made many of us reflect and even slightly quake.'[1] He clearly got the message – but I didn't think of it as a fiery sermon. I didn't raise my voice or wave my arms or point or peer down at the congregation. A gentle, insistent tone was all that was needed.

But the point is, sometimes you have a chance in a local community, a town, or even a nation, to say something of value that will have an effect beyond the occasion itself and the people present on the day. And people are never paying closer attention than in the face of death. The sermon is perhaps the most obviously rhetorical one in the whole book, but is not intended to be showy; instead, the intention is to communicate to the congregation that I realize this is a formal event, yet it's one in which I've been invited to say something significant and so I'm going to use time-honoured ways of saying significant things that owe debts to orators from days gone by. My style is to go quiet, not shouty, for the key moments – I have no facility to be demonstrative and explosive. Everyone must find their own wavelength. But humility or shyness must sometimes give place to calling, and when there's an occasion to step up, the preacher needs to take it.

The last sermon in this chapter concerns an almost uniquely global figure – Desmond Tutu. Because St Martin's sits beside the South African High Commission, and because the church played an active role in the Anti-Apartheid Movement, relations with the High Commission are still close. Hence, I was asked to preach at the UK memorial services for Nelson Mandela and, several years later, for Desmond Tutu. I adopted a technique I learned from Bill Clinton, who, at a memorial service at

---

1 Andrew Marr, 'Andrew Marr: Twitter fooled everyone during this election', *The Spectator*, 21 December 2019, https://www.spectator.co.uk/article/andrew-marr-twitter-fooled-everyone-during-this-election/ (accessed 3/05/2023).

Duke Chapel while I served there, coined a memorable phrase about the deceased that he repeated throughout the sermon and that I can remember to this day. He hardly needed to say anything else. It was all in that phrase. Hence I strove for an opening sentence that did the same.

A little man who made a big difference
Luke 19.1–10
21 *February 2022, on the death of Desmond Tutu*

Archbishop Desmond Tutu was a little man who made a big difference. In fact, he probably made a bigger difference than any Anglican of the last century. His countless admirers could well claim him as the greatest Anglican of our lifetimes. In the words of the psalm, he has shown us the path of life, in his presence there was fullness of joy; in his right hand there are now pleasures forevermore.

The Arch, as he was often known, will be celebrated in the church for centuries to come, for two reasons. He showed us how to stand up to tyranny, enduring setbacks without despair. And he showed us how to make peace once the transfer of power had taken place, ensuring a future bigger than the past.

I want to take four lines from the story of Jesus' encounter with Zacchaeus that may help us grasp both the wonder and the mystery of this little man who made a big difference. First, we read, 'He was short in stature.' Desmond had polio when a child, at a time when the disease killed a quarter of those it afflicted. His right hand never recovered. Tuberculosis permanently weakened his lungs. Those who fought apartheid trusted in arms or sanctions. Desmond trusted in God. For him, apartheid was idolatry, because it maintained that the colour of your skin was more important than your status as a child of God. And apartheid was blasphemy, because it turned God's grace for all people into God's favour for some and scorn for others. For the Arch, when you had God on your side, however small you may have felt, you were always in the majority. It was better to fail in a cause that would finally succeed than to succeed in a cause that would finally fail.

Then in the story of Zacchaeus we read that, 'All who saw it began to grumble.' Desmond's life was a bobbing buoy in a sea of controversy. He was the first to say that apartheid disfigured the perpetrator more than the victim, but many doubted his conviction that there was a place for all races in the struggle for freedom. He was surrounded by people who believed he was too ambitious, changing jobs so frequently, who argued he was naïve, preferring peaceful protest to armed resistance, who suggested he was too political, demanding apartheid be dismantled rather than simply asking people to abide together in peace, who argued he was too merciful, seeking reconciliation rather than judgement and punishment. The Arch had two tactics that disarmed all critics. One was example. When, in 1981, 15,000 mourners showed up for the funeral of Griffiths Mxenge, and one was identified as an informer, a necklace killing looked certain. But Desmond threw himself over the accused man and, with his cassock blood-stained, took him to his car and drove him away. The good shepherd lays down his life for his sheep. The other tactic was humour. He told the conflict-averse Pentecostals, who doubted his political commitments, 'You're the only people I know who can put your heads in the sand and wave your hands at the same time.' This was his genius. Even his enemies couldn't defeat his humour.

Next in the story we read, 'Today salvation has come to this house.' Despite his Nobel Prize in 1984, despite his role in preventing interracial war in the 1980s, despite his presenting the freed Mandela to the South African people, the Arch's greatest achievement was surely the Truth and Reconciliation Commission. He taught the world the difference, and the relationship, between judgement and mercy. He demonstrated that reconciliation was no idle process, but required the demanding, sometimes agonizing, sometimes traumatic, work of truth-telling, testimony, confession, listening, reparation and finally rehabilitation. Time and again, people would say, 'It has been good for me to tell my story.' One said, 'Today the nation cried my tears with me, and I can begin again.' The process created a sacred space, in which the possibility of forgiveness and the possibility of repentance were made real. Every time there was a moment of repentance and forgiveness, the Arch would say, 'We need to pause. Something holy has happened. Something that will change us.'

Finally in the story of Zacchaeus, we read, 'The Son of Man came to seek out and save the lost.' We're here today, not just because we want to honour a person who did so much to turn despair into hope, death into life – but because in his life we see a parable of the kingdom of God. Like the Arch, Jesus dwelt among his people and shared their existence in the face of oppression. Like the Arch, Jesus put his life on the line by refusing to step away from danger if it meant stepping away from truth. Like the Arch, Jesus transformed relationships by example and humour, leaving his enemies speechless and challenging those who presided over cruel domination. Jesus too was a little man who made a big difference. We're here today not just because no one can ever tell the story of the transfer of power in South Africa without honouring the role of Desmond Tutu, but because of something even more important: Desmond Tutu denied himself, took up his cross, and followed Jesus, as powerfully and transformatively as anyone in our lifetimes. We celebrate the Arch, not just because he spoke to our hearts, not just because he captured the heart of a nation – but because he offered us a window into the heart of God.

In this case – as later with Queen Elizabeth II – there were numerous written and spoken tributes and the skill lay in finding something to say that transcended the commonplace and the clichéd. While not every preacher gets an invitation like this, most will have an opportunity to write or communicate words on the death of a global public figure, so I include this sermon as an example of how one might go about doing so.

2

Preaching at a Wedding

For a preacher with an ego, a wedding is a healthy lesson: you're not the centre of attention. You can finesse a glorious occasion, but the glory lies elsewhere. It's best to remember that; because the biggest mistake you can make is to make the occasion about you.

Even if you didn't previously know the couple, in a preparation session on the order of service and another on life together (I call them 'the wedding' and 'the marriage'), you're almost bound to get to know them pretty well; and these two people are entrusting you with one of the most sacred moments in their lives, so the whole experience is precious and honoured.

Like a funeral, those on the front row might be so consumed by arrangements, arguments and emotion that they can hardly hear what you're saying. But the uncle six rows back or the neighbour ten rows back or the godparent obscured by the absurd hat may be at a crossroads in their marriage and may be listening with breathless attention. Your ministry is to everyone present on the day, not just to the couple.

Here are some guidelines for preaching at a wedding.

1. Go easy on the jokes. Both in officiating and in preaching, the temptation is to give in to the tension and nerves and infuse or defuse it with humour: 'If anyone knows any reason in law ... Speak now – this is your last chance!' People will laugh because of the nervous tension. But it's not funny. This is an immensely serious moment, in a culture that struggles with the whole notion of a vow: your job is to be the still centre that can cope with solemnity and depth. You're not the best man. Get out of the way.
2. Harness the emotion but don't be overcome by it. A lot of people cry at weddings – your sermon may well make people cry – but don't you be one of them. Rehearse your script in such a way that you anticipate the parts that could hit you, and only look at the couple during the parts where you're in full control. This is also about deflecting attention from yourself.
3. Don't confuse marriage preparation with the sermon. Some things – like any reference to bodily love – are appropriate for the privacy

of the preparation, but not helpful in a sermon. A sermon isn't an opportunity for giving advice, nor a moment to denounce contemporary culture, for whatever you deem inadequate about it.

4. A sermon is about how God shines through the extraordinary and the ordinary in the combination of wedding and marriage. It's not a pious gloss on an earthly rite of passage; it's genuinely elevating people's imaginations at a moment they're very willing to have them elevated.
5. There are three big differences about weddings from 50 years ago: each makes the preacher's job easier. Getting married in church is now a minority pursuit. That means the couple really want to be in church and are so much more open than in the past to the preacher's ability to perceive the Holy Spirit laced through the contours of their lives.
6. Meanwhile, the great majority of couples have lived together before they marry. So the tension at a wedding is not the sexual tension it once was. The fact that the couple probably know more about sex than the preacher means the preacher can relax and explore other mysteries of marriage more freely.
7. A consequence of having lived together means the couple has doubtless already experienced some of the downside of marriage and found a way through together; so any counsel is building on experience, not speaking into naïveté.
8. Be positive. Everyone is aware marriage can be difficult, burdensome and imprisoning – but this isn't the day to dwell on it. Much better to raise expectations for what marriage can be than to embark on a therapy session in public. The couple have made a positive choice to be married: your job is to explain what a wonderful choice that is.
9. Marriage is no longer just a boy–girl thing. The church may not formally conduct weddings for same-sex couples; but the world does. Make sure your remarks are translatable into a same-sex context and enriching for couples from diverse backgrounds.
10. There are doubtless many at a wedding for whom church is unfamiliar – and some for whom it's a place of foreboding. You communicate to them as much by your gentle demeanour, quiet composure and receptive engagement as by what you say.
11. Be brief. No one has turned up to hear you speak. If possible, write a new sermon for the occasion, so it's as new for you as for the couple, and if you're given the opportunity to choose a reading, choose one you've never chosen before, apt for this couple.

PREACHING AT A WEDDING

The sermon below was preached in what I could call ideal circumstances: two people very much part of the congregation, for whom an enquirers' course had been significant in cementing their relationship, where Christian language and culture was welcome and invited. Because the couple had met in musical theatre, I chose a theme to suit their genre. I've anonymized the parties to the wedding in this and the sermons below, using letters instead of names.

I wanna know what love is
1 John 4.7–21
4 June 2022

A and B, I want to portray for you three pictures of your future. The pictures are ones I'm just imagining. The point is not whether or not they *come* true. The point is whether or not they *are* true. In the part of the First Letter of John we've just read, the author is wrestling with what love means. I'm not breaking any secrets by telling you you're going to spend the rest of your lives with each other wrestling with what love means. So here are three pictures to help you find out.

Here's picture one. It's in three years' time. You love your house. But you think it's time you explored the basement. You're beginning to open up the basement and you discover a horrendous, ugly, smelly mess just where the staircase reaches the bottom. You're both gasping for clean fresh air. You've got five choices. Option one: A cleans it up. Option two: B cleans it up. Option three: you both close your eyes for up to 15 years and hope it will go away by itself. Option four: you inveigle a relative or friend, or pay a contractor to deal with it. Having rapidly surveyed the options, one of you presses Spotify and starts playing the 1984 Foreigner song. One of you belts out at the top of your voice. 'I wanna know what love is.' The other one replies, just as loud, 'I want you to show me.' And you realize there's option five: you can do it together.

Here's picture two. It's in five years' time. You have a lovely baby infant. You're mindful of the climate crisis, so you decide to go for washable nappies. The final episode of the epic Netflix drama is on the TV and you've planned your whole week around watching it and beholding a thrilling denouement that will never be forgotten. Your little tot starts to get a bit whiffy. You start to add up events of the last couple of days and realize the household is experiencing diarrhoea of biblical proportions. The costume drama is incredibly tense and gripping but this tot can't wait. You've got five choices. Option one: A can deal with it. Option two: B can deal with it. Option three: you can both close your eyes for 15 years … actually, that's not an option. Option four: you can get someone else … actually, that's not an option either. This won't wait. So what happens? One of you belts out at the top of your voice. 'I wanna know what love is.' The other one replies, just as loud, 'I want you to show me.' And you realize there's option five: you can do it together.

Here's picture three. It's in 60 years' time. You're wrestling with whether one of you needs to go into a full-time care home. This time the smell isn't coming from the basement. This time the smell isn't coming from your baby's backside. This time it's coming from one of you. You run through the options. There aren't many options now. Option three – sorry, you ain't got 15 years. Option four – no one's going to sort this out for you. You belt out, 'I wanna know what love is.' But no words come back. Your partner of 60 years isn't on that register anymore. Option five isn't an option. You can't do this together.

Or can you? Think about it. You've spent a lifetime laughing as one sang, 'I wanna know what love is,' while the other sang back, 'I want you to show me.' You've spent a lifetime discovering that the answer to that question lay in the single word, 'Together.' So this is the moment that you realize, 'Actually, we're still going to do this together. At the beginning I tore your trousers off because I adored and desired you. Later we took our baby's trousers off because sometimes a nappy just needs changing. But today I'm going to help you take your trousers off because you can't go and do your business on your own. We'll face this together.'

The Bible is a story of a people who fitfully, fleetingly and faithfully realize that God is constantly saying, whispering, imploring, the word 'together'. 'I want to do this with you. I want to be with you.' Over and over, God and humanity say to each other, 'I wanna know what love is,' and reply, 'I want you to show me.'

And that's what marriage is. It's two people wrestling with what love is. It's two people, in the passion of youth, in the partnership of parenthood, in the companionship of old age, whispering, singing, hollering, 'I wanna know what love is,' and replying, 'I want you to show me' – and then realizing, however smelly the task, however daunting the project, however fearsome the challenge, however humiliating the confession, however sad the news, however overwhelming the endeavour, the answer lies in that single, faithful, enduring, simple word: together.

The sermon is a homily because it's all circling around the single word 'together', seen from several angles. The power of the sermon lies in its simplicity and with the accuracy of its observation. Accordingly, I checked with a mutual friend on my first example and was informed their house didn't have an attic but did have a basement – so I changed it. A detail like this can make a big difference in credibility.

I'm not a great singer, but many people at the wedding were, so I managed to build up a call and response by simply singing 'I wanna know what love is' and cupping my ear for a response. That made it difficult – but poignant – to curtail the response in the third example.

There are no jokes here, no nervous humour, but plenty of lightness of touch. The best way to preach a sermon like this is very, very slowly and very, very gently. Every word counts. Make it count.

The next sermon is in a more complex context: where there's an Atlantic Ocean between the couple, where one half has had to leave home and familiarity to cross the sea; but also where there's been a previous marriage. One half of the couple is in the military, which is a serious commitment with consequences that need acknowledging. So the sermon is subtler – but perhaps because of that, more tender.

Intreat me not to leave thee
Ruth 1.16–17
6 August 2022

I want you to get an appreciation of how astonishing are the words we've just heard, and of how remarkable they are as a template for the marriage we're gathered here to witness.

Outside the book of Ruth, there are only four conversations between women in the whole Bible. But this little book of four chapters has eight such conversations. And it begins with this conversation between Naomi and her two widowed daughters-in-law, Orpah and Ruth. Both young women are foreigners, from Moab. It's a time of famine and their husbands, Naomi's two sons, have died, along with Naomi's husband. There's only one thing to be done – the young women obviously have to return to their home country, which Orpah does. But Ruth refuses, despite Naomi's insistence. Ruth binds herself to Naomi, in some of the most profound and moving words in the whole Bible. Ruth faces the moment of truth in her life on which she bases all future truth.

She says five things. Where you go, I will go. Where you live, I will live. Your people will be my people. Your God will be my God. Where you die, I will die. In other words, our relationship will be the basis for every other decision I take in my life. Let's look at those five commitments.

Where you go, I will go. Well, C and D have made a start on this one. You may have noticed we're sitting in England, not in Canada. But this isn't just about geography. This is about sharing existence in whatever form it comes. You're going to retrain in mid career: I'm going to share the poverty and hope of that with you. You give birth to a child with multiple disabilities: we're going to do this together. You find yourself afflicted with PTSD: I'm by your side. Where you go, I will go.

Where you live, I will live. The life of an army household involves a lot of moves and flexibility. There are going to be times when one of you says, 'Oh, not again.' But your search for home is already over: from now on, you say to each other, 'Home is where you are.' In fact, we all know home is where Henry the golden doodle is. Again, it's not just a physical thing. It's saying, we're going to learn to flourish together in whatever circumstances we find ourselves. We are never going to say, it would be so much easier if I were with someone else. We're going to say, our relationship will be the basis for every other decision I take in my life. Where you live, I will live.

Your people will be my people. This can be a hard one. It's saying, I won't poke holes in your family and constantly assert that my family is less weird than yours. I don't expect everyone in your family to be my first-choice best friend. But I commit to seeing and enjoying the best in each of them, and encouraging you to do so. We're going to live together a life of gratitude, not resentment. Your people will be my people.

Your God will be my God. We are going to make our deepest convictions about truth, meaning, purpose and eternity the heart of our relationship. We're doing so by beginning our marriage at this altar. If we have children, we're going to bring them into a sense of belonging with the love that will never let them go. We'll respect our disagreements and receive each other's perspectives as opportunities to go deeper. Your God will be my God.

Finally, where you die, I will die. I'm not just hanging out with you until I get a better offer. This moment, right now, is the moment of truth in my life on which I base all future truth. There is no well-being for me outside well-being for you. You are not a means to my flourishing. I have no flourishing that's outside flourishing with you. Where you die, I will die.

Christians read these precious words that Ruth says to Naomi because they show us what it means to bind ourselves to one another. But they also show us what Jesus means. Jesus is God saying to you and to me, Where you go, I will go. I'm going to experience everything about human life. Where you live, I will live. I'm going to move into your neighbourhood. Your people will be my people. I'm going to have a mother, cousins, neighbours, just like you. Your God will be my God. I'm going to know what it means to need God, as well as to love God. Where you die, I will die. I'm going to love you right until the very end.

C and D, say these astonishing words to each other today. Whisper them to each other between the sheets every night. Speak them to each other over the babble of a room full of children and responsibilities. Repeat them to each other in the intensive care unit when you're not sure the other is going to make it. Write them on your hearts; remember that they're written on God's heart. For this, right here, right now, is the moment of truth in your life on which you will base all future truth.

Five is a large number of points to make in a sermon lasting around 6–7 minutes, but the passage demanded it and because the words come straight out of the text there's nothing arbitrary or forced about it. The structure is the same as the previous sermon – you think this is all about marriage but a paragraph from the end, you discover it's actually a description of the incarnation. The challenges – moving from Canada, adopting an army life – are not hidden, but made part of an exposition of what commitment entails, framed in a way that's positive ('Whisper between the sheets') rather than bleak. Rather than say, 'A marriage is about life, not the wedding day' – which rather takes the air out of the wedding balloon – the intention is to highlight the wedding day as the moment you gladly make commitments you earnestly later seek to keep.

The next sermon came in an extraordinarily complex context. There was relational complexity – a previous marriage, four children, two of school age; enormous geographical complexity – a 6,000-mile distance between the couple's homes; and then exasperating pandemic complexity – a wedding twice postponed only days before the event due to Covid, and endless concomitant quarantine challenges. I've never experienced a wedding taking place against so many odds.

So I tried to keep the sermon as elegantly simple as I could and, resisting the temptation to make much reference to the catalogue of trials in the background, sought to transcend the context and enable the couple to contemplate the characteristics of the years ahead of them.

Three little words
16 July 2021

There have been so many complications getting to this moment that everyone involved could be forgiven for forgetting the simplicity of the reason we're here: E and F love each other and want to get married. I want to suggest three words to which F and E may return should they ever forget that same simplicity in the years to come. Each word requires the unlearning of another word.

The first word to unlearn is 'if'. Some arrangements are pervaded by the word if. If you keep your side of the bargain, I'll keep mine. If you weren't so annoying, exasperating, infuriating, I'd be kind, gentle and understanding. Today's the day you dispense with that word if – and replace it with the word 'always'. Your love is no longer conditional: it's permanent. If is the language of contract; always is the language of covenant. If is provisional, always is unconditional. Time to replace if with always.

The second word to unlearn is 'for'. For is the curse of marriage. Do you know how many hours I've spent making a nice dinner for you? Have you any idea what it costs me to work so hard for you to have a comfortable future? For names the accumulation of unspoken resentment, until like a bursting dam it all cascades down and floods a relationship. For is based on guesswork, assumed benevolence, a private sense of unrecognized moral superiority. Quietly put that word away today. Replace it with the word 'with'. For is about entitlement; with is about sharing. With requires constant relating, regular recalibrating, honest rebalancing. The point is never to do it well, or quickly, or efficiently – but to do it together. It's not a performance to make the world applaud – it's a mystery to enter together more deeply. It doesn't matter what you do, what matters is to do it with you.

The third word to unlearn is 'ask'. You've done all the asking already. Did you love someone before me? Did you ever do something you're still ashamed of? Is there anything you haven't told me? Asking is good, but the questioner sets the agenda. It's time to cease asking and begin something deeper – something called wondering. To share your memories of the past is an act of trust and tenderness. To share your wonderings about the future is intimacy of an even higher order. I wonder what you're looking forward to. I wonder what you're afraid of. I wonder who you most want to talk to. I wonder what you most need from me. A wondering isn't a question. It doesn't set an agenda, it sets a stage. It says, dream with me, ponder with me, explore with me, discover with me. When you ask, you almost always have an idea of the right or desired answer. When you wonder, you're both opening your hearts to something neither of you yet know.

Three little words. 'Always' takes away the fear of the future. 'With' means you'll never be alone. 'Wonder' means the future is an adventure.

These are the three ways we relate to God. With confidence that God is never going to go away. With joy in the word together. With awe at God's glory. Marriage is our way to practise the always, the with and the wonder of being together, that we may be better able to comprehend the always, the with and the wonder of being with God. Three little words, which sum up marriage, and sum up our approach to God: always with wonder.

If you're going to strive for elegant simplicity, you need to be succinct. This sermon was only four minutes long. But the brevity is part of the message: amid all the complications of the journey to the altar, the couple only have to remember three words. The fact that the three words fit together in a little phrase makes it more satisfying, and more memorable. Again, the structure is to make the points and then twist them around to point out the theological frame of reference and conclude by suggesting those points work both for marriage and for faith.

The next sermon is again in challenging circumstances: a previous marriage that involved significant pain, and subsequently young children being ferried to and fro, with uncertainty until the very last about whether they would attend the wedding. So a lot of 'noises off' to take energy and attention away from the wedding day. This is therefore a very different sermon, one in which the mood is restoring joy after sadness, rather than simply beginning a journey with hope.

The day of the Lord's favour
Isaiah 61.1–3, 7–11
12 May 2018

G and H, the Spirit of the Lord is upon you. The Lord has anointed you.

I want to talk about these precious words of Isaiah and about what they mean to you and to all of us gathered to celebrate with you today. The book of Isaiah is in three parts. The first part is a series of warnings: things are not good in Israel and the prophet says so. In part two, Israel has faced calamity: its people are in exile in Babylon; their lives have fallen apart. And yet, proclaims Isaiah, God is in Babylon too – and in exile, Israel sees a new face of God, who through suffering sustains steadfast love and who shares Israel's burdens. And then in part three, from which we read today, Israel has returned from exile and is exploring how to live a wiser, more grateful, more generous life.

I believe the story I've just told is very close to the story of G and H, and to what today is about. To understand the true joy of today we have to touch on a story that isn't all about joy. All the words we need are in Isaiah's description. Just listen to these words: broken-hearted, darkness, mourning, grieving, shame, disgrace. They're all different words for exile. I want to say out loud what everybody here knows: H and G know what exile means. They know grief, and darkness, and what it means to be broken-hearted.

And because of what they have known, I want you to feel with them the power, the love and the glory of these stirring, transformative and amazing words. 'To bestow on them a crown of beauty instead of ashes, the oil of gladness instead of mourning, and a garment of praise instead of a spirit of despair. They will be called oaks of righteousness, a planting of the Lord for the display of his splendour.' Just let me say that again: 'A crown of beauty instead of ashes, the oil of gladness instead of mourning, and a garment of praise instead of a spirit of despair.' We're talking about a future that's bigger than the past. We're talking about coming out of exile and entering a new world, where new life can grow, wisdom can flourish, tenderness can be shared like never before. And there's more. 'Instead of their shame my people will receive a double portion, and instead of disgrace they will rejoice in their inheritance. And so they will inherit a double portion in their land, and everlasting joy will be theirs.' Everlasting joy. How 'bout that. God says, 'In my faithfulness I will reward them and make an everlasting covenant with them. All who see them will acknowledge that the Lord has blessed them.'

G and H, this is your day. The day of the Lord's favour. G you are the kindest, most big-hearted, patient and faithful person a man could ever wish to meet. H, you are the most gentle, humble, enduring and tender man a woman could ever have known. God has brought you together not just to create a beautiful story, not just to give you a crown of beauty and oil of gladness, but for something more. Go back to the first things Isaiah says. You have been given the Spirit of the Lord for a reason. That reason is to bring good news to the poor, to bind up the broken hearted, to bring freedom to the captives and release to prisoners, to comfort those who mourn, and provide for those who grieve: not just as parents, vital as that is, but as oaks of righteousness. To be oaks of righteousness means to be a great spreading canopy under which the vulnerable, the isolated and the rejected can shelter. You have known what exile means: your lives will not be sustained efforts to forget that experience, but you now have a calling to translate what you have known of grief into medicine for the soul of those who continue to struggle. You have been brought together to be a blessing.

Because remember this isn't the only place these words appear in the Bible. Jesus says these words at the very start of his ministry, in the synagogue in Nazareth. He's saying that in his body he has become Israel, and in his body he will experience Israel's exile, and take upon himself the broken heart, the imprisonment, the shame and the disgrace. He's saying that his cross will grow into an oak of righteousness in which all will find shelter. He's saying that, in him, exile has come to an end.

And that's his promise to you today, H and G. Today, this Scripture is fulfilled. God has clothed you with garments of salvation and arrayed you in a robe of righteousness, as a bridegroom adorns his head like a priest, and as a bride adorns herself with her jewels. Today you receive a double portion: new life, and a new life together. A crown of beauty instead of ashes, the oil of gladness instead of mourning, a garment of praise instead of despair. And through you, God has shown us a glimpse of the most precious gift of all: the glory of Christ and the real significance of what today means to those who know you and love you. For this is a new beginning, a future that's bigger than the past, a dazzling phoenix of beauty from a shroud of ashes. This is resurrection.

If you're going to preach a sermon like this, you really need to check with the couple that they're prepared for you to express awareness of difficult things – even in the context of transforming those things. It's always preferable to be in a context where you can tell the truth, if only in part – but it's not your role as preacher to be breaking news to a congregation where half the people there, for example, don't know one of the couple has been married before. A conversation with the couple where you say, 'Are you happy for me to talk about your children … your grief … in vague terms, as a preface to talking about your joy in each other and the gift this marriage presents?' can be very significant: some approach marriage hoping it will provide some magic dust to take the strains and sadness of the past away, and if that's the case you need to be more deft and ambiguous. There's a difference between getting a gut feeling and taking a risk and naming an elephant and clumsily ruining the day by thoughtlessness and lack of consultation.

However, if you do take a risk like this and you do get things right, you really can find that the truth sets not just the couple but everyone free.

I finish this chapter with a sermon it would be difficult to replicate, because I based it around three hymns from a service that included five hymns. About six weeks before the wedding I was singing the hymn 'Be thou my vision' when I was struck like never before by the line, 'Heart of my own heart, whatever befall' – and realized it summed up marriage, and summed up the incarnation. The rest of the sermon flowed from there.

Heart of my own heart
26 November 2022

One lesson that clergy never learn is that people don't come to church to listen to sermons; they come to church to say prayers and sing hymns. So on this wonderful occasion I want to talk about the prayers contained in three of the hymns J and K have chosen for us to sing this afternoon. The first comes from 'Be thou my vision'. Listen to these words very carefully: 'Heart of my own heart whatever befall.' Feel how much is expressed in those seven words. We often use the phrase 'one flesh' to describe marriage, but I find that somewhat too graphic, not to say salacious. I'm suggesting J and K say to one another, every night, 'Heart of my own heart.' And in a moment, L will lead his daughter and son-in-law in these vows: 'For better, for worse, for richer, for poorer, in sickness and in health, to love and to cherish, till death us do part.' But if those vows sound to you not only scary but somehow heavily momentous, maybe you could simply edit them down to this: 'whatever befall'. Has ever a more dazzling yet humbling promise been made? 'Heart of my own heart whatever befall.' K and J, sing those words to one another every morning, every night.

Now let's turn to the hymn 'Jerusalem'. Again, just before the end, we sing these words: 'Till we have built Jerusalem.' What William Blake is saying is that life isn't a passive waiting for things to come to you or an entitled assumption that you deserve things or an acquisitive claiming of things for yourself; life is a project – what one author calls a 'long obedience in the same direction,' a seeking after an ultimate goal. J and K, your marriage is a project. You are deciding today to commit yourselves not just to each other, but perhaps more importantly to something beyond either of you that you can only attain together. That may include family but it's not just family. None of the rest of us knows what your Jerusalem is. But there's a project that only you can realize; and you can only realize it together. That's your life project; and it begins today. Ask each other, every wedding anniversary, every New Year's Eve: 'How's Jerusalem going?'

Then third, a hymn we've already sung: 'Love divine, all loves excelling'. Yet again, direct your attention to the very end. Ponder these words – possibly the most evocative words in any hymn in the language: 'Lost in wonder, love and praise.' Never lose the impulse to praise each other. It doesn't have to be froth. It doesn't have to be superlative. But every day, try to say, 'I really appreciated the way you filled the dishwasher before coming to bed,' or, 'I admire the way you gave the credit to your colleagues and didn't keep it for yourself.' The more good things you notice, the more good things there'll be to notice. And never lose the capacity to wonder. Wonder at the gift of life; wonder at the gift of another person; wonder at the mystery of existence. Get praise and wonder right and love will look after itself.

We think of hymns as what we sing to God. But consider this. Hear God singing to you, 'Heart of my own heart whatever befall.' That's the whole Bible – there, in one sentence. Hear God saying, 'You and I are going to build Jerusalem together.' That's what creation is all about. Hear God saying, 'Lost in wonder, love and praise.' That's how we're going to spend eternity.

So K and J, don't just sing these three hymns today. Sing them to each other every day. Because they tell you everything God believes about you, and everything you need to know about marriage. May you build Jerusalem together. May you be the heart of one another's heart, whatever befall you both in this earthly life. And may you be lost in wonder, love and praise forever.

3

Preaching at a Baptism

Around 40 years ago, a generation of clergy entered ordained ministry convinced that baptism was the welcoming of (most often) a child into a worshipping community and therefore that baptisms should take place at the main Sunday service of a parish. Around the same time, baptism shifted from being normal to unusual, and having had maybe 50 baptisms a year a parish would often have fewer than 20. So the new conviction was practicable, but in most parishes it never became satisfactory.

The reasons are many. A big day of suits and dresses for the family and godparents sat uncomfortably with a routine Sunday for the regular congregation. A long service with few concessions to visitors somewhat contradicted the language of 'welcome'. A young baby, often accompanied by young children among siblings, cousins and godparents' offspring, could work up quite a racket, leading to painful moments that test the boundaries of what welcome entailed. Thus, an occasion of celebration and welcome could quickly turn into one of discomfort and antagonism.

One simple change can take away a lot of the angst: shifting the baptism itself to the beginning of the service and removing most of what would take that space until the gospel lesson (or the lesson on which the preacher will speak). This significantly shortens the service, offers an opportunity for restless infants to step outside without missing the baptism, and avoids the sermon turning into a fight with competing voices.

It also permits a proper sermon. The sermons in this chapter aren't homilies: they're sustained engagements that take the opportunity of a baptism to focus and exemplify the commitments of discipleship. The sermon below had multiple contexts: a first child, the later stages of the pandemic and Harvest Festival. It turned out these had more in common that might at first appear.

Restoration
Joel 2.21–27
3 October 2021

Imagine a plague that no one saw coming, affected the entire population, caused hardship and grief in every household, felt like the judgement of God and left people shellshocked and impoverished, picking their way through wreckage like survivors in a bomb crater, shrouded by damage and loss. There are tears, moans and wails, but most of all, a numb silence – a silence that goes on for a long, long time: a silence of exhaustion and despair and defeat.

That's the situation portrayed in the book of the prophet Joel. He's describing the aftermath of a plague of locusts – what the story calls the hopper, the destroyer and the cutter, or what an advert might call a locust that cuts as it destroys as it hops. Israel is left hungry, desolate, without grain to make food. But into this apocalyptic situation God speaks a word of astonishing transformation. 'I will restore to you the years the swarming locust has eaten.' Listen to those words a moment at the bottom of your heart. 'I will restore to you the years the swarming locust has eaten.' What do those words mean? That's what I want to explore with you this morning.

Rose Tremain's 1989 novel *Restoration*, also a 1995 film, describes the fortunes and misfortunes of Robert Merivel, a medical student in the early years of Charles II's reign. With the restoration of the monarchy in 1660, the Puritan austerity of Oliver Cromwell has been displaced by the gaudy revelry of Charles' lavish court. Robert Merivel succeeds in curing the king's sick puppy and is installed as the royal doctor. He lives a wild, carousing life, culminating in a royal commission: looking for a veil of respectability to hide his kingly desires, Charles commands Robert to marry Celia, one of the royal mistresses. In return, Robert receives from the king a magnificent estate in Norfolk and a pension for life. Robert is riding high.

But then Robert, in a parody of the fall, does the one thing he must not do: he falls in love with his wife. Charles ruthlessly strips him of his estate and income. Like Icarus plummeting from the sky, Robert descends from the highest echelons of society to the lowest. He reconnects with his friend John Pearce, whom he'd left behind in his days of fortune and favour, and resumes his medical career at a Quaker hospital for the mentally ill. Here he becomes a sober, serious and sympathetic character and grows to love one of his patients, Katherine. John perishes in the Great Plague and Katherine dies in childbirth, but

Robert demonstrates his new-found character by entering a burning building during the Great Fire of London to rescue an elderly woman. News of his heroism reaches the king. Moved by Robert's change of character, Charles sends Robert and his daughter back to the same estate in Norfolk, saying, 'What was taken from you is restored, in return for the man you have become. It is your house, Robert, and I shall never take it from you.'

'I will restore to you the years the swarming locust has eaten.' The novel is about restoration on several levels. Robert gains, loses and then receives again prosperity, the king's favour and his grand Norfolk estate. Sending Robert to Norfolk, Charles says, 'The plague is coming. Some will be spared, and some will die; but all of us will awake.' Thus the story is about restoration after a pandemic. Meanwhile, we observe the restoration of the monarchy and how an exuberant England displaces the curmudgeonly Puritan era. We also see royalty restored from a purveyor of excess into a rewarder of virtue. Rose Tremain later said she wrote *Restoration* in the late eighties as a critique of the late Thatcher era, saturated in self-centred superficiality, riding for a fall.

The story shows us what restoration is and is not. Restoration is almost never the reinstatement of a situation identical to that which came before loss. Restoration incorporates wisdom gained during loss. Restored reality is transformed from desolation. It's also wiser, truer and more abiding than the original state of affairs. Picture a beloved pottery teapot that sits above the kitchen sink. Someone comes to stay and clumsily hits it against the fridge door, knocking the spout off it. They may say, 'I'll get you a new one,' but the truth is, *you don't want a new one* – you want the old one restored, even if it means the spout's a bit wonky and dribbles a bit – because that teapot has warmed the heart of many a friend and stranger and epitomizes the wisdom of those conversations in a way a new teapot never could. You can't have the old teapot back, but you don't want a replacement – you'd rather have a restoration that makes the breakage a chapter in a bigger story of craftsmanship and hospitality.

When Robert goes back to that Norfolk estate, it's not the same as it was before. It's not just that he no longer owns it himself. It's that he's an older and wiser man. He's not captivated by his lust for the beautiful Celia; he's shadowed by his grief for the tender Katherine. He's not footloose; he's the father of a young girl. He's not a hedonist; he's laid down his life in mental hospital and burning building. The swarming locust has taught him something about the value of people, kindness, medicine, parenthood. Restoration won't obliterate those things; it'll incorporate them into a richer story.

Why is the tiny three-chapter book of the prophet Joel in the Old Testament? Because the locust plague it describes is a metaphor for a larger story. The book was written around 400 BC. A hundred years before, the people of Judah had begun to return from 50 years in exile in Babylon, 500 miles to the east. The years the swarming locust had eaten represent those 50 years of exile. It's no exaggeration to say that the Old Testament was written as Israel came to terms with the catastrophe of exile. The whole Old Testament is one long exploration of what it means for God to say, 'I will restore to you the years the swarming locust has eaten.' But when Israel came back from exile, things were not the same as before. To use the teapot analogy, Israel didn't get a replacement teapot. It got the old teapot with a decidedly dodgy reattached spout. More importantly, Israel wasn't the same as the Israel that was taken into captivity. Like Robert Merivel in seventeenth-century England, restoration didn't mean simple return to the status quo before the disaster: it was something new, combining what was good in the previous era with what was true about the challenging one.

'I will restore to you the years the swarming locust has eaten.' I'm thinking of a woman who finally found the courage to put her child in the back seat of a car and drive away from a marriage that had diminished and humiliated her for 15 years. How was she to look back on that time? 'I will restore to you the years the swarming locust has eaten.' I'm thinking of a young man who, in a student prank, set light to a building, and the fire got out of control, and he spent 13 years in prison, shrouded in grief and shame. How was he to face life when he'd spent his whole adulthood behind bars? 'I will restore to you the years the swarming locust has eaten.' I'm thinking of a boy with a debilitating illness that meant he hardly went to school. By the time new drugs had been found, he was in his twenties and his whole education had been scuppered.

None of these three people could turn the clock back. None of them could simply buy a new teapot to replace the broken one. But all of them found a future that was bigger than the past, made from the broken spouts and ravaged crops that littered their personal histories. I wonder if your story resonates in some way with their stories. I wonder whether, when you hear the words, 'the years the swarming locust has eaten,' you know exactly which years those are. Maybe you're in the middle of those years right now. If so, hear those words spoken to the prophet Joel in your heart today: 'I will restore to you the years the swarming locust has eaten.' I will restore them. They are not wasted. They are not forgotten. They do not have the last word. I will restore those years. Maybe you can look back and see how God has done exactly that, redeeming your exile, your devastated fields, and restoring you to life and love.

We read the words of Joel at harvest festival not simply to recall that some harvests are not happy ones. We read them to realize what harvest is. Harvest is the moment all the good growth of the season is gathered in, together with the damage and failed vegetation. The good crops are separated out for food, while the rest is turned into feed for pigs or returned to the ground to enrich the soil. In other words, harvest is restoration: everything that is harvested either finds its fulfilment or is turned into something useful for the future. Harvest is terrifying if we think of it as the moment of judgement that separates the worthy in us from the bad; but the good farmer throws nothing away, and is able to turn even the foolish, fragile and fallible parts of our lives into fodder for another year. That's how restoration works.

At the start of the book of Joel we read these words: 'Hear this, all inhabitants of the land! Tell your children of it, and let your children tell their children.' Today we gather around a precious child, Philippa Rosenwyn, as we celebrate her baptism. We gather to tell her the story. It's the same story Joel is telling us in his prophetic book. Israel knew the years the swarming locust had eaten. It had known slavery in Egypt. It had wandered 40 years in the wilderness. It had dwelt 50 years in exile. The early church knew these stories and in them saw Jesus' story, saw his cross as the years the swarming locust had eaten, saw its own persecution as another exile or slavery. And in baptism ever since, Christians have gathered round a child, just as Joel instructed us, and told the story of how the world is but a shadow of what God created it to be, but God in Christ restores the years the swarming locust has eaten. And we tell stories of how we too have heard God saying, 'I will restore to you the years the swarming locust has eaten.' And today we realize, as we look back on 19 months of the pandemic with its death and despair, that God is speaking those same words to us, 'I will restore to you the years the swarming locust has eaten.'

Hear those words in your heart right now. Hear those words cover the tears of your lost years. Hear those words echo around our whole world in the grief and desolation of the pandemic. Hear those words as we inscribe precious Philippa into the story that gives us life. 'I will restore to you the years the swarming locust has eaten.' Hear those words and realize what it is you are experiencing. You are realizing what happens when restoration and harvest and Jesus and baptism all come together. You are discovering resurrection.

PREACHING AT A BAPTISM

There are few more powerful sentences in the Bible than the one that begins, 'I will restore.' When I identify the hinge of a sermon, in this case the word 'restore', and the way it applies both to Israel after exile and society after the pandemic, I then sit still for as long as it takes to identify something in my history, in literature or film, or in second- or third-hand experience that feels the way that word feels. Sometimes it takes a while – not long ago, I spent a whole evening getting nowhere with this exercise. In this case what came was Rose Tremain's novel, which I'd read 30 years before, so I reacquainted myself with the novel and watched the film for the first time. This yielded extraordinary treasure – notably the prescient line, 'The plague is coming. Some will be spared, and some will die; but all of us will awake.' This was an occasion where there was simply so much appropriate material to explore, the discipline was to leave much of it out in order to keep the sermon uncluttered and light enough for a family to enjoy while attending to insistent youngsters.

Here are some guidelines for preaching at a baptism.

1. Don't ease up – the family, friends and congregation deserve a proper sermon; but you need to arrange the liturgy and hospitality in such a way that a sermon doesn't become a fight for volubility.
2. Go big – it may not be a special occasion for the congregation, but for the family, especially if it's a first and long-awaited child, it's a huge day, so you should put on your wedding voice and relish how precious the moment is.
3. Don't feel you need an extensive-theology-of-baptism sermon: let the process emerge naturally and you're bound to find where one part of the sermon or even its whole direction is enhanced or highlighted by the fact that there's a baptism taking place.
4. The basic theology of baptism is of crossing the Red Sea and leaving sin and death (represented by the Egyptians in the Exodus story) behind. A baptism sermon should have some sense of leaving behind and taking up.
5. The other chief theme of baptism is commissioning for ministry. The term 'initiation' isn't especially helpful, because it glazes over this sense that ministry begins at baptism. Perceiving what this child (or adult) is being called to concentrates the mind of the congregation on vocation and commissioning.
6. Like marriage, a lot of the work of baptism is done in private, in preparation with parents. Don't mix up private preparation with public preaching. A sermon isn't a lecture on how to be a good parent or how to raise your child in the faith. It's an encounter with God.

The sermon below is one that coins a phrase and repeats it throughout, also making it the title. Repetition can seem infantilizing, but provided the term coined is both descriptive and memorable, it can hold a sermon together, draw out its different angles and messages and be memorable long after the day.

Unbelievable yet unforgettable
John 12.1–8
3 April 2022

A couple of weekends ago, on the last day of the Six Nations Rugby Championship, Wales were playing Italy. Wales, the defending champions, hadn't had a great season, but were glad to finish up by playing lowly Italy, the also-rans of the tournament, who'd lost their previous 35 games in a row. Italy put up a fight, but with two tries, the Welsh left wing, Josh Adams, single-handedly dragged Wales into the lead. Maintaining a rather foolish tradition, with two minutes to go, the commentator announced the man of the match, awarding it to Adams. The co-commentator said, 'Hang on, this game isn't over yet, you might have spoken too soon.' Sure enough, the Italians rampaged close to the Welsh line. Then the Welsh hoofed the ball far beyond the half-way line, and the co-commentator said, 'No worries, looks like you're off the hook.' Whereupon, in one of the great moments in recent rugby history, the young, sylph-like Italian fullback, in his first international start, weaved past Josh Adams' flailing tackle and all the way to the line where his killer pass enabled his wing to score and sensationally win the match for the Italians in the dying seconds. The Welsh players were distraught; the Italians, ecstatic. Unbelievable. Yet unforgettable.

But the best was yet to come. In a quiet moment a few minutes later, while still on the pitch, the disconsolate Josh Adams walked over to his young Italian opponent, whose brilliance had brought about the winning try, and handed him his man-of-the-match medal, saying, 'This needs to come to you.' Somehow Adams rose above the disappointment of losing, the wretchedness of having missed the crucial tackle, the recognition that his great performance had been in vain and the competitive spirit that befits an athlete, and made a gesture that will stay in the memory long after his career is over and the result of the game forgotten – a gesture that transcends sport and speaks of humility, generosity and appreciation for another human being. To employ an over-used sporting expression, it was an iconic moment. It was like a sign – a sign pointing to a bigger world of true reverence and genuine respect. Unbelievable. Yet unforgettable.

John's Gospel is made up of signs. Jesus makes his way around Galilee and back and forth to Jerusalem and in every place, he performs signs – turning water into wine, giving sight to the man born blind, raising Lazarus from the dead. The most significant sign of all is the sign of the cross. Each of these signs is a depiction of who Jesus is and what kind of life he's inviting us into. But there's one sign that's different from all the others. The difference is that, whereas Jesus performs one sign after another, this sign isn't performed by Jesus. It's performed by Mary, the sister of Martha, and of Lazarus whom Jesus has just raised from the dead. Rather like Josh Adams handing over his man-of-the-match award, Mary's sign transcended its setting in a meal, maybe a meal to celebrate Lazarus' return. No one remembers what they ate that night; but what Mary did has never been forgotten.

So what did Mary do? She did three things, all of which were, in different ways, both extraordinarily beautiful and utterly outrageous. First, she wasted a huge sum of money. If you go by the figure Judas quotes, you're talking about the average annual wage of a person in first-century Palestine, or £30,000 in today's money. That's a lot of money to spend on perfume, and it's even more money if what you're going to do is pour the whole lot over someone's feet. You can see the open mouths. It's shocking, but mesmerising. Unbelievable. Yet unforgettable.

The second thing she did was to break social taboos on a grand scale. Feet more or less correspond to the nether regions in the first-century imagination. They need washing, because this is not a culture that has a fully developed appreciation for woollen socks, but that washing was generally the job of a non-Jewish slave. What feet weren't used to receiving was the touch by an equal; touching by a woman, horror of horrors – this is intimacy to a spectacular degree – and not just touching by hands, but rubbing, caressing and surrounding by hair. Hair! Can you imagine? Let's not pretend our so-called permissive society doesn't have sexual taboos. But can you imagine a culture in which for a woman even to be seen in public with a man outside her family was pretty racy goggling at what's going on here? You can hear the cartoon eyes popping out on stalks. Everyone's horrified: but they can't look away. It's erotic – but it's something more powerful even than that – it's a sign of utter devotion. Unbelievable. Yet unforgettable.

The third thing Mary did was to prepare Jesus' body for burial. This kind of perfume was what you put on a dead body to stop it rotting before you put it in a tomb. Presumably she'd put a cheaper version on

Lazarus not long before. But if pouring away a huge amount of money was reckless, and washing the oil off with her hair was salacious, this was either morbid – or inexplicable. Here's a man in the prime of life, with a host of followers and doing miracles for toffee – and you start preparing his body for the grave. What on earth does she think she's doing? Unbelievable. Yet unforgettable.

Why does it matter? Why is this more than a faraway story of faraway people in a land long ago? Because this isn't fundamentally about £30,000 of perfume, or a woman having the courage to cross a few boundaries out of sheer devotion, or about being the only one in the room to realize the person you all love is about to die. This is about God. This is about a God who crossed a thousand boundaries to kneel at our feet. This is about a God who was so devoted to us as to face death for us. This is, fundamentally, about a God whose life is so poured out in love for us that the odour of devotion doesn't just fill the whole room – it fills the whole universe. The reason this sign is so important is that a disregarded woman portrays for us the truth at the heart of all things. God's reckless, transgressive, death-defying pouring-out of all the wealth and glory of the universe into the embodiment of love for us in Jesus. And Mary, pondering the wonder and the mystery of her brother's being raised to life, is the first person in John's Gospel not just to realize who Jesus is, not just to appreciate the enormity of what he represents, but to set about imitating him in all his overflowing and superabundant extravagance. Mary realizes Jesus doesn't just want our worship, he wants us to follow his path. The best form of worship is to do just as he does. Imitation is the sincerest form of flattery. Mary turns her life into an icon of God's love. It's ridiculous, embarrassing, criminal, dangerous, wasteful. But she doesn't care. *Because so is God.*

Judas is having none of it. He does the maths. He's using what philosophers call the felicific calculus – he's working out what will bring about the greatest happiness for the greatest number. He wants to sell the perfume, parcel out the proceeds into little bundles and make sure the benefit goes in some degree of relief for those experiencing food poverty. He's trying to manage the unmanageable. The question for Judas is, 'Is your scheme a way of imitating God's extravagant love, or is it a way of so managing a problem that it no longer requires extravagant love?' Judas and Mary represent contrasting ways to respond to Jesus. Judas fixes problems with rational answers so that passionate displays of extravagant love are unnecessary, and all human challenges can find suitable solutions. Mary jeopardizes her economic security, sexual reputation and social standing by imitating the wondrous love of God.

Today we have before us young baby George and young baby Estella.

We've just performed a sign, by which we've reenacted the Hebrews' crossing-over from slavery to freedom, and our own crossing-over from death to life. The question for George and Estella is, how are you going to use that freedom; how are you going to live that life?

I wonder how you think about your life. We don't get long: threescore years and ten, maybe fourscore; sometimes a lot less. Is our life fundamentally a shrewd calculation of how to squeeze the most out of scarce resources, a sober estimate of days to be lived, materials to be consumed, impact to be measured, marks to be left? Or is our life to be like Mary's: an icon of God's desire for and devotion to us? Imagine your whole life crystallized into one portrait: wouldn't you want it to be a portrait that embodied God's extravagant love? There comes a moment for each of us when all our striving, studying, searching, surviving is stilled into one iconic gesture: Mary shows us a gesture that fills a whole room, a gesture of a love whose fragrance pervades the whole universe. Mary was no one special: someone's sister. But we're still talking about her, because she made a gesture that embodied a thousand prayers, a sign that pointed to the heart of God.

Baby George and baby Estella, may you have parents who love you with the extravagant love of God. May you grow up in a community of faith that embodies divine abundance and isn't caught up in parcelling out and managing human scarcity. May you be a person of whom people say, 'That's taking it a bit far!' or 'Watch it! You're wasting all those resources on something as useless as devotion and passion and beauty.' May you be a person of whom others are embarrassed because you're uncomfortably like Jesus, a person whose gestures are remembered in 2,000 years' time because they depict heaven, a person whose life is an icon of God's wondrous love. And may you grow to be a person who, like Mary, does something unbelievable. Yet unforgettable. As unbelievable and unforgettable as the revelation of God's extravagant desire for us.

Like confirmation, it can be difficult to remember that baptism is something God does for us, rather than something we do for God. And the message that God is lavish and extravagant rather than curmudgeonly and killjoy, and thus that we imitate God in our generosity and grace rather than in our prudence and sobriety, is a helpful one if a church is crowded with those who seldom join in worship.

The final sermon in this chapter, and last in the book, reflects on the process of what takes place in baptism – dwelling not on the scriptural antecedents, nor the words uttered, but on the moment when the parent hands the child over to the priest. For a family that has longed for a child, this seemed an indirect way to ponder the precious yet fragile nature of life and the gracious, assured character of God's love. But it also provides a suitable moment, unusual at a baptism, to talk about death.

Out of hand
John 10.22–30
8 May 2022

I was 4 years old. I was in Bath, the city nearest to the village where I grew up. We were at the top of Milsom Street, which was the main shopping area. My older sister, all of 7, set out to cross the road; but she'd only thought seriously about the cars coming from the right. When we got to the middle, a car sped towards us from the left. My sister panicked, let go my hand and scooted across in front of the oncoming car to the pavement beyond. I was left alone in the middle of the road. I did what I have always done in a crisis ever since: nothing. I stood still as the car shrieked to a stop, touching distance in front of me. Eventually, my heart thudding, the car driver gesticulating (in retrospect probably more petrified than I was), I ran at top speed to join my sister. We were glad to see each other again. In the confusion of emotion, we resolved that these things were probably best not shared with our parents.

I've taken funerals for children whose similar stories turned out differently.

Of all the dilemmas of parenthood, one of the most poignant is to work out when to hold tight and when to let go. If my parents were still alive to hear me tell of that moment etched on my childhood memory, I suspect they might wonder where they were in the story and conclude that that day they'd perhaps erred a little too much on the side of letting go. As a child, each of us has corresponding contrasting impulses. From quite early on we perceive the utter isolation of being totally alone, try to put in place relationships that mean it will never come to pass and develop strategies that enable us to survive should it ever do so. Yet at the same time, any child who's been lifted up away from a place of temptation, conflict or danger knows what it means to wrestle out of that grip and with a determination to shape their own destiny and face life's challenges in their own way.

Back in the days when I was single and was pondering whether I was called to remain so or instead to meet a partner and raise children together, I was deeply struck by a practice I read about in a book by the American pastor Raymond Bakke. Leading a church in urban Chicago, he and his wife decided that their children needed to experience the city for themselves, not just from behind their parents' trouser legs. So in turn, when each child reached the age of 10, Bakke would give them $10, drop them off on the far side of town and let them find their way home any best way they could. This was the seventies, so there were no mobile phones. Those children were little fish swimming in a big urban sea. It was a rite of passage: Bakke and his wife would answer any questions their child had, talk with them about the day a few weeks ahead and prepare a celebration for their homecoming. Needless to say, it was a transformative experience for each child – a kind of baptism in which the children discovered when to trust other people, what they'd learned from their parents, how to rely on themselves and what it feels like to depend on God.

The baptism of a child has many poignant moments. The parents and godparents are asked to make a public declaration of faith, which is unusual in our culture, where it's rare to make public declarations of faith in anything other than the likely success-rate of a vaccine or the veracity of a witness in a libel trial. The pouring of water on the baby's head evokes both the daily bath time of a parent's care and the liberative parting of the Red Sea to free the Hebrews from slavery. The anointing with oil commissions this tiny tot for a unique future, affirming that God creates each one of us for a purpose and that we eventually find that purpose in God. The candle displays the conviction that God lights a fire in each of us at baptism that may burst into flame as we find an adult faith later in life. But for all these resonant moments, for me the most poignant of all is when, as the priest, I ask the parent to hand over to me their precious child, their child that in some cases they've waited years for, made sacrifices for, prayed for, longed for, nurtured from tiny birth to stocky infanthood, who is to them more precious than the rest of the world combined. And as I ask them to hand this child over, I look into their eyes, as you do when you receive a priceless gift from someone, and as they search my soul to ask if they can trust me with this bundle of infinite worth, I search their soul to enquire if they really know what they're doing.

And what are they doing? The answer lies in this morning's gospel reading. Jesus is contrasting three kinds of characters: the *wolf* who comes in and steals, perhaps the Roman occupying army in his context; the *bad* shepherd who fails to protect and guide the sheep, perhaps the Jerusalem leadership that was soon to connive for Jesus' demise; and himself, the *good* shepherd, who knows each of his sheep by name, whose sheep recognize his voice, and who lays down his life for his sheep. Here, Jesus makes perhaps his greatest theological claim in all the gospels: he says, 'The Father and I are one.' But notice the context in which he does so. He repeats the phrase that's crucial to what we've been doing together this morning in baptizing Freddie. He says, 'I give my sheep eternal life. *No one will snatch them out of my hand.*' Then he says the same thing in a different way. 'What my Father has given me is greater than all else, and *no one can snatch it out of the Father's hand.*'

Think about that word, 'snatch'. It's a childish word. It's what we say to young children who are arguing. 'Don't snatch baby Jesus from Mary. Joseph and Mary were friends.' But the word connects with our deepest fears about a child: that something, someone – some disease, some stranger, some disaster – will snatch that child from our hands.

We want to create an entirely safe, completely protected world around a child, where no sickness, hardship, danger or threat can jeopardize their security, well-being, growth and development. But the truth is, such safety is impossible. When a parent comforts a child who's just had a nightmare and says, 'I'm here. I'll always be here,' they're not telling the truth. But beyond being impossible, such safety isn't even desirable. One of the reasons Covid has been so devastating in this country compared with many African countries is that in most of Africa, people are routinely exposed to so many diseases, they become largely immune to them at an early age, so Covid was pretty small fry; whereas here, we hide children from disease, meaning they've got no protection when a new and virulent one comes along. Raymond Bakke was a brave man when he asked his children to find their own way across Chicago, but he wasn't a fool. Eventually, we all have to find our way through uncharted, unknown and potentially hostile environments, and the earlier we learn that this is what life involves, and develop the capacity to navigate it, the better.

So when, in the baptism ceremony, the parent hands their precious child over to the priest, it's not the case that they're transferring the baby from the assured security of home to the precarious embrace of the church. Because the painful truth is, a parent can never say to a child, 'No one will ever snatch you out of my hand.' The parent does have to let go eventually, however foolish the child's choice of lifestyle, however ghastly their friends, however dangerous their career, however unspeakable their choice of life partner. Suffocating with self-serving love is just as dangerous as letting go too early and invariably counter-productive.

But the point is, Jesus *can* say, 'No one will ever snatch you out of my hand.' Jesus *does* know your child by name. Jesus *does* lay down his life for your child. Jesus *will* embrace and walk with your child forever. 'Ah, but,' we understandably say, 'who *is* this Jesus who claims to be and to do all these things?' Jesus says, 'I and the Father are one.' In other words, Jesus says, 'I am inseparably bonded to the essence that is before and beyond this present existence. When I say, "Nothing can snatch you out of my hand," that means not just the conviction of now, but the embrace of forever. Your child's destiny is as secure as being held and cherished by the eternal loving hands of God.'

In infant baptism, the parent hands the baby to the priest; one of the most difficult and trusting things a parent can do. But it's not handing over from security to danger. It's handing over from the love and care of a *parent*, which for all its passion, sacrifice, commitment and attention can never be permanent, impermeable or total, to the love and care of *God*, which can be and is all of those things, now and always. That's why I find looking into the parent's eyes at that moment so profound. Because they're handing over their child from now to forever. It's perhaps the most significant moment of our lives, besides the moment of our death. Because death is the other moment when we transfer from now to forever. And here's the crucial thing: just as Raymond Bakke was saying, 'My child is way better off having faced the fear and danger of the city from an early age, and thenceforth living in the light of it, not in denial of it,' so young Freddie's parents, in handing him over to be baptized, are saying, 'This is a rehearsal for a final goodbye, the separation of death. It's a statement that if we can face the truth of this handing over from now to forever, we can face the final one too.'

Because in the end, the Christian faith is simply this. God chooses not to suffocate us with love, but to hand us over to existence. That means God lets us go into a world of danger, temptation, distress and challenge: all of which lie inside that little word, 'snatch'. But when we turn to the risen Christ, we see one whose hands bear the nail marks of love, nail marks that say, despite everything it costs, 'I will never let you go.' That could be a tragic gesture. What turns it into the entry to eternal life is what we discover in John chapter 10: Jesus and the Father are one. Baptism is the moment we recognize our mortality, and Christ's divinity.

If we are safe in Christ's hands, we are safe with the essence of all things forever. Nothing can snatch us out of those hands.

Nothing, never; whatever, forever.

Index of Biblical References

Old Testament

Genesis
2.4b–9, 15–end   139–43

Exodus
32.1–4   182–7

Ruth
1.16–17   279–81

2 Samuel
7.1–14   188–92

1 Kings
17.8–16   89–93

Job
19.23–7   192–6
38.1–7, 34–41   58–63

Psalms
1   267–9
23   51–6

Proverbs
8.1, 22–31   202–6

Song of Songs
8.6   187
8.6–7   265–7

Isaiah
43.17   120–4
43.16–21   198–202
45.1–7   63–7
61.1–3, 7–11   283–5
64.1–9   77–81

Joel
2.21–7   289–93

New Testament

Matthew
1.18–25   95–9, 100–4
2.1–12   116–19
4.1–11   134–8
6.1–6, 16–18   131–3
11.2–11   89
20.1–16   219–23
24.14–30   224–8

Mark
5.21–43   213–17

Luke
1.26–38   104–8

3.15–17, 21–22	120–4	**2 Corinthians**	
4.14–21	124, 125–9	4.1–12	238–43
5.1–11	208–12		
18.9–14	228–32	**Galatians**	
19.1–10	272–4	1.11–24	243–7
24.13–35	163–6	5.1, 13–25	31–5
24.36–48	153–8		
24.44–53	168–72	**Philippians**	
		3.17—4.1	13–17
John			
1.1–14	110–13	**Hebrews**	
10.22–30	298–301	10.11–14, 19–25	249–54
12.18	294–7	11.29—12.2	254–8
20.1–18	149–51		
21.1–21	158–62	**2 Peter**	
		3.8–15a	83–7
Acts			
2.1–21	174–8	**1 John**	
		4.7–21	158–62
Romans			
4.13–25	234–7	**Revelation**	
5.1–8	37–41	1.10, 22—22.5	19
		21.1–4	5–8

Index of Names and Subjects

Adams, Josh 294–5
Advent season 82–94
Advent Sunday 71–81
Alter, Robert 202
annunciation 55, 95–9, 100–4, 104–6, 170
Aquinas, St Thomas 158, 251, 270
Ascension 167, 207
  Sunday after 167, 168–72, 227
Ash Wednesday 130–3
attention, seeking 83–7, 136–7
Austen, Jane, *Pride and Prejudice* 120

Bailey, Kenneth, *Jesus Through Middle Eastern Eyes* 223
Bakke, Raymond 298–9, 300, 301
baptism 122–4, 225, 288–301
  and identity 9, 16–17
baptism of Christ 119–24
Barth, Karl 87
Being With course 156
belief 255–8
Bell, Bishop George 54
Berry, Wendell 125–6, 129
Best of Both Worlds (TV series) 95–6, 97–9
Bethlehem, and Jerusalem 116–19
Blake, William 286
blasphemy 184, 272
body, human 100–4

Brexit 4–9, 25, 31
Bridgerton (Netflix series) 120–2, 124
Brittain, Vera, *Testament of Youth* 43–5

Calvin, John 172
Campbell, Ffyona 37–41
Carnegie, Andrew 20
carol services:
  Advent 71
  Epiphany 116
  preaching at 109
Christ *see* Jesus Christ
Christmas 109–15
  and Ascension 169–70, 172
  preaching before 94–108
Christmas Eve 109, 110
Christology 3, 128–9, 202
church
  current condition 197, 198–201
  destiny 85–6
  and the edge 60
  and the Holy Spirit 85–6, 92–3, 167, 173, 206
  humility 176
  and Pentecost 173–6
  and politics 13–17
  as priest 251
  and social infrastructure 21–3
Church Times 238–9
Clinton, Bill 271–2
congregations xii–xiii, 12

and trust in preacher 77, 94,
  109–10, 113, 149, 254
context xii–xiii, 18, 202, 248
cost of living 24, 25–9
courage 270–1
Covid pandemic 25, 105, 107,
  141, 153, 156–8, 281, 292, 300
  and normality 153
  and work 219–22
Cronin, A. J., *The Citadel* 240
crucifixion 14, 72, 84, 155, 157,
  165, 170

Dahl, Roald 163–4
dependency 25–9
desire 77–81
disability 57–68, 90–1, 127
Disability Sunday 57, 64
discipleship 130–3, 160–2, 251,
  254–5, 288
Doerr, Anthony, *All the Light We
  Cannot See* 229–32
doubt 152, 154, 157–8

Easter 144–51
Easter season 152–66
Emmaus road disciples 152, 160,
  163–5
emotion, in sermons 46, 77–81,
  99, 138, 149, 196, 243–7, 275
end of the world 71–81
Epiphany 116–29
Epistle 248–58
eschatology 19–24
  and Advent 71–7, 82
ethics 119
Eucharist 161–2, 225
Examen, Ignatian 128
exile 121–2, 155, 186–7, 197–
  200, 249–50, 283–5, 291–2
existence, human 105–6, 114–15
exorcism 89

faith 39, 236–8, 246, 251, 254–8
First World War 42–6
Foreigner, 'I wanna know what
  love is' 277–8
forgiveness 156, 160, 169, 221–3,
  268
Four Tops, 'Reach out and touch'
  168
freedom 30–41
Freud, Sigmund 190
Frye, Northrop 228
funerals 261–74

Gabriel, Marius, *Goodnight
  Vienna* 27–8
God *see* grace; Holy Spirit; Jesus;
  love; Trinity
Godden, Rumer 26
Goodhart, David, *The Road to
  Somewhere* 13–14
Gospels
  and the Ascension 169
  and Old Testament 121–4, 181
grace of God 39, 81, 88, 103,
  221, 231, 237
Graham, Billy 175
grief 78–80, 148–9, 157, 261–2,
  263, 266–7, 283–5

harvest festival 292
heaven 83–7, 111–13, 170
Hebrew Bible 182, 204
Holy Saturday 144
Holy Spirit
  and the church 85–6, 92–3, 167,
    206
  and conception of Jesus 98,
    100–4, 107
  and disability 63, 65–7
  and mission 22–3
  and the Old Testament 181, 197
  and parable of the Talents 224–7

INDEX OF NAMES AND SUBJECTS

and Pentecost 167, 169, 173–8
and preaching 68, 82
and reconciliation 50
homilies 109–10, 114–15,
  116–19, 130–3, 144, 145,
  149–51, 277–9
hope 39, 246, 251
  against hope 234–7
hourglass 110–13
humility, and church 176
humour 10, 109, 129, 133,
  163–6, 172, 178, 203–4, 275
hunger 77–81

identity
  and baptism 9, 16–17
  Christian 7–8, 10, 14–17, 175
  national 6–8, 10, 14, 43
idolatry, as sin 182–6
incarnation 109
incarnation, *see also* Christmas
irony 18, 117–18, 161, 163, 203,
  228–32
Israel
  Babylonian exile 64, 106, 121–2,
    155, 186–7, 197–202
  Mary as 102–3

Jerome, St 158
Jerusalem, and Bethlehem 116–19
Jesus Christ, baptism 119–24
  crucifixion 170
  as high priest 250–3
  and parable of the Talents 224–7
  resurrection 84, 113, 144–51,
    152–66
  second coming 71–7, 82–3, 88
  sermon at Nazareth 124–9
  as shepherd 51–6, 161, 299–300
  temptation 118, 135–6
  see also Trinity
John the Baptist 82, 88–93, 116

Jones, Norah, 'Come away with
  me' 141
journalism 267–71
joy 40, 222–3, 284

kingdom of God 16, 84–5, 92–3,
  226–7, 273
  calling from the edge 60–1
Klinenberg, Eric 19–21, 23

Lazarus, raising 147, 150, 295–6
Lent 130–43
  First Sunday 130, 134–8
life, eternal 79–81
locust swarms 263–4, 289–92
love 39, 169, 251
  and death 266–7
  extravagant 295–7
  in marriage 277–9
Luther, Martin 53

magi 117–19
Marr, Andrew 271
Mary of Bethany 295–7
Mary Magdalene, meeting with
  Jesus 145–9, 150–1
Mary of Nazareth, annunciation
  to 55, 95–9, 100–4, 105–8, 170
McKnight, John 23
ministry 160–2, 293
miracles 207–17
mission 161–2, 163
  and Holy Spirit 22–3
Mitchell, Joni, 'Both Sides Now'
  139–40
Monty Python
  Life of Brian 91–2
  Spanish Inquisition sketch 192,
    194, 196
Mothering Sunday 130
My Sister's Keeper (Jodi Picoult;
  book and film) 31–5

names 66–7
Nazareth, Jesus' sermon at 124–9
New Year's Day 104–5, 107
Newton, John 97
Nietzche, Friedrich 239
normal, new normal 153–7

Old Testament
  and disability 57–67
  and the Gospels 121–4, 181
  and Holy Spirit 181, 197
  and Jesus 155
  narratives 181–96
  poetry 197–206, 238
Orwell, George, *Animal Farm* 116–19

Palm Sunday 130
parables 218–32
  of the Labourers 219–23
  of the Pharisee and the Tax Collector 228–32
  of the Talents 223–8
parenthood, and letting go 298–301
Pascal, Blaise 131–3, 158
Passion Sunday 130
Paul, St 233–47
peace, joy of 37–41
Pentecost 167, 172–8
Picoult, Jodi, *My Sister's Keeper* 31–5
politics 3–17
  and freedom 30
Pride and Prejudice (Jane Austen) 120
priesthood 248, 249–54
promise of God 56, 85, 91, 121, 151, 195, 222, 236–7

questions 58–9, 61, 83–6, 152, 188–92, 282

Ready Steady Cook 174
reality 111–12
recognition 163–6
reconciliation 41, 67, 264–5, 273
redemption 49–50
relationship, with God 8, 60, 75, 132, 169–71, 185–6, 190–1, 199–200
relationship, Trinity as 84, 169–70, 183
Remembrance Sunday 46, 47–50, 123
restoration 289–93
revelation 158–60, 163
  and Scripture 248
Russia, invasion of Ukraine 51–6

salvation 90–3, 99, 127–8, 194–6, 221, 223
Scripture xiii, xv, 3–4, 87, 226
  and disability 57, 62–8
  and priesthood 249–54
  and revelation 248
  see also Epistles; Gospels; Old Testament
Second World War 47–9
Sermon on the Mount 91
sermons
  exegetical 3–4, 104–8, 158–62
  pastoral 3–4, 5–11, 88–93
  personal 56
  preparation xi–xii
  prophetic 4, 11–13, 269–72
  teaching 82
shepherd, Jesus as 51–6, 161, 299–300
sin
  of blasphemy 184
  and creation 11
  and crucifixion 205, 212
  of idolatry 182–6

INDEX OF NAMES AND SUBJECTS

society 18–29
Sole, David 243–4, 246
Stoicism 235–7
Stoppard, Tom, *Rosencrantz and Guildenstern are Dead* 58, 61–2
Sunday after Ascension 167, 168–72
Sunday before Christmas 95–108

tangent 114–15
Taylor, Sonya Renee 153, 156–7
temptation of Jesus 118, 135–6
tension 3
theology
  and Ascension 171–2
  and disability 60–2
  and ethics 119
Thurman, Howard 51
Tiananmen Square 244, 246
treasure in clay jars 241–2
Tremain, Rose, *Restoration* 289–93

Trinity, as relationship 84, 169–70, 183
trust
  of congregation 77, 94, 109–10, 113, 149, 254
  in God 21, 39, 54–5, 141–2, 160, 171, 188, 191, 193, 195–6, 236–8, 245–7, 256–8
truth 270–1, 280–1, 285, 300–1
Tutu, Desmond 271–4
Tyler, Anne, *Saint Maybe* 135

Ukraine, invasion by Russia 51–6

virgin birth 102–3
vocation 60–1, 67–8
waiting 77–81
  and hastening 83–7
war 42–56
weddings 275–87
wisdom 204–6
wondering 282–3, 287
work 219–23

www.ingramcontent.com/pod-product-compliance
Lightning Source LLC
Chambersburg PA
CBHW031056080526
44587CB00011B/712